The Tough Alchemy of Ben Okri

Pen and ink portrait of Ben Okri
by Rosemary Clunie *That Magical
Absorption* (2004) (94.3' × 5.8'),
Collection of the artist.
Courtesy: Rosemary Clunie.

The Tough Alchemy of Ben Okri

The Writer as Conceptual Artist

Rosemary Alice Gray

BLOOMSBURY ACADEMIC
LONDON • NEW YORK • OXFORD • NEW DELHI • SYDNEY

BLOOMSBURY ACADEMIC
Bloomsbury Publishing Plc
50 Bedford Square, London, WC1B 3DP, UK
1385 Broadway, New York, NY 10018, USA
29 Earlsfort Terrace, Dublin 2, Ireland

BLOOMSBURY, BLOOMSBURY ACADEMIC and the Diana logo are trademarks of
Bloomsbury Publishing Plc

First published in Great Britain 2021
This paperback edition published in 2022

Copyright © Rosemary Alice Gray, 2021

Rosemary Alice Gray has asserted her right under the Copyright, Designs and Patents Act, 1988, to be identified as Author of this work.

For legal purposes the Acknowledgements on p. xxiii constitute an extension of this copyright page.

Cover design: Eleanor Rose
Cover image © Rosemary Clunie

All rights reserved. No part of this publication may be reproduced or transmitted in any form or by any means, electronic or mechanical, including photocopying, recording, or any information storage or retrieval system, without prior permission in writing from the publishers.

Bloomsbury Publishing Plc does not have any control over, or responsibility for, any third-party websites referred to or in this book. All internet addresses given in this book were correct at the time of going to press. The author and publisher regret any inconvenience caused if addresses have changed or sites have ceased to exist, but can accept no responsibility for any such changes.

A catalogue record for this book is available from the British Library.

Library of Congress Cataloging-in-Publication Data
Names: Gray, Rosemary (Emeritus professor of English), author.
Title: The tough alchemy of Ben Okri / Rosemary Alice Gray.
Description: London ; New York : Bloomsbury Academic, 2021. |
Includes bibliographical references.
Identifiers: LCCN 2020010909 (print) |
LCCN 2020010910 (ebook) | ISBN 9781350152991 (hardback) |
ISBN 9781350153004 (ePDF) |
ISBN 9781350153011 (eBook)
Subjects: LCSH: Okri, Ben–Criticism and interpretation.
Classification: LCC PR9387.9.O394 Z69 2021 (print) |
LCC PR9387.9.O394 (ebook) | DDC 823/.92–dc23
LC record available at https://lccn.loc.gov/2020010909
LC ebook record available at https://lccn.loc.gov/2020010910

ISBN: HB: 978-1-3501-5299-1
PB: 978-1-3502-4939-4
ePDF: 978-1-3501-5300-4
eBook: 978-1-3501-5301-1

Typeset by Newgen KnowledgeWorks Pvt., Ltd, Chennai, India

To find out more about our authors and books visit www.bloomsbury.com and sign up for our newsletters.

To my beloved late husband, Derek, whose presence is ever absent and whose absence is ever present; to our offspring: Peter, Alan and Carolyn (Canna), who have shared in our loss; to Ben Okri – a citizen of the universe whose mission is to persuade humankind that all life is worth preserving and whose mercurial writings have inspired me for more than two decades.

Contents

List of figures	ix
Preface	xi
Foreword	xix
Acknowledgements	xxiii

Part 1 The alchemy of life: 'To find life in myth and myth in life'
(*Birds of Heaven* 1996) 1

  1 Ben Okri's aphorisms: 'Music on the wings of a soaring bird' 3

  2 Epistemic ecology and 'diminishing boundaries of a shrinking world' in 'Heraclitus' Golden River' from *Wild* 13

  3 Ontopoiesis in Okri's poetic oeuvre and *A Time for New Dreams* ... 25

  4 Recovering our true state of being in 'The Comic Destiny' 33

Part 2 Rebalancing the triadic elements of life 45

  5 Apologia pro *In Arcadia*: A neglected masterpiece? 47

  6 'Domesticating infinity' in *Mental Fight* and *Astonishing the Gods* ... 57

  7 Redreaming ways of seeing: Intuitive creativity in *The Landscapes Within* ... 69

  8 Promoting the poetic cause in 'stokus' from *Tales of Freedom* 85

Part 3 The mercurial imaginary: The writer as 'demiurge' (artist/craftsman) ... 99

  9 Sowing 'a quilt of harmony': Eco-phenomenology in 'Lines *in Potentis*' ... 101

 10 'A clear lucid stream of everywhereness' in *Wild*: A postmodern perspective ... 109

 11 Survivalist culture in 'Laughter beneath the Bridge' 117

 12 The poetic muse of archaeology 129

Part 4 The wheel of transformation: The writer as lodestar (guide) ... 139

13 Sublime transformative paremiology in *A Way of Being Free* ... 141
14 'The Standeruppers': The frightening irony of the Anthropocene ... 149
15 Conscious reveries in *The Magic Lamp: Dreams of Our Age* ... 157
16 'The Incandescence of the Wind' (1982): 'Rain wisdom down upon the earth' ... 167

Part 5 In search of the marvellous: The sacred ziggurat
(symbolic celestial mountain) ... 175

17 Protean magic in *The Mystery Feast* and *The Magic Lamp* ... 177
18 'An Interval in the Enchantment of Living': *The Age of Magic* ... 187
19 When chaos is the god of an era: Rediscovering an
    'axis mundi' in *Starbook* ... 199
20 In conversation with Ben Okri ... 213

Notes ... 223
Bibliography ... 243
Index ... 267

Figures

1	Cropped cover of *The Landscapes Within* (1981)	75
2	The false mirror redrawn by Renato Tomei	75
3	Ben Okri	221

Preface

Ben Okri (OBE) has invested his lifeblood at the rock face of the true stuff of literature. It is hoped that the readings in this monograph will lead to an appreciation of Okri's creativity and to a deeper understanding of the literary strategies, contexts, themes and modes he employs. While he is connected to several realms and ages of writing, he belongs to no single one.[1]

The aim is to show that Okri transmits to close gaps, to create bonds. His is an inimitable conceptual artistry; his writings urge us towards upliftment, pointing the way to a Higher Consciousness for the well-being of humankind and planet earth. I attempt to show that for this contemporary alchemist, the 'Imaginatio Creatrix' (creative imagination) is transformational and transcendent, allowing us to confront the untenable in the sociopolitical environments in which we live and move, and to meditate on the incomprehensible mysteries of earthly life in both its quotidian and spiritual spheres.

For over a century, African writers have tended to foreground a dystopian sociopolitical vision embraced by literary sociologists. As a native pan-Africanist, my concern is to examine how African authors sustain elements of a utopian society. Okrian scholarship reflects the dystopian-utopian dichotomy: there are those who follow the neo-Marxist magical realist mode[2] and those who attempt to journey through studies in African renaissance into a New Enlightenment. The Okrian oeuvre invokes such resonances of a resilient cultural, existential and spiritual identity. Okri transmogrifies the ingenuity, artistry and imaginative force of our society through narrative allegory and personal revelation, transmuting the anxieties of politico-historical conditions into a unique alchemy of symbolist imaginary to penetrate behind reality in search of an ideal world. Never didactic, his writing suggests through cumulatively graphic, often abstract imagery how the past may be purified and crystalized through the passage of time and intuitive creativity to enlighten readers so that they can transcend the human condition through the enjoyment and stimulation of great storytelling.

Sharing my research into the existential angst portrayed in Okri's work is a deeply felt personal goal. The monograph is the culmination of over forty years of extensive reading of colonial/postcolonial/neocolonial texts that deal with liberation as modernity's political ideal. I ask philosophical, eco-phenomenological and esoteric questions to explore the writer's vision in redefining occidental hegemony. My mode centres on detecting and revealing how Okri alerts us to an African energy of life, actuating within the reader a vivacious enthusiasm. Questions underpinning these chapters include: How has each encounter with an Okrian text presented a new dynamic? How does each reveal a cumulative logic in his work and the vacillation between recording and reflection that propels his actors into action? To what extent is each transformative? What new vision of life does Okri suggest? Why does each text open a state almost beyond words and imaginative images? What is African epistemology? Such questions are rehearsed and explored in his work, while they and his fictive replies to them resonate with the legitimately appropriate query into decolonizing colonized minds and institutions.

Okri is at the cutting edge of debates about decolonization – rediscovering our origination/Africanness, our part in the maternal continent from which we are all sprung. History is an important theme for Okri, but he comes at it obliquely, defamiliarizing the particular to probe familiar global historical and legendary narratives. The call for decolonization or reassertion of our mother continent's truths is international and urgent. Literary scholarship has a duty to search out those thinkers who have defined paths of African philosophies. One of these continental observers is Ben Okri who does not wish to equal or parallel European thought but to show us how to consider our own issues in a way that is congruent with the traditions and cultures not only of the African continent but also of the world at large. My arguments show that Okri has much to teach the West in its consumerist, hegemonic and in some respects avowedly desiccated belief systems. Although never didactic, Okri's writings demonstrate a deeply felt concern for life on planet earth, both in terms of ecology and human community. His essential message is one of an expanded sense of the multiplicity of realities to be discerned and exploited creatively in literature and life. For him, this transfiguration includes the preservation of Nature. Forests, flowers and birds are leitmotifs throughout his works. For Okri, renewal lies in and through the potential of creativity.

As my subtitle testifies, Okri is a conscious artist whose writing demonstrates the complexity and transformative power of African culture and thought; it suggests how this culture engages with modernity. His art demands attention, intellectual focus, if it is to be understood. It requires effort: a will to engage, a participation that redefines the words 'art' and 'artist'. He sounds a call for those willing to heed it, to hear what is said and not said. This is nowhere better illustrated than in his aphorisms. The phenomenon of aphoristic expression as formulated by Okrian practice evidences astute syntactical arrangements and a complex interrelationship among human behaviour, spiritual affinity and the natural world. These maxims elaborate our internal states and tendencies, effectively creating new vistas of meaning. His sublime transformative paremiology (study of aphorisms) is especially relevant in demonstrating the joy of lucid organization; all form part of a perspicacious unity. His attitudes are synaesthetic – conveyed by the cognitive meaning of the aphorisms and, at the same time, evoking corresponding feelings in the reader. Okri recalls an Edenic Africa before the intrusion of industrialization. His recollection of our being in Nature parallels Wordsworth's concern to remind humankind of their true existential, spiritual oneness with the green-created world.

Throughout Okri's aphorisms that percolate my readings, the power of revivification comes from the reminder of the powers that are latent in all human souls. This is what he suggests when he says that creativity is indicative of the transhuman. As with the entire corpus, the aphorisms do not merely expose the fallacious aspects of post-industrial, postcolonial realities, nor do they simply amplify the private vision of the writer; they provoke reflection and imperceptively lead to inner transformation. More than a statement of the composer's thoughts and attitudes, the aphorisms revivify the reader's sense of being, ameliorating the crowded troubles of postmodernity's obsessive need for surround-sound and hyper-connectivity. As concise emotive and mental utterances, the aphorisms induce sensibility and intellectual responsiveness; they may even modify the reader's attitudes towards existence, implying a sublime ontology.

This monograph comprises reworkings of selected essays that I have written on Okri's work over the past decade. The journey is far from complete. It has been and continues to be labyrinthine. It has enhanced self-actualization, an appreciation of and for the mysterious chinks that Okri opens into living and how to live spiritually, which I wish to share with potential readers.

It behoves me perhaps to express the tentative nature of my readings of this complex modern writer. Steeped in classical and contemporary myth, Okri's oeuvre justifies the title of this monograph; it is alchemical in numerous ways because, what shines through the darkness of the impending Sixth extinction, is the consolation – for those of us who have the stamina to undertake an arduous, but no less worthwhile, literary quest – of Okri's vision of a better world for all, as encapsulated here. In the aphorisms, especially, he has created his own myth of a promise, however uncertain, that the sun will rise again.

Okri's impulse parallels the teleology of the Romantic and Modernist traditions in that it implies that anyone can improve one's circumstances by questioning the status quo, thinking creatively, giving rein to the imagination, acknowledging a universal soul. Okri is a visionary symbolist who enlightens humankind. His works interrogate existence – what being human signifies. If T. S. Eliot mourned the desiccation of the twentieth-century soul, wrecked by industrialization of land and technological warfare, then Okri recalls the aspects of the soul and imagination as crucial to human existence in the twenty-first century. What Wordsworth and Blake saw so clearly as the horrific consequences of losing one's soul, greenness, imagination and oneness with the cosmos Okri seeks to correct, forgiving the rude intrusion of Westerners, gun happy and gold hungry, and teaching them to reconnect with the elements of salt, sulphur and mercury that the Wisdom Corpus of Paracelsus understood as the balancing agents of life and living. Paracelsus determined the 'Tria Prima' (three primary spiritual forces), represented as the mercurial/volatile intellect, sulphur, which mediates in the position of the soul, and the salt of life, which he believed coordinate the spiritual, emotional and physical aspects of humanity and in turn associate cosmic forces and planetary directions.[3]

Okri revives the Wisdom Corpus; reminiscent of Paracelsian thought, he is acutely aware of humanity's need to be respectful of the 'Tria Prima': he is insistent that the mercurial and sulphuric are as real and substantial in our lives and living as the physical. This is what informs the chosen sectional divisions. Okri senses that Western thought has been too bonded to the physical, fiscal and material, at the expense of the mercurial and sulphuric. In his works incorporated here, he alerts the reader to this dissent, re-creating the realms of the mercurial and sulphuric to widen and expand the margins of a world reduced to mechanistic materialism and even unbelief – we need only to think of the spiritually emaciated and impoverished Western travellers in his masterpiece, *In Arcadia*. Okri adopts a powerfully Blakean critique of industrialized humanity and the individual psyche; we have gained so much in the salt realm, the physical, but have sold our mercurial and sulphuric souls to darkness. Paracelsus's three categories of chemistry relate to principles of our beingness and are then related to cosmic elements, as do Okri's. Okri is a mystic, a contemplative artist. Embedded in the notion of 'contemplation' is a striving for the highest spiritual knowledge possible to humankind while still in this life. Okri follows a psychic and elemental path that coordinates and aligns natural with supernatural cycles. He does not regard the universe as a giant Newtonian clock with laws and predictabilities but rather as a filmy, mobile, evanescent whole which is here and then not, visible and as quickly invisible.

Although this monograph is conceived of as a unified tapestry of essays, I have devised a convenient organizing structure that reflects my theme of alchemy (transformation, not sorcery). There are twenty essays in five parts, each with a subheading to indicate the general alchemical thrust of my critiquing lens. Chapters are ordered according to broad themes and begin with a chapter on selected Okrian aphorisms – the only one of its kind thus far, serving to illuminate the ancient wisdom in the writings from the works under review.

The Wisdom Corpus is therefore evoked in each section heading. In Part 1: The Alchemy of Life, the subtitle 'To Find Life in Myth and Myth in Life' serves as a convenient Okrian credo, for myth – that which embodies 'truth' – is fundamental to the symbolic canons of all cultures. The title to Part 2 encapsulates the Paracelsian tripartite conception of the essence of being, a coalescence of body, mind and spirit. Part 3 celebrates the writer's craftmanship, his versatility as a conceptual artist, while Part 4, a transformative guide, begins with a second essay on the carefully chosen maxims from a relatively early text, *A Way of Being Free*, a collection that includes a brilliant essay on Shakespeare's *Othello*. This second exploration of Okri's maxims, like that in Part 1, also represents an initial study on his aphorisms; in it I have tried to show the importance of these in imparting his visionary aesthetics. It is, however, notoriously difficult to write consecutive prose about something so atomized as a section of aphorisms. It is even more challenging to detect the author's vision that informs the ideas he propounds so lyrically and seductively. One detects classical, Christian and traditional African motifs that interact in Okri's work. This I have tried to illustrate by also incorporating many of his aphorisms throughout my readings. I have invoked the sacred ziggurat in Part 5, a term denoting a pinnacle, a cosmic or celestial mountain, central to several religious mythologies. The ziggurat is the quintessential symbol for the alchemy wrought by the creative imagination, operating ontopoietically (heightened awareness). As a portal to the spiritual realm, the ziggurat – a natural geological feature, replicated in church spires and minarets – evokes a moral ideal for humankind, and Nature is seen as an agent of spiritual truths. This section returns my interpretations to their starting point, effectively closing the hermeneutic circle.

Okri's thinking animates life and herein inheres an essential part of the connotation of the epithet, 'tough', in the monograph's title. His output is also 'tough' because it is no easy read; it demands conscious attention to diction, syntax and rhetorical device for understanding. It demands rereading, coupled with in-depth research to throw light on the vast scholarship that underpins the works. Okri's writing is 'tough' because of its no-nonsense or steadfast undercurrent – the vision this writer enjoys of contemporary life is founded on rock-hard and sometimes uncomfortable truths.

Why study the Okrian oeuvre?

Relevance: In the enormous angst of unresolved issues of materialism, of loss of faith – in a higher order as well as in indigenous knowledge systems – of the defeat of nationhood, the primordial sap, global warming, the Fourth Industrial Revolution, the Covid-19 pandemic and general disillusionment of the twenty-first century, a study of Okri's works hints at 'how the future can have a future' (to borrow from fellow Nigerian Odia Ofeinum). Okri suggests that even as a labour of Sisyphus, these issues that are the concern of modernity, postcoloniality and decoloniality should not be abandoned. The corpus manifests an awareness of the crisis facing our planet as the Holocene bears its poisoned fruits for mankind, subtly paving the way to a better future for all through love and creativity. Lines from 'The Ruin and the Forest' pertain: 'Habit is thus a great / Force of nature. / When used blindly, / Without wisdom, / In the creation of art / It cultivates a fruitful mediocrity. / Hitched to a great new dream / Or vision it is the creation of marvels / And enduring pyramids of creativity' (*Wild* 2012: 45, ll. 43–52).[4] Here is the voice of the way forward: 'Let the energy of commerce flow. / Let the vision of art heal. / Technology, provide the tools. / Workers of the world / Re-make the world / Under the guidance of inspiration / And wise laws. / Create the beautiful music / Our innermost happiness suggests. / Delight the future' ('Lines *in Potentis*' 2012: 27, ll. 39–48).[5]

Literary excellence: Okri's work is shot through with a profound ecological understanding; it is cerebral, yet accessible; the political dimension is interwoven with a powerful sense of the interconnectedness of all things; its Homeric foundations and African mythological themes connect Okri with the deep beginnings of literature. His guiding principle is nowhere better expressed than towards the end of *Songs of Enchantment* (from *The Famished Road* trilogy) when, from the silence of 'unblindedness', Azaro's father, in conversation with his son, an 'Abiku' (spirit-child), is moved to muse that '[t]he light comes out of the darkness' (1993: 287). In reading a work by this visionary author, one is imperceptibly led to believe in our obligation to address contemporary dilemmas. With this guiding principle, storytellers must consider '[h]ow to make those intuitive leaps that can transform humanity, how to make this mysterious faculty available to all' (2011: 27). Okri is peerless in his ability to make attentiveness to our world an imperative of consciousness. His writings intimate that art is directed by consciousness; that the complex self has access to reflection; the objects of reflective cultural creation can provide 'the true turning point in the future history of civilization' ('Interview with Ben Okri' 2012).[6] The works emit the intoxication of encounter with the best self and that self for the betterment of all.

The body of work and its uniqueness: The corpus is vast. More importantly and testifying to the craft and versatility of this writer, it encompasses all the literary generic categories, each challenging in some way the boundaries and possibilities of art. Okri's work is that of a consummate artist, one who has mastered the art of expressing ideas and emotions, not by describing them directly, but by suggesting what these ideas and emotions are, by re-creating them in the mind of the reader through the use of unexplained and intriguing symbols.

Scholarship and debate: There is a sustained and growing body of criticism with special issues of international journals dedicated to the oeuvre. Okri's creative output spans multiple generic and sub-generic categories: areas pertinent to genre studies. His cross-generic works – poetic prose, dramatic short stories, the invention of the 'stoku' (an amalgam of short story and *haiku*) – and dark poetic film scripts encourage lively scholarly debate and research. A linear thread is dismay at humankind's inhumanity, whether the topic is slavery, racism, internecine strife, colonialism or other examples of humankind's propensity for domination, coupled with a dream of a better world in which love, beauty and cosmic awareness can lead to redemption. Eschewing the stance of the subaltern and pointing to decolonization of the mind through the agency of the creative imagination, his works explore three burning theoretical issues in today's fraught sociopolitical climate: decolonial turns, postcolonial shifts and cultural connections.

Dissemination of scholarship, partnering in global knowledge production: Reading circles, tertiary institutions and multimedia platforms around the world are interacting with one another to discuss the import of Okri's work.

Intercultural unity: Okri's work typifies what Homi Bhabha calls 'cultural hybridity'. His own reading is massive and cross-cultural. Through his storytelling ability and wide intertextual nuggets from literary and filmic sources, he pays tribute to fellow writers by synchronizing his ancient and modern, Western and Eastern analogues to transcend arbitrary cultural divisions.

Cultural icon and literary service to the wider community: Writing for over four decades, Okri has become an international cultural icon, always in demand. He is engaged in an enormous amount of literary service through extensive readings, lectures, occasional writing, adjudications, conversations, book festivals and interviews throughout the world. More than reading and thinking, Okri cultivates a deeper understanding of Nature, demonstrating a green economy consciousness. He gives back in reciprocity indicative of generosity of spirit, a communal ethos or what in South Africa is termed 'Ubuntu' (I am because we are).

Capacity-building and social consciousness: His participation in countless panel discussions, workshops and interviews on creative writing has stimulated and will continue to stimulate potential new writing.

Stimulation of the act of reading: As human and transcendental symbolist, Okri's purpose is to re-create in readers visual impressions of the dark quality of contemporary life with possible ways in which to re-dream our world. He invokes a Nietzschean 'will to power', a redemption of suffering, in which suffering is willed, transfigured and deified to become a form of great delight through reading or viewing its artistic representation. Okri's innovation inheres not only in transdisciplinary and cross-generic insights and modes that flow into his larger body of literary production but also in their accommodation of the poetics of narrative synthesis in which oral and literate forms and styles interfuse. In the context of hyper-connectivity – smartphones, social media and the like – Okri urges the reader to 'stop, stop for a moment – just stop' and to read slowly. His aim is to restore the pleasure principle, for readers to think about and enjoy the pure act of reading.

Serious literary consideration: Two main principles of the African oral tradition infuse Okri's work: authority and association. An idea is given validity by being placed side by side with another idea that bears the stamp of communal approval and by its being linked to the storehouse of collective wisdom. Okri at once globalizes and poeticizes such wisdom as evidenced in his extensive aphoristic, fictional, non-fictional, dramatic, poetic and word/image output. What is new and relevant in all the categories and in the essential questions Okri asks of reality, of history, of consciousness (themes grand and intimate) in the realization of each work, is the poetic intelligence so strongly built into the structures of meaning, feeling, thought and expression.

Promotion of the global tongue: Okri's impeccable use and command of the English language serve to promote best practice of the current lingua franca.

Vision: Okri's desire is to 'Spread illumination through this darkening world' ('Heraclitus' Golden River' 2012: 94, ll. 82 and 83).[7] A paradox is that his work is imbued with a feeling of perfect happiness and, by implication, a picture of paradise, whilst conveying a mood of black despair. In the final analysis, it is the work, its value, the light it gives, the clarity it engenders, the hope it sustains, the magic it awakens and the beauty it spreads that entice study of the Okrian corpus.

Foreword

A writer's body of work is like a vast lake. Sometimes it is like a river. Often with a glance you can encompass it. But when you dive into it, the body of work seems to have no end. This is not because the work is endless. Even Shakespeare's plays have a definite number and the collected works of Homer that have come down to us intact come to the grand infinite total of two. But they are both endless. Any true writer's work ought to be endless. You track its secret courses, its sources, its influence, its art, its meanings, its contradictions, its journey through time, and a measurable body of endeavour grows, multiplies, fractures, morphs, changes aspects, reveals unsuspected concerns, displays hidden erudition and concealments, mirrors universes and bodies of thoughts, refutes theories and schools, and turns out to be more sinuous and suggestive and receptive to constantly new interpretations than could ever have been suspected at the time of its initial reception.

The writer's work is always there, to be enjoyed, to be savoured, to be lived in the reading. But beyond all that, there is another dimension to the writer's work, to each book they write, if it is a true book. And that is the dimension of interpretation. Often we read a book once and, in accordance with our level of development, or the state of our minds at that particular time, we read the book that we are capable of reading. Often to read a book once is to cast one's eye over its contingent surface. Rarely, indeed never, at a first reading do we register in the depths of our minds the complex hidden understructure of the work, the resonant chain of its metaphors, the secret mountain ranges of its allusions, its contrapuntal arrangement of events and motifs that speak to and transform one another in a rich symphony operating just below the superficial level of the text. In short, every good book is a complex living organism that reveals its ever-changing depths to the reader who reads and rereads and then tracks down, like a detective combining uncanny intuition with great research and study, the multidimensionality of the work and the many things that it says without saying, hints without hinting, awakens without trying to awaken.

This takes a special reader, one who perhaps secretly grasps that the text, like the world, is a universe of enigmas and signs, some of them political, others metaphysical, and still others yet constantly hovering, like those quanta that become one thing or another depending on the observer, between one kind of reality or another, or between many realities at the same time.

In the decades since many declarations have been made about the death of the author, in which textual analysis has undergone many revolutions, in which many schools and sub-schools, in which ideologies and methods had penetrated the domains of literature, from theory to postcolonial studies, from feminism to transgender studies, in ever-increasing branching of mode after mode – through all this, literature has survived the many prisms; through all this, the primal activity of writing and writing well remains as perilously difficult as ever. Now it seems that the value of a text can no longer be spoken of in the fundamental mode of its quality; this seems to be increasingly of least concern. We come to a text, in the academy, not seeking first to grasp its excellence, its beauty, its craft, but a thousand other things of cultural and temporal importance. But it seems that this cannot long survive, for texts cannot be kept alive purely on their interest or value to this group or that group but finally only on how they speak to us, to our humanity, through their art and through the infinite refraction of their meaning.

The value of the true critic has never been more crucial; the need for those who can, with minds ranging wide through the literary disciplines of their times, see deep into texts and release hidden genies of understanding, become for us more urgent. We live in times when we read less and know less about the world's cultural heritage, times in which we are more and more fracturing into clans and tribes of thought and concern, in which many walls are erected around enclaves and preserves, where each thinker is encouraged to become a specialist of their one way of reading, in territories of contested value and ownership. We need critics who still bring rigour and imagination to their challenging tasks, who are not easily fooled and bullied by hounds of shallow reviewers who, not taking time to read a work properly and with due respect, dismiss it at the first sign of difficulty; critics who have the courage to pass over where there is an overwhelming tide of superficial convergence, where thousands agree on the value of a work because thousands have agreed on the value of a work; critics who can look into books that others have ignored and restore to them the legitimacy of their pressing concerns; critics who peer into what everyone else has overlooked, sometimes out of familiarity, sometimes out of laziness, and found therein new revelations, new angles, new songs, that have been lying there in the texts awaiting the right kind of sensibility; critics who, with the strength of their gaze and interrogation, smash apart a text to reveal the miraculous sub-particles, behaving in strange and unpredictable ways, that animate the inner world of the texts, giving rise to that shimmering, changing surface that we call a work of art.

Somewhere Proust wrote that 'the better the telescope, the more the stars', or something of that order; hinting that the world is really only as good as the subtlety of our seeing and maybe also the subtlety of our feeling and of our grasp of the mysterious nature of reality. That the world is a book and the book is a world is already an old mode of aphoristic thought that still has enough energy in it to start a few more interstellar journeys. The fact is that works of art speak the language of enigma amidst the language of the everyday, the language of politics, the language of change.

In these twenty essays, spanning over a decade, Professor Rosemary Gray brings a fresh eye and a fresh dimension to a consideration of the works of Ben Okri. She looks into areas other critics have ignored, pays attention to works that seem in a minor key and reveals them to be quite central to his artistic project, and brings a new discipline of literary criticism to bear on the works to see what they yield when seen through the lens of the metaphysical, the philosophical and the cultural. It could be said that the critical perception of Ben Okri's work has not begun to do justice to the complexity of the body of work, to the richness of its techniques, to the scale of its political and aesthetic engagements, to the wealth of its hidden allusions, to the implications of its innovations. And Rosemary Gray's essays attempt bravely an exploration of Ben Okri's worlds. Her rereadings of a work like *In Arcadia* have compelled a critical re-examination of that somewhat neglected text; her encounter with the new prose form that Ben Okri invented, called 'stokus', has helped the realization that they too, in their quantum state, reflect the complexity at the heart of his aesthetics; and her study of his aphorisms has helped draw attention to the philosophical concerns that run beneath the longer fictional texts, showing that after all in a writer's work, world reflects world and different parts of an oeuvre throw unexpected lights on other parts, that the small is not so small, the refracted not so fractured and the prosecution of reality that can be said, whether in political implication or in existential extrapolation, to lie somewhere at the heart of the literary programme, finds its praxis in all the domains of the writer's dream kingdom.

In these essays, Rosemary Gray shows her wide reading and her eclectic mind. The essays burst with energy and critical fizz. Often the excitement of discovery can be discerned; often the surprise at intuitive delight can be felt; and often the sheer scale of the research undertaken yields lovely rewards. But mostly it is the yoking of disparate critical disciplines, brought to bear on a new reading of Ben Okri's work, that delivers the interest and the fascination.

Rosemary Gray began these essays late in her professional life, and they represent for her a kind of renewal. It seems she found in Ben Okri's body of work a subject that was conducive to her critical gifts. It is a rare pleasure when a writer finds in a subject a rich seam of exploration that allows them to renew themselves in their discipline. This is strangely fitting, for renewal is also a keen vein running through the secret terrain of Ben Okri's work. It is his terroir. Renewal of Africa, renewal of the art, renewal of the psyche of a people as it is possible through literature. That and the art of enchantment.

When all is written and read, it is the enchantment that lasts the longest and goes on working long after the times and the breath and the bones have ceased whispering in the wind. The writer may have many aims, intentions and purposes in mind as they create their work; but something greater and more mysterious than their intention is what lasts. It is that something which fascinates, which haunts, which stimulates and which makes us want to go on asking questions of those works. It is that something which is at the heart of criticism, whatever form it takes now and in the future. And that something must also shine from criticism, in the intelligence, the detective work, the quality of thought, the depth of analysis, the weaving of Ariadne's threads through the labyrinths of language and structures.

While it must be stated that this way of looking at Ben Okri's work is not exclusive, that there are as many ways of studying a body of work as there are keen minds to undertake such a study, Rosemary Gray does take ownership of this way of studying it. That is to say, so thoroughly does she invest her sensibilities into this metaphysical, spiritual and cultural reading that she makes this kind of reading her own. In its way, perhaps she has shaped her own aesthetic mode, her personal hermeneutics. In this way also, both the critic and the artist have revealed something distinct about each other through the encounter in these critical essays. The light that shines on the work shines also on the one that shines it. Like a painting you perhaps saw once of a family in a laboratory watching an experiment by a new form of light. You notice the light, the faces and the experiment. Every critical essay is an experiment in understanding. Every act of reading is a laboratory. When you read these essays, something of the light shines on you too. The light comes from the subject, the experimenter and the reader. It is hoped that when you read these essays, you might return to the books themselves and see them again in a new, expanded light.

© Ben Okri
Little Venice, London
September 2018

Acknowledgements

I thank my students at the University of Pretoria and Derek's and my offspring, Peter, Alan and Carolyn, for sharing my enthusiasm for Okri's creativity; our daughter, Canna, for travelling this journey with me, accompanying me to international conferences (her PowerPoint presentations illustrating my readings have been enjoyed by conference participants worldwide); Dr Matthew Curr and Alan for proofreading; and my academic peers for steering my interest towards the Okrian oeuvre.

I have granted licence to publish earlier versions of several of the essays to journals – *Academic Journal of Interdisciplinary Studies, English Academy Review, English in Africa, Imbizo: Journal of Literary Studies, Literator, New Directions in the Humanities, Research in African Literature, The International Journal for African Renaissance Studies* and *Tydskrif vir Letterkunde* – and books – *Analecta Husserilana* – as acknowledged in the references that follow each chapter and reused with the permission of the original publishers; those incorporated here are all double-blind peer-reviewed *new* or substantively reworked versions.

I thank Rosemary Clunie for granting permission to use her beautiful cover painting and the frontispiece pen and ink portrait of Ben Okri, and Matt Bray for the Okri photograph. I acknowledge both my deep appreciation to Renato Tomei for redrawing the image of Magritte's *Le faux miroir* and to Ben Okri whose writings inspired this monograph and keep me ever-wakeful. Last but not least, I thank Bloomsbury Academic Publishers for their inimitable professionalism.

About the Author

Rosemary Alice Gray is Emeritus Professor in the Department of English at the University of Pretoria, South Africa. She is a rated researcher, specializing in Anglo-Saxon, Middle English and Pan-African texts; her current research interest is the work of Ben Okri. She has written or presented thirty-one papers on Okri's oeuvre in the past decade. She is Honorary Life Vice President of the English Academy of Southern Africa and Managing Editor of the *English Academy Review: Journal of English Studies*. Her book publications include *Broken Strings: The Politics of Poetry*, *Sounding Wings: Short Stories from Africa* (with Stephen Finn, Longmans), *Light Comes Out of the Darkness: The History of Expo for Young Scientists* (OUP) and *A Glass Half Full or Half Empty? The Challenges of Political Succession and Elections in Africa* (Ssali).

Part One

The alchemy of life: 'To find life in myth and myth in life' (*Birds of Heaven* 1996)

1

Ben Okri's aphorisms: 'Music on the wings of a soaring bird'

Introduction

In a chapter that explores the what and how of a collection of nuggets of wisdom, it is apposite to begin by asking why writers such as Ben Okri, who have accepted the post-enlightenment critique of reason, use reason to convey grand notions conceived to give meaning to individual and collective life. One surmises that the answer might lie in a belief in the changeability of the human condition. Okri subscribes to the philosophy of the transhuman, expressed by Sebastian Seung (2013: 273) as being 'the destiny of humankind to transcend the human condition'.[1] Okri stresses the centrality of 'great stories', for instance, because they provide an overarching explanation of human life or suggest universal moral principles (2015: 1042). A fragment in *Birds of Heaven* highlights the moral purpose of Okri's aphorisms: 'It is precisely in a broken age that we need mystery and a re-awakened sense of wonder: need them in order to be whole again' (1996: 40 no. 84). 'We are all wounded inside in some way or other,' Okri insists. 'We all carry unhappiness within us for some reason or other' (ibid.). One deduces, therefore, that Okri's maxims serve as a (moral) corrective to ameliorate both postmodernity's material culture and the resultant discontent with contemporary life.

Reviving the Wisdom Corpus from antiquity, this multitalented Nigerian writer provides a guiding paremiological exemplum in *A Time for New Dreams* to counter postmodernity's obsession with the pleasure principle, fast living and hyper-connectivity: 'And out of the wilderness / The songbird sings / Nothing is what it seems. / This is a time for new dreams' (2011: 147). Based on Italian Renaissance's Desiderius Erasmus's ([1540] 1982) view on the luminous benefits of concise thought, the argument is that the quintessence of aphorisms or proverbs is their pithy wisdom. A basic premise is that the 'Imaginatio Creatrix' communicating in poetic-prose aphorisms provides fertile ground for new connections, new depths and new transversals as well as epiphanies or what Okri terms the alchemy of 'serendipity'. The cross-generic outpourings of this conceptual artist reveal an almost boundless quest for improvement to counter the hurt – possibly accruing from egotistic values – through intuitive creativity and heightened consciousness leading to intellectual growth and spiritual upliftment. These aphorisms are thus transformative.

The African worldview, as Wole Soyinka reminds us, turns on belief in 'the continuing evolution of tribal wisdom through an acceptance of the elastic nature of knowledge as its one reality, as signifying no more than reflections of the original coming-into-being of a manifestly complex reality' (1995: 53). Integral to Okri's probing of rationality is the evolutionary process of epistemology and 'the emergence of human creativity as the stimulus to the development of human culture with its aesthetic, moral, and intellectual senses' (to borrow from Jadwiga Smith 2011: 17).

In Okri's vision that informs his aphorisms, one detects classical, Christian and traditional African motifs. In contrast to the biblical book of Proverbs or its Hebraic Deuteronomy, Okri is neither prescriptive nor doctrinaire: he prods us gently towards the light. This is encapsulated in the title to this chapter, derived from Okri's publication *The Magic Lamp* (2017), itself an intersectional text featuring a selection of Rosemary Clunie's art and Ben Okri's accompanying ontopoietic intuitions on Nature and the nature of being. The metaphor 'Music on the wings of a soaring bird' serves to illustrate Okri's synaesthetic mode.[2] While the immediate appeal is to the auditory and mental, our visual as well as sensory faculties are simultaneously stimulated. Okri's view of reality, reflecting that of phenomenologist Anna-Teresa Tymieniecka, 'encompasses three ontological categories: the physical, the vital and the meaningful' (Smith 2011: 18).[3]

Interdisciplinarity and transdisciplinarity in Okri's aphorisms

Okri has spared no genre or medium in his creative impulse, erasing artificial disciplinary and generic boundaries. Not only does he argue for the healing power of poetic truth, but he also sees a symbiotic relation between the language of literature and that of philosophy, coining in *Birds of Heaven* a cultural aphorism that '[p]hilosophy is most powerful when it resolves into story. But story is amplified in power by the presence of philosophy' (1996: 40). According to Ron Grace (n.d.: 4), etymologically, philosophy is the 'love of wisdom'. In revivifying the ancient philosophy of the Wisdom Corpus, embracing its ideas, points of view, ways of life, systems of belief and so religious myths in his pithy observations, Okri demonstrates its synthesis with the African folkloric tradition that contains 'a general truth', itself the definition of an aphorism in *The New Oxford Dictionary of English* (1998: 76).

An early Okrian aphorism asserts unequivocally that '[t]he greatest religions convert the world through stories' (Okri 1996: 20 no. 12); and Okri elucidates on the role of fiction in the perpetuation of religious mythologies: 'All the great religions, all the great prophets, found it necessary to spread their message through stories, fables, parables' (ibid.: 19). This echoes the claim of Italian theologian, Desiderius Erasmus ([1540] 1982: 17), who suggested that the overlap between philosophy and theology is such that theology is served as much by proverbs as by philosophy. The book of Proverbs in the Christian Bible, with its principle theme of wisdom, testifies to this view.[4] 'The Bible is one of the world's greatest fountains of fiction and dream,' Okri (1996: 19) aphorizes.

Ronald Grace (n.d.: 4) suggests that faith provides the deepest level of wisdom, akin to what Okri terms 'serendipity', in its advocacy of an integrative underlying order. His poem, 'On Klee' (1996: 45), provides his poetic objective correlative: 'Wisdom reigns in hidden symmetry / And colours are but charmed invisibility. / What lingers in the soul / Often bypasses the eye / And the birds of heaven, without wings – / How much more sublimely do they fly' (Stanza 4).

In contradistinction to Roger Fowler's notion that ' "Art" … like "good" must be simply a commendatory word covering a multitude of incompatible meanings' and – more insightfully – that 'Art, as all know who are in the know, is not Life' (1973: 12), Okri avers in an aphoristic correlative that 'All art is a prayer for spiritual strength' (1996: 12 no. 8). Evocative of the notion of a universal soul, he adds: 'If we could be pure dancers in spirit, we would never be afraid to love, and we would love with strength and wisdom' (ibid.). Erasmus's articulation on the efficacy of aphorisms or proverbs, such as these, concurs in greater detail:

> To weave adages deftly and appropriately is to make the language as a whole glitter with sparkles of Antiquity, please us with the colours of the art of rhetoric, gleam with jewel-like words of wisdom, and charm us with titbits of wit and humour. In a word, it will wake interest by its novelty, bring delight by its concision, convince by its decisive power. ([1540] 1982: 17)

The trajectory of Okrian aphorisms

This discussion traces the trajectory and suggests the import of Okri's blueprints for regaining our true state of being, for loving 'with strength and wisdom', conveyed via his aphorisms in *Birds of Heaven* (1996), *A Time for New Dreams* (2011) and *Callaloo* (2015: 1042–3). Broadly speaking, the trajectory comes together in the form of a secular sermon on ontopoietic 'beingness', a term used by phenomenologists as a synonym for Heidegger's 'Dasein'.

Predicated on the twin aphorisms that 'Africa breathes stories' and '[w]e are part human, part stories' (Okri 1996: 24 and 26), *Birds of Heaven* explores the notion of humankind as 'Homo fabula'. As a variation of the myth of faith and faith in mythmaking, Okri aphorizes enigmatically: 'To find life in myth, and myth in life' (ibid.: 42 no. 95). This prefigures a later aphoristic gem – 'Great literature is almost always indirect' (Okri 2015: 1042 no. 6). Predictably, given the thrust, a swirling cosmic dance of Okrian maxims has to do with the imagination and creativity, illustrating the writer's conceptual artistry and transdisciplinary mode. For instance, he asserts that '[t]he imagination is one of the highest gifts we have' (1996: 42 no. 93), but with the proviso that imagination operates best when unbounded, as implicit in '[t]he higher the artist, the fewer the gestures' and explicit in '[t]he fewer the tools, the greater the imagination' (ibid.: 40 nos 81 and 82). Musing that '[c]reativity is a secular infinity' and that '[c]reativity is evidence of the transhuman', he asserts that '[c]reativity is the highest civilizing faculty' (ibid.: 41 nos 86, 87 and 88), a concept reiterated in my interview with the writer in 2011 (the closing essay in this monograph). Such twinned adages are perspicacious, for, as Anders Sandberg attests, 'Transhumanism, broadly speaking, is the view that the human condition is not unchanging and that it can and should be questioned' (2014: 1). This resonates with Soyinka's claim for the evolutionary and plastic growth of wisdom, mentioned earlier.

Foregrounding the primacy of love and creativity, Okri intertwines art and spiritual love, moral codification, thankfulness and politics in numbers 90, 93, 98, 99 and 101 with:

> Love is the greatest creativity of them all, and the most blessed.
> Creativity is love, a very high kind of love.
> Humility is the watchword at creativity's gate.
> Creativity is a form of prayer, and the expression of a profound gratitude for being alive.

And then, in another transdisciplinary observation, a mode that is core to his aesthetic practice, Okri avers that '[p]olitics is the art of the possible; creativity is the art of the impossible' (1996: 41–3). The astute anaphoric wordplay implies alchemy at work.

To adopt Joseph Addison's view, if clarity and perspicacity were all that were needed, 'the poet would have nothing else to do but to clothe his thoughts in the most plain and natural expressions' (Jones [1922] 1963: 239). Although pared down to their essentials, the aphorisms in *A Time for New Dreams* develop mythmaking, inviting us to rethink our human condition.

Here, Okri is perhaps more methodical in his exhortations. In a section entitled 'Seeing and Being', he provides ten aphorisms on this chosen theme, nine of which are variations on the indivisibility of seeing and being, as captured in '[t]o see, one must first be' (2011: 23 no. 5); while the tenth, 'It takes a work of art to see a work of art' (24), illustrates an aphorism from *Birds of Heaven*: 'All great stories are enigmas' (1996: 43 no. 97).

The next quiver of aphorisms in *A Time for New Dreams* occurs in a section entitled 'The Romance of Difficult Times'. In line with this oxymoronic section heading, these maxims turn on paradox, where paradox, as defined by Fowler, is an 'apparently self-contradictory statement, though one that is essentially true' (1973: 136). Fowler cites an example from Schopenhauer by way of explication: 'The more unintelligent a man is, the less mysterious existence seems to him'; as well as one from Shaw that evokes the pathetic fallacy: 'The man who listens to reason is lost: reason enslaves all whose minds are not strong enough to master her' (ibid.). Both paradoxes are proverbial or aphoristic. Okri's adage that '[s]tory is a paradox' (1996: 31 no. 48) in *Birds of Heaven* can perhaps be better understood in aphorisms 19 and 21 that are, when paired, clearly paradoxical: 'In the beginning there were no stories' and 'The universe began as a story' (ibid.: 22). To a Western believer, the allusion would seem to be to Genesis. But I would argue in line with Emmanuel Obiechina (1995: 123) that these aphorisms perform an organic and structural function. They allude to 'a return to the roots movement in African literature as a means of giving maximum authenticity to the writing' by sustaining 'traditional solidarities' and espousing 'values, beliefs, and attitudes conditioned and nourished by the oral tradition', to interpret, that is, by evoking an indigenous poetics of myths, folktales, fairy tales, animal fables, anecdotes and legends that precede the written tradition.

In *A Time for New Dreams*, difficult times are invoked in paradoxical aphorisms mediated by communal consciousness and impulses arising from group sensibilities (as suggested in the Obiechina quotations (1995: 124)) as in Okri's: 'There can be no rise without a fall, no fall without a rise' and 'There can be no prosperity without adversity that has been wisely transformed' (2011: 39 nos 2 and 3). More ontopoietic is the aphorism 'Difficult times do one of two things to us: they either break us or they force us back to the primal ground of our being' (ibid.: 40 no. 6); while more acute is a doxographic aphorism from antiquity: ' "Sometimes the way up is the way down," Heraclitus said' (ibid.: 41 no. 17).

In Apostolic times, Christ's followers were enjoined to practise the virtue of hospitality as concretized in the parable of the loaves and the fishes. Emulating the earlier Messianic Jewish Laws on the spirit of hospitality (Lev. 19.33 and 34), a virtue much esteemed by civilized peoples (Cruden 1949 [1971]: 314), as well as 'one of the most treasured laws of the African social existence' (Soyinka [1976] 1995: 21), Okri includes a series of aphorisms on the topic in his compendium of wisdom in *A Time for New Dreams* (2011). Having provoked with a delightfully rationalistic counterargument of 'Philosophically there is no such thing as hospitality because we are all guests on this planet, we are all guests in life' (ibid.: 54 no. 15), he expounds on the virtues of hospitality, once again transcending disciplinary borders. For example, he braids holism with alchemical psychology and the science of relativity, and with ancient Chinese philosophy and creative openness to the world of ideas in the following hospitality aphorisms (8, 17, 18 and 12):

> Hospitality is a secret affirmation of the oneness of humanity, a sort of secular kinship. Hospitality is something we should be able to extend not just to our friends, but even to our enemies.
> It is quite possible that we are guests in the universe and guests in the condition of mortal consciousness.
> Hospitality is therefore temporary, finite, and subject to the continual changes of the human condition.
> According to Lao Tsû the truest hospitality is when the host is like a guest, and the guest like a host. (Ibid.: 52–4)

This set climaxes with an inner or heightened consciousness aphorism in 'There is also intellectual hospitality, the hospitality to ideas, to dreams, to ways of seeing, to perception, to culture' (ibid.: 55 no. 20). Okri implies that intellectual hospitality is akin to 'Logos'; it is 'the most important of all …' (ibid.). Thus, mindful hospitality is a hold-all for all facets of hospitality. His evocation of the term 'guest' in these maxims illustrates his own intellectual hospitality. Etymologically, the word 'hospitality' derives from the Latin 'hospes', 'a guest' (Brewer's [1952] 1970: 349) as in 'hospice' or the Knights of St John.[5]

Considering the challenges that confront us in our postmodern age and in our creative or critical endeavour, Okri offers three other significant sets of aphorisms in *A Time for New Dreams*: those on childhood, on Form and Content, and on Healing Africa, which will be touched on briefly. In contradistinction to the book of Proverbs that tends to focus on the once popular adage of 'spare the rod and spoil the child',[6] Okri's adages on childhood have to do with the need for educated parenting as opposed to biological inevitability. By contrast to early Judaeo-Christian thought, he sees childhood clearly as a paradoxical period: a 'focus of love – real love and confused love' (2011: 77 no. 2). Underlining the paradox of the vulnerability, but also the innate cruelty of childhood, he avers: 'Childhood: the place of all society's experiments, its disastrous ideas of conscious engineering' (ibid.: 78 no. 6); but 'a time also of innocent cruelties, tearing off the wings of butterflies, cutting up worms, ganging up on the weakest, the newcomer, or the strange one' (ibid.: 78 no. 5); and 'the meeting place of an endless chain of failures and successes, hopes and fears, marvels and disasters, disorders and joys, and the hidden narrative of ancestors' (ibid.: 77 no. 6). These adages show that modern insight into the psychology of both parenting and childhood, particularly in today's diffuse nuclear family unit, denied the wisdom of tribal elders.

As expected, the section 'Form and Content' relates at once to general truisms about literature and to an ontopoietic take on artistic creation, as in, 'Form endures longer than content' (Okri 2011: 125 no. 2) and 'Nothing can live in art or in life that does not find the form unique to itself by which its individual soul can be expressed' (ibid.: 120 no. 8). More poetically and perhaps even reminiscent of the Romantic era, Okri states, 'Form is the visible manifestation of spirit' (ibid.: 127 no. 13) and 'The medium is higher the more levels it has within it that correspond to the levels within us' (ibid.: 128 no. 16).

The main axis of these latter aphorisms is the phenomenology of life and of the human condition informed by cosmic creativity: a pointer to the creative function of transhumanism.[7] An excerpt from Soyinka's *Myth, Literature and the African World* serves to elucidate:

> Where society lives in close inter-relation [sic] with Nature, regulates its existence by natural phenomena within the observable processes of continuity – ebb and tide, waxing and waning of the moon, rain and drought, planting and harvest – the highest moral order is seen as that which guarantees a parallel continuity of the species. (1995: 52)

Acknowledging attitudes towards Africa of dismissal, patronage, exploitation and even insult, Okri provides a slipway into his aphorisms on the healing of Africa within by reminding us that 'Africa is difficult to see because it takes heart to see her. It takes simplicity of spirit to see her without confusion, / And it takes a developed human being to see her without prejudice' (2011: 59). It follows that '[t]o see Africa one must first see oneself' (ibid.: 60), lending meaning to lives that were robbed of it by prejudice. This implies being at once childlike – innocent and pure, and mature – insightful and tolerant: seeing without bias.

Sustaining the metaphor of seeing, Okri has a three-pronged aphorism on cognitive perception: 'If we see it, it will be revealed. We only see what we are prepared to see. Only what we see anew is revealed to us' (2011: 137 no. 20). He recaps with the anthropological reminder that Africa is the cradle of humankind: 'There is a realm in everyone that is Africa ... We all have Africa within (ibid.: 134 no. 6). It is a given, therefore, that love is an essential response in an axiomatic exhortation, 'To clear the darkness from the eyes of the world' (ibid.: 136 no. 18), 'We have to learn to love the Africa within us if humanity is going to begin to know true happiness on this earth' (ibid.: 137 no. 23). Okri is clearly convinced that our contemporary world requires that reflective intelligence that plays a key role in human life and cognition. This brings me to the final set of aphorisms to be discussed: those in *Callaloo*'s special issue on Ben Okri (2015).

Suggestive of the centrality of numerology for Ben Okri, the alchemist, a triad of themes dominates a dozen maxims in *Callaloo* viz. modes of reading, freedom and creativity. The first and third reflect those on 'Form and Content' in *A Time for New Dreams*, while the second incorporates reading and creativity and encapsulates a pivotal preoccupation for Okri, as testified in titles such as his *A Way of Being Free* ([1989] 1997) and *Tales of Freedom* (2009), and explored in depth in his novel, *The Famished Road* (1991). Aphorism number 12 (2015: 1043) is a terse definition of freedom: 'The genius of inner freedom'. This adage echoes the philosophical underpinning of an extract from *A Way of Being Free* which reads:

> It is possible that a sense of beauty, of justice, of the inner connectedness of all things, may yet save the human species from self-annihilation. We are all still learning how to be free. Freedom is the *beginning* of the greatest possibilities of the human genius. It is not the goal. ([1989] 1997: 132; emphasis added)

The other freedom aphorisms (Okri 2015: 1042 nos 2 and 3) highlight the necessity for untrammelled freedom:

> The essential thing is freedom. A people cannot be great or fulfilled without freedom. A literature cannot be great without it either.
> The basic prerequisite for literature is freedom. The first freedom is mental freedom.

And, paradoxically, 'It is possible to be free in the world and unfree in your head' (2015: 1042 no. 4), an idea that Okri explores in his 2019 novel, *The Freedom Artist*.

Elaborating on cognitive freedom, Okri asserts: 'Reading slowly reveals the hidden dimensions of a text' (2015: 1042 no. 1). Speed reading or scanning, so popular in our information age, can lead to misunderstanding. By contrast, 'Slow Reading restores sanity to a world where we grasp less than we hear, take in less than we are told, and miss the meaning of our most significant experiences' (ibid.: 1042 no. 11). Okri's injunction is to '[l]aunch the Slow Reading movement throughout the world' (ibid.). He believes that '[t]he most striking thing about great literature is the strength of freedom that flows through its pages' (ibid.: 1042 no. 5). This is because '[i]t is art, rather than its subject, which makes a work always mysteriously relevant to us … It is its art alone which keeps a work alive through the long ages' (ibid.: 1042 no. 10).[8]

Conclusion

One cannot dub Okri a Deuteronomist or ancient lawgiver![9] His is not a collection of commandments. He does not instruct or preach. His wisdom comes painstakingly gift-wrapped with the message: 'We are all, quietly, invisibly, at the vanguard of how our world turns out' (2018: pers. com.). Fellow Nigerian Obiechina explains the tradition of proverbializing that thrives on analogy and association in African narratives:

> [T]here are in African novels movements forward and backward along symbol-referent trajectories that radically influence their plots … the embedding of the narrative proverbs necessarily reduces the tempo of narrative, since the reader is constantly compelled to slow down in order to absorb the full import of the newly embedded story, to decipher it as a symbol or image, to relate symbol/ image to its referent, and to relate them (story, symbol/ image and referent) to the structure of the novel's total meaning. (1995: 127)

The appeal for slow reading is itself symbolic: it encapsulates what Okri seeks to achieve with his aphorisms – to stop and stare, to reflect and so take time perhaps to reformulate our thinking.

It is the mystery of the creative impulse, the secret workings of the artistic mind, the withdrawal from the world into the inner sanctum of creativity that engages Ben Okri. His demonstration of the creative process constitutes a personal aphoristic statement that, not without irony, is given to the Abiku child's drunken father in *The Famished Road* to voice. Azaro's father leads the Party of the Poor with a Churchillian 'cri de guerre' (war cry/call to arms): 'THINK DIFFERENTLY,' he shouted, 'AND YOU WILL CHANGE THE WORLD.' / No one heard him. / 'REMEMBER HOW FREE YOU ARE,' he bellowed, 'AND YOU WILL TRANSFORM YOUR HUNGER INTO POWER' (1991: 419–20; original emphasis). With such a powerful paremiological outburst, it seems to me a paradox that only one other critic appears to have been drawn to comment on Okri's aphorisms. Historian Richard Bauckham, in his erudite survey of the aphorisms in the Epistle of James, mentions Okri together with Francis Bacon, La Rochefoucauld and Elias Canetti (2002: 109) as belonging to a major tradition of aphoristic writing.[10] More perspicaciously, he draws attention to a similarity between James (3.5-8) and Okri's reflection on 'the potential of words to do harm' (ibid.: 205). Jesus' disciple James points to the paradox that man is able to tame a large horse with a small bit and steer a huge ship with a tiny helm but is unable to 'tame' the 'fire' of the tongue, one of the smallest members of the human body. In Jas 3.8, we read: 'But the tongue can no man tame; it is an unruly evil, full of deadly poison.' This does indeed correlate with an aphoristic fragment from *Birds of Heaven*. Okri muses: 'It seems to me that our days are poisoned with too many words. Words said and not meant. Words said *and* meant. Words divorced from feeling. Wounding words. Words that conceal. Words that reduce. Dead words' (1996: 3; original emphasis). This kind of moralizing is atypical of Okri, whose didacticism is generally more veiled as in a fragment in *Birds of Heaven* that both summarizes my argument and highlights the subtle moral purpose of Okri's aphorisms, mentioned at the outset: 'It is precisely in a broken age that we need mystery and a re-awakened sense of wonder: need them in order to be whole again' (ibid.: 40).

2

Epistemic ecology and 'diminishing boundaries of a shrinking world' in 'Heraclitus' Golden River' from *Wild*

Introduction

Ephesus, the home of Heraclitus,[1] stands in the Maeander Valley, south-east of the mouth of the Maeander (Cayster) River in modern day Turkey. The river flows into the Mediterranean. South-west of the city is Mt Koressus (Bülbüldag); on the east is Mt Pion (Panayirdag), and there is a plain of arable land northwards between the city and river. Ephesus's harbour lay about four miles inland from the Mediterranean with a man-made canal cut to run eastward from the Maeander. Heraclitus's Ephesus was rich enough to boast one of the Seven Wonders of the Ancient World, the Temple of Artemis, and it later contained the massive Library of Kelsus; as a centre of trade, it was unrivalled (see Greaves 2010). Then what happened? The river gradually silted up despite Herculean efforts to keep the canal open, and, now, a visit to the ruins of Ephesus leaves one feeling hot and dusty. But for Heraclitus and his contemporaries, the Maeander was the most significant physical feature of the city's wealth, trade and fame. These geophysical aspects were perhaps the impetus behind Ben Okri's poem, 'Heraclitus' Golden River', with its central theme of the change/no change dialectic and its catalytic river motif.

Okri stands in a long tradition of persons moved by the reading of the pre-Socratic cosmologist, Heraclitus, whose fragments of writing are sufficiently enigmatic for him to have been called 'the Obscure'. The archaic thinker made elliptical commentaries on the phenomenological world, especially about how things change. The statements were not from a rationalist, Aristotelian viewpoint. Heraclitus's oracular statements belong to the tradition of 'wisdom literature' which flourished from Babylonia to Ionia and into Sicily and Egypt in ancient times and tended to the pithy, the contradictory, the obscure (Lazaridis 2007: 219–20, 243).

Okri's own oeuvre displays a similar virtuosity in making profoundly oracular, elliptical statements. Moreover, his speculative worldview ('Weltangschauung'), intimating a phenomenological realm between subjective and objective reality, is in line with Heraclitus's comprehension of the world. Yet, whereas readers of the contemporary Okri can make a clear distinction between what is considered rational, scientific and provable, and set that in opposition to what is imaginative, poetic and metaphorical, it is more difficult to do so when faced with the fragments of the Sages in pursuit of wisdom some 2,600 years ago. Okri's is a bold enterprise to gloss the archaic words of Heraclitus in his poem, 'Heraclitus' Golden River', and bring them within the understanding of a modern reader in his anthology, *Wild* (2012). The contemporary audience he addresses makes little distinction between urban and wild except as part of a private tourist programme. Unlike Okri, we tend to take for granted writing as signs disinvested of their numinous power to give access to potent wisdom, and it is commonplace that our wise folk, like Udita Goswami (actress), William Arntz (producer) and Werner Heisenberg (philosopher), can end up in pseudoscience films for the masses, such as 'What the Bleep Do We Know!?'

Epistemic eco-phenomenology and the river of creative inspiration

In an uncanny echo of the film's title, Ben Okri states in his 2011 *A Time for New Dreams* that '[t]he universe grows more mysterious around us even as we find out more about it' (28). He suggests that the reason behind this paradox is that 'we are taught to see less in ourselves, to ask no questions about our true inner nature' (ibid.). Elaborating on the need for self-discovery, or what fellow Nigerian and Nobel laureate, Wole Soyinka ([1976] 1995), terms man's 'gravity-bound apprehension of self' as 'inseparable from the entire cosmic phenomenon' (3), Okri posits that

> [k]nowing ourselves, we will know others. Only by knowing ourselves can we begin to undo the madness we unleash on the world in our wars, our destruction of the environment, our divisions, our desire to dominate others, the poverty we create and exploit. (2011: 29)

The excerpt suggests that Okri apprehends big movements in philosophy through reading and imagination – so, he goes from the wisdom literature that counsels self-control to the full-blown philosophical idea of 'Know thyself'. He thus extends Soyinka's ethics. His epistemology, akin to that of Heraclitus, embraces both ethics and politics. By '[k]nowing ourselves' or exercising our own 'logos', Okri suggests, 'we will know others' and so come to realize that the external 'logos' of the cosmos entails an 'ethical and political scheme in which one is persuaded by the best person, who can only be the one who exercises this capacity best' (Kahn 1979: 24), that is, by the knowing self.

Indicative of epistemic eco-phenomenology would be the poet's green economy awareness, his deep concern for, and the need to grapple with, current as well as perennial issues, issues vitally significant to the survival of humankind, at the heart of which lies a tension between education (what we are taught) and knowledge of self. 'Only through self-knowledge,' Okri insists, 'can we reverse the damage we do with all the worldly knowledge we have, which is only a higher ignorance' (2011: 29).

What then is the inspirational role of art in countering our 'higher ignorance', in providing intuitions and/or new ways of thinking to address or redress culturally imposed indoctrination and man's destruction of the planet – the frame of Part 1 of his poem entitled 'Heraclitus' Golden River' (2012: 92–4)? The answer, as implied in Part 2, resides in a symbiosis of the impetus and equipoise of one-world consciousness.

An Okri aphorism, 'To see a work of art or the truth in a work requires a solid foundation in ourselves' (2011: 24), coupled with the poem's reiterated pivotal injunction to '[s]pread illumination through this darkening world' (2012: ll. 82–3), encapsulates impetus. His claim in *A Way of Being Free* ([1989] 1997) that '[t]he poet turns the earth into mother, the sky becomes a shelter, the sun the inscrutable god …' (2), together with the poem's lines: 'Poets pray to the goddess of surprise / Love is seduced by change, / Itself unchanging' (2012: ll. 28–30), reflects equipoise.

Ultimately, the poem advocates discretion, which moves to self-knowledge, as a metaphysics of life: basic tenets of 'wisdom literature'. The proposition is evidently a review and revival of a pre-modern, mythopoeic relationship with Nature as a living, sentient interlocutor and of life rather than man as 'the measure'.[2] This resonates not only with the poem's title but also with Theodor Adorno's claim that art 'suspends self-justificatory, teleological rationality' (2002: 138), an aspect integral to Okri's poetic enterprise.

'Heraclitus' Golden River'

Part 1 of the poem under discussion reflects our 'darkening world' of dispossession, 'war' and 'rage', while Part 2 is a meditation on the dance of illumination through knowledge of self and our cosmic oneness. Consideration of Okri's poem occurs here within an epistemic ecology in which Nature and the poetic consciousness conjoin as dialectically twinned tropes. Heraclitus's oracular fragments inform the thrust of the poem; its title, for example, invokes Heraclitus's doctrine of flux and, by implication, a unity of opposites. Reminiscent of Okri's deployment of the phrase 'Et in Arcadia ego' – the inscription on the tomb in Poussin's painting of *Les Bergers d'Arcadie* – in his 2007 novel, *In Arcadia*, with its multiple signification,[3] Heraclitan fragments are couched in a comparably complex, twinned and epigrammatic style. Consider, for example, two of the river fragments: 'On those stepping into rivers staying the same other and other waters flow ("ἕτερα καὶ ἕτερα")' (Dk22B12)[4] and 'Into the same river we step and do not step, we are and are not ("ποταμοῖς τοῖς αὐτοῖς … εἶμεν τε καὶ οὐκ εἶμεν")' (B49a).[5] As Prier observes,

> It is the dyadic phrase 'ἕτερα καὶ ἕτερα' that dictates the oppositional nature of the [first] fragment itself because of the strict sense of disjunction yet identity the words imply. Yet, everywhere the *underlying third term*, or the *Logos* as unity, is symbolized by the river – the river that … [in the second fragment] unifies life and death, the ultimate opposition for man. (1976: 70; original emphases)

The relation between eco-phenomenology and the fluidity of artistic creativity foregrounds our embeddedness in the cosmos. A close observation of natural forces and a metaphysics of life, arising from an expectation that the imagination will bring us into an understanding of the phenomenological wild with its immense complexity, is at play.

The opening lines of 'Heraclitus' Golden River' – 'Change is good, but no change / Is better' (ll. 1–2) poeticize Heraclitus's river insights in its dialogue on the change/no change dichotomy. This, in turn, is a reflection on the tension between Nature's ebb and flow and humankind's 'iron will[,] [o]ur willed philosophies' (l. 32), vainly bent on trying to stem cyclical change, coupled with the hermeneutics of being-towards-death (to invoke Heidegger's term).[6] The implication is that a mythic conjunction between poetry and ontopoiesis might awaken the superconscious to its true value and so to our relation to the cosmos. The motif of the 'diminishing boundaries / Of a shrinking world' (ll. 24–5) within a theme of the inexorability of mutability deals with the 'great and ultimate' questions, to use Husserl's phraseology (1970: 299). Such questions are implicitly pondered over in Okri's poem.

Although her viewpoint is one of philosophy rather than phenomenology of life, Nicoletta Ghigi expresses the project as being

> to reappropriate the role, drawing from psychology and the other sciences (i.e., anthropology, psychoanalysis, etc.) of being, the 'indicator of the sense or meaning of living' or, as Aristotle said, to teach one to reach that which is generally called wisdom. (2014: 4)

Okri's eco-phenomenological thrust points to the wisdom of 'beingness' as testified in the poem's nexus: 'But the river flows, and so must we. / Change is the happy god Heraclitus / Glimpsed in the golden river' (ll. 79–81).

Non-duality, reciprocal interdependent relationships and the concurrence of being and 'logos' are also integral to African thought (see note 17) as reinforced by Okri's statement in an interview with Hubert Essakow about his Booker Prize novel:

> *The Famished Road* is fed by the dreams of literature. I devoured the world, through art, politics, literature, films and music, in order to find the elixir of its tone. Then it became a perpetual story into which flowed the great seas of African dreams, myths, fables of the world, known and unknown … The novel was written to give myself a reason to live. (2016: 2)

Okri's Heraclitan preoccupation with the metonymic river of life is manifest in the flow of 'the great seas', above, and in this poem, as well as in his opening gambit to *The Famished Road* ([1991] 1997) which reads: 'In the beginning there was a river. The river became a road and the road branched out to the whole world. And because the road was once a river it was always hungry' (3).[7] A comparable philological strategy – that of transforming symbolic phenomenon into structural ones through syntactic juxtaposition – is revealed in Heraclitus's archaic sense of identity in opposition as in 'The road up / down, is one and the same' (Prier 1976: 60). For Okri, indicative of the conflation of time where future and past coalesce, this paradox is evidenced in the notion that the river 'became' a road that 'was once' a river. In eco-feminist discourse, the 'river beneath the river', which runs through the psychic 'Otherworld' is perceived as the Divine Feminine or, as Clarissa Estés notes, the 'Wild Woman archetype ... the One Who Knows' (1998: 26), and from whom all instinct and deep knowing emanate. As already quoted, not only does Okri state in the poem under discussion that 'Poets pray to the goddess of surprise' (2012: l. 27) but, correlating with the notion of a divinely feminine muse, he also picks up on the metaphysical and geophysical nature of the poetic enterprise, asserting that '[p]oetry is also the great river of soul murmurings that runs within humanity' (2011: 4). He avers that '[p]oets merely bring that river to the surface for a moment, here and there, in cascades of sound and suggested meaning, through significant form' (ibid.). Lines from Stanza 3 of Okri's poem highlight this aspect: 'And as we keep / Things the same, the river / Works beneath us. / The god works ironies / On our lives ...' (2012: ll. 13–17). The alchemy of the river motif thus encompasses both heightened sensibility and the 'law of change and decay' that underpins natural *and* human life, endorsed in 'The river runs, / Fields unfurl strange / New mushrooms, libraries yield / New books in the charged / Margins of the old' (ll. 17–21). Here, the 'charged margins' of old texts alludes to the glosses, such as those encountered in ancient texts, dictated by 'reason', an indictment of a propensity towards the rational as opposed to the intuitive imaginary, while the 'strange / New mushrooms' allude to an increasingly dark and barren earth, a no longer fructifying wilderness that is at once eco-phenomenological and mystical. The implicit indictment prefigures the realization that the old dogma ('iron philosophies' and 'willed philosophies' (ll. 22 and 32)) perpetuates a metaphorical delimitation and contraction of our world in what follows, 'And reason, trapped in iron philosophies, / Turns on itself, and prowls / The diminished boundaries / Of a shrinking world, / Shrinking because of the horror / Of the devils at the gates' (ll. 22–7). The chiasmus in the last lines in this excerpt ('Of a shrinking world, / Shrinking because of the horror') encapsulates the resonances of a poetic imagination confronted by the horror of the 'diminished boundaries', in other words, of our 'destruction of the environment', quoted at the outset. In Hegel's reading of Heraclitan thought – and, as evidenced in these lines, to Okrian understanding too – the most pertinent characteristic is 'the structure of an oppositional logic divorced from, but regulating entirely, the objective world of naïve sense perception' (Prior 1976: 59–61).

However, Okri suggests that poets have, through imagination, a way of re-entering his notion of the 'wild', where they can 'pray to the goddess of surprise' (2012: l. 28) and where, related to such numinous experiences, poets know that 'Love is ... unchanging' (ll. 29–30), to counter the 'horror' of humankind's destructiveness. The implication is that it is possible through the capacity of those who are poets to resist a reason which is 'trapped in iron philosophies' (l. 22) and to resist changing beliefs, ensuring that 'Old ways [are] kept / Old' (ll. 7–8). Poets have been suggesting their connection to means other than those of ordinary mortals in accessing extraordinary realities for a long time – easily since the hieratic functions of priests in their relation to the divine were taken on by the 'inspired'.[8]

In this poem, Okri creates, imaginatively, the distant beginnings of observations made by the cosmologists about the mysterious contradictory phenomenological reality of the world. A few elite men in antiquity were beginning to question that phenomenological world in all its apparent illogicality and to substitute for the religious and mythical explanations of the great poets such as Homer other causes than divine intervention or 'deus ex machina'. Okri declares, '*Change* is a god that Heraclitus saw / In the ancient river' (ll. 11–12; emphasis added). This interpretation of Okri's poem, 'Heraclitus' Golden River', from his third anthology, rests on his own conception of 'wild' as energy meeting freedom, art meeting the elemental, chaos honed. The reading celebrates mystical unrest viewed from an eco-phenomenological appreciation of sublime alchemy, attempting to show that, for this Nigerian poet, 'wild' is perceived from an ontopoietic or heightened consciousness perspective; it is 'our link with the stars' (*Wild*; see also Gray (2009) and Chapter 19). This cosmic aspect accords with what the American poet Robert Frost called 'wildness', that 'wild place' or 'the unconsidered land' where life itself '… sways perilously at the confluence of opposing forces' (Baym 1965: 716)[9] and to which the poet must go, alone and in silence, to ignite his/her creativity.

The creative imagination at work in this poem is all too evident in its treatment of its subject matter, viz. the unfathomable nature of existence. Through poetry and the manipulation of the truths of the imagination, rhetoric can play its true role of revealing through its manifestation the relation of things to things. One may, through a consideration of rhetorical devices, thus arrive at a better understanding of self, and so, life. Consider, for example, the deployment of paradox, itself a reflection of syntactic opposition: rational/artistic, in 'The words rang / Through the great hall / As they have resounded / Silently through bygone ages' (2012: ll. 2–5). The onomatopoeic 'r' alliteration clanging 'silently' is, at once, suggestive of subliminal indoctrination and, reminiscent of the muezzin's call, of organized religion's resistance to change. This is implied in 'the great halls' (l. 3), presumably of culture or received knowledge and in the evocation of the desert setting of Ephesus in 'The air is dryer where no change / Is better' (ll. 6–7), where 'Old ways are kept / Old' (ll. 7–8). The 'bygone ages' which Herodotus (a key author for Okri) describes in his famous histories are useful to contextualize Heraclitus and the milieu and world in which he lived and worked. Heraclitus is an Ionian Greek, not a Mainland Greek. Okri is particular. Generally, Ionia in its extent is conveniently demarcated by historians so as to include the cities of the Ionian 'dodekapolis' (league of twelve cities) named by Herodotus (1.142).[10] It stands on the west coast of Asia Minor, and although it was Greek speaking from the time of the Luwians, the Achaeans and Mycenaeans had occupied it since the twentieth century BC; yet Ionia shared much in common with all its Anatolian neighbours and the successive invaders who had come before – war craft, building styles, ideas, ways of honouring the gods. Okri's emphasis in the poem on 'gates' (l. 27) for keeping devils or demons out of the city and its 'walls' (ll. 38, 42, 49, 50) built by 'giants' (l. 38) is full of the imagery of ruins of bygone empires and dynasties such as those Heraclitus himself would have observed and travellers in modern Turkey can see. Cities that have gates and walls suggest technological expertise and a level of civilization which was prized in antiquity. Yet, says Okri,

> The giants who built walls
> Meant to be proof against
> Time and the desert ravages

Found in their sleep
That the walls had become
Change, had moved, had dissolved;
Or worse, that the feared things
Had seeped in underfoot,
Or through the air;
Or changed the frontiers
Of their rigid dialogue.

(ll. 38–48)

The earlier description of 'iron philosophies' (l. 22), reiterated through a variation with 'the frontiers / Of their rigid dialogue' (ll. 47–8), is evidently Okri's commentary on the madness of swapping one set of ideologies for another equally vain and rigid set which, in time, will trap the very invaders themselves and turn them, paradoxically, into giants who must build walls of a different kind again and again. His meditation on the destruction wrought over time on cities as centres of civilization and places where the greatest thoughts could emerge is skilfully brought up to date, into 'our age' (l. 61), through the imagery of 'oases' by alluding to the oasis cities of antiquity which were bombed and ransacked.

It is no longer the greedy devils and demons full of their unvirtuous 'thumos' as Heraclitus describes it: 'It is hard to fight against rage/ passion/ desire; for whatever it wants it buys at the expense of soul' (Kahn 1979: 77). Now great kings and emperors do not conquer; rather, 'the unlucky, the unfortunate, / The dispossessed' (2012: ll. 58–9) who are full of 'rage' at the 'Protected places, illuminated / By time' (ll. 56–7) do; these are the fanatics who blow up temples like those of ancient Palmyra, a great oasis city in Syria with monumental ruins. Arguably, too, the paradox in 'Walls invite invasion' (l. 49) could possibly allude to fellow Nature poet Robert Frost's 'Mending Wall' with its telling line, 'Something there is that doesn't love a wall' (1914: l. 1). In this poem, walls, irrationally erected between two orchards (apples and pines), are mysteriously eroded by natural forces and/or wild hares.[11] Walls, symbolizing unnatural physical barriers, are emblematic in English poetry. Their collapse may be wrought by erosion or a conscious force in Nature, as in Frost's poem, or by divine intervention, as illustrated in what follows. Hadrian's Wall, for instance, built by the Roman invaders of England, from the west coast to the east, to protect the Roman settlers from the indigenous Celts and Picts could, in its ecological transfiguration, be evoked in Okri's caution, discussed above, that 'Walls end up trapping within the demons / Meant to be kept out: for / The demons merely turn into / The giants, grow in them / Like silent cancer' (ll. 50–4).

After the departure of the Romans, the Anglo-Saxons referred to the remnants of the Roman constructions with awe and wonder as the work of giants, destroyed by 'Wierds', the pre-Christian Fates, as captured in Michael Alexander's translation of an Old English fragment, which reads: 'Well-wrought this wall: Wierds broke it. / The stronghold burst … / Snapped rooftrees, towers fallen, / The work of Giants, the stonesmith's/ moulderith.'[12]

The multiple intertextuality seems intentional: there is also the wall of Jericho that 'fell beneath itself' in the late fifteenth century BC (the late Bronze Age), rendered in biblical mythology as 'fell flat' (Josh. 6.20) to indicate the miracle of the Israelites' conquest of the Canaanites. In the earlier quoted stanza, the reference to 'the feared things' that 'Had seeped in underfoot' (ll. 44–5) is suggestive of the walled city of Jericho that had within it a copious natural spring.[13] The ambiguities serve to mystify interpretation.

Calling for knowledge of self, discussed earlier, the need to reflect upon existence is suggested by other teasing allusions, such as the reiteration of 'the devils at the gate(s)' (ll. 8–9, 27). Is the allusion to the Christian dogma of Hell Fire? Does this evoke Heraclitus's view of fire as the source and nature of all things, and the transformation of elementary bodies, emblematic of natural change, as indicated in his belief in 'The turnings of fire: first sea, and of sea half is earth, half fireburst' (B31 [a]). Is this perhaps the origin of the Big Bang theory, or is it the Canaanites' fear of the nomadic Israelites as harbingers of change and decay, or is it rather Heraclitus's Ephesus now lying in ruins, with its Maeander a dry riverbed? As is characteristic too of Heraclitan scholarship and the tough alchemy of Ben Okri, interpretational difficulties abound!

This reading illustrates Okri's propensity to pack multiple meanings into seemingly simple phrases: every word is meant to be experienced in order to decipher meaning. Hegel too endeavours to describe the incorporation of the objective world into the phenomenological state of consciousness in terms of human experience. He is quoted by Prier as saying that 'experience is called this very process by which the element that is immediate, unexperienced … externalizes itself [i.e. is felt by the subject as 'external to himself'], and then comes back to itself from this state of estrangement, and by so doing is at length set forth in its concrete nature and real truth, and becomes too a possession of consciousness' (1976: 59–61). This kind of linguistic density and resonance characterizes Okri's treatment of his dichotomous theme of change/no change, which is most tellingly reflected in his use of the coincidence of opposites. The penultimate stanza, for instance, points to an idyllic Arcadian scene of the Augustan peace that followed the Roman civil war: 'It is natural to want calm places / Where stillness grows. / It's natural to want / Virgil's spreading beeches' (2012: ll. 75–8). The image of the 'spreading beeches' that offer shelter from the weather echoes the earlier part of the poem. In Part 1, the image of an oasis in the desert (discussed earlier) prefigures this 'calm' place, a shelter from the inclemency of the desert of Asia Minor. In his reference to Virgil and the Augustan peace, Okri centres the poem on the longed-for idyll of a benign state where the age-old pursuits of bucolic citizens can be pursued. Hence, it is 'natural' to hanker after Virgil's beeches. Both the oasis and the trees convey the notion of ethical composure (not structurally contrived as in neo-Marxists' Corbyn or Sanders) but sensed from within and lived out from that inner conviction. The images imply a democracy of soul and mind perceived and reflected as the composing unity of nature.[14]

Such glimpses of a constructed, well-organized state in perfect balance, a piece of paradise, contrast with the preceding stanza's man-made destruction wrought by 'ambition' (l. 70) and the detritus of 'wars' (l. 72); these serve to highlight the inexorability of change. This epiphanic vision is thus coupled with an enumeration of ecological changes, such as continental drift and cosmic chaos in 'All around, leonids, planets / Stars are whirling. / The cosmos shrinks and grows / It dreams and flows / Beneath the immutable spell of change' (ll. 62–6). Here, Chaos, the theory of how the universe is organized according to laws that we do not easily understand, is envisioned as a 'spell'. The mysterious flux of the universe in Heraclitus's oracular fragments is typically poetic. Okri's cosmogony of wonderment, wedded as it is to his comprehension of mankind's destructiveness, both dovetails with and modifies Heraclitus's philosophy of human affairs, likewise expressed in didactic literary form as in: 'You must recognize that war is common, strife is justice, and all things happen according to strife and necessity' (B80). Okri evidently attributes the cosmic destructiveness to humankind's perpetuation of a futile heroic ethos of valour and courage – what he consolidates into 'ambition' – as precipitating the demise of dynastic and imperial achievements; they 'cave in', 'give up the ghost', and lives 'collapse' (ll. 67–70) as 'wars eat up fathers and frail sisters' (l. 72). In Okri's ascetic ideal, humanism can contribute nothing to his society of knowers, should it remain fixated on the image of strong and opinionated men and women.

Insisting on the redemptive role of poetry, which comprises 'the magic of listening' (2011: 3) to those who can access the 'wild', Okri writes in *A Time for New Dreams*:

In a world of contending guns, the argument of bombs, and the madness of believing only *our* side, *our* religion, *our* politics is right, a world fatally inclined towards war – we need the voice of poetry that speaks to the highest in us. (Ibid.; emphases added)

Conclusion

The necessary destructiveness of war returns the argument to the initial Okri extract on the need for knowledge of self, as well as to the opening of *The Famished Road*, now seemingly alluding to the wrath of Ogun, Yoruba god of war and the road (an African correlative of the Roman Mars or Greek Deimos), but also, by extension, to the Greek anathematizing of 'unhallowed speech' in governance, as in, 'And roads break out / Into unhallowed speech' (ll. 73–4).[15]

As the messenger of the gods, Ogun is the mouthpiece for the ancestors and so for antiquity or the pre-Homeric conception of moderation or excellence ('sophrosyne') that is encapsulated in the aphorisms of the Seven Sages: 'Know thyself', 'Nothing in excess', 'Measure is best' (Kahn 1979: 27–32), reiterated in Okri's pivotal injunction to know oneself and his call to 'Spread illumination through this darkening world' (ll. 82–3).

Okri thus keeps the Heraclitan illusory material intact but conflates 'logos', the guiding principle for Heraclitan cosmology that he calls 'fire', with the river's flow, making Nature's 'change' the guiding principle of this poem, as exemplified in the lines: 'The river makes all things / Dance to the music they / Never understood at the time' (2012: ll. 35–7). The acoustic resonance here recalls the Shamanistic trance dance, a universal in deep antiquity and expressed in more modern times by such examples as the Khoisan ritual to heighten consciousness in order to heal society, encapsulated in Okri's plea to 'spread illumination'. It is the river transformed from being a metonymy for change to a metaphor for 'Logos', the guiding principle that makes 'ta panta' (all things) dance to a music, which they could not have understood at the time. The ambiguous use of 'they' makes Okri's statement enigmatic. Nevertheless, poets are engaged in a ritual of prayer to 'the goddess of surprise' and the road/river should not utter blasphemous words at this time. Of course, the poet Okri stages a model of the world in the kind of powerful suggestions that ritual makes about social reality under the aegis of spiritual authority. This might not be fulfilled, as he reminds us in the rhetorical question posed in *A Time for New Dreams*: 'Who can weigh a word on a scale, even against a feather of truth?' (2011: 5) This possible allusion to the weighing of souls in the afterlife in Egyptian mythology (Spence [1915] 1925: 119) is countered with an oppositional adversative, 'And yet', suggestive of the need to redream the world and Okri's indebtedness to antiquity, a tribute enshrined in the title to this poem, 'Heraclitus' Golden River': 'see how much words weigh in the heart, in the imagination, in dreams, echoing down the ages, as durable as the Pyramids' (2011: 5). The appeal to the senses of sight and sound culminates in one to the ontopoietic intellect, invoking another of the four basic elements of the cosmos: 'Words, lighter than air, are as mysteriously enduring as lived time' (ibid.). And so, at the end of the poem, the poet entreats us to '*Spread illumination* through this darkening world. / *Spread illumination* through this darkening world' (ll. 82–3; emphases added).

His choice of 'One thunderbolt strikes root through everything' as epigraph to his collection, from Heraclitus's 'One thunderbolt steers all things' (B64), does, however, indicate Okri's recognition of a guiding force of the world that, in turn, is a correlative of an African epistemology of holism and enlightenment, captured in the term 'Ubuntu' – which translates loosely as 'I am, because you are'.[16] Daniel Graham clarifies the cosmic thrust in the context of Heraclitan thought: 'The fiery shaft of lightning is a symbol of the direction of the world' (2014: 8), the thunderbolt being an attribute of Zeus, the storm god/a.k.a. life.

Okri's explication of the power of poetry, in its exalted condition as 'a descendant of the original word [read 'logos'] which mystics [read poets] believe gave the impetus for all creation' (2011: 5), coupled with his insistence that '[p]oetry incarnates that which shapes, changes, transforms' (ibid.) transmutes Heraclitus's thunderbolt into a metaphor for poetic agency. This is captured in Okri's belief that '[p]oetry hints at the godlike in us and causes us to resonate with high places of being' (ibid.). Okri concedes that '[t]he ancient oracles may be silent; and we may not believe in the many ways the gods speak to us, or through us' (ibid.). And, as is customary in Okrian oracular sayings, he follows this with a qualification, introduced with the adversative 'but' in: 'But living means that we are the focus of many pressures: the demands of society, the strange pressures of being itself, of yearnings, inexplicable moods, dreams, and of feelings powerful with all currents of mortal life' (ibid.). He clinches his cyclical argument on the ecological dance of life in his closing couplet with an appeal for 'sophrosyne', an evocation of the 'wild', where 'chaos' can be 'honed': 'No change is good, dancing / Gracefully to change is better' (ll. 84–5).[17]

So, what is ultimately significant in Okri's treatment of the oppositional change/no change dichotomy, that is, of his dialectic of opposites ('Gegenstände'), is that the poet reinvests the words with a numinous power they had lost. His speculative method of thought, as witnessed in the hierarchical and heuristic progression of this two-part poem, not only allows Okri to deal validly with his overt as well as deeper subject matter – the inexorability of change and the need for enlightenment – but also to embed a collection of Heraclitan ideas that permits the coexistence of change and no change, and so of being and not-being on an equal footing, making quite clear the necessity for a new interpretational stance and a new attitude to existence through an ontopoietic epistemic ecology.

3

Ontopoiesis in Okri's poetic oeuvre and *A Time for New Dreams*

Towards an understanding of the symbiosis between poetry and ontopoiesis in Ben Okri's aesthetics and poetry

Drawing on one of Okri's non-fiction publications, *A Time for New Dreams* (2011), this chapter adopts a literary aesthetics approach. Arguing that poetry is an intrinsic physical human attribute, Okri asserts that '[w]e are, at birth, born into a condition of poetry and breathing' (ibid.: 3). 'Birth is a poetic condition,' he continues in the same phenomenological vein: 'it is spirit becoming flesh' (ibid.). Then, pointing to the mythic conjunctions inherent in such a non-dualistic cosmogony and the indissoluble cycle of life, he avows: 'Death is also a poetic condition: it is flesh becoming spirit again. It is the miracle of a circle completed, *the unheard melody* of a life returning to unmeasured silence' (ibid.; emphasis added). Although at first seeming radical, such pronouncements recall the holistic philosophies of ancient times: 'In Asian and European antiquity ... man did, like the African, exist within a cosmic totality, [man] did possess a consciousness in which his own earth being, his gravity-bound apprehension of self, was inseparable from the entire cosmic phenomenon,' asserts fellow Nigerian and Africa's first Nobel laureate, Wole Soyinka ([1976] 1995: 3).

Apart from the centrality of holism, two important tropes underpin Okri's aesthetics: the contiguity of life and death *and* music. In my 2011 interview with the author, he prefigured 'the unheard melody' of the cycle of life becoming death becoming life. He highlighted the synergy of all forms of life and music by sharing *his* consciousness of reality: 'A piano with only five keys is a reality. But, if we include all the keys, the white keys and the black keys, this is a different reality.' Not only does Okri perceive reality as being equated to a melody, it also 'depends on our cultural perception of the keyboard of life.'[1] Insisting that 'poetry is not just what poets write' (2012: 4), Okri metaphorizes: 'Poetry is also the great river of soul-murmurings that runs within humanity.' The poet is an agent or channel, merely bringing 'this underground river to the surface for a moment, here and there, in cascades of sound and suggested meaning, through significant form' (ibid.). Pertinently, the discussion of Okri's poetic *oeuvre* – which begins with his first anthology, *An African Elegy* ([1992]

1997) – attests to a harmonious melding of poetic theory and literary product, to the interdependent web of life.

An African Elegy

A stanza, taken from *An African Elegy* ([1992] 1997), invokes forces of the cosmos to *evoke* an ontopoietic promise of new life. Alan Singer and Allen Dunn define phenomenology or the ontopoiesis of life as 'an attempt to give a philosophically rigorous description of the essential features of different types of experience' (2000: 134). Edmund Husserl refines this thought, explaining that it is futile to attempt 'to understand either the mind or the world in isolation from one another' (ibid.: 122). Husserl's phenomenological method describes the interrelationship between the mind and experience reflected in Okri's 'An Undeserved Sweetness', the third stanza of which reads: 'And now the world is assaulted / With a sweetness it doesn't deserve / Flowers sing with the voices of absent bees / The air swells with the vibrant / Solitude of trees who nightly / Whisper of re-invading the world' ([1992] 1997: 14). This allegorical poem is a synechdochic force; at dusk, the trees surrounding the 'malarial slums / In the midst of potent shrines / At the edge of great seas' form a heuristic (enabling discovery by oneself), inspirational catalyst for cultural revitalization. This is not a promise of a sudden revolutionary change but an almost imperceptible, 'nightly' evolutionary change wrought by the natural forces of life. As in so many of Okri's poems, this one invokes the idea of a metaphysical force, a 'wind' that not only 'lifts the beggar / From his bed of trash', in the opening lines but also 'bends the trees' into the poet's 'dreams' in its closing lines. Here, a vibrant, vital Nature creates anticipation and opens up multiple and multivalent (many meanings) possibilities of renewal in both the poet's and the listener's heightened imagination. This is poetry that goes beyond the body towards the expanses of the soul in an implicit injunction for an expansion of consciousness. 'Poets,' avers Okri in an evocation of ontopoiesis or conscious awareness, 'want nothing from you, only that you listen to your deepest selves' (2011: 6). The poem is transformed into an Aeolian harp, enabling the wind to play 'Handel on the set mysteriously', resuscitating a long-forgotten memory of 'the long / Hot nights of childhood' so that 'Dreams of the past sing / With voices of the future' (1997: 14). The poem has Romantic vitality born of the struggle to transcend and transform quotidian reality. 'Poetry,' argues Okri (2011: 5) 'is the descendant of the original word which mystics believe gave the impulse for all creation.'

That poetry is synonymous with 'logos' is open to debate, but Okri does intimate his belief in the ontology of leading a poetic life. 'Poetry hints at the godlike in us and causes us to resonate with high places of being' (2011: 5), he declares. And traditional oral African poetry was, like its Western counterpart, born as a song; it developed as praise chants to be heard, not read. 'The voice of poetry,' says Afro-Egyptian writer Ali Ahmed Said a.k.a. Adonis (1992: 13), in corroboration, 'was the breath of life – body music. It was both speech and that which went beyond speech. It conveyed speech and also that which written speech in particular is incapable of conveying.'

Informed by this tradition, a second poem from *An African Elegy*, recollecting a spring fair on a wet Easter Sunday in 1988, serves to illustrate the way in which the signifier is not just an isolated word or phrase but a word or phrase bound to a voice, becoming 'a music word, song word', as Adonis puts it. The opening gambit of 'The Cross is Gone', reads: 'It was a day of fairs / Yellow music on the wind, feathers / Of dead birds whirling beyond / The green trees' ([1992] 1997: 15). These lines embody an energy replete with cosmic signs. As with those from 'An Undeserved Sweetness', they are not merely an indication of a single meaning. Anticipating the climactic lines of the poem taken from *The Book of Common Prayer*: 'Christ has died / Christ is risen / Christ will come again –' (ibid.: 18), the sentient trees 'bore / The features of dying men'. The trees look back – recalling for the reader the paradox in the Anglo-Saxon poem 'The Dream of the Rood', in which the cross speaks of its honour of being, at once, the faithful retainer and the bejewelled instrument of death. They too have witnessed 'the sordidness / And the miracles ...'. They 'were heaving / Their comrades had fallen / The great spirits trapped in their monstrous / Trunks sang ... / Songs of white mermaids / Corrupted beyond their time'. Looking forward, these trees are depicted as 'Breathing lamentations on the unforgiving earth / Into which they will not be reborn'. Foretelling of an apocalypse, 'The trees sang to us of a darkening age / With mysterious dying / And yellow spirits in the wind' (ibid.: 15). These lines recall the poem's setting on 'the graveyard of the Heath', with its sodden 'deceptive grass' and 'karmic hurricanes' (ibid.). The transferred epithets in these two metaphors are potent portents of inexorable change. As the persona and his partner[2] – described as 'the innocent journeyers / Into forbidden zones of dying gods' – reminisce about the 'tyranny' of the past, 'Noting the character and psychology / Of each surviving tree' (ibid.: 16), they gain the summit of Parliament Hill above the Thames and gaze upon the cross, dreaming the city of London '... better / Than it dreams itself' (ibid.: 17). Then, in a *volte-face* and in an evocation of the 'awe-ful' prophecies of the book of Revelations, the personae 'saw all the world laid out / Before us in the air', a city perceived 'in a moment's enchantment' but 'Whose history / weighed down with guilt and machines / Laughed all around us like ghosts / Who do not believe in the existence / Of men' (ibid.). The dichotomies in the portrayal of the city of London as full of both possibilities and tyranny foreshadow the fateful closing lines of the poem, which sombrely declare: 'The cross – that cross – is gone' (ibid.: 20). These lines could point to a loss of faith, showing the organic link between poetry and lament, and so indicate that Okri's poetry is at once hymnal and dirge.

However, if the emphasis were to be read as 'that', that is, the Judaeo-Christian cross specifically, the symbolism is at once broadened, leading to a wider interpretation and one suggested in an awareness of the sentient character of Nature, of 'each surviving tree'. As the cross is an ancient symbol, predating the birth and death of Christ, an equally plausible, if more veiled allusion, is to a serendipitous recall of the 'quincunx' (the four directions and four elements of the globe conjoining at the fifth point, the centre). In this context, the absence of the cross on which Christ was crucified opens the way to a meditation on the cross in alchemical tradition as our psychic compass, permitting 'conscious orientation in space and time' (Stevens 1998: 142).

The emotive and affective content of 'The Cross Is Gone' and 'An Undeserved Sweetness' typify the profound congruence between the poetic voice and the acoustic values of speech in both *An African Elegy* and *Mental Fight*. This congruity is clearly articulated in *A Time for New Dreams*: 'Words, lighter than air, are as mysteriously enduring as lived time' (2011: 5).

Mental Fight

Motifs of cosmic conjunctions inform Okri's *An African Elegy* ([1992] 1997) and, more especially, his Blakean *Mental Fight* (1999). Subtitled 'An Anti-Spell for the 21st Century', this second collection suggests that the notion of cosmic conjunction is inherent in the concept of ontopoiesis or in the self-induced development of consciousness as propounded by Anna-Teresa Tymieniecka's (2000 'Logos and Life' CX: n.p.) phenomenology of life. Ontopoiesis is seen to embrace the self-creative activity of consciousness: 'All our creativity, our innovations, our discovery,' says Okri in *A Time for New Dreams* (2011: 27), 'come from being able first to see what is there, and not there; to hear what is said, and not said. Above all to think clearly; to be nourished by silence. And – beyond that – the art of intuition.'

Section 2 of Okri's epic poem for the new millennium, tellingly entitled 'Time to be Real', opens with an ontopoietic injunction: 'Allow uncontemplated regions / Of time to project themselves / Into your sleeping consciousness, / Inducing terror, or mental liberation' (1999: 4). Drawing on varying responses to death-confrontation – despair, emptiness, enlightenment – the poet enjoins us to 'explore our potential to the fullest', to dispense with 'our fear of death … Having gained a greater love / And reverence for life / And its incommensurable golden brevity' (ibid.). Okri's idea of love and being-towards-death[2] can here be seen as an a priori to embracing his anti-spell. He does not aim at realizing anything, at solving life's difficulties,[3] but rather at awakening a realization of the marvellous: 'so long as poetry sends our minds into realms of gold and questions, and touches our deep and tender humanity,' Okri (2011: 5) states, 'then it will always be a force for beauty, for good, in the world, neutralising slowly the noise of guns and hatred.' In this sense, the wind and the sentient trees are metaphors for poetry itself in the two poems from *An African Elegy* discussed at the beginning of this chapter.

Prose too has this same transformative quality. In conversation with Okri, I raised the import of an aphorism from his *Songs of Enchantment* (1993: 287). From the silence of momentary 'unblindedness', Azaro's blind father, in conversation with his son, a 'spirit-child', an 'Abiku', is moved to say that '[t]he light comes out of the darkness'. Okri elucidated: 'We either return to blindness or make a leap to a now. There are only two options: retreat to the cave or leap. This is primal. We have inherited from the ancestors. This must take us forward not back!' (Gray 2012a: 12). In *A Time for New Dreams*, he muses: 'How to make those intuitive leaps that can transform humanity, how to make this mysterious faculty available to all – this will be the turning point in the future history of civilization' (2011: 27). The implied call is for future generations to live more responsibly, with greater sensibility.

'We ought to conjoin faith with a need for self-discovery,' Okri (2011: 28) exclaims, expressing true apprehension of self (to deploy Soyinka's terminology ([1976] 1995: viii)). True self-apprehension or self-individuation – also referred to as ego development – correlates not only with the Zen notion of mindfulness but also with ontopoiesis, as seen in lines from Section 2 of Part 7 in *Mental Fight*, which read: 'The world is not made of labels. / The world, from now on, / Will be made through the mind' (1999: 55). 'Practising mindfulness in Buddhism means to perform consciously all activities, including every day, automatic activities such as breathing, walking.' It is to assume the attitude of 'pure observation' (Shambhala [1991] 2010: 145). This mindful infiltration is, at once, performative and transformative in that language brings man and his world into conscious existence. This emerges in the next lines which explain what Okri conceives of as the optimum operation of mindfulness. He admonishes us to '[a]ccept no limitations to our human potential' as, in his opinion, transformation is wrought 'Through great dreaming, great loving / And masterly application' (1999: 55) of spiritual values to our lives. His language is charged with imaginative creativity. It is neither mimetic nor expressive but 'pure poetry', characterized as a product of a synthesis of thought and imagination. Such language shapes consciousness and perception. 'Poetry,' says Okri (2011: 5), 'incarnates that which shapes, changes, transforms.'

In *A Way of Being Free* (1997: 2), Okri declares: 'Poets seem to be set against the world because we need them to show us the falseness of our limitations, the true extent of our kingdom.' In the poem preceding the one just discussed and in ontopoietic language that is simple, yet profound, calling a phenomenology of life into being, the poet emphatically asserts: 'The mind of humanity is such a force. / New worlds wait to be created / By free minds that can dream unfettered, / Without fear, turning obstacles / Into milestones towards luminous glories' (1999: 54). Comparably, he maintains in *A Time for New Dreams* that '[w]e ought to step out of our old, hard casing. We think we are one kind of people, when in fact we are always creating ourselves. We are not fixed. We are *constantly becoming*. Constantly coming into being. Writers hold out a mirror to the bright visions of what can be' (2011: 18; emphasis added). In a similar vein regarding what Tymieniecka terms, even more precisely, 'beingness-in-becoming' (2004: 17), she has elaborated:

> Taking up the Kantian aspiration to a definitive critique of reason – albeit with a Husserlian twist – as we descend the phenomenological ladder of objectivities to the very end, but without postulating 'things in themselves,' the ontopoiesis of life reaches the incipient point of intentionality and unveils the prepredicative level of the becoming of life. (Ibid.)

Throughout *Mental Fight*, Okri is searching for true conjunctions between the individual and the world, between national hermeticism and absorption into a cosmic unity beyond time. The excerpts quoted reiterate his affirmations expressed in the earlier discussion of *Mental Fight*. Part 5 opens with an implied 'carpe diem' assertion: 'Now is a material event / It is also a spiritual moment / And the blinding light of the real / Can pierce through and tear / Asunder the unreal. / Every moment thus carries / The ordinary and the monumental' (1999: 7). Unblinded, the 'celluloid' stripped from our eyes, 'behind it all we see things / As they could be' (ibid.). *Mental Fight* is, like Okri's first collection, clearly predicated upon ontopoiesis/self-induced development of consciousness. Quoting from two other pieces in this collection, the new millennium is 'richly potent' (ibid.: 18), because humanity is on the 'cusp' of new beginnings, 'transcending the political / Hinting at the evolutionary' (ibid.: 16). Clinching his argument, Okri affirms that 'In time's ovulation / We are now at a rare intersection / That magic favours' (ibid.: 19).

The seventh or final poem in a section subtitled 'Signs from the Old Times' points to the conjunction between the temporal and the divine, or between his/her story and poetry: 'How often have great minds / In the past prayed, and wished / For better favoured moments / In time to unleash their best / Gifts of humanity?' (Okri 1999: 20). The poet responds to his rhetorical question, unequivocally declaring the ripeness of the time for spiritual awakening: 'This is one such conjunction: / It fills the heart with too much humility / And amazement to behold' (ibid.). And the poem closes with a plea: 'we must behold it, with minds calm, / With aspirations clear, / And with a smile in the soul / That only those fortunate people have / Who find themselves at the right time, / At the perfect mythic conjunction / That is also a living moment, / A moment lived through' (ibid.).[4] The injunction encapsulates Soyinka's notion of self-apprehension as the key to cultural and personal liberation. It prefigures the thrust of *A Time for New Dreams* in which the entreaty is to '[l]et life inspire you, and teach you always how to be free, and to encourage freedom in others, if they so desire' (2011: 95). Okri's belief is of unified beingness: 'All of humanity is really one person. What happens to others, affects us' (ibid.). Transcendence and transformation are the keys to existence: 'There's no way out, but up. Let's all rise to the beautiful challenges of our age, and rise to our true mysterious luminosity' (ibid.). It is this quest for individual and communal freeing of the self that runs passionately through the writings of both anthologies of poetry.

Described as either '[a]n anthem to mark the end of an age, or a hymn for the future' (dust cover), *Mental Fight* is shot through with a synthesis of celebration and heedfulness. It is described on the dust cover, which quotes *The Times*, as '[a]n angry, hopeful, weary, wary, epic reveille to the human spirit'.

Conclusion

The argument has attempted to show that ontopoiesis is inherent in Okri's non-dualistic cosmogony. It employs his ontopoietic aesthetics as seen in *A Time for New Dreams* to interpret selected poems from the two anthologies. 'We ought to conjoin faith in evidence with a need for self-discovery,' Okri asserts in this non-fictional work (2011: 28). In his poetry, a higher state of consciousness or 'illumination' is proffered as the basis for life's transitions, wrought largely through spirit awakenings via a retrieval of traditional geo-cosmic horizons.[5] In the poems in *An African Elegy* ([1992] 1997) and the tellingly entitled *Mental Fight* (1999), borrowed from William Blake's visionary 'Jerusalem', such transitions accrue from a conscious reconstruction of the human self, affected by materialism, pitted against the forces of the cosmos. 'Now is a material event, / It is also a spiritual moment. / And the blinding light of the real / Can pierce through and tear / Asunder the unreal,' Okri states in his *Elegy* ([1992] 1997: 7), intuiting Soyinka's affirmation: '(For let it always be recalled that myths arise from man's attempt to externalise and communicate his inner intuitions.)' ([1976] 1995: 3).

Aligning himself with Mario Vargas Llosa's Nobel acceptance speech (7 December 2010: 11), Okri also attributes the transition from barbarism to civilization to creative artists. 'Literature and civilization are different but not different,' he stated in my early interview. He elucidated: 'The society that gave rise to the Divine Comedy flowered as a renaissance; the society that gave rise to Shakespeare led to a greater civilization. Literature does not create it, but there is an inspirational link, like mercury and the alchemist's stone. Literature shows the presence and reveals and enhances a psychic strength, pulls it out to reflect a greater civilization' (2012: 12). In *A Way of Being Free*, Okri credits creative artists with this same civilizing capability through a revitalization of one's psycho-spiritual life:

> The poet turns the earth into mother, the sky becomes a shelter, the sun an inscrutable god, and the pragmatists are irritated ... The problem is with those who are frightened of the rather limitless validity of the imagination, frightened of people who continually extend the boundaries of the possible, people who ceaselessly reinvent existence; frontiers people of the unknown and the uncharted. (1997: 20)

This excerpt indicates that Okri sees the poet's role as one of guiding humankind in the search for a mode of existence that could irradiate the mind, counter prejudice and so liberate the timid psyche. Poetry thus enables one to think beyond the canopy; it affords the opportunity to experience the transcendence of truth. Okri's aesthetics and poetry coalesce in a reflective intelligence that should, as Tymieniecka (in Low 2011: 32) reportedly avows, 'have an important role in human life and cognition'.

4

Recovering our true state of being in 'The Comic Destiny'

Introduction

Ben Okri's 'The Comic Destiny' from *Tales of Freedom* (2009) is a sobering modern fable that represents a new form of dialogue within the context of dispossession, slavery (in its broadest terms) and fragmented human relationships. Okri confronts familiar history across borders. Profoundly affected by the Nigerian Civil War, Okri confesses to a preoccupation with justice, a key theme in the story. For Okri, a poet-seer, justice alludes to the existence of the ideal lying beyond reality, within a protorationalistic world view. This chapter briefly discusses the fable as fictional mode and the symbolism of the forest as setting and is a contribution to clarifying Okri's gnomic fable with reference to the use of literary, historical and imaginative moral echoes. It suggests that the text contains allusive cross-references to his own *Starbook* (2007) and to Samuel Beckett's *Play*, reproduced as a film called *Comédie*.

Okri situates his fable within a delicate web of allusions, a web that reverberates with the idea of places of entrapment – be these a forest clearing, medieval castle, inferno, mouse trap, refurbished guest house or life itself. He generalizes the motif of entrapment by having his enslaved protagonist conclude that life is 'a bloody prison, a bird cage, a trap' (2009: 90). In reading the text as a fable, the reader anticipates a moral pointer as its conclusion; fables are about teaching how to live rightly. Perhaps given the title of the collection, we expect the moral to be about freedom, and in 'Beyond', the last of the five sections of 'The Comic Destiny', the moral becomes clear – there is the potential to go back to a prelapsarian state at the 'source' and so to be free again: 'Let's go back to the source,' said New Woman. / 'Of rivers.' / 'Of worlds.' / 'Of dreams.' / 'Of realities.' / 'Of friendship.' / 'Of fellowship.' / 'Of what the heart feels' (ibid.: 104). The rhetoric of a punctuated list – source, rivers, worlds, dreams, realities, friendship, fellowship, what the heart feels – is a typical call by Okri, alluding to what it means to live rightly: to be able to make sound judgements in living and to be imbued with artistic sensibility and in tune with the imagination, as intimated in his *A Way of Being Free* ([1989] 1997). New Woman, the speaker in the quotation, is one of the characters in the fable who most fully represents these qualities. The catalogue underpins the message in both 'The Comic Destiny' and the earlier novel, *Starbook* (2007). At the climax of the list, the statement of impassioned belief that 'what the heart feels' can be a remedy against lack of fellowship and friendship – some of the causes of the multiple ills of the world – is familiar in other works by Okri.

The fable creatively dramatizes the human condition. Humans are unable to communicate successfully; their relationships are characterized by that pitiful state; we ourselves have created the condition. The unequal power relations among humans, dispossession, cruelty, the ruin of Nature and so on are contained in the phrase 'human condition'. Modern thinkers add the adjective 'biopolitical' to the word 'condition'. Okri's fable is a dramatic representation of our condition with an Old Man, Old Woman, the slave Pinprop or Mada, an escaped murderer, as well as a young woman and a young man, in a forest clearing. The biopolitical condition in which human action happens is described by Pinprop:

> Too much neurosis and disease and new diseases ... And the shrinking of cages till we can no longer fly[1] ... And squabbles and lies and terror. Self-destruction and the willed destruction of other people. And sickness, sir, sickness in the throat and stomach and food and streets and faces and the air ... (2009: 10)

Fables hark back to the earliest human stories in writing. *The Panchatantra*, 'Five Principles', exists in a Sanskrit form but is only a copy of earlier versions of animal fables with moral pointers (Hertel 1915). There is the apparent simplicity of the fable format: the use of satire, a limited number of actors with easily identifiable names, a straightforward plot, action that is confined to a stereotypical place and an outcome which reveals that the wisdom of one at least of the characters is belied by the wisdom of the moral pointer. Okri's use of rich and complicated echoes and allusions from his literary, historical and imaginative worlds points to the profound truth that is hidden in the fable.

This reading aims to clarify Okri's gnomic fable with reference to his use of literary, historical and imaginative moral echoes. The forest as the dystopic setting of the fable about life and human relationships is a typical device of fable (although Okri's version takes place in the early twenty-first century). It is not a specific physical place, but one of imagination. By using the topos of the forest for the action of the fable, Okri places his fable in a tradition in literature which began some ten thousand years ago in writing. The *Epic of Gilgamesh* from the Land between the Rivers (part of modern-day Iraq) has a famous scene in a 'locus horridus' when Gilgamesh and his friend Enkidu fight Humbaba in the forest of the Cedars of Lebanon. Dante's *Divine Comedy* opens in a 'selva oscura' ('dark wood'; *Inferno I*, l. 2).

Where the order of things in the Mesopotamian story and the Italian medieval poem is ruled by divine plans and the destiny of the characters is ordained and so redeemed, the same is not true of modernity's characters. The clearing in the forest cannot be read out of its context of modern African and European history. Forests are not Sherwood or Arden nowadays, but Rwanda, Biafra, Katyn, Piatichatki, Bykivnia and Mednoye, the terrifying list of forests in which the massacres of thousands, the 'self-destruction and the wilful destruction of other people' (Okri 2009: 10), happened during the twentieth century; this is also close to Okri's own experience in the Nigerian Civil War (1967–70).[2]

In the context of human dispossession, enslavement and destruction, all the characters in this fable – except for the slave Pinprop – are trapped in dysfunctional human relationships and a communicative impasse. In the forest clearing, a site of 'exhaustion', 'fear', 'terror' and 'disorientation', Mada Pinprop functions as the voice for right living. Mada is clearly a palindrome for Adam or original man, who ate of the fruit of the forbidden Tree of Knowledge. Analogously, Pinprop functions as the originating spokesman for those banished from Eden, entrapped by a colonization of the mind, to use Ngugi wa Thiong'o's (1986) term, and the willed destruction of self and other.

It is the slave, Pinprop, who catalogues the disconcerting terrors of contemporary life – speaking out against key moments in history, of internecine strife, of slavery and the slave trade, of colonization and destruction, and also of 'boredom', a syndrome of modernity and a linear motif in 'The Comic Destiny'. Reminiscent of Omovo in *The Landscapes Within* (1981), Pinprop is 'broadly a figure for the people who are disenfranchised, powerless to stop the violence' (Coundouriotis 2015: 1091). This unlikely protagonist, Pinprop, foreshadows the possibility of an ultimate return to a prelapsarian state, which is indicated in the epilogue. Okri suggests that we 'stop running … searching' (2009: 90), that we live a just life.

The fable is an appropriate vehicle for conveying a profound message simply. This is the antidote for the spirit which is '[b]eaten, crushed underfoot, prey to a thousand seasons of sickness. Tedium, neurosis, boredom'. Underlining the point, while also alleviating its thrust, dancing and laughing, Pinprop intones: 'And so again and again, in our epic journey, in exile, after falling and rising toiling and becoming hunchback, I find only silence, How crude' (2009: 94).

Okri interrogates injustice, past and present, and represents this fictively; his motive appears to be practical: to find out how human life and conduct can be improved, as W. K. C. Guthrie notes in the context of Greek thought ([1950] 1978: 17). Okri's project is a ceaseless dialogue with his own 'Imaginatio Creatrix' and with his ancestors, on behalf of the dispossessed and disenfranchised, confronting what Ato Quayson terms 'a traumatic history of disability' (1999: 66). In the hands of a poet-seer such as Okri, 'endowed with the power to see behind and beyond the objects of the real world to the essences, concealed in the ideal world' (Chadwick [1971] 1973: 3), justice, as a remedy for socio-historical and contemporary ills, alludes to the existence of the ideal lying beyond reality. As in nineteenth-century symbolist thought, true reality springs from a vision of paradise regained, where a just sensibility operates, as implicit in the appeal to behave appropriately, to take the 'right action' (Guthrie [1950] 1978: 7). Right living inheres in 'escap[ing] to what I am[,] [g]row[ing] on my own cross' (Okri 2009: 90). In his poem 'Heraclitus' Golden River', Okri's reiterated injunction is to '[s]pread illumination through this darkening world' (2012: 94, l. 82).

With its largely unnamed, world-weary characters lost in an infernal clearing in the forest, a complex symbol that embraces lack of enlightenment as well as terror, 'The Comic Destiny' has New Woman remind us that the way forward is, paradoxically, to go back: 'back to the source', to Nature, to right conduct – the ancient meaning of justice – to holism. The West African worldview, akin to that of Eastern protorationalism, considers the physical universe as being an infinite whole made up of infinite wholes (fractal objects) and governed by infinite synthetic principles.[3] For Okri, an avid Homeric reader, 'justice' is symbolic of ancient wisdom; it has its original non-moralistic meaning.[4] The dialogue and action in 'The Comic Destiny' presuppose the need for both 'dike' (justice) and 'arête' (virtue or excellence). For the Greeks, language and thought were inextricably interwoven and interacted upon one another (Guthrie [1950] 1978: 4). As a concept, 'illumination' involves 'theos', a god, or a more than human power or force observed everlastingly 'at work in the world' (ibid.: 11): transcendental symbolism at work in the text (see Chadwick [1971] 1973).

As in the title of Dante's epic, Okri's use of the term 'comic' for his fable does not denote that which is simply amusing; it derives from commedia, meaning 'a poetic composition in the style intermediate between the sustained nobility of tragedy, and the popular tone of elegy' (Dante 1909–14). Dante's work is introduced here as an intertextual bas-relief. The forest in which the action of 'The Comic Destiny' takes place is a 'mise en scene' that directs the reader to Cantos I and II of Dante's *Inferno*. The principal theme for both texts is a journey through the misery of life. Their symbolism is comparable: evocations of bleak suffering and a search for light beyond human experience. Allegory for Dante expresses the experience of the human soul, painfully struggling from sin, through purification, to the beatific vision. For Okri, the allegory is a quest for our 'destiny' where the mysteries of life can be unravelled and where 'justice' is achieved for all – our true state of being.

Okri's hope is to spread a beyond-the-norm conception of living. He has long been preoccupied with justice, as indicated in his interview with Caroline Jowett (1995). He makes this even clearer in *A Way of Being Free*: 'There are some things on earth that are stronger than death. One of these is the eternal human quest for justice.' Believing that 'fables are made of this [quest for justice]', he adds that 'a people cannot live without it [justice], and in due course they will be prepared to die to make it possible for their children' (1997: 108). As in his corpus, 'The Comic Destiny' is a quest, in this case, in the form of a modern fable, for conduct that eschews evil. For Okri, sin or evil is devoid of religious connotations and is simply the obverse of the word, 'live' (l-i-v-e). It is a failure to live a just life, as he suggests in *The Age of Magic* (2014). In this novel, he argues that living without evil is a palindrome (live) signifying how not 'to die in life' by 'living in the present moment' (ibid.: 29, 28; see also Gray 2017).

An interview by Asis De sheds light on Okri's symbolist mode. Asked for his views on culture, Okri decodes his complex notion of living in the present, in the heat of the moment: 'CULTURE is a secret ingredient in civilization. It is the frozen things we bring with us from the past, transformed by the ever-living fire of the mystery of being' (2015: 251; emphasis added). This situates 'The Comic Destiny' in a mythic, non-temporal zone. His writing exemplifies what Homi Bhabha describes as a postcolonial aesthetic of cultural hybridity (1994; see also Mathuray 2015: 1104).

In 'The Comic Destiny's' utopian periphrastic thrust, New Man and New Woman, a naked pair, advocate a return to the first day 'when all love was ours' (2009: 107). Okri's other unnamed characters, symbolizing a spectrum of the dispossessed, are all in search of a place to rest: 'A room to let' (ibid.: 95). This manifests as a 'white building' with a 'blue door' (ibid.: 96), an Eden beyond from which New Man and New Women emerge at last, and to which Old Man, Old Woman and their slave are ultimately destined. The symbolism epitomizes a fusion of the phenomenal and mystical worlds, by way of an elegiac fable.

'We are in a comic position,' says Okri, aligning his view with that of Novalis. 'We are living not with a sense of absurdity, but with a sense of disjunction' (Guignery 2015: 1060). In 'The Comic Destiny', 'evil' is exemplified by Old Man and Old Woman's maltreatment of their slave ('Old Man kicked Pinprop beneath the table'; 'Old Man and Old Woman … carried him off to the woods … dumped him on the ground with a thud … chained him' (2009: 5, 12)). Another manifestation of eviling/not living rightly is the couple's obsession with past reminiscences: 'each lost in their separate monologues' (15). This is reminiscent of Samuel Beckett's characters, who likewise epitomize the way in which personality obstructs reception and communication. Old Woman, in search of a 'happy ending' (ibid.: 17), struggles to gather the threads of her life that manifested as 'signs on the trees' that 'had been scattered all over the place' (ibid.: 14, 15) throughout the forest. Old Man's rememberings are more sinister and historical: of 'the skeletons that strange tribe built their houses with … [sic]' (ibid.: 14). The fable draws upon a rich tapestry of allusive nuggets from literary and filmic sources; the principal one is Okri's own slave-fable novel. *Starbook* (2007) is important in this regard, as is Beckett's radio drama, *Play* (1964). Of necessity, the discussion is limited to two interrelated references to these texts: 'The Comic Destiny' and *Starbook*.

Eleni Coundouriotis wisely cautions against reading Okri's fiction 'too literally, as factual'. She adds: 'Okri defamiliarizes the particular to prod us to reconsider familiar historical narratives' (2015: 1090). 'Stories,' Okri reminds us in *A Way of Being Free*, 'are either dangerous or liberating because they are a kind of destiny' ([1989] 1997: 112, no. 17). Destiny, the mysteries of life and justice are the imponderables that Okri explores in 'The Comic Destiny' and in *Starbook*, Okri's narrative of the prince and the maiden, which is likewise a fable. *Starbook* is a tale told a child by his mother, 'a myth', because '[s]omeone has to turn a life into a legend' (2007: 415). It begins with a mythical description of a pre-colonial Eden, complete with a palace and a shrine house:

> In the heart of the kingdom was a place where the earth was dark and sweet to taste. Everything that was planted grew in rich profusion. The village was built in the shape of a magnificent circle … The forest was dense about the village, and it seemed that those in the heart of the kingdom lived in a magic dream, an oasis of huts and good harvest in the midst of the enveloping world of trees. (ibid.: 3)

By the end of the novel, white slavers and colonial forces have ruined this idyll:

> That night the white spirits fell on the tribe and carried away its strong and its young. They destroyed the village and scattered its inhabitants among the hills. Those who were caught were gagged and bound and sent across the seas; many of them perished in the crossing; those that made it over, in their suffering, spread an unconquerable spirit in the new land; because their spirit, from ancient times, has always been strong. (ibid.: 410)

These two extracts from *Starbook* inform the content and the elegiac tone of 'The Comic Destiny', while also reversing the narrative trajectory. The sequel – the correlating fable – begins in a 'locus classicus': 'Old Man and Old Woman sat in the forest. Pinprop sat at their feet. They were in a clearing. They listened to footsteps running in their direction, and to a siren wailing in the distance. After a while the footsteps receded' (2009: 5). The once-flourishing kingdom of Benin, raped and pillaged by imperial forces, is now a global 'clearing' in the forest, with a slave-owning elderly couple. And as intimated earlier, 'The Comic Destiny' ends with a vision of Paradise regained, with the three initial characters together 'in the white building' (ibid.: 98). Endorsing their debilitating ennui expressed in 'We are too old to chase ideals,' said Old Woman and 'We are too old to seek new beginnings,' said Old Man (ibid.: 61), the old couple remain in darkness, while their slave is sitting 'in the light' (ibid.: 98). That it is left to the new generation to see the light is reinforced by a sleight of hand: the transmutation of Young Man and Young Woman into New Man and New Woman, who appear to have regained their erstwhile love for each other. 'Let's be happy again,' said New Man. 'As on the first day.' / 'When all love was ours.' / 'As it still is.' / 'And always will be,' they both said together, as one (ibid.: 107). And, in an echo of black Eden in *Starbook* and of Okri's plea to 'spread illumination through this darkening world' (2012: 'Heraclitus' Golden River', l. 82), the recovered pair 'spoke like children discovering light'. In this epiphanic moment, New Man had suggested a fresh start, involving going 'back to the earth.' / 'To simple beginnings.' / 'To what nourishes.' / 'To what grows.' / 'To sunlight.' / 'And flowing water.' / 'To inner light' (2009: 103). This other listing pre-empts that of New Woman, quoted at the outset. The anaphora, here, mimics the gnomic catalogue of what constitutes 'beginnings'. In *The Diversity of Life*, entomologist Edward Wilson coincidentally provides a useful scientific explanation for the seductive appeal of 'beginnings' and their mythological association with an Edenic Africa: 'The human species came into the world as a late product of the radiations that, 550 million years into the Phanerozoic, lifted global biodiversity to its all-time high. In a more than biblical sense, humanity was born in the Garden of Eden and Africa was its cradle' (1992: 211).

It is testimony to Okri's skill as a word-weaver and to the ways in which he evokes notions of Edenic bliss and new beginnings that the novel and its 2009 fable sequel are seldom recognized as chronicles of rampant evil: terror, dispossession and slavery, although their trajectories are marked so plainly from black Eden at the start of *Starbook* to white occupation at the end of the novel. In 'The Comic Destiny', this pattern is inverted, as already noted, and while there are repeated pointers to the evils of the slave trade and its legacy, the fable concludes with a more generalized search for inner light, for a true way of being.

In Okri's two texts, there are also unmistakeable pointers to a postcolonial writing back to the imperial centre. For example, in 'The Comic Destiny', Old Man recalls that the 'strange tribe had built an unhealthy routine round the skeletons. They didn't realize that the skeletons were alive and subversive. And so their routines became hellish and the people became afflicted with diseases that only a final destruction could cure' (2009: 15). This is a clear intertextual flashback to Okri's fable on the looting of the Benin Bronzes and the iniquities of enslavement in his novel *Starbook*, written two years earlier. The novel speaks of the 'White Wind', symbolizing the imperial and colonizing moment. In the sequel, Old Man, presumably a former neocolonial big wig, muses: 'The tribe thought it had finally arrived and then one night in history the owners of the skeletons turned up and began to remove their bones and skulls. The buildings collapsed, and only the artefacts remained' (ibid.). This foreshadowing of the collapse of colonialism, and the optimistic cargo cult of neocolonialism in 'The Comic Destiny', can be seen in two ways. On the one hand, there are the linear motifs of light, birds, water and dreams; on the other, there is a search for a room to let – arguably an allusion to the biblical Mary and Joseph finding no room at the inn prior to the birth of the Christ child. This is framed by the intermittent screech of a siren.[5] Pinprop satirizes the colonial endeavour as a quest 'in search of violence', 'Looking for a place to die?' The slave expounds on the early Christianizing mission as '[u]gliness ... and the cruelty of myth' and indicts the slave trade in graphic terms: 'The excessive stench of putrefying bodies. Too much blood and tiredness, and iron in the throat. Small places turning septic, and large spaces tumbling into confusion. And people becoming hell. And hunger bloating too many bellies' (ibid.: 9). This cascade of negative images can be associated with the existential angst of Samuel Beckett. It provides a counter-narrative to the prosaic verse listings of New Man and New Woman that point to a recovery of a true state of being.

'The Comic Destiny' and Samuel Beckett's *Play*

The allusive network is masterfully interwoven by Okri to present a composite portrait of human ennui and of his understanding of how to counter the effects of the sense of alienation, something that is central to Beckett's writings. In his monograph, *Proust*, Beckett perceives alienation as endemic to the human condition: 'Man is the creature that cannot come forth from himself, who knows others only in himself, and who, if he asserts the contrary, lies' (1931: 66). Paul Lawley's interpretation of this credo in the context of Beckett's short radio drama, *Play* (1964), is usefully insightful. Because *Play* focuses on failed relationships as the result of an inability to communicate, it is, I believe, more pertinent than *Waiting for Godot*, often cited by other critics as an important intertext for Okri.[6] Lawley accepts Beckett's belief about self-delusion but reinterprets it as akin to classical 'virtue', discussed earlier. He argues thus: 'The desiderated "truth" not a moral truth the opposite of which is a lie (the word is significantly absent from the Play) but an ontological truth, a "truth" of being the opposite of which is the parody of being we are witnessing' (Lawley 1984: 25). Okri's 'The Comic Destiny' goes beyond communicative impasse to re-enact just such a 'parody of being' before culminating in an opposing ontological truth; what Lawley has called 'a truth of being'. Axiomatic to Beckett is his belief: 'The Observer infects the observed with his own mobility' (1931: 17).

Beckett's characters in *Play* (M, W1 and W2) and most of Okri's in 'The Comic Destiny' (Old Man and Old Woman; Man, Young Man and Young Woman, Man) are portrayed as having exhausted their capacity for what Lawley terms 'inventing': they 'say the same things over and over'. Both sets of characters are imprisoned within language as they are imprisoned within the parody of presence. Lawley comments: 'As we watch the Play we realize that the one kind of imprisonment determines the other' (1988: 8). Okri's appeal is ultimately against communicative impasse brought about by being imprisoned in the past and so living in isolation: what he indicts as the 'ritual of remembrance again, speaking without hearing the other, interrupting, overlapping, in their inward speech outwardly spoken' (2009: 61).

The indictment is against dehumanized interpersonal relationships, implied in the inability of the characters to engage in a meaningful exchange of ideas. As noted, Old Man and Old Woman reminisce endlessly about totally separate past experiences yet, paradoxically, they communicate enthusiastically on ways in which to 'enslave' their slave. Young Man and Young Woman do not appear to be aware of the presence of the elderly couple, nor do they themselves interact physically. The young married couple, with a baby out of sight but not out of earshot, lie on the ground in the forest clearing with fingers barely touching and even when standing up to look for a place to recall their 'unity and love', 'they still kept the distance between them' (2009: 70). This is indicative of the constant arguing that represents the primary form of communication in a lost relationship. The situational irony is that, while purportedly looking for 'a place to learn how to dream again' (ibid.: 65), they believe – to adapt an aside from Beckett's *Endgame* (1958) – that '[a]ny old dustbin is fine' as a place to live (Okri 2009: 66). They thrive on arguing, thus masking the boredom of a love that once incited jealousy (ibid.: 49–51). The young wife even rejects her husband's recollection of the miracle of the birth of their child, focusing instead on the memory of pain. This suggests that the narrative technique is one of verbal interrogation by way of exposure. The young couple stand for the paradox that 'a tolerable hell is better than an impossible heaven' (ibid.: 48). Okri here hints at a possible redemption of suffering, through a striving to regain their true state of being. This manifests in the representation of their emergence from the forest into enlightenment and transformation into New Man and New Woman. In addition to being suggestive of Dante's journey through Hell, the forest is thus a synecdoche for Okri's lost and dysfunctional human ciphers, and a simulacrum for Beckett's communicative impasse. But, it is also the site of the lost black Eden of *Starbook*.

Pinprop's description of the effects of colonialism, quoted earlier, is an elliptical way for Okri to sublimate the horrors of colonialism, neocolonialism and slavery – injustice. His deft incorporation of related allusive references by Pinprop to the play-within-a-play, 'The Mouse Trap' in *Hamlet*, as well as to Aesop's fable of the goose that laid the golden eggs, supports this interpretation. Echoing the legendary founder of fable, Aesop, it is the worldly wise and verbally acute slave who cites these exempla: conventionally read as fables of murderous greed and self-betrayal.[7] The story of the goose is common to many cultures and appears in many variations. It is commonly a fable about the consequences of greed; the farmer's wife kills the goose to retrieve more than the single egg per day. In Shakespeare's *Hamlet*, Claudius's reaction to the play within a play – 'The Mouse Trap' – can likewise be read as illustrative of cause and effect, as exposing a greed. Claudius murdered his brother, King Hamlet, usurped the Danish throne and married the widow, Gertrude, setting a chain-reaction in motion. In both cases, meaning dawns slowly and cumulatively through analogy. Both function as rhetorical instruction on the need for illumination to counter 'evil'.[8]

There is also, for Okri, the power of the creative imagination: 'Life is a masterpiece of the imagination,' says his Young Man (2009: 72). This is the power of a fruitful dream, one that can counter the barrenness of a finite analytic paradigm expressing the way our finite senses and brains function. In the concluding section of 'The Comic Destiny', New Man in conversation with New Woman advocates a counter paradigm, an infinite synthetic paradigm of a proto-reality, through the agency of new beginnings: ' "Let's dream again," said New Man. / "Like we used to as kids." / "Of Eden when it was new" ' (ibid.: 105).

This serves to highlight what Okri calls 'the dream logic of his work' (Guignery 2015: 1058). As is his custom, Okri is specific. He avers: 'Imagination dreams that which knowledge makes real. It could be said that imagination is the protoreality' (2015: 15). This returning movement to a holistic or synthetic approach to reality can, as New Man suggests, restore an earthly paradise. His advocacy of 'love', 'courage', 'patience' and 'wisdom' (2009: 105), coupled with New Woman's desire to go 'back to the source' (ibid.: 104) and of 'learning to play again / As on the first day' (ibid.: 106) in the garden, is invoked as a counter agent to the ennui of postmodernity, and encapsulates the fable's moral.

Jeremy Lefkowitz reminds us that, in antiquity, the Graeco-Latin fable was 'linked to the lower classes and affiliated with slaves' (2014: 1), noting: 'The Life of Aesop also stages the emergence of fable from the world of slavery … [It] also emphasizes a number of thematic connections between Aesop's status as a slave and animal fables for which he became famous' (ibid.: 13). Okri's protagonist and the only named character in 'The Comic Destiny' is an Aesopic slave, known to his keepers, the new neo-colonial 'corruptors' of the land, Old Man and Old Woman, as Pinprop. Not only is he intelligent and knowledgeable, as already suggested, but he informs Man, an escaped murderer, that he is called Mada. Naming is important in this fable. This reference to the power of language could allude to the biblical 'logos' in Genesis; and the legend of Adam and Eve's eating of the fruit of the Tree of Knowledge, and the couple's subsequent hiding from the wrath of God, newly aware of their nakedness.

Okri transposes the legend, and New Man and New Woman seemingly get a second chance, while Pinprop ultimately basks in the 'light'. 'The Comic Destiny' has been performed, as a staged drama, called *Comédie*. The name Pinprop can therefore also be adduced to evoke notions of a props man of modern, realistic theatre, a pivotal stage prop or theatrical device, a pinpoint or focal point that brings the separate points of view together. In the penultimate section of 'The Comic Destiny', we read: 'Old Man and Old Woman sat in the white building. Pinprop sat at their feet. Everywhere else was in darkness, except Pinprop. He sat in light' (2009: 98). Pinprop symbolizes an enlightenment. Both Old Man and Old Woman are slavishly dependent on him for he alone can create. Pinprop can be seen as the correlative of the light in Beckett's *Play*, the light (whether of God or Satan) that obliges M, W1 or W2 to speak. Lawley (1988: 10) explains: 'It is the inquisitor-light which confirms and reveals, indeed in a sense creates, so that release from the light would mean from this state.' He cites the following punning interchange from *Play* in illustration: 'When you go out – and I go out. Some day you will tire of me and go out … for good' (Beckett in ibid.). For Beckett's W1, speech – her use of language – is dependent on the stage light shining on her. By extension, she is portrayed as evidently believing that it must be something in language which is required by the light. Okri's usage parallels this. Pinprop mocks his keepers and presumably a religious ethos that permits humankind's inhumanity, by laughing, singing then shouting, 'into the silence': '"Slave, slave, let there be light." / Silence. / "Let there be light, slave," he shouted' (2009: 98). Then in a *volte-face* and a subtle allusive cross-reference to Beckett's *Play*, the narrating voice quips: 'The light that was on Pinprop turned instantly to darkness'. Pinprop's 'ex cathedra' retort is 'Ah … the word made manifest. Now for some peace' (ibid.: 99), and in a second unscripted stage direction, beyond solipsistic communicative impasse, we are told that silence follows. Okri thus 'defamiliarizes the particular to prod us to reconsider historical narratives' (Coundouriotis 2015: 1090).

Conclusion

As in Okri's 'The Comic Destiny', Beckett's *Play* is full of obvious Christian echoes, but it contains fewer marked historical and anthropological allusions. The references discussed treat conventional social behaviour through satire to mask the central question: What are we doing here? There is a marked tension between subject and form: the farcical proceedings of life and fractured communication keep the reader/audience's attention away from the despair of life.

The importance of the double versions of Okri's 'The Comic Destiny' (text and staged play) and Beckett's *Play* (staged play and film) is that visual media are preferred modes for contemporary dissemination of knowledge. In addition to the topicality of subject matter, the appeal accrues from the intense theatricality, despite the fact that nothing much happens in either writers' plots. Bamber Gascoigne pertinently observes that 'the endless cross-talk … is always funny and at the same time sad'. He elaborates: 'good cross-talk acts are very funny, and sad because their main reason for talking at all is just to pass away the time, to fill the void' ([1962] 1990: 184–5). As Verna Brown asserts: 'When the pact is not renewed between past and present, or between people, there is a fragmentation into separate dynamisms that cannot cohere' (2009: 70). Gascoigne concludes: 'Under the farcical ripple of dialogue lies a serious concern' ([1962] 1990: 185).

The question arises: Is a fable a subtle way of talking about the politics of control – which inscribes and proscribes life? Okri seems to wish not only to foreground sociopolitical malaise but also to suggest possible remedies besides Dante's eternal providence. To do so, he has devised fables in which the questing imagination follows the movement suggested by the subtitle to Tolkien's germinal work, *The Hobbit* ([1937] 1995): 'there and back again', to borrow from W. R. Irwin (1961: 578) although in a different context.

What then does the tapestry of allusive side-references suggest? All conjoin in a thematic web of entrapment, highlighted by their settings – be they the 'locus classicus' Dante-esque forest (Dante and Okri); a royal castle (Shakespeare's *Hamlet*); a refurbished guest house (Agatha Christie's ([1952] 1965) Monkswell Manor in *The Mousetrap*, now in its sixty-seventh year on the London stage); and ordinary farmhouse or an actual mouse trap (in the fables of yore) or Beckett's love triangle – most featuring a murderous taking of life. All signify this darkening world, in need of light. The call for right living seems to be embedded in the implied moral: the need to engage with one another in the community of the entrapped. Either implicitly or explicitly, the allusions conjoin to remind us that we are all connected, that every action becomes an interaction: 'There is much to escape from.' / 'And nowhere to escape to' (2009: 56).

Having all but universalized the fable of life, Okri hints at what is 'worth dreaming about' (ibid.: 56), 'since we got lost' (ibid.: 55). Typical of Okri, no grandiose remedy is prescribed to recover our true state of being. As Young Man and Young Woman, the new generation, ultimately realize, it is simply 'A room where we can go on creating beautiful spaces, and expanding the universe.' / 'Yes, really pushing it all back and making it real with our vitality' (55). In a topsy-turvy world, Okri's project in this fable is idealistic: to spread light, following the legacy of Romanticism as, for instance, in Keats's (2009) yearning for renewal in 'On sitting down to read *King Lear* once again': 'When through the old oak forest I am gone, / Let me not wander in a barren dream, / But when I am consumed in the fire / Give me new Phoenix wings to fly at my desire' (ll. 11–14). 'The Comic Destiny' re-dreams of 'new Phoenix wings' for, as Okri states, 'All the high road stories have been told, but not the hidden roads stories that lead to the true centre' (2015: 29). In an early poem, 'An African Elegy' – a meditation on death – Okri concludes with the affirmation that 'The Sky is not an enemy / Destiny is our friend' (1992: 41). Elsewhere, he intimates a rationale for his new fable: 'The greatest stories are those that resonate our beginnings and intuit our endings (our mysterious origins and our numinous destinies), and dissolve them both into one' (1997: 114, no. 26).

While Okri is never prescriptive, 'The Comic Destiny' resonates in just this way. The closing scene, with Pinprop, Old Man and Old Woman together in the white house with the blue door, coupled with the appeals by New Woman and New Man for new beginnings, is illustrative of dissolving both our beginnings and endings 'into one'. It is, as this fable suggests, our true state of being to reconcile hierarchical social constructs, to strive to dissolve erstwhile disabilities such as fear, dispossession and slavery by getting 'back to the source' (2009: 104), to Nature, to seemly behaviour (the ancient meaning of justice), to right living.

Part Two

Rebalancing the triadic elements of life

5

Apologia pro *In Arcadia*: A neglected masterpiece?

In Arcadia ([2002] 2003)¹ has suffered surprising critical neglect. The paucity in critical judgement is typified by remarks such as '[a] considerable challenge is involved in taking on such an idiosyncratic, complicated and intellectually obscure work of fiction' (Anon. 2008) and 'Okri has chosen a big and bold subject and a highly original approach to it' (Bruce 2003). Is this perhaps indicative of a failure to read Ben Okri on his own terms?

Okri's first new millennium novel takes its impetus from both 'A Moment in Timelessness'² – his inaugural millennium lecture at the 1997 Edinburgh Book Festival – and *Mental Fight* (1999) – his Blakean intertext, subtitled 'An anti-spell for the twenty-first century'. Like Melville or Schreiner or Woolf or Joyce, Okri reincarnates his own genre of fiction as a reflection, in words, of his own belief system and right to invent:

> A great challenge for our age, and future ages: to do for story-telling what Joyce did for language – to take it to the highest levels of enchantment and magic; to impact into story infinite richness and convergences; to make story flow with serenity, with eternity. (1996: 20)

Art, initiation and a dynamic stillness inform Okri's conscious artistry. 'We have entered a new age. We must be prepared … People who use only their eyes do not SEE. People who use only their ears do not HEAR,' writes Okri towards the end of *The Famished Road* (1991: 498; original emphases). As if in elucidation, he concludes *Starbook* with '[t]he ways of time are indeed strange; and events are not what we think they are. Time and oblivion alchemise all things, even the great suffering' (2007: 421). The reciprocity of time is a primary narrative device in *In Arcadia*.

In this context, there may be alternative reading strategies for appreciating a novelist who is set to subvert and, at the same time, enliven the structures of old-world writing and reading. The proposition is that, narratologically, this three-part novel evinces a cyclical structure delineating three phases of spiritual growth: breakdown, breakthrough and emergence, interlinked by a linear motif of Akashic still points or 'intuitions' (i.e. numbered meditations of poetic insight).³ The argument draws upon Okri's philosophical decoding of the labyrinthine symbolism in Nicolas Poussin's famous painting *Les Bergers d'Arcadie*, as well as on a modification of Steven Harrison's progression of spiritual life in *What's Next after Now: Post-Spirituality and the Creative Life* (2005),[4] and closes with further justification for the chosen critical approach.

Although there have been one or two positive reviews of *In Arcadia*, negative criticism predominates even among those who do address narrative technique. Consider Bruce King, for example, who dismisses the novel with:

> Except as a metaphor of life as a journey, the story in itself seems purposeless as there are few events and little narrative development ... The plot is mostly an excuse for a meditation on notions of Arcadia with its resonance of paradise, a lost Eden, innocence, the pastoral, and its consequent associations with the Fall, anxieties, unhappiness, and death. (2003: 86)

King follows the tone set by Jeremy Treglown, who was even more dismissive: 'Realism apart, *In Arcadia* has no narrative tension and the characters are ciphers. The long philosophical-cum-cultural-historical rants which it mainly consists of, with their outbreaks of Latinity[5] ... are shapeless, repetitive and trite' (2002: 68). What both King and Treglown fail to take cognizance of is the integral relationship between story and artefact, idea and form, in the art of fiction-making. Henry James uses a graphic metaphor to make the point about this interrelationship: 'The story and the novel, the idea and the form, are the needle and the thread, and I never heard of a guild of tailors who recommended the use of the thread without the needle, of the needle without the thread' (1963: 9).

Narrative technique in Okri's novels is likewise not something superadded to the content but, rather, a fundamental and deliberate means of structuring perceptions. This three-part novel can be read as a three-phase narratological experiment tracing, first, modernity's breakdown (the fires of transformation); then, the individual's breakthrough (confronting the actual); and finally, emergence and creativity, as already intimated. Evocative of this tripartite reading, in *Birds of Heaven* and *A Way of Being Free*, Okri states: 'Maybe there are only three kinds of stories; the stories we live, the stories we tell, and the higher stories that help our souls fly up towards the greater light' (1996: 42; 1997: 126). As will be shown in the fuller discussion of the metafictional elements in *In Arcadia* later in this chapter, particularly for such 'higher stories', 'Chaque romancier, chaque roman, doit inventer sa propre forme. Aucune recette ne peut remplacer cette reflexion continuelle.' (Every novelist must devise his own appropriate form for each text. No formula can replace this constant or on-going consideration (own translation)) (Robbe-Grillet 1963: 11). As a conscious artist with an instinctive sense of form, Okri shares Alain Robbe-Grillet's insistence on the centrality not only of form but also of organic creativity. It would be simplistic, therefore, to suggest that an African author as profound and as daring as Ben Okri would, or even could, divide his text slavishly into these three kinds of stories – his interest lies in sacred geometry, not simple arithmetic. 'The greatest stories are those that resonate our beginnings and intuit our endings (our mysterious origins and our numinous destinies), and dissolve them both into one,' opines Okri in *Birds of Heaven* (1996: 24).

A brief outline of the story line serves to demonstrate this cyclic patterning. *In Arcadia* traces the journey, from London to Paris, of a motley group of out-of-work professional misfits, commissioned by a mysterious producer, whose identity is never revealed but who provides 'clear instruction' (2003: 28) at intervals, to make a television documentary about the meaning of Arcadia. En route aboard the *Eurostar*, they interview the train driver and later film his suburban Paris garden as well as other versions of bucolic ideals at Versailles and in the Louvre. Periodically, members of the crew receive cryptic notes or inscriptions. Symptomatic of the cyclic pattern of spiritual growth, the novel closes with the film crew re-commencing their journey, this time to and then from Switzerland presumably en route for the original physical Arcady in Greece. Lao is the narrator of the first part of the novel, at once, film presenter and intrusive authorial commentator.

The tellingly unnamed sections overlap, reflect on themselves and foreshadow what is to come. Part 1 is divided into two. Book 1 serves to introduce the characters 'all shipwrecks and derelicts on the ruined shores of the city' (Okri 2003: 5) and sets the scene for the start of the journey and the gathering of the film crew at London's Waterloo Station. Evoking the breakdown phase that necessarily precedes spiritual growth, Okri depicts a dismal, contemporary world of social malaise, with 'all on the verge of nervous breakdowns' (ibid.). A device that parallels the breakthrough phase, the proposed TV documentary on Arcadia provides an opportunity to escape 'from the dehydrating boredom ... in this inferno that we call the modern world' (ibid.). Stephen Abell's estimation that 'the first section of the book [is] a bilious – and charmless – invective against modernity, a monologue that blazes a narrative trail to which any reader will struggle to warm, and which Okri himself only half-heartedly pursues' (2002: 23) thus fails to appreciate the thrust of this novel. He misses both the mode – that of contemporary journalism's deliberately exaggerated caricature – as well as aspects of narrative intrigue, such as the suggestion that the coming together of this motley team is in response to an unspoken 'summons' (2003: 5) by Malasso, a 'mysterious force' (25), an invisible 'metteur en scéne' (27) reminiscent of a 'Procous' or 'Prospero' (26),[6] and the warning to 'Beware of inscriptions' (24). Lao is the first to receive a tantalizing warning note about his personal path, which he implies results in 'unusual irradiations of perceptivity' (ibid.: 26), this, in the context of confronting reality: a diatribe against the distortions of the photographic image or what Okri terms 'the faintly disreputable middle-class aspirations' (ibid.: 30) for fame and money. As if awakening from the first Akashic still point, Lao realizes that hope is born of the recognition that 'in living there are no resolutions at all' (ibid.) and this section closes with: 'And so this journey must be a sort of dying for me; a dying of the old self; a birth of something new and fearless and bright and strange' (ibid.: 32).

Okri does not simply argue against Judaic/Western notions of a singular experience of the spirit-in-the-flesh world; he brings to fictive life the notion of the individual soul re-born from bliss spirit to suffering mortal shape:

> One of the reasons I didn't want to be born became clear to me after I had come into this world. I was still very young when in a daze I saw Dad swallowed up by a hole in the road ... I was seven years old when I dreamt that my hands were covered with the yellow blood of a stranger. I had no idea whether these images

belonged to this life, or to a previous one, or to one that was yet to come, or even if they were merely the host of images that invades the lives of all children. (1991: 7)

This is the profound rationalization regarding life of the 'Abiku' child, Azaro, who expounds further, but now esoterically:

> When I was very young I had a clear memory of my life stretching to other lives. There were no distinctions. Sometimes I seemed to be living several lives at once. One lifetime flowed into the others and all of them flowed into my childhood.
> As a child I felt I weighed my mother down. In turn I felt weighed down by the inscrutability of life. Being born was a shock from which I never recovered. (Ibid.)

The spirit world of Okri is not necessarily the 'ad terminum' growth or 'Bildung' of a Western epic, an Odyssey; his bodies are embodied, flitting between life and life.

Steven Harrison explains the breakdown phase which makes spiritual transformation possible. Collapse begins as he states with one's self-perception: 'The fundamental deception we construct is the idea of the self. This prime organizing assumption is the progenitor of all the other deceptions, and it is generated by thought itself as an integral part of the arising of thought form' (2005: 20-1). He adds that '[w]hile we are in the centre of this projected universe, the lack of full dimensionality in the flat world of thought suggests to us that there is something fundamentally untrue about everything', before concluding that it is cosmic interference with our dreamworld that is like a mortal blow: 'The subtle disturbance is the actuality of the universe impinging on our dream world. The awakening from the dream appears from the perspective of the dream as death' (ibid.).

Book 2 of Part 1, reflecting the Fires of Transformation, introduces the eighth member of the party, a young, redheaded ingénue, by the name of Mistletoe (an evergreen plant itself a sacred symbol of immortality). An amateur artist, she is the agent for a discussion of Vermeer's 'The Music Lesson' which provokes her own artistic credo: 'It ought to be like true breathing, breathing the way God ... intended us to breath, but which we've forgotten' (Okri 2003: 53). This painting, with its mystical inscription,[7] 'an allegory of liberty and bondage' (Gowing, in The Royal Collection, 2) adumbrates the interpretations of Poussin's inscription, in the third section of the novel, which features a second mysterious note as well as four subsections entitled 'Intuitions in the Garden', each a correlative for an Akashic still point.

The garden is, of course, a metaphor for a return 'to the original world, with Eden's dawn in the air' (Okri 2003: 40). The idyllic sunlit garden recalls the memory of the cyclic pattern of life and pastoral bliss, ultimately concretized in Poussin's painting that the group view in the Louvre:

> And then, alone with all its beauty, the earth discovered the moving forms of birds and animals and humanity, and it fell in love with them, and made a home in its womb for them when they died, and provided them with all they needed when they were born. (Ibid.: 41)

The second and third re-awakenings continue the central theme: 'Creation and destruction were both part of the same song' (ibid.: 42); and the natural world '[h]ad chosen joy at self's existence, and freedom followed … had chosen the love of self's regenerativeness, and prosperity followed; the necessity of self's presence, and stillness followed; the certainty of self's growth, and power followed' (ibid.: 44). Taken in context, the quartet of abstractions – freedom, prosperity, stillness and power – allude to the great psychic and moral readjustment afforded by a return to the source. As Phyllis Hodgson explains: 'Such is the aim of all mystics, to rise in consciousness to this spiritual level which is unattainable by the normal faculties of knowing' (1967: 10). The prose flow in the excerpts is as fluid as the sentient double lives of Okri's spirit-in-life beings. A meditative silence is the leitmotif of all three intuitions. However, in the fourth intuition, man's desire for power resuscitates the memory of the Fall: 'And then we dreamt of paradise, because we had lost it' (2003: 45). Part 1 closes with the breakthrough: confronting actuality; re-visioning the purpose of the journey: to recapture 'the matchless mysteries of mortal life' (ibid.: 58).

Part 2 elaborates upon 'the stress of the world that had given rise to the Arcadian legend' (Okri 2003: 64), appropriately eliding into five subsections called 'Intuitions in the Dark', all evoked by speeding through the underwater tunnel that links England to France, where all reality becomes pure inscription without words, where 'the mind contracts. The spirit folds inwards' (ibid.: 67) and 'the world surrenders to an omnipotent darkness' (ibid.). Meditations on light and dark proliferate, concretized by the disappearance and reappearance at different points of three of the characters. On arrival in France, Lao realizes that the imagined second Arcadia 'is more true [*sic*] in the mind than on earth' (ibid.: 82); it is 'our secular Eden' (65). As if in explanation, Harrison states:

> The great liberation is actual and requires nothing, gives nothing, contains nothing and creates nothing. We are all done, whether we like it or not, whether we are spiritual or not, whether we agree with this or not. When we cease to characterise life as a process with attendant goals, we apprehend what has always been the case, an acausal world in which manifestation is absolutely true and description is relatively not. (2005: 21)

In summary, he notes: 'The great liberation then is not a state, but an energetic manifestation, an actuality, not an idea' (ibid.).

Born of silence, three Akashic still points propel the narrative forward. First, the narrator reiterates the Arcadian dream: 'Our modern neurosis is Pan's revenge. Our craving for Nature is our craving for reunion with the sublime, for oneness, for rejuvenation' (2003: 66). Akashic memory then surfaces in the rhetorical question: 'Is the visible life the deposit of all one's thoughts and deeds?' (ibid.: 102). Finally, dropping his habitual mask of cynicism, Lao is encircled: 'because he lived, in spirit, within humanity's abstraction, within the oneness of it. He believed, deep down beyond thought, that all are one' (Okri 2003: 105). Okri here replaces rather than displaces Judaeo-Christian notions of the spirit world.

The imaginative forum of African writers such as Schreiner, Lessing and Okri is not weakly reactive or predictably adversarial towards the old world. It is vigorous in its certainty of describing and inscribing new places, relations and intellectual structures. It has the verve of discovery and the gloss of newness that Sir Philip Sidney sensed at the quick point of Renaissance English. The key to Okri's *In Arcadia* is arguably Mistletoe's intuition: 'Arcadia is the chiaroscuro of the mortal and the immortal, of happiness and death, of eternity and transience, beauty and the grave' (2003: 179). Shepherd Hoodwin clarifies the concept:

> The instinctive (neutral) center is the location of a person's individual akashic records; it interpenetrates the other centers and stores their memories there; it is the seat of the subconscious. The individual instinctive center is, in turn, connected to larger 'storehouses,' such as the collective consciousness of humanity.
>
> Ultimately, it is connected to the whole, so when we clarify our instinctive center through self-knowledge and healing, we are contributing to the clarification of the entire universe. (n.d.: 2)

This is the third phase of spiritual growth, explored fully in the third part of Okri's novel. Reminiscent of Eliot's 'The Still Point' in 'Burnt Norton',[8] Harrison elucidates on this erasure of space/time duality: 'The source of quantum creativity is non-located; … it is located in its entirety. The creative utilises the locus, utilises time and space, but is not these qualities, certainly not limited to their boundaries' (2005: 21). And in *Birds of Heaven*, Okri reiterates this sentiment in relation to literature:

> Like music, like painting, literature too wants to transcend its primary condition and become something higher. Art wants to move into silence, into the emotional and spiritual conditions of the world. Statues become melodies, melodies become yearnings, yearnings become actions. (1996: 5)

Part 3 of *In Arcadia* is devoted to the film crew's visit to the Louvre and a discussion of Poussin's artwork. Set in an idyllic pastoral scene, the painting features three shepherds and a shepherdess seemingly examining the enigmatic inscription on a large gravestone, 'Et in Arcadia Ego'. Andrew Gough[9] states that the painting 'is considered by many to conceal unspeakable esoteric secrets'. Okri echoes this by having his film-maker observe that the inscription is one 'which no one could decode' and, reflecting back on the earlier excerpt about 'Le Jardin des Tuileries' (Tuileries' garden), that the painting depicts 'a place of immortal bliss, in a land that used to be called Eden, but which was renamed Arcadia, and it is all the lands of the earth' (2003: 193). Characteristic of Poussin, the figures overlap, suggesting dynamic interaction, while the interplay of light and shade is a principal painterly technique. As the group examine the painting, they receive a warning given to the producer in a dream:

> Don't forget that the landscape is greater than the tomb. Death is merely Time's inscription, a beautiful absence. Don't dwell too long in Arcadia. This is fatal. For

if you dwell too long there, you will become the tomb, and your life its inscription. (Ibid.)

Musing upon the nature of art, in general, and of painting, in particular, Okri states:

Painting is the illuminated record of invisible realms seen in glimpses. Intimations of re-incarnation. *Akashic still points.* Painting is indeed one of the places where Hades is averted. It is the hint of a sort of immortality within. It comes from the same place inside us where gods are born.
    Painting is one of the most mysterious metaphors of Arcadia. (Ibid.: 190; emphasis added)

This excerpt perhaps explains why King assumes that '*In Arcadia* is a variation on *Astonishing the Gods*' (ibid.: 86). The latter novel does feature an invisible realm, but it does so to the exclusion of the earthly realm. The lead character in *Astonishing the Gods* is invisible, a seeker after divine grace, whereas that in *In Arcadia* is very much flesh and blood, a character whom Treglown describes as 'an arrogant, garrulous, paranoid misanthrope' (2002: 68). Of interest, however, is the reference to 'Akashic still points' which, in the context of describing *Les Bergers d'Arcadie*, Okri suggests are 'the resting point[s] of an idea that has travelled thousands of years in the mind of humanity' (2003: 204). The purpose of such resting points is to help one organize and integrate what one already knows, thus leading to new and creative insights.

In *Science and the Akashic Field: An Integral Theory of Everything*, Ervin László states: 'The Akashic records (Akashic is a Sanskrit word meaning "sky," "space" or "aether") are … understood to be a collection of mystical knowledge that is encoded in the aether, i.e. on a non-physical plane of existence' (2004: 4). Hoodwin (n.d.: 1)[10] explains that 'the core of the akashic records is the akashic plane, the neutral plane' and '[i]t is the overall record for the universe'. Of Okri's interpretations of the artwork, *Les Bergers d'Arcadie*, King emotes: 'There is a complicated argument here about the imagination projecting the artist's emotions on the world through art, plus some common sense and psychobabble about happiness being within, something one chooses' (2003: 87). Although he concedes that '[t]he form is interesting – as the novel becomes art criticism, cultural history, meditation', King is quick to insist that 'the great truths offered appear as clichés' (ibid.).

Stephen Abell's review endorses these negative sentiments. In the context of interpreting 'Et in Arcadia Ego' ['I too have lived in Arcadia' / 'I too have been here' / 'Death too is here'], the inscription on the gravestone in Poussin's *Les Bergers d'Arcadie* (and the novel's central enigmatic symbol), Abell expatiates: 'The difficulty of the work comes to symbolize the uncertainty of the world, the inscrutability of the inscription testifies to the elusive nature of all meaning' (2002: 23). Quoting Okri, he continues: '[A]rt becomes a "condition of unease, of dislocation, of being out of it all, an exile"'. But then, Abell continues:

Reading Okri at his most ripe … is something like submerging your head in aromatic water: pleasant to begin with but none the less liable to drown you … this novel inhabits the same plane of awkwardness [as the art work], enacting – archly refusing to succour – the struggles of life, by asking questions without providing reassuring answers ... This ... reveals the core of inadequacy that undermines the entire book. Okri is, in fact, sheltering in his own ideal of awkwardness, a false aesthetic of failure, as he comforts himself with a sense of his own unforgiving perspicacity ... Such inconclusion, filled with its own question marks at the end of the novel, is as frustrating as it is lazy. (Ibid.)

However, '[c]ertainty,' says Okri in *A Way of Being Free*, 'has always been the enemy of art and creativity; more than that it has been the enemy of humanity' (1997: 30).

This novel is neither 'trite' nor 'clichéd'. The elegiac ethos of the past tense 'I too once *knew* Arcadia' / 'I too *have been* in now' (own translation; emphases added) recalls us to an identifying landscape of the soul and field which cuts against rationalist organization, political schemata and mercantilist compensation. And far from being either 'psychobabble' or 'lazy', Okri clearly points to reading the painting as a metonymic Akashic record:

Lao found himself thinking not of the inscription as such, but of an idea through time. He was thinking about the journey of an idea from a real place to a poem; from the real Arkadia in the Peloponnese to the idyllic and pastoral poems of the Greek poet Theocritus, and from Theocritus to Virgil. (2003: 206–7)

Virgil's Bucolics are political: the suppliant appeals to Caesar Augustus not to reassign his land. Virgil sings of the sacred bond between 'farmer', 'shepherd' – read human being – and the humanizing influence of a known landscape. This follows the epistemology of the German 'Naturphilosophie' or that of English Romanticism where Nature is seen as transformational or even as a portal to the spiritual realm. The theme, or knowledge, of this gained meaning runs straight from Theocritus to Okri. We are the land; the land is our mother! As a further guide to his interpretation of the painting, an intrusive authorial voice declares: 'With Virgil, Arcadia became the seed of an ideal, a dream, and a lyric meditation on the mystery of creativity' (ibid.: 207). This metafictional comment guides interpretation of novel and painting in accordance with Chinese principles. George Rowley articulates these principles in a chapter entitled 'Spirit and Matter':

We will begin with the basic contrast of spirit and matter. In the west the gulf between them has been impassable. For us spirit belongs to the life of prayer and worship, matter is the concern of science. This has directed our art to the extremes of religious meaning and naturalistic representation ... The Chinese created a unique conception of the realm of the spirit which was one with the realm of matter. This meant that their painting would never become religious, imitative, or personally expressive as our painting; and it also meant that art would tend to take over the functions of religion and philosophy and would become a prime vehicle for man's most profound thoughts and his feelings about the mystery of the universe. (1947: 5)

In a poem to the painter, entitled 'On Klee' (1996: 45), Okri muses: 'So you too were on the journey / To the East / Where mystery / Is the stuff of the feast.'

As noted at the beginning of this chapter, Okri interprets *Les Bergers d'Arcadie* as an Akashic still point. Predictably, Part 3 consists of meditations, rhetorical questions, intuitions: 'ideas that have travelled thousands of years in the mind of humanity' (2003: 204). Thus, for Okri, this is 'an open painting', 'a true enigma', 'a visual koan', 'a perpetual quest' (ibid.: 203), 'an idea through time', 'the journey of an idea' (206). 'And so Arcadia and death are inextricably intertwined. Immortality and death are conjoined. Beauty and death are linked, happiness and death are coupled' (ibid.).

'This unique conception of spirit and matter,' says Rowley 'was embodied in the Tao' (1947: 5). Okri's lead character is a black Lao. Lao Tsû is the old philosopher of Tao Têh Ching. Rowley explains this natural mysticism: 'It is said of the Tao: / Being great, it passes on; / Passing on, it becomes remote; / Having become remote, it returns' (ibid.: 7). In addition to direct references to Taoism and Akashic still points, eight characters participate in this journey, a journey into the soul. In Chinese culture and for symbolists, the figure eight is a sacred number, a metaphor for eternity. Compare Okri's fellow Nigerian Wole Soyinka's 'Modius' (read Moebius as illustrated in Max Escher's painting): 'multiform / Evolution of the self-devouring snake to spatials / New in symbol, banked loop of the "Modius Strip" / And interlock of re-creative rings, one surface / Yet full comb of angles, uni-plane, yet sensuous / Complexities of mind and motion.'[11]

In closing his novel, Okri recommends that '[l]iving ought to be the unfolding masterpiece of the loving spirit. And dying ought to set this masterpiece free' (2003: 230); this as the antidote to the despair, terror and cosmic emptiness of modernity, to the 'finely drawn out ritual of humiliation and meaninglessness' (ibid.: 121). 'What ultimately remains on the akashic plane,' writes Hoodwin, 'is the distillation, what was learned, which is what is relevant for the universe to carry forward into the future' (n.d.: 2).

'Pace' (despite) misreadings, Okri thus ascribes a porous world of soul and body which moves in circles of spirit, landscape, past and present: the pure essence of which may be that timeless plane of Akashic still point but which the world is severely at odds with the linear progressivism and obsessive materialist expression of the egocentric Western ideology of the glorious individual.

6

'Domesticating infinity' in *Mental Fight* and *Astonishing the Gods*

Introduction

The argument in this chapter is predicated upon the notion of temporality as a state of becoming within the stillness of time and connected to the chosen literary texts, where the text is a compendium of becoming. It begins by exploring the pertinence of its title in a reading of *Astonishing the Gods* ([1995] 1999) inspired by Ben Okri's poetry anthology *Mental Fight* (1999). The notions of 'timelessness' or 'domesticating infinity' are discussed – tacitly acknowledging Alexander Gunn's (1929) triple definition of eternity as an unending extent of time/timelessness/and that which, while including time, somehow transcends time – before an exploration of the mode of the novel is undertaken.

One of the most intriguing features of *Astonishing the Gods* is Okri's self-reflexive dialogue with time. In this experimental novel, the author's contemplation of a present that has almost entirely lost contact with its past leads fluidly, not into a future time, but into a placeless timelessness within the present. His invisible protagonist – the embodiment of an aspirant spirit undergoing initiation into the esoteric mysteries and learning to accept abstract ideas to develop – experiences the narrative incidents beyond rationality, when such rational categories as time, space and causality have been dissolved. Deepak Chopra's view of eternity throws further light on this seeming conundrum when, in his non-fictive *Life after Death*, he surmises that death accomplishes the following 'miraculous things':

> It replaces time with timelessness.
> It stretches the boundaries of space to infinity.
> It reveals the source of life.
> It brings a new way of knowing that lies beyond the reach of the five senses.
> It reveals the underlying intelligence that organizes and sustains creation.
> (2006: 25–6)

This suggests that, in its transformative renovations, the alchemy of death provides consolations beyond the sentient and knowable in life. For the invisible querent, continuous time dissolves into unconnected moments of the iterative present (the eternally now).

The novel, like the poetry in *Mental Fight*, can thus be read as Okri's (pre)text for an interrogation of a timeless eternity: his project is to 'domesticate infinity', to point a way on where there is no way out by seemingly embedding his narrative within the esoteric Perennial Tradition.[1] Okri has contributed immensely to metafiction and to the ameliorative purpose of storytelling, as he opines in *A Way of Being Free*: 'When we have made an experience or a chaos into a story we have transformed it, made sense of it, transmuted experience, domesticated the chaos' (1997: 113 no. 22).

Initiation into the mysteries of Perennial philosophy – embraced 'inter alia' by Hermeticism, Gnosticism, Cabbalism and Sufism – consists of eight guided steps: (1) to allow the spirit to reunite with the Higher Consciousness; (2) to release the spirit from the spell under which it is held in bondage in the body; (3) to bring the body and mind to quiescence; (4) to free the Higher Consciousness from the enthralment of the ego consciousness; (5) to reunite the spirit with its lost universality; (6) to separate the higher subtle feelings from the gross sense feelings; (7) to free the spirit from any misconceptions; and (8) to allow the spirit to travel to higher realms (Livergood n.d.: 1). The relevance of this tradition will become apparent in the discussion of narratological strategies in *Astonishing the Gods*.

'Philosophy,' says Okri in *A Way of Being Free*, 'is most powerful when it resolves into story. But story is amplified in power by the presence of philosophy' (1997: 125 no. 85). He then highlights the difference between fiction and politics: 'Politics is the art of the possible; creativity is the art of the impossible' (ibid.: 127 no. 101). Yet, Robert Bennett is moved to lament that

> *Astonishing the Gods,* continues to develop the same kind of spiritual, mythical vision and lyrical aesthetic that Okri develops in *The Famished Road* and *Songs of Enchantment*. Unfortunately, however, it lacks much of the political engagement, experimental energy, and complexity found in Okri's previous novels: its characters are less developed, its narrative structure seems more amorphous than complex, and its mythical vision fails to develop the same intensity because it is not counterbalanced with realistic dimension. (1998: 368)

While political and realistic elements are hardly 'de rigor', this chapter seeks to address Bennett's issues with the novel's 'narrative structure' and its 'mythical vision'. As intimated, my reading aligns itself more nearly with Ato Quayson's assessment of Okri's oeuvre prior to the publication of *Astonishing the Gods*:

> By implying that the state partly shares the *abiku* condition[2] ... Okri suggests that the cyclicality of arrested development can become endemic if it is not recognized for what it is. That he chooses to pose the issue as a function of the potential relationships between the real world and that of spirits suggests that the condition of post-colonial arrested development cannot be adequately grasped within the rationality of Western discourses. The rationality of indigenous belief systems has a part to play in the understanding of the African condition. (1995: 157)

Okri's existentialist aesthetic in this novel and in his second poetry anthology is as much concerned with the reintegration, revitalization and synthesis of selfhood as it is with the literal impossibility of this. His narrative is an empowering quest for spiritual self-realization that initially inheres in unravelling the 'secret of visibility' (Okri [1995] 1999: 4), of becoming more 'real' in a Lacanian sense.

Jacques Lacan builds on Plato's (1994) notion of the 'really real', or the 'Forms' which 'constitute a realm of unchanging being to which the world of individual mutable objects is subordinate. Because the forms are immutable, they are more real – and more true [*sic*] – than the changeable material world' (Leitch 2001: 34). Lacan perceives three 'orders' or dimensions of the psyche; he defines 'the real' as that which is outside reality:

> The Real [as opposed to the Imaginary and the Symbolic] is the easiest to define and the hardest to talk about. In fact, it *can't* be talked about; any such discussion is 'impossible'. The moment it becomes an object of discourse, it ceases to be the 'Real' because it becomes real *for someone* and it becomes the 'truth'. We are used to the real. The truth we repress … The truth is always disturbing … But what is disturbing can be disturbing only *for someone*. The Real can thus only be studied in its effects on the other two dimensions, the Imaginary and the Symbolic. (Ibid.: 1281; original emphases)

In the realization of his integrated philosophic-theological theory of the Real/truth, Okri combines dream and desire with myth in his exploration of time/eternity within an imaginary city of the mind. The objective is 'to discover the hidden unifying laws of all things, to deepen the spirit, to make more profound the sensitivities of the individual to the universe, and to become more creative' ([1995] 1999: 66). Directing the reader to the novel's mythical title, Okri adds: 'And sometimes – very rarely – but sometimes nonetheless, our highest creative acts, our highest playfulness, our self-overcoming, our purest art, our ascending songs, by some mysterious grace transcend so many boundaries and enter so many realms that we occasionally astonish even the gods' (ibid.: 148).

'We do not wish to be remembered,' says the last spirit guide in the story. 'We only want to increase the light, and to spread illumination' ([1995] 1999: 149). This pure light is, we are told, 'a symbol and *dream* of the gentle master who had been visible to his followers for only three days before ascending into invisibility, and becoming one of the greatest forces for light in the spirit and imagination of the world' (ibid.: 92, emphasis added). ('Trust in dreams,' says Kahlil Gibran (2001: 109), 'for in them is hidden the gate to eternity'.)

In *Astonishing the Gods*, Okri effectively conflates Lacan's three orders of the psyche. 'We are learning to be masters of the art of transcending all boundaries. We are learning to go beyond the illusion that is behind illusion' ([1995] 1999: 148). Here, the intellectual currents of German transcendental philosophy – with its will to transgress the boundary between the human and the divine – and the Judaeo-Christian tendency to confront 'almost without mediation the problems of the absolute and its promises' (as Achile Mbembe (2004: 10) points out) form a singular theory of temporality, where temporality constitutes a state of becoming within the stillness of time. Consider, for example, Okri's single stanza poem from the closing section of his collection (inspired by William Blake's 'Jerusalem, the Golden') entitled *Mental Fight* (1999).[3] Tellingly called 'Turn on your light', the poem provides the germ for my discussion: 'The illusion of time will give way / To the reality of time / And *time present is made / Before time becomes present. / For all time is here, now, / In our awakening*' (ibid.: 67; emphasis added).[4] Invoking the time – as space – equation,[5] where 'time present' is an a priori becoming, the poem is evocative of timelessness, of eternity and, more importantly, of spiritual regeneration. In 'Human kind' [*sic*], Okri muses: 'Human kind cannot live long / With the notion / Or the reality / Of *timelessness*. / Only in the mind. / Only in the spirit' (ibid.: 6; emphasis added).

What Okri proposes in *Astonishing the Gods* is loosening the fetters of the past and visualizing universal justice 'through careful spiritual and social evolution' (1999: 72). A similar suggestion is given in an untitled poem, where Okri's injunction is to 'Allow uncomplicated regions / Of time to project themselves / Into your sleeping consciousness / Inducing terror, or mental liberation' (ibid.: 4). Here, facts become subservient to imagination and beauty. The linear flow of timelessness in this poem coupled with the oxymoronic notion of timelessness inducing the 'terror' of 'mental liberation' implies that the treatment of time in *Astonishing the Gods* can be seen as a literary device, functioning as a substructure upon which the nature of the protagonist's inner time is superimposed. The poetic plea thus points not so much to self-knowledge as to self-enlightenment or, as Dominic Bradbury puts it in an almost Okrian echo, learning 'how to make possible the impossible, how to turn the ordinary moment or mind into the legendary, how to turn darkness into light' (1999: n.p.).

Okri's project is, essentially, to discover how to turn spiritual exhaustion into spiritual energy; how to distil human experience. What he experiments with, is how to *domesticate the infinite*. His opening, untitled poem in *Mental Fight* explicitly points *the way*:

> An illusion by which we become
> More real.
> A moment unmarked by the universe,
> By nature, the seasons, or stars.
> Moment we have marked out
> In timelessness.
> Human moment.
> Making a ritual, a drama, a tear
> On eternity.
> *Domesticating the infinite.*
> Contemplating the quantum questions,
> Time, death, new beginnings,
> Regeneration, cycles, the unknown.
>
> (1999: 3; emphasis added)

In line with Perennial philosophy, the way to 'domesticate the infinite' suggested here is by meditating upon the cyclic nature of time. It is also via 'mystical initiation, consisting of multiple experiences' (Holroyd 1989: 87) based on the premise that man is saved not by faith but by knowledge ('gnosis'). And 'such knowledge is vouchsafed by secret lore or obtained through mystical illumination' (ibid.). This is perhaps clarified by another extract from 'Turn on your light':

> You can't remake the world
> Without remaking yourself
> Each new era begins within.
> It is an inward event,
> With unsuspected possibilities
> For inner liberation.
> We could use it to turn on
> Our inward lights.

Liberation and enlightenment are symbiotic:

> Infect the world with your light.
> Help fulfil the golden prophecies
> Press forward the human genius.
> Our future is greater than our past.
>
> (Okri 1999: 67)

Two adjacent, axiomatic paragraphs from *Astonishing the Gods*, featuring Okri's invisible initiate's reaction to the marvellous city he finally encounters, reflect this dawning of inner illumination. The first is contemplative and invokes ancient mythology in:

> He contemplated the overwhelming mystery of the square. He studied its bronze equestrian rider. He gazed upon its sea-god and horses emerging from a giant fountain of adamant. And he pondered its guardian figure of an ancient prophet-king who stood poised in dreaming marble before his own mystic annunciation of courage. (1999: 87)

In its more descriptive mode, the second paragraph re-enters a dazzling world of pseudo-religious certainties, where everything is possible:

> The equestrian rider was on a high diamond platform. With the hand bearing the shining sword of truth, he was pointing ever-forward to a great destiny and destination, never to be reached, because if reached the people and their journey would perish. He was pointing to an ever-moving destination, unspecified except in myth, the place of absolute self-realization and contentment which must always be beyond the reach of the brave land, but not so much beyond reach that the

people would give up in perfection's despair, and set up tent somewhere between the sixth and final mountain. (Ibid.)

In this novel, Okri resorts to the popular device of travel, but, here, the journey is an ongoing spiritual quest. *Astonishing the Gods* is a resolute reclamation of a spiritual home. Reinforcing the numerologically resonant seven-year sea journey and the three physical feats to shed the temporal body that precede this vision, this pivotal extract is from Book 4, Chapter 3, and so is evocative of the union of the temporal (four) and the Divine (three).

The extracts from Okri's anthology of poetry *Mental Fight* and from his novel *Astonishing the Gods* conjoin to define his poetic and fictive modes. Okri is a notoriously difficult author to write about, because he seems to evade categorization within the categories critics normally employ for African writers (Anthony Chennells, pers. com.). Variously defined as 'non-realist' (Quayson 1995: 144); 'classic magical realism' (Cooper 2003: 412); or, by implication, the prose of nativism or 'counter-realism' (Mbembe 2004: 13), Okri's oeuvre is, I argue, original and inimitable. His narrative mode is a philosophic-theological one, with a mystical Perennialist bent. His is a conscious, spiritual artistry, as he himself acknowledges in *A Way of Being Free*: 'Poets seem to be set against the world because we need them to show us the falseness of our limitation, the true extent of our kingdom' (1997: 2). In an immanent world,

[t]he poet turns the earth into mother, the sky becomes a shelter, the sun an inscrutable god, and the pragmatists are irritated ... The problem is with those who are frightened of the rather limitless validity of the imagination, frightened of people who continually extend the boundaries of the possible, people who ceaselessly reinvent existence; frontiers people of the unknown and the uncharted. (Ibid.)

Informed by such thinking, his vision in *Astonishing the Gods* and *Mental Fight* is predicated upon the paradigm of rhizomatous growth and 'possible worlds', inevitably drawing upon a dynamic interdisciplinary network of cosmic understanding. As Stalnaker (quoted in Doležel [1998] 2000: 14) observes, 'possible worlds have transcendental existence, they reside in the omniscient divine mind'.

In another key passage from *Astonishing the Gods*, the author imagines, supposes, believes in, wishes for and dreams about (an)other reality, a reality beyond – where building a nation derives from three qualities: 'amazing things' accrue from conscious knowledge and 'extraordinary things' from inner knowledge. But when a nation or an individual creates things 'sublime' or 'miraculous', 'they create always from the vast unknown places within them. They create always from beyond. They make the undiscovered places and infinities in them their friend. They live on the invisible fields of their hidden genius' ([1995] 1999: 51). The aesthetic was later to be reiterated and transposed in *The Mystery Feast*: 'Stories are the infinite seeds that we have brought with us through the millennia of walking the dust of the earth. They are our celestial pods. They are *our alchemical cauldrons*' (2015: 12; emphasis added). Okri then expatiates on the magical transformations stories make possible: 'If we listen to them right, if we read them deeply, they will guide us through the confusion of our lives, and the diffusion of our times' (ibid.).

Featuring an invisible querent[6] in the chthonic realm, *Astonishing the Gods* is thus a metaphysical conception: a liminal utopia in a timeless zone 'beyond'. This is a text in which (as the extracts show) the creative energy of fictional pretence has primacy over mimesis. Both Lubomir Doležel and Gilles Deleuze/Félix Guattari privilege this kind of fiction-making over verisimilitude. For Deleuze and Guattari, the text is 'a pragmatic assemblage or tool kit of becoming' (Leitch 2001: 1594), while text writing is, for Doležel, 'the art of making and understanding the world' ([1998] 2000: 42). Both these postmodern theories are integral to my reading of *Astonishing the Gods*, because both posit an alternative world, generating a philosophy of becoming;[7] both detach themselves from a static, hierarchical order; both are concerned with the effect of duration. Motifs common to both heterocosmica and rhizome theory are artistic invention, a convergence of aesthetics, ethics and politics, and the absence of either mimesis or diegesis. These too are tropes central to both *Astonishing the Gods* and Okri's 1999 poetry collection.

As if extending Deleuze and Guattari's critical theory of becoming and exteriority as opposed to being, derived from the paradigmatic shift from the knowledge metaphor of the tree of life with its static, binary logic, to that of the rhizome, 'conceived as an adventitious mode of thinking that grows between things and produces offshoots in unforeseen directions' (Leitch 2001: 1594–5), Okri's creative philosophy likewise attempts to free 'the forces that have been constrained' (ibid.: 1594). But its focus is more spiritual than that of Deleuze and Guattari (2001). Consider, for example, the following extract, with its echoes of the book of Revelations in the Christian Bible:

On that great day a marvellous sign came upon the people. As the rituals were coming to an end, there was an extraordinary flash in the sky. Then the heavens, as if in a mysterious annunciation, revealed their splendours and their luminous glories. And when the people freshly arisen from the ocean beds looked upwards, they saw a fabulous sight. They saw the shining doubles of themselves, clothed in the miraculous light of perfection.

To realize a little heaven on earth, that was the glory of their promise.

The beauty of the moment was overwhelming. Suddenly, looking about him, he saw poets dancing with angels, musicians levitating over happy pastoral scenes, scientists discovering unknown sacred places. (Okri 1999: 131–2)

In his non-fictional *A Way of Being Free*, Okri elucidates this transcendental philosophy when he asserts: 'The poet as quantum physicist, as healer, as angel and demon of the word cannot afford to disdain the world, cannot feel superior to it any more than the scientist can feel superior to thunder, to mountains, or to the constellations. There are no superiorities of function, only ascendancies' (1997: 6–7). In *Astonishing the Gods*, the depressingly 'dusty' malaise of rationalism masquerading as physical science[8] and the customary African writers' fare of narratives of loss and victimization are countered by the hopeful, if 'shadowy', epiphanies accessed through suffering and love. As Okri insists, quoting Saul Bellow in *A Way of Being Free*: 'It's too bad, but suffering is about the only reliable burster of the spirit's sleep' (ibid.: 12). Through the reaction of his central character to the purpose of his quest, Okri elaborates: 'The possibility of a whole people approaching, in their humanity, the condition of divinity, scared and astonished him [the initiate]. The thought that suffering could give people insights into the intersection of life and eternity filled him with amazement' (ibid.: 73). Capturing the mood and atmosphere of Judaic-Teutonic mythology (close to his native Urhobo/Igbo cosmogony, as the two texts under discussion suggest),[9] with its convergence of the rational and the spiritual, the extract serves to crystallize Okri's message.

In this cross-cultural, transdisciplinary African fable of 'possible worlds', Okri does indeed 'astonish the gods' by seeking to reveal the myths and magic of the air and by exploring alternatives for a possible (re)construction of an essential and mystical unity of body, brain-mind and soul: 'The purpose was to discover the hidden unifying laws of all things, to deepen the spirit, to make more profound the sensitivities of the individual to the universe, and to become more creative' (1999: 66). Likewise influenced by theories of chaos and complexity, Deleuze and Guattari claim to 'study subjectivity where it emerges, society where it mutates and the world where it is recreated' (Leitch 2001: 1596).[10] Okri's oeuvre thus manifests a parallel thrust. As Ato Quayson observes:

> From the short stories onwards, when [Okri] began experimenting with non-realist modes of representation, there has been an effort to problematise protocols of representation by routeing several aspects of narrative discourse through a prism of indigenous beliefs about spirits and their relationship to the real world. The area of setting, for instance, is progressively de-neutralised so that it takes on a hallucinatory potential and has a direct impact on the structure of narrative events. (1995: 148–9)

Astonishing the Gods features an imaginary celestial island landscape, seven light years away (the significance of the numerology has already been mentioned), 'discovered only once in a lifetime – if you're lucky' ([1995] 1999: 7), where 'light poured upwards from below, as if the island's relationship with the moon and sky had become inverted' (ibid.: 8). In his rejection of the popular conception of African identity as rooted in its historico-geographical milieu, Okri's vision seems to rest on rhizomatic theory:

> In literature, Deleuze and Guattari do not look for meaning ... In reading ... they look for the lines of flight by means of which ... writers detach themselves – and their texts – from an immobilizing order. In becoming, such writers 'deterritorialize' themselves from and within official culture before 'reterritorializing' themselves elsewhere. (Leitch 2001: 1596)

In *Astonishing the Gods*, Okri complements a personal history (the story people tell) with a 'possible world' geography (that 'ground' that the spirit inhabits), to sprout (an)other reality elsewhere.

Adopting the personae of a series of four guides, the author describes the creation of a fabulous 'new civilization' (Okri 1999: 35) and outlines the four stages of his invisible initiate's solitary search for 'the truest grace' (ibid.: 39), which, in turn, incorporates the eight stages of initiation into the 'Corpus Hermeticus' mentioned earlier. The first stage takes the form of a solitary negotiation of an elemental bridge. This correlates roughly with the first two stages of an initiation into the mysteries of the Perennial Tradition (viz. allowing the spirit to reunite with the Higher Consciousness and releasing the spirit from the spell under which it is held in bondage in the body, as noted earlier). In the second stage, in the realm of the marvellous, protected by the bridge made of mist, just referred to, and a huge golden gate, where silences have melodies, sounds have colours, tenderness has fragrance and smiles are heard – images redolent of Keatsian synaesthesia and negative capability – Okri's pilgrim finds himself in a 'city of sensitive stone': 'It was a city of stone and fire, but its true inspiration was water … It was a place that understood that the good things should be visible, but the best things should be hidden' (ibid.: 64). Despite the evocation of three of the four basic elements, coupled with that of spirit of place, the paradox and rhetoric here speak of an all-but-mystifying mysticism teleporting the reader beyond space and time. Yet, such trenchant and vivid prose is enlivened by the introduction of pithy maxims – a characteristic Okrian technique – that fix themselves in the memory, as in 'the good things should be visible, but the best should be hidden'.

Apprised, by his first guide (invisible like himself), that the first law of the city is 'that what you think is what becomes real' (1999: 46) and that 'anything you are not aware of you have to experience again' (ibid.) – evocative, respectively, of the power of thought in its echoes of Berkeleyan Philosophical Idealism ('esse est principi' (to be is to be perceived)) and of a Hermetic mystical rebirth, with its promise to be silent – the initiate learns to bring body and mind to quiescence and to free the Higher Consciousness from the ego consciousness (the next phases of initiation into the mystical Hermetic rites). The description of this otherworldly cityscape is a fine example of Okri's interest in the elemental as representative of timelessness. It is here that Okri's *Everyspirit* (as opposed to the more traditional Everyman (my coinage)) learns that the basic law of this civilization is 'a permanent sense of wonder at the stillness of time' (1999: 47).

Taking the form of a Socratic dialogue, the conversation that follows transforms the 'Alice in Wonderland'-type question of the nature of time[11] into a reuniting of the spirit with its lost universality:

'Is time still?'
'Does time move?'
'Yes.'
'Where to?'
'I don't know.'
'Have you seen it move?'
'Yes.'
'Where?'
'On a sundial.'
'That is the measurement of a motion. Time itself is invisible. It is not a river. While you are in time all time is still. As in a painting.'

'But day turns into night.'
'Yes.'
'So time moves.'
'No. The planet moves. Time is still.'

(Okri 1999: 47)

Here, the evocation of timelessness reflects the growing scientific awareness of the bygone Victorian Age but also serves to suggest a postmodernist flight from the horrors of history in this late-twentieth-century text. In the above extract, Deleuze and Guattari's philosophy of 'becoming' becomes – in the hands of Okri – a blueprint for 'becoming more real'. But, in a novel that turns on the enigmatic, on the paradoxical ('The season's fashion was for paradoxes, and the market place, even at night, was abuzz with fresh-minted paradoxes and ancient riddles …' (ibid.: 74)), the initiate, after resisting a number of temptations of the flesh, is ready to learn that 'the real things can't be seen' (ibid.: 107).

Failing to comprehend his first lesson in time and motion, Okri's querent is apprised of the second law of the city: 'When you need to know it you will find out' (1999: 48). This transcription of the orthodox 'Seek and ye shall find' leads to the seventh step in the mystical initiation, that of freeing the mind from misconceptions, here transcribed into a new way of seeing: 'When you stop inventing reality then you see things as they are' (ibid.: 49).[12] What strikes one most is the compositional unity of effect. Okri's interest in the interplay of light and time ('the sunlight of unwritten ages'), 'the invisible centuries of unwritten but differently coloured ages' (ibid.: 3) and of dream and memory rather than objects implies an interrelationship (however tenuous) among an African past, the universal human condition and Okri's imagined way into a transformation of an iterative present beyond. The unity between man, microcosm and macrocosm is evident not only in the declared purpose of the quest but also, for example, in the chiaroscuro effect created by 'parts of him … dissolving in the effulgent lights' (ibid.: 10) and in the coalescence of real time and dream time, of movement and stasis, while the single city mirrored in 'an infinity of perfect realms' (ibid.) is suggestive of the indeterminacy of quantum measurement.[13] This, in turn, is implied in Deleuze and Guattari's rhizomatic notion that the official 'molar' line of a social and political position is replaced by a 'molecular' line that begins to separate itself from a first molecule from which the second splits off. It is thus elucidated in Okri's Doležellian imaginary city, the magnificent empty buildings of which, suffused in radiant light, 'all reflected themselves in an oddly terrifying infinity' (ibid.: 8). And, owing to 'an eternal motionlessness about everything' (ibid.: 5), the pilgrim fancies that he has 'wandered into a disquieting dream' (ibid.), where '[t]he moonlight, glowing on the chessboard patterns of the town's magnificent square, filled his heart with a beautiful solitude that would haunt him for the rest of his life' (ibid.).[14] The chessboard symbolizes both pattern and essence, for it is here, before the 'Great Basilica of Truth', likewise iridescent with refracted light, that he sees a unicorn (symbol of wisdom)[15] and the 'forgotten sword of Justice' in the middle of 'a green lake' (ibid.: 11),[16] and learns of the infinite nature of things when he complains to his guide that he cannot understand anything that he has seen. He learns telepathically that '[t]hings are what they are. That is their power. They are all the things we think they are, all the things we sense they are, and more. They are themselves' (ibid.). The extract then presents the opposing logic in: 'If they meant something they would be less. What you see is your personal wealth and paradise. You're lucky if you can see wonderful things. Some people who have been here see only infernal things. What you see is what you are, or what you will become' (ibid.). From an ontological perspective, the extracts suggest that Okri's rhizomatous world is unitary in its diversity.

Ultimately, Okri's method is to interleave, juxtapose and unify the existential and the mythic, the illusionary and the labyrinthine, the theological and the philosophical. Thus, his initiate learns in his third stage of re-education to separate the higher subtle feelings from the gross sensory ones, personified by pain in the form of an injured bird, and by a beautiful, seductive temptress fleeing the higher realm of existence for sensory delights. Unlike realist or socialist realist African writers, Okri is concerned more with essence than with processes that fuse the temporal and the eternal.

The fourth stage of initiation (equivalent to the eighth and final stage of esoteric Rebirth, that of allowing the spirit to travel to higher realms) is anticipated as early as Book 2 of Okri's eight-part novel, when the guide of the aspirant pilgrim points to the significance of triumphing over 'all that is flux': 'There is a time for inventing reality, and there is a time for being still. At the gate of every new reality you *must be still*, or you won't be able to enter properly' (1999: 50; emphasis added).[17] Before departing, the guide prepares the initiate for this last stage in his journey, teaching him that sublime knowledge creates the potential for an earthly paradise (ibid.: 51), that the key to immortality is unseen suffering in silence (52–3), and that his role is to herald change (53).

Re-entering the magnificent city gates alone, he finds himself in a terrifyingly mutable domain, the elemental city of paradoxes and mythical creatures, where 'the open air seemed eternal' (1999: 80). Then, joined successively by an archetypal silent, boy-child guide (Book 3), a tall, lean youth and a misshapen dwarf (Book 4), and a goddess (Book 5), he encounters the prophet king (already mentioned) and the great earth mother, and learns that this civilization is dedicated to a simple goal: 'the perfection of spirit and the mastery of life' (1999: 67). The impulse is towards a Sufi yearning for and striving towards the 'God self'. In Okri's utopian culture, the merchandise is ideas (ibid.: 75); the currency of banks is thoughts of well-being, wealth and serenity (69); libraries are places to deposit intuition, dreams, memories and prophecies; hospitals are for the joyfully healthy (69); and universities are places 'for self-perfection, places for the highest education in life' (66), that is, for the acquisition of the knowledge of 'the art of self-healing' (70).

The remainder of the book is devoted to temptations reminiscent of those in Bunyan's *The Pilgrim's Progress* ([1678] 1960), and to a never-ending striving after the four major historical types of knowledge: experiential, holistic, analytic and experimental, with the discourse and symbolism shifting from ritual-mythical, through initiatic-religious, philosophical and scientific, to artistic. Okri's pilgrim's destiny is the great convocation, where three 'masters of illumination' (1999: 143) tell him of his true quest, that is, 'creative wisdom' (ibid.); henceforth, in an echo of the Hermetic sublime, he must dedicate himself to 'increase the light, and to spread illumination' (1999: 149).

The final message of the novel is that 'it is dreams that create history' (1999: 115) and '[o]nly those who truly love and who are truly strong can sustain their lives as a dream' (ibid.). And it is these spiritually enlightened, higher-order beings who can consecrate their master dream: 'to initiate on earth the first universal civilization where love and wisdom be as food and air' (1999: 131). This, then, is Okri's singular theoretical framework to counter misfortune and wrongdoing: a rhizomatic renewal – a non-canonical philosophy of temporality, reflecting a universalist, mystical cosmogony. In this new cosmic order, the initiand is able to meditate, in 'the silences for a millennium' (ibid.: 140), silences born of suffering:[18]

> The silences came from mountaintops covered with snow and the depths of unfathomed oceans … from angels and diamonds, from the heart of Time and the languid countrysides, from the hidden dimensions and the hidden heaven, from all the dead and all whose hearts quicken to the highest love, the silences came, and they passed through him, and they altered no spaces, and he noticed how real the room of meditations was for such dancing eternities. (Ibid.)

In Okri's *Astonishing the Gods*, as with his *Mental Fight* poems, the mythic dimensions of the hereafter, of infinity, are explored, familiarized and domesticated, while the small, ordinary objects, experiences and thoughts are raised to the level of the mythic, affording a glimpse of an ideal wholeness accruing from the invisible growth of the human mind and soul. This personal mystical yearning is also evident in 'The Poet Declares' from Okri's *An African Elegy*: 'Let the music irradiate my spirit / And I shall travel farther than allowed / to find the gifts of the new / light' (1992: 79).

7

Redreaming ways of seeing: Intuitive creativity in *The Landscapes Within*

Introduction: The role of intuitive creativity

That Ben Okri's *oeuvre* reveals a preoccupation with an interweaving of dream, creativity, ways of seeing and intuition is borne out by a seminal statement in 'Plato's dream', a subsection in *A Time for New Dreams*: 'All our creativity, our innovations, our discoveries come from being able first to see what is there, and not there; to hear what is said and not said. Above all to think clearly; to be nourished by silence. And beyond that – the art of intuition' (Okri 2011: 27). This resonates with Carl Jung's adage: 'Who looks outside, dreams / Who looks inside, awakens' (Jung 2018: n.p.).

The narrative of Okri's novel, *In Arcadia* (2002; see Gray 2009), is interspersed with 'Intuitions', described by Bel Mooney in *The Times* as 'meditations of poetic insight and sometimes incantatory beauty, building towards a conclusion of reluctantly tender optimism'. This is an example of what 'intuitive creativity' signifies. A pertinent for instance of 'intuitive creativity' can be found in *A Way of Being Free*: 'Stories are one of the highest and most invisible forms of human creativity,' says Okri (1997: 120 no. 59). To awaken 'the art of intuition' is thus to invoke poetic insight or mystical serendipities through heightened consciousness or ontopoiesis.

Prominent phenomenologists, such as Anna-Teresa Tymieniecka, hold that phenomenology or the ontopoiesis of life[1] and contemporary scientific inquiry can meet 'because the creative act of the human being offers royal access to the common enigmas of both' (2004: ii). 'All great stories are enigmas,' Okri avers in *A Way of Being Free* (1997: 126 no. 97). In *The Mystery Feast*, Okri asserts that civilizations are distinguished by their 'imaginative dimension' (2015: 15). Reflecting on evidence of imaginative productivity in ancient Greece and Egypt, he declares that it is the imagination that 'dreams that which knowledge makes real' (ibid.). He concludes that 'imagination is the proto-reality' (ibid.), as intimated in Jung's adage and my opening quotation from *A Time for New Dreams*. Similarly, the basic tenet of George Rowley's thesis in his discussion on the principles of Chinese art is the close kinship between artist and mystic. Reinforcing the affinity between artist and mystic, Rowley argues that while the mystic seeks 'life more abundant', the artist 'becomes a creator' (1947: 3). This resounds with Okri's belief in the primacy of the imaginary: the creative discovering act in storytelling and, in turn, defines the numinous notion of 'intuitive creativity'.

The intention here is to explore a tentative idea of the creative horizon of Okri's notion of redreaming ways of seeing. 'One of our much-neglected qualities is the creative ability to reshape our world. Our planet is under threat. We need a new one-planet thinking,' says Okri in *A Time for New Dreams* (2011: 145). The phrases 'redreaming ways of seeing' and 'intuitive creativity' are invoked to show that Okri's continual play of referentiality between and within his multi-generic texts foregrounds the composite or holistic nature of an Afro-Western historical-cultural context and heritage. As a Nigerian-born Londoner, Okri's entrapment through nature and nurture is in pre-existing patterns of thought, motif and form that tell of an inner conviction of mysticism and the eternal presence of the ancestors. As Rowley attests, these spiritual roots 'lie deeply buried in the early orientation of the different cultures' (1947: 3). 'They are,' he elucidates, 'the intangibles which embody the hopes and longings of a people; they are the incommensurables which determine the answers to the three basic issues of experience, Nature, Man, and God' (ibid.).

The symbiosis of the role of the dreaming imagination and intuitive creativity in art can be illustrated in the opening stanza to Okri's poem, 'The difficulty of seeing' in his anthology, *Wild*, that points to the enigma of experience: 'It feels odd to look long / At a corpse or a leaf: / It disturbs one's belief' (2012: 62). This tercet alludes to the mystical conjunction between life (leaf) and death (corpse), and the way in which seeing impacts upon believing. Then, moving from a general observation to the inner affect, the poet is specific, 'I found it hard to see / My mother's face; / The more I looked, / The more her face eluded me. / I see her perfectly / In dreams, or when I don't try' (ibid.). The closing couplet to this insight into the elusive nature of visual recall or eidetic memory is movingly evocative. It reads: 'Then long afterwards / I wonder why I suddenly cry' (ibid.). Here, a synaesthesia of the senses coalesces: a mirage becomes a fleeting illusion of reality, but only in dreams, while the elusion of perception evokes the heartfelt grief of bereavement as the poet attempts to re-imagine the beloved visage of his late mother. This poem at once echoes incidents in *The Landscapes Within* and reflects on the opening poem in *Wild* entitled 'My mother sleeps' (2012: 9–10). Both poems transpose Okri's aphorism, 'Love is the greatest creativity of them all, and the most blessed' (ibid.: 125 no. 90).

Given that the basis for such creation or recreation is the imagination, coupled with the elixir of love plus such faculties as the senses, intuition and belief, the resultant artistic product must, paradoxically, be both intuitively universal and culture specific. The artwork itself (be it performance, text, sculpture or painting) embodies and reveals the spirit of a people. As Rowley posits: '[T]hat spirit is so manifest that we seldom stop to ask why this pottery is Greek or that sculpture is Hindu, or why this figure must be Italian or that landscape English … Each culture seems to have had a special bent' (1947: 3). Yet, as intimated in the opening stanza of 'The difficulty of seeing', that spirit also transcends cultural borders.

Acclaimed South African sculptor and poet Ptika Ntuli notes that 'the concept of African art, has been, and continues to be much contested' (2010: 10). It is important, therefore, to expand upon how Ben Okri's intuitive creativity can be defined. His extensive travels, cross-cultural reading, incisive mind and artistic temperament inevitably impact on his ideological frame of reference. 'Anagnorisis' or discovery of the true nature of one's own situation, keen observation and the absorption of influences from other times and other spaces are natural correlatives. Not unnaturally, therefore, his world view/'Weltanschauung' is one of interconnectedness, interrelationships and interdependence, on the one hand, and of cosmic relationships, on the other. His role as creative artist is not unlike that of an inSanusi, such as Ntuli, or a high-ranking healer, a mystical thinker.

The introduction criss-crosses reference to several Okrian texts to illustrate my contention that for Okri – as for other African writers – the way of seeing is not primarily through religion, philosophy or science but, as indicated in the amalgam of Okrian quotations cited, through art as the product of a grounded imagination. 'When we see the unseen, hear the unspoken, that will be something amazing' (2014: 256), says the intrusive authorial voice in Okri's novel, *The Age of Magic*. The plain prose meaning of this periphrasis is 'redreaming ways of seeing'.

In *The Landscapes Within*, Okri (1981) imagines ways in which to ameliorate multifaceted losses brought about by the bleak societal dysfunction in Nigeria. As he avers in *A Way of Being Free*, '[w]hatever resilience has kept wounded people and devastated continents here, alive, can be transfigured to make them strong, confident, and serene. They have to question everything, in order to rebuild the future. They have to *redream* the world' (1997: 132; emphasis added).

Redreaming perception in *The Landscapes Within*

Set in war-torn Nigeria in the aftermath of the Biafran War, the story of Omovo in *The Landscapes Within* opens 'in medias res', with the recollection of a recurring nightmare, indicative of the subconscious mind grappling with the trauma of having witnessed the brutality of an economically induced civil war, and aligning the narrative with petro-fiction. Not only does the dream-inspired discourse predate both diegetic time and time of narration, but the narrative is also situated within a collective African unconscious. The novel is prefaced by two nightmarish dreams recorded in a real/ fictive notebook; dreams which, in turn, become embedded in the text as a dreamtime echo of the novel's first climatic point at the end of Part 1 of this four-part novel. The narrative incident as formulation of the dream is a night-time encounter by two lost youngsters, Omovo and his journalist buddy Keme, with the mutilated body of a young girl child in a park, bordering the beach. The incident and its dream replay dismantle essentialist notions of Nigeria; they leave an indelible 'stain' of 'guilt' (Okri 1981: 67) on the mind of 20-year-old Omovo. This is exacerbated by his fictive memory of having helplessly (eye)-witnessed, at the age of nine, the wanton brutality of government forces against the Igbos during the Nigerian Civil War of 1967–70.

These 'incidents' not only create a hybrid portrait of the atrocities of civil war – underlined by later reference to past atrocities: the slave trade and colonialism, as well as to the present tragedy of neocolonial economics – but they also suggest that the sharing of horrific sights can connect human beings in empathy with one another, as Sope Maithufi (2015: 86) notes in his critique of *Dangerous Love*. Through these exophoric dynamics, the reader is projected into the historic or profane, concomitant with the mythic or sacred within the fictional, as observed in my reading of 'Divinatory simulacra in Margaret Atwood' (Gray 2000: 854). What is important for the general reader is that dream and intuitive creativity supersede anthropological or ethnographical factors.

According to Jane Wilkinson, Okri articulates 'two kinds of realities' (1992: 80) in *The Landscapes Within*. There is the tale of life in the slums of Lagos and the sociopolitical situation in post-civil war Nigeria; and then there is the tale of the inner workings of the mind of the young artist, Omovo, and the creative process in which he is intuitively involved. This section focuses on the trajectory of the latter which is towards 'the moment' (1981: 272) when, in an epiphanic illumination or 'axis mundi' (cf. my critique of *Starbook*, 2013b: 128–45), 'the landscapes without synchronise with the landscapes within' (Okri 1981: 206). The synchronicity effectively illustrates intuitive creativity within a specifically African perception of proto-reality. Contrary to a reality that maintains 'clear ontological boundaries between what … is usually designated as observed and imagined experience, material and magical phenomena, and real and fictional worlds', for Okri, as Derek Wright observes, 'different and disparate worlds appear to coexist; there is an indeterminacy with regard to where literal reality ends and metaphor begins, a habitual elision of figurative and narrative space' (1997: 140).

This early novel can be read as an inquiry into ways of seeing informed by the process of intuitive creativity, as seen through the eyes of a prescient young black artist. Here, words seem to cast off their usual idiomatic sense; expressions fall painfully apart as the artist's vision shifts between what is seen and not seen. Consider the scene when, embarrassed but creatively aroused by the reaction of two men for having chastised some youngsters for taunting a goat and having experienced a lengthy 'dry season' (Okri 1981: 4), Omovo rushes home to his drawing. In a prime example of intuitive creativity, '[h]e worked and reworked the tentative lines, curves and shadings a hundred times … In the end he felt he had captured something more strange and real than the original sensation' (ibid.: 7). Of significance, here, is the conjoining of the sensual and the visual, as illustrated in Okri's poem about the difficulties of seeing, quoted in my Introduction. This novelistic incident concludes with the forcefulness of the creative process, devoid of logic – a recreation of the seen that plunges the experience and the telling thereof into the surreal:

> Omovo experienced a pure strain of joy.
> He spoke quietly to the drawings: *I have never seen you before. But it is wonderful that you are here.*
> 'Omovo-o! Wetin be that you draw?' asked one of the compound boys.
> 'Why you draw the tree so?'
> 'Who tell you say na tree, eh?'
> 'If no be tree den wetin e be?'
> 'Mushoom. It be "like big mushroom."'
>   'Na lie!'
>
> (Ibid.)

The implied distillation of sense experience and perception, the 'pure strain of joy' in the act of creation may have been fleeting – the reverie broken by mundane reality – but it evokes the mystical. The young artist is at once surprised and enchanted by his own drawing thus created and is moved to address the anthropomorphized artefact directly in hushed tones, one suspects, so as not to disrupt the mystical experience. Becoming conscious of the 'trifling argument' the work was causing, and looking at 'the many sweaty, intent, indifferent faces', 'a certain panic rose inside him'. 'Look,' he said aloud. 'Why don't you people just go away and leave me alone?' (1981: 7). Then, refusing to respond to a stranger's offer to buy the painting for resale to 'Europeans', Omovo signs his charcoal etching and entitles it 'Related Losses' (ibid.: 8). The appellation encapsulates the pivotal theme of loss in this novel, prefiguring the later filching of the etching as well as the theft of his final painting of a faceless dead girl from his dream, likewise entitled 'Related Losses'. This recalls the opening stanza to Okri's poem, 'The difficulty of seeing' (ibid.: 62), quoted in the Introduction, although the poem was written much later than his second novel.

In a different but pertinent context, John Berger considers what may be gained or lost by the intuitive creativity at play here: 'The painter's way of seeing is reconstituted by the marks he makes on the canvass or paper' ([1972] 2008: 3). Berger then shifts to reception aesthetics, saying: 'Although every image embodies a way of seeing, our perception or appreciation of an image depends on our own way of seeing ... the more imaginative the work, the more profoundly it allows us to share the artist's experience of the visible' (ibid.). Paradoxically, Omovo's fictional audience is either 'indifferent' or lacking in artistic perception – unable to distinguish between tree and mushroom, causing a sense of 'panic' in the young artist. Is the implication perhaps that civil war not only kills innocence but also stultifies creative sensibility in ordinary citizens caught in the fray, so that loss of life and loss of spirit are two sides of the same coin in internecine strife? As noted in my earlier reading of the novel as an unfinished symphony, the pivotal trope (or figure of thought) in Okri's novel is the interweaving of an ever-shifting pattern of loss and revelation, experience and (artistic) formulation, dream and reality (Gray 2013a: 21–31).

Okri perceives of all art as storytelling, insisting in *The Mystery Feast* that '[a] painting on a cave wall of a man pursuing a bison is a story. The frescoes of Giotto in Assize are distilled stories' (2015: 15). It can be argued, therefore, that Omovo's designation of his paintings signifies the untold story(ies) of deprivation, trauma and longing embedded in the psyche of the emergent young artist who produces the art works, as well as in those of his fellow audience. Elaborating on the alchemy of artistic product – be it painting or story – in *A Way of Being Free*, Okri muses: 'It is easy to forget how mysterious and mighty stories are. They do their work in silence, invisibly. They work with all the internal materials of the mind and self. They become part of you while changing you' (1997: 120 no. 58).This fragment concludes with a sombre caution to both reader and teller that doubles as a comment on the reactions of Omovo and his onlookers to his mysterious mushroom tree painting: 'Beware of the stories you read or tell: subtly, at night, beneath the waters of consciousness, they are altering your world' (ibid.). Suggestive of the enigmatic nature of story, Okri elucidates in *The*

Mystery Feast: 'when we tell stories the ages awaken, when we listen to stories our future takes clearer shape' (2015: 15).

Citing the opening incident of the artist's decision to shave his head, and soon thereafter standing in the rain savouring 'the flesh of his head tingl[ing]' (Okri 1981: 6), Alain Severac notes that the 'scene constitutes the luminary aesthetic statement' postulating 'a flayed sensitivity as a prerequisite of artistic creation' (1999: 76). In the context of Okri's claim in *A Way of Being Free* for the imagination as 'one of the highest gifts we have' (ibid.: 126), coupled with the meaning of the Benin name Omovo – a (male) child from above – the shaven head is a complex symbol: a local signifier of loss (Omovo had just lost his mother); but it is also a way of 'feeling the body from within' (Tolle 2005: 78) to use Eckhart Tolle's term, of self-awareness stimulating the imaginative faculty. The 'child from above', an 'Abiku' or spirit child, exists liminally 'somewhere in the interspace between the spirit world and the Living', says Okri (see Ross 1993: 337). He explains that the 'Abiku', the central figure in his famed *Famished Road* trilogy, lives 'simultaneously at different levels of consciousness and in different territories' (see Wilkinson 1992: 53). It can be argued that the sensation of rain beating on Omovo's bald head allows Okri's desire for 'a new one-planet thinking' or the joy of being to flow into everything. Rain on the shaven head facilitates insight, enabling the young artist to be more alert, to *see* more clearly. In effect, it opens what Albert Camus calls 'a whole proliferation of phenomena' (1983: 27) to intuition, to the heart.

An awakened consciousness (what Tymieniecka calls ontopoiesis) leads to what Okri repeatedly refers to as 'The Moment' (1981: 206, 272, 286). This is metonymic for enlightenment or 'satori', a flash of insight.[2] The shaven head thus evokes 'the transcendence of the egoic mind and the possibility of living in an entirely new state of consciousness', of '"learning all over again to *see*, to be attentive, to focus consciousness" … turning every idea and every image … into a privileged moment', to invoke Camus (1983: 26; emphasis added).

By contrast, Berger would perceive images – such as the shaven head or the mushroom tree – more objectively, as 'a direct testimony about the world which surrounded other people at other times' ([1972] 2008: 2–3). He imagines an unspoken dialogue with the visible world, 'an attempt to explain how, either metaphorically or literally *you* see things, and an attempt to discover how "*he* sees things"' (ibid.; emphases added). Roland Barthes is more linguistically inclined, asserting that 'there is no perception without immediate categorization' (1977: 28). In this context, both these images – the bald head and the mushroom-like tree – are devoid of denotation: they have their own 'inner metalanguage'. This is closer to both Rowley's and my earlier argument about African ways of seeing. Barthes explains that this language is that of perceptive connotation embedded in 'its very social existence' (ibid.: 29), likewise alluded to in the discussion on African epistemology. Barthes explains: '[T]he text constitutes a parasitic message designed to connote the image, to "quicken" it with one or more second-order signifieds' (ibid.: 25). However, contrary to my reading, the shaven head signifier would, in these terms, seemingly remain a culturally deferred sign, rather than a more complex conflation of signifier and signified. Pondering the purpose of the signifier, Barthes muses, 'its purpose is less the analysis of the sign than its dislocation' (ibid.: 166). As already intimated, in a Nigerian cultural context, shaving

Figure 1 Cropped cover of *The Landscapes Within* (1981).
Courtesy of Ben Okri.

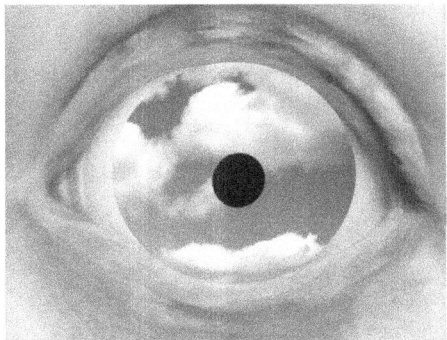

Figure 2 The false mirror redrawn by Renato Tomei.
Courtesy of Renato Tomei.

one's head is a customary sign of bereavement. In this poetic novel and in the context of redreaming ways of seeing, the experiential rests on the perceptual and sensory, giving rise to the cerebral and ultimately the spiritual. In this context, rain on the shaven head is symbolic: it signifies an awakening of a sleeping world, of making what is seen vivid to the mind, and perhaps even of seeing with the third eye (as suggested by the cover illustration to *The Landscapes Within* (Figure 1) as well as a painting of an all-seeing eye by Omovo's mentor (discussed later), themselves a transliteration of René Magritte's *Le faux miroir* (the false mirror; Figure 2)).

The similarity between Magritte's famed eye (redrawn for inclusion here) and Okri's cover illustration provides the lens through which I view this novel – as invoked by both Omovo's irritated response to the village youngster's well-meaning but naïve questions and the young artist's heightened consciousness.

Notions of coexistent proto-realities are explored and extended throughout this novel via the interplay between sharply etched reflection or daydreaming, on the one hand, and an imaginative recreation in Omovo's mind and, thence, onto his canvass, on the other. Privileging the complexities and contradictions inherent in the process of self-awareness – made manifest in the bald head trope – sharpens the perception that this narrative, as an art form, is incapable of miming or mirror-reflecting a single perspective; it is non-mimetic and suggests that dreams create the kind of speculation that is most fruitful for artistic creation as in Magritte's 'La clef des songes' (the key to dreams). And, as with the Magritte cameos of the interpretation of dreams, Okri tends to resist the idea that meaning is a given or can, indeed, be given in *The Landscapes Within*. This typifies the mode of the nineteenth-century French symbolists, whose art of expressing ideas (and emotions) eschews direct description and even similes and metaphors. Okri follows their strategy: one of recreating the ideas/sense impressions in the mind of the reader using unexplained symbols (see Chadwick [1971] 1973).

This then is the story of the operation of intuitive creativity in a developing artist in a Lagos ghetto. Intense visions suggest a desire to encapsulate the creative process within a chaotic slum milieu. Omovo consoles, suffers, dreams, etches, paints and has visions. Consider, for example, his eerie encounter with a huge painting of Christ on the cross which, coupled with witnessing a figure dying tortuously of stab wounds outside the church, culminates in momentary night blindness with his soul being 'plunged in a soft hued area of nothingness' (1981: 221), precipitating a new knowledge of self. To see what is going on in the art of great writers or painters, one must first of all be established in 'the art of oneself' (2011: 23 no. 2), says Okri in *A Time for New Dreams*. Seen through Omovo's eyes, the painting is described as an emanation of a 'danse macabre':

> The cross was done in thick black and was rather like a stake with jutting spiked ends, a thing of incarnate evil. Christ was depicted as a diminutive madman and the suffering rendered on his face, from which foam issued strangely, seemed so intense that it did not look like suffering or anguish. It looked like maniacal laughter. The blood that blurted from his impaled hands and feet was the colour of red wine streaked with violets and whites. It was a crude painting. (1981: 220)

Omovo's blinded perception of Christ's crucifixion is of the grotesque: blackness, evil, insanity, distortion and exaggeration, symbolic of the darkness of life. In a shocked *volte-face* (about face), the depiction transmutes into a metonym for the suffering of his own people as the artist is drawn to identify with the 'diminutive madman' portrayed in his own likeness, as a tiny black-skinned figure rather than the customary white bearded shepherd of Western iconography:

> The painting might not have been about Christ at all. Then he looked at the face again. A shock exploded inside him when he realised that the face had been done in black and his thoughts seized and his mind ran riot and he had no control over the pains and the pains threatened to drown his mind and he wanted to scream madly and he opened his mouth and the sounds and furies fought themselves. (Ibid.)

The identification is enhanced by the choice of 'seized', the onomatopoeia serving to endorse the resultant speechlessness; the 'intense pain' that caused both mind and voice to 'seize'.

Barthes's claim in *Image, Music, Text* that 'the image no longer *illustrates* the words; it is now the words which, structurally, are parasitic on the image' (1977: 28; original emphasis) seems to pertain to this excerpt. It is as if the mystery of art – and books dealing with artistic endeavour, such as *The Landscapes Within* – can only be confronted rather than interpreted. Art, like life, is here seen as a revelation of the horror of inhumanity posed against the mystery latent in all things. In sum, therefore, as Barthes states, 'it is not the image which comes to elucidate or "realize" the text, but the latter which comes to sublimate, patheticise or rationalise the image' (ibid.).

Okri's view is therefore closer to that of Barthes than to Berger's as is also captured in his statement in *A Time for New Dreams* that '[t]o see the true art or the truth in a work requires solid foundation in self' (2011: 24 no. 7). In his text, *African Art*, Ivan Bargna elucidates this Okrian aphorism, stating that 'African art can be considered a relational field in which the identity of everything that exists depends on the strength that is in everyone, which in turn depends on the position it occupies in the web which makes up the world and whose map is furnished by tradition' (2000:15).

So, whereas Berger points to the centrality of reception aesthetics, to the reciprocity between the artwork and viewer response, Okri's canvas is more deeply personal and cultural. Like Bargna's, it is also mystical, presupposing an engagement with the unknowable by the reader. 'Otherwise,' Okri explains in *A Time for New Dreams*, 'like light passing through a transparent object the work of art passes straight through an unformed mind and heart' (2011: 24 no. 9).

As argued in my earlier reading of this novel (Gray 2013: 21–31), the initial, graphically rendered dream is of an endless trek through a '*terribly* dark forest' (Okri 1981: 3 and 64; emphasis added), where trees became *coloured* mist then mutate into a vision of the faceless corpse. In the second interrelated nightmare, the artist's mind is confronted by a huge, '*terribly* blank canvass' (ibid.; emphasis added). A kaleidoscopic milieu of '*coloured* mountains', 'turbulent and calm seas' and 'primeval forests', reminiscent of Magritte's 'The key to dreams' mentioned earlier, form the backdrop for the appearance of the dead girl 'seen' walking towards, but never quite reaching, Omovo, before he again wakes in shock with a sense of unutterable loss and 'a mad urge to capture' (ibid.) the elusive vision on canvass, a feat that he manages only towards the end of the novel – tellingly a painting, like the dream and Okri's own haunting attempt to recapture his own dead mother's face, 'without a face', and also entitled *Related Losses* (ibid.: 281), as noted. The loss echoes that of Omovo's stolen painting of emaciated children playing around a mushroom-like truncated tree (ibid.: 5), already discussed.

These dreams dictate the narrative thrust and tone of Okri's second novel becoming, in turn, simulacra for the mercurial nature of the creative process (of both painting and writing) reminiscent of Ted Hughes's poem, 'The Thought Fox'.[3] Okri's imaginative rendering of the workings of the subconscious mind penetrates deeply into the narrative thread and structure of *The Landscape Within*, defining its section themes of Loss, Mazes, Masks and Fragments, and culminating in the focal character's brief insight into the meaning of 'The Moment' (1981: 286).[4] Ultimately, the novel offers an imaginary resolution to sociopolitical and personal conflicts: 'It's about surviving,' Omovo comes to understand, 'but it's more about becoming a life artist' (ibid.).

Okri repeatedly attributes the oneiric (dreamtime) records in *The Landscapes Within* to 'painter boy' (1981: 4, 35 and 197), Omovo. The dreams of the mutilated body 'haunt the novel and [are] returned to again and again', as noted by Adewole Maya-Pearce (1992: 92). This recurrence is integral to the author's way of seeing, coupled as it is with Omovo's obsessive recording and rereading of the dreams in a notebook, itself implying that self-reflection is an intuitive creative imperative. This is highlighted by an internal reflection on a drawing Omovo had done at the tender age of 7 of 'a series of squiggly lines that went round and round and formed different shapes', which his teacher and his father had eulogized as capturing 'life' (ibid.: 95 and 96), but which he was never again able to emulate. The intrusive authorial voice explains why: 'The boy somehow understood that he had done it once but could not do it again till he really knew how' (ibid.: 96). The reminiscence is typically Okrian, typically oblique. Is the implication, to borrow loosely from Anna-Teresa Tymieniecka, that, in the impoverished theatre of slum life, 'all the forces and dynamisms of human existence stew'? (2004: 26) And, owing to the freely inventive nature of a very young boy's creativity and his struggle to capture something of the essence of existence, the artistic enactment loses its foothold, becoming detached from any foothold. An additional implication is that art is not and cannot be complete; the artist continuously mediates life's predicaments, especially when these recur throughout history. I. A. Richards's insight into lines, circles, triangles, such as those in the child's painting, endorses this interpretation: 'The lines of geometry belong to the world of Being; those the geometer may draw to the world of Becoming. He uses them to help him to *think* about Forms – in the world of Being. Forms themselves are not able to be seen or drawn, but they can be thought of' ([1966] 1972: 7).

So, far from developing into a 'Bildungsroman', the novel remains – and this, paradoxically, is its brilliance – an unfinished 'Kunstlerroman' (art novel), climaxing in the young geometer/artist's recognition of the elusive evanescence of insight/knowingness: 'I'm still learning' (1981: 286), Omovo insightfully explains to Keme before reading him his elder brother, Okur's poem, which captures the same ephemeral nature of seeing: 'Searching for bright pebbles / and strange corals' (ibid.) on the seashore as a small child, Omovo's brother writes that the poetic persona sometimes *saw* them 'hidden and clear', but found 'other things too / like half-defaced sketches on the sand / pointing a way through the tormented seas' (ibid.). Here, the 'half-defaced sketches' encapsulate not only the mystery of how an empty sea shell can bring forth a musical echo of the sea: a melding of the concrete and the abstract, but also the illusory fleetingness of artistic insight: 'The world of Becoming is indescribable – except through Forms (Ideas) of the world of Being' (1996: 7), says Richards in his edition of *Plato's Republic*.

Earlier in the novel, Omovo shares a comparable moment of illumination/intuition with the young Ayo, son of the chief in the village near to the city of Lagos where Omovo has sought respite after the triple losses of an evanescent vision of his beloved dead mother (revisited in 'The difficulty of seeing'); losing his job; then the loss of his lover, Ifeyinwa, who has been shot, a casualty of internecine strife, in the forest near her home while escaping from her abusive elderly husband. 'I had an unconscious glimpse into profound and magical, solid and undefinable beauty; its strange and soundless music; its vanishing and unearthly lights' (1981: 270), he tells Ayo. Attempting to recapture the 'quintessential' and 'beatific' vision, Omovo laments that he felt 'desperate and empty ... seeking for so much as another glimpse through the tiniest crack of that door' (ibid.). The triple losses shift the vision into a metaphysical dimension evocative of Coleridge's *Aids to Reflection* that reads: 'Nothing is wanted but the eye, which is the light of this house, the light which is the eye of the soul' (1840: 70). (Here, the word 'wanted' is, of course, used in its archaic sense of 'lacking'.) The eye, Coleridge continues, is: 'This *seeing* light, this *enlightening* eye, is Reflection. It is more': 'it is what a *Christian* ought to mean by it and to know, too, whence it came ... of what light even this light is but a reflection. This too, is THOUGHT, and all thought is but unthinking that does not flow out of this, or tend towards it' (ibid.; original emphases).

Inner reality: 'The landscapes within'

The catalytic dreams/nightmares, and their incorporation into the narrative, are thus methodological, defining not only ways of seeing in this novel but also intuitive creativity. In *The Landscapes Within*, Omovo's paintings parallel his dreams as 'a means to explore the deeper, more unconscious meanings and miasma of his life and the landscapes about him' (1981: 85).

His painting and, by extension, his dreams are 'a part of his response to life: a personal prism' (1981: 85).[5] The landscapes within thus become axiomatic to both the narrative point of view and the novel's symbolism, effectively supplanting Omovo as lead character and making Omovo's creative imagination, his heightened consciousness, the eponymous hero of this early novel. The signifier and the signified conflate, becoming an awareness, a mode of perception: a presence rather than an agent. The spirit child's brief 'moments' of insight evoke the Zen moment of no-mind and total presence, incomprehensible to the intellect. Both Okri's title and the narrative itself tacitly refer to the 'landscapes of the mind' (ibid.: 18), suggestive of both transcendence and individuation. Anthony Stevens sheds light on the meaning of the term 'individuation' from a Jungian perspective: it 'designates that process of personality development which leads to the fullest possible actualization of the Self, (the central nucleus of the personality which contains all the archetypal potential with which an individual is innately endowed)' (1998: 235).

After completing his second painting (of a scum pool) and before it is confiscated by the authorities as unpatriotic (as 'caricaturing the nation's progress' (1981: 139)), Omovo intuits 'that the future was contained somewhere in his mind' (ibid.). Mystified by the furore that the picture engenders, Omovo states: 'I simply painted a scumscape as I *saw* it' (ibid.: 139–40; emphasis added). The recurrent scum motif is thus externalised in the painting that he calls *Drift*. As Magritte famously, or infamously, retorted when pressed for the meaning of an artwork: 'visible things always hide other visible things. But a visible *image* hides nothing' (Sylvester 1992: 318). This aligns itself with petro-fiction and Barthes's insistence that every image is a complex text.

Omovo's mentor, Dr Okocha, had painted a single eye on his work shed door: 'a brooding green eye, with a black pupil and a gathering red teardrop': which 'stared all-seeingly at the teeming streets and back into its own darkness' (1981: 35). As stated, this painting features on the cover of *The Landscapes Within*, and it seems to be an analogue for a public prism, reminiscent of Magritte's 'Le faux miroir'. The eye is a simulacrum for the mind's eye, evocative of the quest for wholeness. In *Plato's Republic*, Socrates provides a useful explanation of the conflation of the extrinsic and the intrinsic:

> [T]he natural power to learn lives in the soul and is like an *eye* which might not be turned from the dark without a turning around of the whole body. The instrument of knowledge has to be turned round, and with it the whole soul, from the things of becoming to the things of being, till the soul is able, by degrees, to support the light of true being and can look at the brightest. (Socrates 518, p. 126, below in Richards [1966] 1972: 5; emphasis added)

In implied comment on its assumed inter-art variant, Magritte's 1935 'Le faux miroir', suggestive of imperfect perception or mystical perception, Dr Okocha's painted eye invokes the neo-Platonic/Coleridgean concept of the '*enlightening* eye', just mentioned and is reminiscent of Okri's notion of the creative process as the inward visionary quest of the dreaming 'soul' opening 'towards infinity' (Wilkinson 1992: 83), cited earlier.

This ontopoietic text concerns itself with 'the imaginative realm, as opposed to the landscapes without, i.e. the physical world' (2004: 96) as attested by Darla Tunca. Even the story within the story, an illicit love affair borne of innocence, is imbued with heightened consciousness. The brief union with Mr Takpo's young wife, Ifeyinwa, with whom Omovo shares a love of reading and art, is one of complementary spirits and yearnings ('caritas') as opposed to carnality. 'He became for her something of a spiritual husband, one that she only confronted fully in her dreams and fantasies' (1981: 103). Ife, also a dreamer, voices her grievance about her arranged marriage to an old and brutal man by saying to Omovo: 'You have your art. I don't have anything' (ibid.: 25), thus forging a link between the two narrative threads and the third-person authorial voice, as I pointed out in my initial reading of this text (Gray 2013). Nonetheless, it is as if, in her suffering, Ife stumbles upon the redemptive nature of artistic creation, enabling a more transcendent way of being even amid abuse, poverty and deprivation.

More euphemistically but equally ephemerally, Okri writes of another pair of his lovers, Lao and Mistletoe in *The Age of Magic*:

> If they knew how, they could have walked through the mirror of beauty into a shining world. In that moment, between strides, they could have seen that nothing was meant to be, but only what they made it. They could have rewritten their lives on the margins of the book of life. (2014: 228)

'The novelist,' asserts Milan Kundera pertinently in *The Art of the Novel*, 'makes no issue of his ideas' ([1986] 1988: 144). 'He is an explorer feeling his way in an effort to reveal some unknown aspect of existence. He is fascinated not by his voice but by the form he is seeking, and only those forms that meet the demands of his dream become part of his work' (ibid.). 'The writer,' Kundera stresses, 'inscribes himself on the spiritual map of his time, of his country, on the map of the history of ideas' (ibid.). As already intimated, the title of Okri's novel is a poetic compression of an Afro-Western

'Weltanschauung'. As Simon Schama asserts, 'landscapes [for the African] are culture before they are [N]ature'; they are 'constructs of the imagination projected onto wood and water and rock' (1995: 61) and, by extension, paper.

For a writer such as Okri, existence in the modern world can best be understood through his literary representations of imaginary landscapes. The episode in which Omovo caricatures one of his work colleagues as the realization of his own imminent dismissal, following the machination of this colleague, dawns upon him underlines my point. 'Drawing made him reminisce; it could be so lonely. In his mind rose the fleeting, blurred images of some of the things he had drawn and painted passionately in the past' (1981: 199); a reminiscence that leads to a stream of consciousness recollection of the classic film, *The Lost Horizon*, and its elusive catchy theme tune: a synthesis of the visual and the auditory.

Okri's early oeuvre is redolent of African influences yet, paradoxically perhaps, speaks to Western sensibilities in a variety of intriguing conversations. As argued in my earlier essay on *The Landscapes Within* as an unfinished symphony, the novel epitomizes the polyphonic mode,[6] blending as it does triads such as dream/narrative/poetry and instinct/intuition/vision. An analysis of any excerpt reveals comparable counterpointing. Consider, for example, the artistic braiding when Omovo tries to explain what he has learnt about the idea of the Moment to his journalist friend. As intimated, first, there is repartee as Keme presses Omovo to divulge what he had said about the Moment; then, Omovo has a vision and a revelation which coalesce in 'I thought I sensed a brilliant shadow of a god. I think I saw, instead, one of those rare faces horribly mirrored in us … But I'm learning something also though' (1981: 286) leading to the bit about surviving and becoming a life artist, already quoted. All facets are bound by a common fugue-like theme: ways of seeing.

In *The Age of Magic*, Okri seems to corroborate this interpretation by having his lead character, Lao, discuss these abstractions and the attendant loss with his artist companion. The conversation goes as follows as Mistletoe continues to muse that '[t]here's much more to life than what we see' (2014: 256). Lao retorts:

> 'Believing only what we see enshrines only what can be seen.'
> 'And so we don't question what we don't see.'
> 'But often we are brought down by the unseen.'
> 'I know: Anxiety, neurosis, stress, cancer.'
> 'By the time we see what they are doing to us it's too late.'
> 'We treat the symptoms, and die.'
> 'But the causes are unseen.'
> 'And because they are unseen we don't believe they exist.'
> 'There's something primitive about the phrase "Seeing is believing", don't you think?' said Mistletoe.

Then pointing ambiguously to the paradox of insight, we hear:

> 'Truth seems upside down'
> 'And inside out.' (2014: 256–7)

The prevailing question in *The Landscapes Within* is couched in a novelistic essay on loss. The essay on loss incorporates a litany of losses: including loss of homeland; getting lost; loss of lives; wives; mothers and lovers; fathers and brothers; paintings; identity (the mutilated girl and Ife become faceless non-entities), fortunes; and loss of face; culminating in the piece of coral without its heart, which Omovo throws back into the sea at the close of the novel. The usage is, however, as much playfully connotative as it is denotative. The word 'loss' is woven into a complex tapestry of symbols and signs.[7] This extracts its significance from its rational context and places it in a context accessible only through the interpretative imagination. Submerged by the indefinable, the metaphor of loss conceals more than it transmits, thus counterpointing the exploration of the other key abstract concepts: intuitive creativity, corruption, dream, integrity, perception and responsibility.[8]

Ultimately, this novel deals with ways of seeing, with subjects that can be thought about but cannot be known; with the fluidity of 'the landscapes within'. What this suggests is intuitive creativity, where 'Creativity is,' as Okri states in *A Way of Being Free*, 'a secular infinity' (1997: 125). The conceptual artist here, perhaps inadvertently, reveals both the *inside* of life, and the *outside*. He is a Jungian dreamer who awakens. To quote Rowley, 'This creation is the product of the imaginative "wedding of spirit and matter"' (1947: 3).[9]

Conclusion

The argument has been that the novel is predicated on the autonomy of art and the autonomy of the real. Kundera elucidates on the significance of the oneiric narrative, saying: 'Imagination, freed from the control of reason and from concern for verisimilitude, ventures into landscapes inaccessible to rational thought' ([1986] 1988: 78). *The Landscapes Within* is a compelling meditation on existence – ways of seeing and intuitive creativity, through the medium of imaginary internal and external landscapes, seamlessly connecting consciousness and unconsciousness. As Wright observes in a coincidental summing up of my argument about Okri's writing: 'There is ... an inward movement away from protest and polemic and towards interior psychic healing; there is also a visionary introjection of the world into the artistic consciousness that places a tremendous emphasis on the redemptive energies of dream, myth and the imagination' (1997: 159). In the context of semiotics and mythology, Barthes pertinently states: 'the new semiology – or the new mythology – can no longer, will no longer be able to, separate so easily the signifier from the signified, the ideological from the phraseological' (ibid.: 166). 'It is not,' he explains, 'that the distinction is false or without its use but rather that it too has become in some sort mythical' (ibid.). This seems to suggest that ways of seeing have undergone an intuitive transformation. Wright points to the operation of intuitive creativity in a comparable mystical context: 'For Okri, redemptive energy is finally not a political but a purely visionary, imaginative quality' (1997: 60). In *A Time for New Dreams*, Okri writes of another young artist, this time a Spaniard, and his first encounter with

African masks, a life-changing looking 'inside' moment of the kind that Jung believes 'awakens' and that serves to illustrate Okri's articulation of the visionary redemptive energy of the imaginary: 'He had been touched into life by the ancient myth of the superman and by the brilliant angel of the beautiful darkness. A darkness that was, in truth, a new light' (2011: 66).

8

Promoting the poetic cause in 'stokus' from *Tales of Freedom*

This reading illustrates the theme of the poetic in Ben Okri's 'stokus' from *Tales of Freedom* (2009). It does this principally through an exploration of this new literary mode and its use of serendipity. As a sudden insight, serendipity becomes a poetic device equivalent to illumination or an epiphanic moment. The introduction is an attempt to show the interrelationship between poetry and thought, on the one hand, and among poetic experience, creative consciousness and serendipity, on the other. A mere two years after publishing his *Tales of Freedom* (ibid.), arguably his most poetic prose, Okri was to write in *A Time for New Dreams*: 'Heaven knows we need poetry now more than ever. We need the awkward truth of poetry. We need its indirect insistence on the magic of listening' (2011: 3). And so, I invite you to listen imaginatively to poetry's most cryptic mode: a *haiku* entitled 'Freedom': 'The hawk wheels and glides; / It does not need to stumble / Over the mundane' (Heese 1997: 11). This African *haiku* illustrates the power of poetry to appeal to the sensory ('the magic of listening' encapsulated in the onomatopoeic 'wheels', 'glides' and 'stumbles') and the cerebral ('the awkward truth of poetry' alluded to in the implied contrast between the preoccupations of humans and the freedom of Nature). African philosophical traditions accept that the experience of wonder, reflected here, is the originating source of philosophy. For a philosophical poet or poetic writer such as Okri, freedom is embedded in the poetic; it inheres in awakening from 'the sleep of reason' (Okri 2011: 70), from the twenty-first century's 'vile dreams … goaded awake by guns' (ibid.) and embracing 'the art of being' (2011: 73), reflected in Heese's hawk and encapsulated, for example, in the serendipities evoked in Okri's 'stokus', which will be discussed more fully later in this chapter. But first, it is pertinent to articulate the central thesis of the coalescence of poetry and thought and the discussion's braided subsidiary themes of poetic experience, creative consciousness and serendipity that inform my reading of Okri's 'stokus'.

Towards an understanding of Okri's poetic aesthetics and the coalescence of poetry and thought

Okri's innovation in the mode of the short story, a distinctive part of his body of work, can be seen notably in *Tales of Freedom* (2009) in his amalgam of the short story and *haiku*, giving rise to the 'stoku', that is, to a marriage between the exemplary compression that characterizes his short story form and an extraordinary flash of landscape and serendipity that epitomize the *haiku*. This is short story verging on poetry – brief yet revelatory in capturing the *spirit of place*. Further, his work manifests a quite extraordinary interrelationship between the African worldview and consciousness, and a postmodernist Western 'Weltanschauung'.

As I noted in an earlier publication that explored ontopoiesis or the self-induced development of consciousness (Tymieniecka 2004: 5) in Okri's poetic oeuvre (Gray 2014: 50), this conceptual artist avers that poetry is intrinsic to humankind. Okri asserts that '[w]e are, at birth, born into a condition of poetry and breathing' (2011: 3). Furthermore, he insists that '[b]irth is a poetic condition … it is spirit becoming flesh' (ibid.). Then, pointing to the mythic conjunctions inherent in such a non-dualistic cosmogony and to the indissoluble cycle of life and death (Gray 2014: 50), he avows: 'Death is also a poetic condition: it is flesh becoming spirit again. It is the miracle of the circle completed, the unheard melody of a life returning to unmeasured silence' (Okri 2011: 3). As also noted in my earlier chapter in *Analecta Husserliana* 116 (2014: 50), such phenomenological arguments recall the holistic philosophies of ancient times that are still prevalent in African philosophical thought as testified by fellow Nigerian and Nobel laureate, Wole Soyinka, who states: 'In Asian and European antiquity … man did, like the African, exist within a cosmic totality, did possess a consciousness in which his own earth being, his gravity-bound apprehension of self, was inseparable from the entire cosmic phenomenon' ([1976] 1995: 53).

Taken together, these quotations by two of Nigeria's philosophical writers serve to underline the symbiosis between poetry and thought. Prefiguring Okri's conception of freedom – embedded in the totality of the poetic experience or serendipity – as embracing 'the art of being' (2011: 73), having awoken from 'the sleep of reason' (70), quoted earlier, Adonis counters any paradoxical separation of poetry from thought through an etymological argument: 'If we go back to the root of the Arabic word for poetry ("shiʿr"), that is to the verb "shaʿara", we see that it means "to know", "to understand" and "to perceive"' (1992: 57).

As if foreshadowing my reminder that when one talks of imaginative wit, one should remember that the word 'wit' is derived from the Anglo-Saxon 'witan' (to know), he adds:

> On this basis, all knowledge is poetry. We call the poet 'shāʿir' (literally, 'one who knows, understands, perceives') in Arabic because he perceives and understands ('yashʿuru') that which others do not perceive and understand, that is he knows ('yaʿlamu') what others do not know. (1992: 57)

So, belying a dualistic epistemological system derived from Western religions (jurisprudence and theology), on the one hand, and the spoken or written word (language, i.e., grammar and rhetoric), on the other, Adonis's holistic epistemology, based as it is on philosophical argumentation, conceives of poetry as 'a continuation of these two systems, adding to their arguments its own particular arguments, drawn from Greek thought' (ibid.). Whether the lineage is Anglo-Saxon, Islamic, Greek,

Japanese, African or even peculiarly Okrian, this conception of poetry is succinctly captured in Heese's 'Freedom' *haiku*, quoted at the outset. This resonates too with Okri's conception of poetry as 'closer to us than politics, ... as intrinsic to us as walking or eating' (2011: 3). Alluding to ontopoiesis/a higher state of consciousness, he asserts that it is 'the voice that speaks to the highest in us', 'to the Gordian knots of our private and natural condition ... to all the unsuspected dimensions that make us both humans and beings touched by the whisperings of the stars' (ibid.). It can be argued therefore that for Okri there is no division between poetic experience (life) and creative consciousness or the self-induced activity of consciousness that Anna-Teresa Tymieniecka (2004: 5) calls ontopoiesis. Okri elucidates: 'All our creativity, our innovations, our discovery come from being able first to see what is there and not there; to hear what is said and not said ... the art of intuition' (2011: 27).

Illustrative of intuitive creativity are Okri's serendipitous 'stokus', stories that incline 'towards a flash or a moment, insight, vision or paradox' (2009: 108), akin to the Japanese *haiku*. The defining characteristic of the *haiku* is the 'wordless line', the white space Okri alludes to in seeing and hearing beyond the norm, that is, being alert to the invisible and the inaudible. His concept of serendipity is arguably a correlative of the white space of a 'sumi-e' or what is unsaid in a *haiku* yet conveys as much as, if not more, than what is set down on paper (cf. Lowenstein 2006: 134).

Whatever the medium, Okri's writing, in general, and his innovative 'stokus', in particular, are in turn characterized by Soyinka's notion of self-apprehension, his 'gravity-bound apprehension of self' as 'inseparable from the entire cosmic phenomenon' ([1976] 1995: 3). The 'higher state of consciousness or illumination' that is the 'basis of life's transitions' is 'wrought largely through spirit awakenings via a retrieval of traditional geo-cosmic horizons, that is, via a crucial link between the soul and the cosmos' (Gray 2014: 56). 'We ought to conjoin faith in evidence with the need for self-discovery' (2011: 28), says Okri in *A Time for New Dreams*, highlighting the indivisibility of poetry, thought and intuition in his higher-order thinking (HOT) aesthetics. His is an aesthetic that permeates the various modes of literary creativity, as indicated in his almost Messianic belief, expressed in *Birds of Heaven*, that '[t]he greatest religions convert the world through stories' (1996: 20 no. 12). Poet and storyteller, Ben Okri uses literature to highlight significant but rare moments of illumination. Put differently and in relation to his 'stokus', his deployment and conception of serendipity as a poetic device are indissolubly linked to interiority, to inner vision.

Why then, one asks rhetorically, is there such a dearth of scholarly criticism on this section of *Tales of Freedom*, a publication that has two components: a long dramatic short story entitled 'The Comic Destiny' and thirteen 'stokus'. Whereas the former has attracted a great deal of scholarship, possibly because of its overt intertextual allusions to Samuel Beckett, the latter appears to have been neglected despite their obvious charm.

Reception of Okri's 'stokus'

As with so much of his writing, the 'stokus' in *Tales of Freedom* (2009) have met with a mixed reception and a paucity of serious scholarly attention. What little there is consists of immediate post-publication, media reviews. An anonymous interviewer for *The Scotsman* (2009), for instance, enshrines the authorial intention by describing Okri's fusion of short story and *haiku* as 'pushing the groundedness of prose closer to the magical shimmer of poetry, just to see if there's another way of touching the mysterious flash of human existence'.[1] By contrast, Lucy Daniel writes somewhat condescendingly in *The Telegraph* (30 April 2009) that '[al]lthough they have some quirky charm, these prose pieces read more like half-formed stories that are far from transcendent', and, reading the 'stokus' via a literalist ontology, she adds that '[i]t's also hard to see what relation they bear to the *haiku* form'. Dismissing Okri's chosen nomenclature and further underlining her tendency to essentialize, Daniel claims that the mode is 'usually called prose-poetry'. I would argue that Okri's 'stoku' modifies and enhances the short story mode – prose not poetry – through allusive *haiku*-inspired compression rather than manifesting as prosaic free verse poetry. Likewise committed to praxis, David Astle retorts reductively: 'I felt happier treating each stoku as a mix of story and Sudoku, staring at each opaque parable in hope of a solution' (*The Book Show*, 18 May 2009). Conscious of Okri's post-structuralist/postmodernist tendency and seemingly more well versed in the Okri oeuvre than Daniel or Astle, Nisha Obano reminds us that '[t]he enigma of arrival is something Okri omits from his creative work'.[2] Jay Parini's summation, by contrast, comes closer to a Romantic viewpoint; he claims that '[t]hese are vague sketches – ill-formed, framed in generalised symbolic language, with only occasional moments of genuine poetry and insight'(2009: 1).

However, as intimated in the discussion of Okri's poetic aesthetics, his writing is fundamentally meditational, as is also evidenced, for instance, in his introduction to the new edition of *Astonishing the Gods* where, recalling an incident that became the catalytic question for this novel, he states: 'The question passed into the inspiration, and a meditation persisted, a meditation on invisibility ... In a world blinded by the visible might not its opposite be fruitful as a contemplation of the human condition?' ([1995] 2014: vii–viii).

The 'stokus'

The reading is premised on the argument that any appreciation of what Okri calls 'stokus' should be predicated not only on the wider Okrian oeuvre and his poetic aesthetics but also – and more importantly – on an understanding of the basic conventions of both the short story and the *haiku*. For, as he states, this then new elliptical form of compressed poetic prose is 'an amalgam of short story and haiku [*sic*]' (2009: 108). The brevity and visual beauty of fellow African writer and critic Marié Heese's traditional *haiku*, quoted at the outset, serves to illustrate the mode. Just as the seventeen-syllable poetic form expresses delight in Nature, coupled with a deeply felt sensibility accruing from contemplation on the nature of being, so too do Okri's 'stokus' implicitly pose philosophical conundrums, such as: What is reality? What is the meaning of freedom? The underlying teasing of the intellect serves to highlight the unification of the poetic and philosophical. His motifs cryptically capture transnational and transcultural ideas, places, customs, festivals and transient pleasures within the *haiku* paradigm while adhering to the morphological pillars of the short story: conflict, character, theme and point of view.

Okri captures the drama of nature – whether natural or human – in his description of the mode of the 'stoku', where images have an existential impact on perception 'like a figure materialising from a cloud, or a being emerging from a vaporous block of marble' (2009: 108). The structural analogy is pertinent, capturing as it does the mysterious power of the imagination. Creativity does not invent but discovers, as Okri implies in '[the "stoku"] is story as it inclines towards a flash of a moment, insight, vision or paradox' (already quoted), adding that '[i]ts origin is mysterious, its purpose revelation, its form compact' (ibid.).

The final entry of Okri's thirteen stokus in *Tales of Freedom* offers an example of the refined quality of his *haiku*-inspired sensibility. Reminiscent of *Piers Plowman* or *The Pilgrim's Progress*, 'The Message' – a quest myth – can be read as a synoptic allegory for a principled life. Having described a lifelong quest, a solitary journey, the purpose of which is to bear 'a message that only you can carry' (2009: 193), the narrator concludes by describing 'the pastel sky ... touched with blue' in the 'dawn sunlight' (ibid.: 197), a poetic allusion to the regeneration, 'the peerless freedom' (ibid.) that accrues from accepting one's lot in life, from avoiding temptation, from living one's true purpose *in* life. Here, the sky and sun are not merely token metaphors for *haiku* idiom and poetics; the evocation of Nature or 'zóka' is, at once, emblematic of *haiku* aesthetics and of Okri's poetic sensibility.³ Writing from a third-person omniscient point of view and employing the dis-unifying strategies of ellipsis and ambiguity, the author redreams the outcome for his symbolic Everyman: 'the true gift of it was in your spirit, your inner liberation ... The sense of being in a new world, a luminous world ... the sense of living an enchanted life in the kingdom' (2009: 196). Lucy Daniel perceptively sees this 'stoku' as a 'hopeful parable' but suggests somewhat fancifully that 'the reader is addressed ... as a weary traveller in a mysterious fairy tale kingdom, whose journey has been the book itself' (2009: n.p.)! In African cosmogony, there is no division between the real world and the chthonic realm as indicated in the Soyinka excerpts quoted earlier. And, as already argued, for Okri, there can be no division between poetry and thought. So, I would venture to argue that 'the kingdom' is an allusion to the non-dualistic cosmic realm in which we live following illumination or 'inner liberation'; in other words, being in this world when the mysterious process of experiencing inner vision (serendipity) has opened for us the kind of freedom that Okri writes about and Heese illustrates in her 'Freedom' *haiku*.

Although the overriding theme of each 'stoku' is freedom, they are almost impossible to codify outside Okrian aesthetics, caught as their serendipities are 'in the air, reverse lightning' (2009: 108). Each 'wheels and glides', like Heese's bird of prey, without 'stumbling on the mundane' (1997: 11). Okri's poetic prose 'stokus' are ignited by a valorization of the quotidian and the complexities that characterize the constructions of non-institutionalized and mobile subjectivities. To borrow from C. S. Lewis, albeit in a different context ([1961] 1995: 89), Okri's writings are 'exquisitely detailed compulsions on a mind willing and able to be so compelled'. In his *An Experiment in Criticism* ([1961] 1995: 88), Lewis draws a contrast between 'using' a work of art and 'receiving' it. In terms of the preferred more open reception aesthetic, he goes on to state: 'When we "receive" it we exert our senses and imagination and various other powers according to a pattern invented by the artist' (ibid.). Underlining such reception aesthetics, Okri asserts that '[l]iterature must persuade first of all through the imagination' (2009). To titillate the imagination, at the heart of the 'stokus', the theme of freedom is teased out through such esoteric subthemes as rejuvenation and validation ('The Message'); overcoming prejudice and social stratification ('The Mysterious Anxiety of Them and Us' and 'The Racial Colourist'); innocence and poetic justice ('The Secret Castle'); self-knowledge ('Belonging'), the futility of war and the virtue of selflessness ('The War Healer'): the texture, colour, flavour and smell of which are conveyed through a focal incident, experienced by a limited number of characters, variously utilizing all three main narrative viewpoints – omniscient; first-person narrating experiencing self; and third-person/central intelligence – within an overriding economy of form. However, as Dominic Head cautions, 'the length question must be secondary to a consideration of technique. It is only when quantity and technique are examined together, as mutually dependent factors, that quantity acquires any significance' (1992: 4). This brings the discussion to narrative strategies or techniques.

Short story techniques, *haiku* and 'stokus'

In his text, *Studies in the Short Story*, David Madden enumerates the basic elements of the short story as 'conflict, character and theme' (1984: iii), stated earlier, the effective development of which depends on the writer's point of view. All elements conjoin to determine style. In *Birds of Heaven*, Okri alludes to style, asserting that '[s]tories can be either bacteria or light; they can infect a system, or illuminate a world' (1996: 33 no. 56). Okri's favouring of enlightenment, as evidenced in 'The Message', is arguably inspired by *Piers Plowman* and *The Pilgrim's Progress*, as already mentioned. This implies an interrelationship between fictionality and spirituality, on the one hand, and life's dramatic events and poetry's awkward truth, on the other.

Mary Pratt notes that 'to some extent, the moment of truth stands as a model for the short story the way that life stands as a model for the novel' (1981: 183). She elaborates: 'The lurking associations are these: if the short story is not a "full-length" narrative it cannot narrate a full-length life: it can narrate a fragment or excerpt of a life' (ibid.). And, more importantly in the context of my argument, 'if from that fragment one can deduce things about the whole life, then the more novel-like, the more complete, the story is'. Pratt thus foreshadows Anthony Burgess's yardstick for the short story which, he says, accomplishes a 'novelistic job' but does so briefly (1984: 38). Okri experiments further, establishing the interrelationship between short story and poetry's *haiku*, the most compressed mode of literary expression.

More importantly and of necessity, as well as illustrative of the amalgamation of short story and *haiku*, compression or brevity goes hand in hand with poetic technique, calling into being the use of such stylistic devices as ellipsis and implication ('I had gone into the house by accident or maybe not' in 'Belonging' (2009: 111)); ellipsis, ambiguity and symbol ('You have come from beyond the snowline. It has been an epic journey … You have travelled alone, bearing a message that only you can carry' in 'The

Message' (ibid.: 193)); allusion and symbol ('it doesn't take much, does it, to unhinge a man. Especially if, in a clearing at night, under a moonlit sky, a mind can't unfix itself from a symbol' in 'The Clock' (ibid.: 127)); irony and paradox ('Who on earth are these children? Has grief unhinged them into genius?' in 'Wild Bulls' (156)); and the pure poetic experience of 'In the world of these special books there is no stress, only a kind of peace, and freedom, and a sense of having been redeemed into the weightless condition of pure beauty. The imagination renews the world like dawn does' in 'The Unseen Kingdom' (ibid.: 138-9). Such poetic devices, coupled with serendipitous insights or epiphanic moments, enhance the effects of the narrative strategies of complication, characterization and theme and the attendant narrative stance or point of view.

The point of view in the Japanese *haiku*, as in the slightly longer 'tanka' or 'waku', is that of a poetic central intelligence, its style and mood, contemplative, inspired, meditative, as can be seen in two of the Zen poet, Matsuo Basho's (1644-1694) untitled poems that follow: 'Clouds come from time to time – / And bring to man a chance to rest / From looking at the moon' and 'In the cicada's cry / There's no sign that can foretell / How soon it must die'. Both these *haiku* illustrate a compression into a simple pattern of the poet's awareness of the natural world, the aporia alluding to the mystical nature of enlightenment: the cloud of unknowing of life and death. The *haiku* is often a medium for spiritual experience as these two *haikus* as well as in Heese's 'African miracle' indicate: 'Shangaans prescribe pain. / The phoenix will rise again / Only through fire' (1997: 37).

Each *haiku* captures rare moments of inner vision, serendipities or interiority. Each encapsulates the solitary contemplative condition in which poetry and Okri's 'stokus', such as 'The Golden Inferno', discussed later, are written. Heese's *haiku* alludes to the Shangaans' practice of shamanism, an African trance dance or devotion to attain spiritual power or cosmic oneness. As Alan Northover argues, through the trance dance and rock art, shamans 'affirmed rather than renounced the suffering and pain of existence, and through their creativity, tried to control it' (2014: 116-17). Both their painting and their dances were, he says, 'an attempt to create meaning and bring order to the flux of phenomenal experience and to the pain of existence' (ibid.). Coincidentally, the dichotomy of suffering as a prerequisite for regeneration in 'African Miracle' and Shamanic activities resonates not only serendipitously with the fact that the *Independent* (2002) dubs the Nigerian-born author Ben Okri '[t]he shaman of modern British fiction' but also with Okri's summation that '[s]tories are either dangerous or liberating because they are a kind of destiny' (1996: 21).

Both danger (that of profligate sexual activity) and the liberation that comes from recognition of this danger are evoked in Okri's 'The Golden Inferno', which features the house that 'was a country' or 'the country that was a house' (2009: 169), the transferred metaphor signifying the cancerous detritus wrought by sexually transmitted diseases (gonorrhoea, syphilis, HIV/AIDS), which have reached epidemic proportions in the country of Okri's birth, as implied in 'Sex cannot be the angel of death of a whole people' (172). Inside are 'thousands of tables and pallets' on which lie 'innumerable men and women stricken with a disease for which, as yet, there is no cure … no awakening except death' (ibid.). Outside is a gutter clogged with a dead cow, more sick people on a hospital bed, books and, possibly, human corpses. The turning point in this 'stoku' is the action of a single woman who 'borrowed some boots and went into the gutter and began to probe and heave' (ibid.). The first-person narrator suggests the paradox of horror: 'We watched and did not watch her' until 'gradually, people joined in' (ibid.). The tension between carnal desire and disease is evoked in the oxymoronic title, 'The Golden Inferno', the intrusive authorial voice suggesting that a resolution can be brought about only when 'the long denial was over' (2009: 173). In a subtle allusion to William Blake's 'Rose', the famed opening line of which is reflected, albeit obliquely, in Okri's telling of the Archbishop's pronouncement that '[t]his is a husband and wife thing, a thing between husbands and wives', while in a dramatic *volte-face*, the omniscient narrator reveals the truth of the matter in 'The plague had plunged the world into gloom' (ibid.: 170).

As already intimated, this 'stoku' reflects the pathos inherent in an existential 'kind of destiny' that both threatens and frees. 'If we master desire we will be transformed. We will become masters of ourselves, the magnet of a beautiful new future' (2009: 172), declares the voice of the central intelligence, serendipitously, in 'The Golden Inferno'. Ultimately, the 'stoku' invokes a renewed aesthetics of depth, such as that which characterized medieval Japan, known as 'sabi' and signifying 'a deep connection with [N]ature', as Ross (2012: Preface) points out. In this context, Nature or 'zōka' can also be defined as the process of 'creation'. Ross elucidates: 'In this Taoist metaphysical understanding, all things are in the sway of process, ultimately arising from and connecting to the Tao or the One. The true poet and artist are also in the sway of this process, when they do their poetry or art' (ibid.).

Consider, for example, Okri's 'stoku' entitled 'Music for a Ruined City'. Witnessing the devastation of a 'city under occupation' (2009: 132), the first-person black narrator – an echo of Lao's experience in Okri's *In Arcadia* ([2002] 2003) – is subjected to an act of racial discrimination; he is singled out for a body search and is forced to relinquish his passport. His response is tellingly revelatory if paradoxical: 'I was annoyed, but my annoyance freed me from illusion' (2009: 133). This 'stoku' turns on a double paradox: the first tragic, the second poetically transcendental. The narrating, experiencing self chides the (likewise black) official for complaining about being under occupation yet 'waiving the rules' (ibid.: 132) for the white occupiers, who were neither searched, nor asked to relinquish their passports, yet treating a fellow African like 'a criminal' (ibid.). The second paradox is that 'somewhere in this tragic city an orchestra strikes up' (2009: 134). Although the music is 'alien to all around it', it casts a spell, transforming the bombed city, promising 'a wiser future rising from the rubble' (ibid.).

The individual, transformative aspect of the poetic is, likewise, succinctly captured in the 'stoku' entitled 'Wild Bulls', in which the narrating, experiencing self finds himself in 'a fabulous house' (2009: 155). In a dramatic sleight of hand, we discover that this 'stoku' is likewise set in the chaotic aftermath of war,[4] where the narrator is charged with teaching a houseful of abandoned orphans. Traumatized by loss – a recurrent theme in the Okri oeuvre[5] – 'they cannot absorb anything yet' (ibid.). Obliged to teach them something ('I am meant to be their teacher' (ibid.)), the narrator turns to art. Illustrative of the author's claim that the purpose of his 'stokus' is 'revelation', already quoted, that is, serendipitous, the teller points to the situational irony in the redemptive nature of art, its ability (as with music in the previous 'stokus') to transform, to reveal an imaginary that can transcend disaster. These newly orphaned and bewildered children 'take to it [art]. They paint and draw freely, for long hours, absorbed and lost in colour, fleeing from grief into a world of mysterious shapes, of bulls, birds, hybrid creatures, and patterns in which are concealed indeterminate beings' (ibid.).

Notwithstanding Daniel's mimicking of the intrusive authorial voice: 'Who on earth are these children? Has grief unhinged them into genius?' (2009), the 'stoku' reflects more nearly Heese's 'African Miracle' *haiku* (quoted earlier) in which the Shangaans accept the pain of existence, attempting to master it through their ritualistic routines. The analogy is endorsed by the authorial comment in this tale on the reactions of visiting international scholars, who are both astounded and bemused in 'It is like beholding, on the walls of obscure caves, works of bold mature colourists, of the stature of post-impressionists, or even the masters of expressionism' (2009: 156). The intellectual subtlety, allusiveness and precision in Heese's *haiku* are enhanced by abounding energy (to borrow loosely from Hodgson 1967: 30).

In a chapter entitled 'The Joys of storytelling' in *A Way of Being Free*, Okri articulates the mysterious process of self-induced consciousness or ontopoiesis and the resultant serendipitous self-awareness and its transformative capabilities:

> We all live our lives on this side of the mirror. But when joy touches us, and when the bliss flashes inside us briefly, we have a stronger intuition. The best life, and the life we would really want to live, is on the other side of the mirror – the side that faces out to the great light and which hints at an unexpected paradise. (1997: 45)

The implied injunction, here, is not to live life as if we are a reflection of our true selves, because, when we face 'out[wards]', towards 'the great light' of enlightenment, then and then only, can we experience 'joy'. The excerpt serves as a blueprint for how Okri's rhapsodies each depict a revelation of 'the art of being' wrought through serendipity.

The 'stokus', 'The Secret Castle', itself a metaphor for happiness within a moment of timelessness,[6] and 'The Unseen Kingdom' serve as illustration. Set in Italy, the former 'stoku' recounts an incident where a bus driver's son, Reggio, engages in small talk with a young lady for whom he has given up his window seat on the journey home from school. The innocent exchange has a dual repercussion. First, the young lad is transported into 'a magical world' (2009: 180). Highlighting the essential paradox within the title, the omniscient narrator elaborates: 'He was within happiness itself, within its secret castle' (ibid.). Then, the labourers on the bus misread the naivety, and one of the workers even wrestles Reggio to the ground when all alight from the bus. This is no fairy tale as may have been anticipated, although the resolution is arguably a little too neat: the bus driver shepherds all back onto the bus and returns them to their original point of departure, where ultimately, the docile young lady leads the troupe of workers off the bus but not before pressing a flower into the young lad's hand. This can be read as a symbolic gesture, acknowledging the unspoken 'joy' she had experienced in the innocent yet profound questions posed by the boy. His opening gambit, for example, is 'Do you like those hills?' followed by 'Do you like that cloud?', then 'Do you like that car going past us?' (2009: 176). The second set of questions follows a similar pattern: 'Do you like fields?', 'Do you like rivers?' and 'Do you like roads?' Seemingly ingenuous, the questions reveal a mature awareness of the opposition between the natural and the man-made world, eliciting positive and negative (yes/no) responses, respectively. They are also indicative of the 'white space' or 'semi-e', already discussed, that characterizes the *haiku*, forcing one to read beyond the words, or to live 'on the other side of the mirror', to use Okri's metaphor for true beingness. As with 'The Unseen Kingdom', the 'stoku' provides a fleeting insight into social psychology as well as pathology and both 'stokus' share an ironic twist.

The second 'stoku' is set in the south of France (perhaps the French Riviera adjacent to Italy). It features an international book lovers' fair, where '[t]here is indeed a mysterious mood about the place, a dawn coloured enchantment, on account of the open books' (2009: 117). Whereas the first comments on the social predicament of modes of perception, the generating circumstance of the second foregrounds the whispered scandal of a rigged prize-winning entry at an international book fair. The closing ironic twist here is that '[t]he rigged condition lingered, but it meant nothing. For here, in this fair, the only thing that matters is the charmed condition of books that endure' (ibid.: 140), an allusion to Lewis Carroll's works and original manuscripts on display at the fair. The poetic insight or serendipity here is captured in the truism that '[i]t is impossible, in the long run, to rig a book into a magic condition, or to make it give off a light it does not have' (ibid.), which flows from an abortive attempt to determine who had tried to rig the results in order to win 'the prestigious festival prize' (2009: 138). The quoted sentiment reverberates Okri's assertion in *A Way of Being Free*: 'Writers have one great responsibility: to write beautifully ... to write well ...' (1997: 60). According to Okri, this means 'being truthful'. The obligation signifies: 'To charm, to amuse, to enchant, to take us out of ourselves'. A 'parallel responsibility' is 'to bear witness in their unique manner to the beauties, the ordinariness, and the horrors of their times' (ibid.). The 'stokus', it would seem, are Okri's realization of this experimental mission.

The consensus of the critics of the 'stokus' in *Tales of Freedom* cited is that the strongest tale is 'The Mysterious Anxiety of Them and Us'. Despite his somewhat cynical analogy between Okri's 'stokus' and Sodoku, quoted earlier, Astle is able to recognize literary quality. Adopting a Carrollinian neologism, he concedes:

> [A] posh banquet is compromised by the presence of hungry eyes watching. As one diner frets, 'To turn around and offer them food would automatically be to see them and treat them as inferior.' Nowhere else has global imbalance been better expressed, and it took a slithy Okrian stoku to do it![7] (2009: 2)

Here, the embedded paradox reflecting both the critical concession and the implied social dilemma of seeing and not seeing wrought by the social divide – them and us, self and other, the haves and the have nots – at the banquet recalls that of watching but not watching in 'The Golden Inferno' discussed earlier. The reader is left with the rhetorical question: 'Did we who were eating feel guilty?' (2009: 120) to which, underlining the paradox, the narrator is given to retort: 'It was a complex feeling' (ibid.).

A less obvious paradox is seen in 'The Legendary Sedgewick', a 'stoku' recounting the relative expertise of two cricketers. Whereas the acknowledged 'legend of the game' (2009: 163) had mastered the 'classical overarm bowl' (ibid.), a retired 'once famous cricketer' (ibid.: 162) usurps this legendary stature and status by cracking 'the arcane art of the spin and speed rotation of the casual throw' (ibid.: 164), thus putting himself 'in an unfathomable class, a different space' (ibid.).

The last of the 'stokus' to be briefly dealt with, 'The Black Russian', implies a correlative paradoxical 'different space'. This 'stoku' recounts the highly successful filming of Pushkin's *Eugene Onegin*, with a splendidly attired black Russian, who happened to be aboard the train, slipping seamlessly into the script, resulting in the virtual relocation of Pushkin's work to Africa. The serendipity in this 'stoku' is somewhat more introspective: 'we knew in our hearts that we had brought home a great Russian classic' (2009: 151), an implicitly serendipitous happenchance.

This brings the argument to a more focused discussion of Okri's use of serendipities in these rhapsodies in prose.

Serendipity

The *Cambridge Advanced Learner's Dictionary* (2008) defines 'serendipity' as 'the lucky tendency to find interesting or valuable things by chance'. As noted, 'stokus', asserts Okri, foregrounding their metaphoric mode, are 'serendipities, caught in the air, reverse lightning' (2009: 108). They are thus akin to fellow African-born writer J. R. R. Tolkien's notion of eucatastrophe. Not unlike Tolkien's eucatastrophic tales, Okri's 'stokus' correspond to the primordial desire – in a world of poverty, injustice and corruption – for the consolation of 'a catch of breath, a beat and lifting of the heart, a piercing glimpse of joy and heart's desire' (1973: 22).

The touchstone in *Tales of Freedom* is, not surprisingly, and as already stated, freedom, but a freedom that accrues from serendipitous self-discovery, from knowledge of self, mirroring the inner state, the state within. In 'Belonging', the first of the thirteen 'stokus', for example, mistaken identity leads first to 'the thrill of belonging' (2009: 112) and then to wilful self-delusive pretence, the enjoyment of role play. Ultimately and in 'a flash', the shock of a younger, fresh-faced narrator (ibid.: 113) being mistaken for 'a black, Arabic, pock-marked elderly in-law' trapped in a fixed role generates the freedom of a serendipitous realization by the ultimately unmasked narrating, experiencing self that 'I wasn't trapped by tradition. I was lithe. I could go any which way. I had many futures open to me' (ibid.). Here, the situational irony of being assumed to belong, wanting to belong, then not belonging, of being uncovered/ discovered facilitates dialectic thinking, engendering self-validation in the joy of the knowledge of freedom of self.

A further example of situational irony coupled with dialectic thinking can be seen in 'The Clock', a symbol for the consciousness of the inexorable passing of time, but also for 'the abomination' (2009: 126) of becoming fixated with the mechanical artefact, itself a metonym for the ambiguities of the physical time of the cosmos, historical time with its emphasis on economic and cultural processes, psychological time and even of the Doomsday Clock[8] or the end of life as we know it. Ironically, the narrator finds himself inadvertently drawn into a support role for a man he only 'partly knew' (ibid.: 125) in a night-time enactment of a courtly duel. All four actors are dressed 'in eighteenth century costume', the enemy sporting 'a large, round, shining clock' (ibid.) around his waist. Seemingly drawing on diverse fields of knowledge to outwit the prevailing discourse and dilemmas of time and space, the opponent is perceived as the embodiment of the complexities of time, entirely unhinging the other duellist's mind. The narrator, at first solicitous and caring, finally curtails his visits to the asylum, abandoning his now insane acquaintance who is obsessed with and possessed by 'the clock' and arrives at 'a sort of freedom' in 'not fixing [his] mind on anything, or anyone' (2009: 127). Whereas Jay Parini (2009: 2) reads this negatively as 'a refusal to engage', the speaker overtly cautions against obsession or obsessive-compulsive disorder (OCD): 'It doesn't take much, does it,' he asks rhetorically, after witnessing his acquaintance's demise into madness, 'to unhinge a man. Especially if, in a clearing, at night, under a moonlit sky, a mind can't unfix itself from a symbol' (Okri 2009: 127), already quoted.

A comparable serendipity occurs in 'The Racial Colourists'. Here, the serendipity is more recognizably a eureka moment. Fleeing from the pursuit by a bespectacled white youth at night during wartime surveillance and realising that there is no escape – 'Where was I running to, where could I run to, where was safe for me?' (2009: 144) – the first-person black narrator stops short to listen – 'in a blue flash of lightning' (ibid.) – to his inner voice, which urges: 'Go towards him. Don't run away. Go menacingly, purposely.' The epiphanic moment inheres in an insight into stereotypical racial interaction: 'He's more scared of you than you are of him' (ibid.). Up close, the erstwhile pursued realizes: 'Behind his glasses he had scared, timid eyes and an ordinary harmless face' (2009: 145). It can be argued, therefore, that this 'stoku' is a parable about the necessity of confronting one's (irrational) fears.

In 'The Secret Castle' and 'The Unseen Kingdom', already discussed, the serendipities appear to lie, respectively, in the happiness born of innocent pleasure and an unexpected gift (of a flower) leading to a sense of self-worth and (in the second 'stoku') in the knowledge that '[i]t is impossible … to rig a book into a magic condition, or to make it give off a light it does not have' (2009: 140), quoted earlier. In 'Music for a Ruined City', another 'stoku' set in a war-torn city (possibly an allusion to Lagos during the Biafran War, although the writer rejects this (pers. com.)), life is sustained by the Mozart effect. Although '[t]his is a music alien to all around it, to the bombed-out city', music casts 'a spell, changing what it touches' (2009: 134). Among the ruins, the conquered 'listen to music that enchants and cleanses the spaces of suffering. There time stands suspended, and a pure joy percolates out from the orchestra, out and up, in a spiral, to the sky and the stars' (ibid.). The transcendent resolution personalises the synaesthetic affect: 'I go on wandering among the broken columns, witnessing the faces of mute grief, with Mozart in my heart, like ice over a wound' (ibid.). Here, the simile of an icy remedy to sooth the disaster of internecine strife effectively captures the post-serendipitous state.

In 'The War Healer', the scene shifts from the ruined city onto the battlefield itself and the serendipity lies in the paradox of the compulsive selfless service of an erstwhile photographer in the face of futility: 'While they murdered one another, he restored, buried, healed' (2009: 190). Ultimately, the intrusive authorial voice intones:

> In a world where no one listens, where no one seems to care, where hatred is greater than love, where hearts are hardened by vengeance and pride, where violence is preferable to peace, what else is there for him to do but heal the wounded, and bury the dead, in a war that could go on forever? (Ibid.)

This excerpt recalls the selfless action of the woman in 'The Golden Inferno'. In both 'stokus', the cause and remedy lie respectively in lack of knowledge and in proactive thinking and action. Deeply philosophical, Okri expatiates upon the paradoxes of human behaviour by, for instance, drawing an analogy as to how human beings confront death. They either react with paralytic fear and despair, or – and this applies to 'a fortunate few' – with total acceptance, embracing life anew with a knowledge of living what Heidegger terms 'Dasein'/'being-towards-death'.[9]

Conclusion

This chapter has attempted to illustrate the way in which Okri's rhapsodies fuse content and style. Emphasis also falls on the capacity of the 'stokus' to capture fleeting moments of life, the seemingly infectious that nevertheless remains unknowable and sublime, and illuminates that which exceeds conscious awareness. As Okri avers in *A Way of Being Free*, '[p]oets seem to be set against the world because we need them to show us the falseness of our limitations, the true extent of our kingdom' (1997: 2).

This innovative art form, the 'stoku', with its stress on literary artifice and more specifically on serendipity, highlights different sources of wonder, 'the true extent of our kingdom' (in line with African philosophical traditions); it has an enduring ability to capture the episodic nature of lived life; it bristles with incandescent hope, transporting the reader from the oppressions of daily life to a glimpse of the way to self-mastery akin to the effects of a Shamanic trance dance, discussed earlier. These ontopoietic, or phenomenology of life, snapshots erase the gap between despair and hope, at the same time showing us – as implicit in the *haiku* form, that the transcendental is unknowable, yet sublime. What remains is a longing for and a meditation on the transcendental, the paradox that 'the truth only exists in all its clarity, that is in all its obscurity, in an experience such as this existential union where thought is poetry and poetry thought' to quote Adonis (1992: 64). Adonis thus synthesizes, in a *haiku*-style synopsis, Okri's earlier quoted statement about our current need for 'the awkward truth of poetry' (2011: 3), with which this chapter began. This reflects the original Arabic meaning of the word poetry as knowing/knowledge, unifying poetry and thought. Like poetry, Okri's 'stokus' are not content with merely feeling things and expressing them poetically but thinking about them also.[10] The creative texts of poets and mystics, such as Ben Okri, transcend epistemological dualisms. Okri's 'stokus' illustrate an organic relationship between poetry and thought. Through their insights or epiphanies, moments of illumination or serendipities, these rhapsodies in prose illustrate the way in which serendipity is linked to interiority, to inner vision, a common theme in the Okri oeuvre, thus opening up a new aesthetic horizon, and also a new horizon of thought (cf. Said 1992: 59).

Part Three

The mercurial imaginary: The writer as 'demiurge' (artist/craftsman)

9

Sowing 'a quilt of harmony': Eco-phenomenology in 'Lines *in Potentis*'

Introduction

This chapter begins with a brief discussion of the poet's view of ontopoiesis (heightened consciousness) and eco-phenomenology. Rooting his argument firmly in ontopoiesis or phenomenology of life, Ben Okri asserts in *A Way of Being Free* that 'the poet is the widener of consciousness' ([1989] 1997: 3). Implicitly invoking an eco-phenomenological standpoint, he explains how this raising of consciousness, or the process of ontopoiesis occurs poetically: '[Poets] speak to us. Creation speaks to them. They listen. They remake the world in words, from dreams' (ibid.). He muses about this mystical dialectic: 'Intuitions which could only come from the secret mouths of gods whisper to [poets] through all of life, of [N]ature, *of visible and invisible agencies*' (ibid.: 3; emphasis added). Underlining the relation of eco-phenomenology to the fluid nature of reality in the same text, Okri explains: 'The poet turns the earth into mother, the sky becomes a shelter, the sun the inscrutable god' (ibid.: 2).

Okri's view of the role of the poet and the source of poetic inspiration accords with the late Anna-Teresa Tymieniecka's concept of eco-phenomenology in her introduction to her *Passion for Place* (1997) as the philosophy of 'our relationship to the earth' ([1989] 1997: 2). In defence of her unique brand of phenomenology, she explains not only its theoretical base but also its application. Drawing an analogy to climate change and the current ecological crisis, she is later to explain in *The Passions of the Earth* that people generally see these as physical problems, resolvable through technological innovation. By contrast, eco-phenomenologists approach these problems from a metaphysical perspective, thus requiring 'a fundamental re-conceptualization of human values and our relationship to [N]ature' (2008b: 2).

For Aristotle, too, natural generation and artistic creation are purpose-driven. And, as with Okri's 'invisible agencies' and Tymieniecka's 'metaphysical perspective' on climate change, there is no impassable gulf between 'physis' and 'poiesis'. Consider, for example, Aristotle's statement in his *Physics* (1941), 'It is absurd to suppose that purpose is not present because we do not observe the agent deliberating. Art does not deliberate' (*Physica* II 8 199B27–31). In other words, this is what constitutes the natural generation, just referred to. Aristotle's illustrations serve to elucidate: 'If the shipbuilding art were in the wood, it would produce the same results *by nature*. If, therefore, purpose is present in art, it is present also in [N]ature. The best illustration is a doctor doctoring himself: nature is like that. It is plain then that [N]ature is a cause, a cause that operates for a purpose' (original emphasis).[1]

'The Wedding Prayer' and 'Lines *in Potentis*' (*Wild*: 2012)

The discussion now illustrates Okri's re-conceptualization of human values in relation to Nature in 'A Wedding Prayer' (2012: 20-2) and 'Lines *in Potentis*' (26-7). It is precisely this natural purposive generation that gave rise to the title of this essay, inspired by a line from Okri's 'A Wedding Prayer'. Evincing an eco-phenomenological viewpoint, Okri writes: 'Love has brought two / Rivers into one way, one dream; / Has *sown a quilt of harmony*. / And scattered some magic / Fragrance upon the sea' (Stanza 1, ll. 6-10; emphasis added). These lines arguably signal the immanence of love: love permeates all matter; it implies that which is divine; all matter is sacred. By extension, human activities such as weaving, pottery, sowing seeds are likewise an expression of the sacred. As Teresa Moorey reminds us, 'The ancient Great Mother Goddess not only presided over life – she existed in it' (1997: 2). The metaphysical conceit of the love of two people having 'sown a quilt of harmony' leading to their commitment to marriage is transcendently eco-phenomenologically sacred; the pun on SOW (connoting regenerative husbandry as in the nurturing of plant life as well as the procreation of life customarily anticipated by newlyweds) and SEW (as in the bringing together of unifying in stitch craft) encapsulates the 'double entendre' of the conscious acts inherent in the decision to spend a life together as well as an allusion to the responsibilities of wedded life. Symbolically, too, SOW invokes the biblical axiom of 'As you sow, so shall ye reap', while SEW recalls Joseph's coat of many colours and all that it signifies.

This occasional poem was commissioned to celebrate the nuptials of a bride and groom and is, at once, profound and idyllic. It is dedicated to Ieva and Ivor,[2] to life and to the procreation of life as expressed in the injunctions to the bridal pair: 'May you never lose your / Laughter, your playfulness, / And your music', juxtaposed with 'Be fruitful in enchanting deeds / And in futures' (Stanza 6, ll. 65-7 and ll. 69-70).

Explicit in the second occasional poem, 'Lines *in Potentis*', are the same epistemic eco-phenomenological motifs of ecology, love, music, dreams, [N]ature, harmony and the divine as the opening lines attest: 'One of the magic centres of the world; / One of the world's dreaming places. / Ought to point the way to the world: / For here lives the great music of humanity' (Stanza 1, ll. 1-4). In this focal poem, the canvas is broader and addresses a wider audience in its intersection of the diachronic with the synchronic, that is, of history and contemporary society. Addressed to the cosmopolitan society of Londoners, the 'Workers of the world' (Stanza 4, l. 42), the poem appeals for '[t]he harmonisation of / Different histories, cultures, geniuses and dreams' (Stanza 1, ll. 5-6). This is not simply a utopian vision for, as Eckhart Tolle explains, '[a]t the core of all utopian visions lies one of the main structural dysfunctions of the old consciousness: looking to the future for salvation' (2005: 308). Commissioned in 2002 for the London Assembly and inscribed around the curving structure of the Greater

London Authority Building [the City Hall], 'Lines *in Potentis*' was read by the poet in Trafalgar Square on 14 July 2005.

Whereas the first poem celebrates the conjoining of human life – a balancing of yin/yang, the second commemorates post-human life after the bombing of London.[3] Okri's prayerful dream, as he recalls the horrors of the Blitz from a twenty-first century perspective, is akin to that of Revelations – his is a vision of 'a new heaven and a new earth',[4] the foundation of both being awakened consciousness or ontopoiesis. The recollection of historical facts is part of a purposive mythic pattern the poet employs to capture a series of moral crises that he not only portrays but also seeks to embody in this poem. This is borne out in the injunction to 'tell / Everyone that history, though unjust, / Can yield wiser outcomes' (Stanza 1, ll. 7–9). An enumeration of a list of contraries that follows articulates just what these 'wiser outcomes' may be: 'And out of bloodiness *can* come love; / And out of slave-trading / *Can* come a dance of souls; / Out of division, unity; / Out of chaos, fiestas' (Stanza 1, ll. 10–14; emphases added). The repetition of the modal verb 'can' serves to highlight the transformative metamorphosis envisaged. Explicit in Okri's Africanist cosmogony is the Blakean aphorism that 'Without Contraries is no Progression' (Keynes, 'Blake's "The Marriage of Heaven and Hell"' (1966: 149)). As Okri too avers in *A Way of Being Free*, '[t]here can be no absolutes: no absolute good or evil, no absolute way of living. No absolute truth. All truths are mediated and tempered by the fact of living. Being alive qualifies all things' ([1989] 1997: 54). 'Poets,' Okri muses in the same text, 'seem to be set against the world because we need them to show us the falseness of our limitations, the true extent of our kingdom' (ibid.: 2).

The epistemological implications are that without paradox, without the various trials and tribulations in one's encounter with what religions call good and evil (but what Blake refers to as Innocence and Experience), one cannot attain perfection of Being. This epistemology reverberates with that of Bertrand Russell who distinguished between two types of knowledge in his *The Scientific Outlook* of 1931. We may, Russell argues, 'seek knowledge of an object because we love the object or because we wish to have power over it' (Chapter 17; quoted by Lenz 2017: 9). Russell's philosophy is that lovers of knowledge, that is, philosophers, poets and mystics, seek 'contemplative knowledge'. This kind of knowledge is inspired by love rather than power; it 'allows us to know and to come to rest in higher purposes that give "delight or joy or ecstasy"' (ibid.). Okri's train of thought in the transformations contemplated in the extract above – killing becoming love; human trafficking becoming 'a dance of souls'; the erasure of divisions and celebrating in nature's chaos – synchronizes with Russell's. Both are lovers of truth, although many paths to truth are possible.

Thus, the vision of London, 'City of tradition, conquests and variety; / City of commerce and the famous river' (Stanza 2, ll. 15–16), as a sacred 'axis mundi' – implied in the 'magic centre' quoted earlier, alludes to an awakening of consciousness – that is, to an awakening to the realization of presence and its power ('potentia') to effect change. The flow of the river (of life) into the sea in 'The Wedding Prayer' becomes the inscrutable flow of the cycle of the seasons, 'Awaiting an astonishing command / From the all-seeing eye of Ra' (Stanza 2, ll. 29–30); in 'Lines …', not only does this aesthetic evocation of the Egyptian sun god transliterate John Keats's 'Hyperion' – 'One moon with alteration slow had shed / Her silver seasons four upon the night' – but it also embodies the awakened consciousness or higher-order thinking (HOT) consciousness. 'When we look out on the world with all its multiplicity of astonishing phenomena,' Okri asks rhetorically in *A Way of Being Free*, 'do we see that only one philosophy can contain, explain, and absorb everything?' ([1989] 1997: 19). He elaborates: 'I think not. The universe will always be greater than us.' As mere microcosms within the macrocosm, Okri suggests that '[o]ur mind[s] therefore should be like Keats's thoroughfare, through which all thoughts can wander' (ibid.: 9). Okri surmises therefore that our minds 'should also be a great cunning net that can catch the fishes of possibility' (ibid.).

In an interview given on the conferment of 'Laurea Honoris Causa' in Philosophy (27 August 2008), Tymieniecka asserted that the very essence of her philosophy – and, evidently that of Okri too – 'is our relationship to the earth and to the cosmos' (2008a: 2).

The appeal in 'Lines *in Potentis*' is for this 'magic centre' of the global village to use its regenerative power to 'Re-make the world / Under the guidance of inspiration / And of wise laws' (Stanza 4, ll. 43–5). In a reworking of the Marxist tenet, 'Workers of the work unite', the injunction here is for the workers to unite, by implication, not because they have nothing to lose, but because the proletariat has everything to lose should they fail to heed the poet's plea. A history of natural and man-made disasters (The Great Fire, the plague and the Blitz) enables London's workers to comprehend their own potency and potential, to 'Tell everyone that the future / Is yet unmade' (Stanza 2, ll. 17–18). Thus, the poem seeks to address mystical unrest, not to counter bourgeois capital. The closing lines resound with this mystique, this eco-phenomenological sensibility in 'I want you to tell everyone / Through trumpets played / With the fragrance of roses, that / A mysterious reason has brought us / *All together*, / Here, now, under the all-seeing / Eye of the sun' (Stanza 5, ll. 57–63; emphasis added). The two pivotal motifs that run throughout world mythologies – wonder and self-salvation – implicitly coalesce in these lines. The mystical is, as Joseph Campbell explains in a chapter tellingly entitled 'Cities of God' from his *The Masks of God*, 'redemption or release from a world exhausted of its glow' ([1962] 2011: 35).

'Lines *in Potentis*' is featured in Okri's anthology *Wild* (2012), as is 'The Wedding Prayer'. Axiomatic to my interpretation is the poet's own conception of *wild* (citing Okri on the dustcover to *Wild*) as 'an alternative to the familiar, where energy meets freedom, where art meets the elemental, where chaos can be honed'. More precisely, for this London-loving Nigerian poet, 'the wild is our link with the stars'. In an interview in *The New Statesman* (29 March 2012), Okri stated: 'I was interested in the wild, not as in wildlife or outside civilization but as a raw, formative energy that artists notice when they look at objects.' This is not aesthetic posturing; it has to do with that which lies beyond reason or rationality. It is predicated on the mystery of eco-phenomenology, on 'enjoyment of literature, of beauty, of the sublime, the elevated, as well as our compassion for the miseries of humankind, generosity towards others … inspired by the subliminal passions of the human soul', to quote Tymieniecka (1997). Okri's concept of 'wild' as that which becomes ontopoietically familiar when creative energy is released to contain cosmic chaos vicariously resonates with Tymieniecka's explication of the Sentience of the Logos which 'is carried in various guises through all the individualizations of life' and 'which from this first germinal coming forth of life, appearance of life, to the fashioning of the individual, which in the case of the human being, with its highest sentient spiritual unfolding … is really carrying the divine' (2008b: 6).

In *The Passions of the Earth* (*Analecta Husserliana* LXXI), Tymieniecka asserts that 'the human being is an ecological fruit … formed by the earth', whose life is sustained by 'the juices of the earth'. This, in turn, explains 'the cosmic dependencies of the human mind and human development' (2008b: 6). Having posited the notion that this has nothing to do with theology but is rather just a metaphysical tendency of life itself, she added, 'the self-individualization of life, which is the basic instrument of ontopoiesis draws on the laws of the cosmos and the earth' (ibid.: 8).

One of these cosmic laws manifests in poetry, according to Okri in *A Time for New Dreams*: 'We are, at birth, born into a condition of poetry and breathing. Birth is a poetic condition: it is spirit becoming flesh. Death is also a poetic condition: it is flesh becoming spirit again. It is the miracle of a circle completed, the unheard melody of a like returning to unmeasured silence' (2011: 3). The cycle of the seasons and the cardinal points of the compass, all of which feature in 'Lines …', are likewise cosmic laws. Significantly, the first season mentioned is spring, a time of rebirth. In the poem, an anthropomorphized spring (invoking its correlative – human birth) 'waits / By the lakes, listening / To the unfurling daffodils' (Stanza 2, ll. 25–7). This, perhaps, is an allusive conflation of William Wordsworth's definitive Nature poems, 'To Daffodils' and 'Tintern Abbey'.

The depiction of summer shares the same esemplastic imagination: it 'lingers with the hyperborean worms', perhaps an allusion to the dragons of yore (Old English 'wyrms') conscientized to nature's purposive way. The choice of the epithet 'hyperborean' endorses the indissoluble link between past and present, between man and Nature, and highlights cosmic unity. The adjective (hyperborean) denotes or relates 'to the extreme north', an allusion to the mythic Peerless Land of classicism, while when applied to the noun, 'worms', it could signify the inhabitants 'of the extreme north' in accordance with the *New Oxford Dictionary of English* (900). Furthermore, embedded in the signifier is a tacit allusion to Greek mythology; the Hyperboreans were members of a blessed race worshipping Apollo (the Greek god of the sun) and living in a land of sunshine and plenty beyond the north wind (ibid.), coincidentally typifying an African setting, while correlating with Egyptian myth's Ra.

Both autumn and winter are likewise anthropomorphized. In an intertextual braiding of Keats's 'Ode to Autumn', 'Ode to the West Wind' and 'Ode to a Nightingale', shot through with Negative Capability,[5] Okri's autumn 'dallies / With the West wind / And the weeping nightingales' (Stanza 5, ll. 50–2). Winter is depicted as clearing 'its sonorous throat / At the Antipodean banquets, preparing / For a speech of hoarfrost / And icicles conjured from living breath' (Stanza 5, ll. 53–6).

Implicit in the evocation of the cycle of the seasons is not only a correlation with human life – a priori Being, birth, life and death and life-after-life or post-human life – but also a veiled bringing together of the four cardinal points viz. north (hyperborean, already discussed), south (Antipodean; the Antipodes is an appellation for Australia and New Zealand), east (the land of the rising sun/Ra/Apollo) and west (the autumnal west wind). The *four* seasons and *four* points of the compass conjoin to unify the cosmos with rebalanced human beings reflected in Okri's vision of the 'harmonisation of different / Histories, cultures, geniuses, and dreams' (Stanza 1, ll. 5–6) already quoted.

Okri's treatment of humankind in both poems discussed here is likewise rooted in eco-phenomenology and the Paracelsian triadic elements of life (see Preface). On the brink of a new life together in London, Viscount Ivor Guest and his bride Ieva (a Latvian beauty) are enjoined to 'Travel / Into one another, as into / A country you have long admired, / And read many fables about, / And now find yourself / Before its famed rivers / Its inspiring mountains' (Stanza 3, ll. 20–6). In correlation, 'Lines …' is addressed to the London populace, possibly the most cosmopolitan in the world, who are enjoined to attune to the 'wild', to the Elizabethan Music of the Spheres, to 'Create the beautiful / Music our innermost / Happiness suggests. Delight the future. / Create happy outcomes' (Stanza 4, ll. 46–9). Londoners, Okri implies, are those who have awakened 'to their essential true nature as consciousness and recognize that essence in all "other, all life forms"' (Tolle 2005: 309); they feel a oneness with the ecological epistemology of the whole, as Okri suggests in 'Lines …', 'Tomorrow's music sleeps / In our fingers, in our awakening / Souls, the blossom of our spirit, / The suggestive buds of our hearts' (Stanza 3, ll. 31–4). This single poetic quatrain foreshadows the closing lines of this poem with its 'trumpets played / With the fragrance of roses', cited earlier, and reflects back to the opening line's 'one of the magic centres of the earth', where heightened sense impressions prevail, where human sensibilities are awakened and optimized.

Ultimately, 'Lines *in Potentis*' can be seen as an eco-phenomenology/Paracelsian blueprint for 'the way' to transform 'nightmare' into 'illumination' (Stanza 2, l. 20), transliterating St Paul's Letter to the Philippians[6] and encapsulating both Revelations' prophetic new earth or Parry and Blake's hymn to the New Jerusalem.[7] All four of these intertexts embody the awakened consciousness that Tolle asserts 'is changing all aspects of life on our planet, including [N]ature, because life on earth is inseparable from human consciousness that perceives and interacts with it' (2005: 308). This statement, in turn, underlines the Aristotelian assertion that there was no impassable gulf between 'physis' and 'poiesis', quoted at the outset of this chapter, as well as an eco-phenomenological epistemology. 'Ours is a condition,' asserts Tymieniecka, 'within the unity of everything alive, which depends on earthly and cosmic laws' (2008b: 3).

Conclusion

In an article entitled 'African Modes of Self-Writing', fellow African phenomenologist Achile Mbembe (2002: 252–3) debates the contention of this unity within the more prevalent discourse of emancipation and autonomy (e.g. in Franz Fanon in his *Black Skins, White Masks* (1972)), which Mbembe terms a 'paranoid reading of history' (2002: 253). He points to 'a tension between a universalizing move' that claims shared membership within the human condition (*sameness*) and an opposing, particularistic move that 'emphasizes difference and specificity' by accenting not originality as such but the principle of repetition (*tradition*) and 'the values of autochthony' (ibid.). This latter invokes a fabricated mask of Africanity:[8] race, culture and the like, whereas my argument is premised on 'Ubuntu' or the brotherhood of humankind in the context of cosmic harmony. It is inspired by the subliminal passions of a contemporary poetic soul.

In the introduction to her *Passion for Place*, Tymieniecka elucidates within an eco-phenomenological logic: 'The soul's creatively orchestrated swings, together with the generative propulsions of imagination, distil the primitive strivings endowed with *specifically human life-significance*' (1997: ix). As an endorsement of an eco-phenomenological passion of place in the hands of a true poet, she observes the resulting Affective Fallacy:

> On the wings of the creative imagination our subliminal passions carry us to unattainable realms, and we exhale beyond our frames with joy or enchantment as our dreams have us roam through shifting dimensions of sublunary reality. All passions 'fly', charting nebulous spheres, as human strivings, dreams, forebodings, desires – in following their particular bents – seek fulfilment by crystallizing in a place … that they imaginatively fashion and qualify with the significance of expectant strivings. (ibid.: xii–xiii)

As a mystical poet, Okri envisages the world as 'A system of co-operation, / Where things are both themselves / And symbols and correspondences' ('Wild': 51). His 'Lines *in Potentis*' aspires to the presence of a vital and rich – perhaps unattainable – realm. His prayer for London is that it comes to represent 'an upward curve / In the moment of a sleeping civilization', to quote the title poem from his second anthology (ibid., ll. 15–16). His vision is of a space where fatigue, work, despair and exhaustion can be transformed by 'that wild inspiration' that 'turns the world / Upside down and therefore / The right way up at last' (ibid., ll. 70–2).

10

'A clear lucid stream of everywhereness' in *Wild*: A postmodern perspective

Taken from Ben Okri's second novel, *The Landscapes Within*, the phrase 'a clear lucid stream of everywhereness' serves to define a postmodern alignment with the theories of complexity and relativity, coupled as it is with the coalescence of time and space in 'Past and present and future disappeared' (1981: 55) and '[t]he whole universe rolled itself into a crystalline moment: and time vanished. Sea, night, sky: all hazed over and became one' (ibid.). The mixed metaphor and transferred epithet in 'everywhereness' and 'lucid stream' neatly encapsulate the cosmic dimension of heightened moments – 'the awakening of consciousness from the dream of matter, form and separation' (Tolle [1999] 2005: 55) – and a striving to achieve 'Dasein' (authentic human existence) through consecrated production. Both inform Okri's poetic vision in his collection of poetry, *Wild* (2012a). The neologism, 'everywhereness', coupled with 'lucid stream' which suggests the inexorable flow of time, is evocative of what Anna-Teresa Tymieniecka calls ontopoiesis,[1] on the one hand, and Tolle's notion of 'the end of time' ([1999] 2005: 55), on the other. Far from evoking a modernist grand narrative, 'everywhereness' is embedded in postmodern, non-teleological complexity, as in Brian Arthur's ([2008] 2012: 165-6) explication of the interrelationship of everything, an interrelationship between the complex approach and total Taoism in which there is, paradoxically, no inherent order. 'The world starts with one,' Arthur explains, 'and the one become [*sic*] two, and the two become many, and the many led to myriad things' (ibid.: 65). In scientific terms, this is the mode of fractals or small, repeating but distinct patterns of the natural world (the irregular regularity of the repeated five florets in a cross section of a cauliflower head, for instance). In postmodernity's Chaos theory that studies the order underlying apparent randomness (see Sardar and Abrams [2008] 2012: 82-3) (as in Taoism), so too in Okri's 'lucid stream of everywhereness', the universe is perceived as vast, forever mutable, yet kaleidoscopically self-similar ('self-similarity implies that any subsystem of a fractal is equivalent to the whole' (Swanepoel 2007: 445)).

The epigraph for this collection of poems is from Heraclitus, the early Greek philosopher (*c*.500 BC) who maintained that all things in the universe are in a state of constant flux and that the mind derives a false sense of permanence of the external world 'from passing impressions of experience' (Delahunty et al. 2007: 299). The false sense is natural:

> It is natural to want calm places
> Where stillness grows,
> It's natural to want
> Virgil's spreading beeches.

Yet, the closing lines of Okri's poetic rendering of the inexorable law of impermanence in the tellingly entitled 'Heraclitus' Golden River', read:[2]

> But the river flows, and so must we.
> Change is the happy god Heraclitus
> Glimpsed in the golden river.
> Spread illumination through this darkening world,
> Spread illumination through this darkening world.
> No change is good; dancing
> Gracefully with change is better.
>
> (2012a: 94)

Postmodern concerns with process, participation, surface, idiolect and interpretation are at play here. The apparent tension between the intertexts, Virgil's bucolic *Eclogues* and Heraclitus's metaphysical *Fragments*, is reconciled in the latter's philosophy of 'universal flux', on the one hand, and 'unity of opposites', on the other, both timelessly foreshadowing postmodernity and effectively 'spread[ing] illumination through this darkening world'. The repetition of this line in the poem mimics or repeats the ecosystem of fractals, already discussed, and referred to in poetics as 'metagage' (repetition that rings the signification of particular words). There is too a symbiosis between Arthur's concept of complexity: 'We are part of [N]ature ourselves, we're in the middle of it ... There is no division between *doer* and *done to* because we are all part of this interlocking network' ([2008] 2012: 166; original emphases) and the postmodern tropes that permeate Okri's collection. Consider, for example, the complex metaphors 'the safari of dreams', 'the wings of death', 'the great abyss' and 'the colour of dawn' from the poem 'Begin with a Leap' (Okri 2012a: 11–12); or the startling personification in 'The Fifth Circle' where 'screams in the air sizzle my flesh', 'History tramps on my nerves' and 'The kettle yells' (ibid.: 65). In an interview with Sophie Elmhirst, Okri describes the creative – and by extension, analytical – process: 'The poem is never complete in the mind. It emerges and then it's like an act of unveiling. The unveiling is the longest and most difficult part of it' (Okri 2012b).

These multiple concerns point to the complexity inherent in the term *postmodern* itself, which seeks to defy demarcation as does Okri's anti-cartographical neologism 'everywhereness'. Both concepts require but resist unveiling. 'Postmodernism means working without rules in order to find out the rules of what you have done' (Appignanesi and Garratt [1995] 2007: 50). Richard Appignanesi and Chris Garratt explain: 'Postmodernism is a confusion of meanings stemming from two riddles ... It resists and obscures the sense of modernism. It implies a complete knowledge of the modern which has been surpassed by a *new age*' (ibid.: 4). One of its principal characteristics is thus indeterminacy, which typifies Okri's: 'There was an extended hissing that heightened and became a primeval sound in the mind. The transport was beyond words or colours' in *The Landscapes Within* (1981: 55). A comparable indeterminacy or deferred meaning inheres in the title *Wild*, explained on the dust jacket as 'an alternative to the familiar, where energy meets freedom, where art meets the elemental, where chaos is honed'. The 'wild,' says Okri, 'is our link to the stars' (cf. Gray [2013], 'When chaos is the god of an era: Rediscovering an "axis mundi" in Ben Okri's *Starbook* [2007]').

Such a link to the stars is evoked in 'The Golden House of Sand', a praise chant to Martin Luther King that culminates in a plea for the Sublime, 'They want to taste the fruits / Of the earth, in music, art, science / And dreams. They want to calibrate / The depth and height of man's spirit' (Stanza 3: 39). In this quatrain, the subliminal or 'what we can conceive of – the infinitely great, for instance – but is not within our power to represent exactly' (Appignanesi and Garratt 2007: 22) is attained through an esemplastic imagination conjoining the senses and sacred geometry. The beginning of this stanza (3) is more prosaic but no less profound. First, the poet cites what is objectionable: 'They do not want to be defined. / They don't want to be limited.' Then he enumerates that which is desired and not desirable:

And they want fire refined.
And they want to love who they want,
And for it not to be an affront,
They do not want to beg for their humanity,
Or for the right to be
Creative, different, or surprising,
Or *wild*, or defying
Of boundaries.

(Ibid.; emphasis added)

Far from evoking the grand narrative of modernism with its Marxist emancipation of workers, or Adam Smith's economic growth of nations, 'The Golden House of Sand' becomes a symbol of the rhetorical ambivalence that is Africa: crisis and opportunity, deprivation and abundance, alienation and identification. As the poem deliberately equivocates, it is a continent of intense loss coupled with the comforting knowledge of belonging (Gray 2007: 194). And, just as participation is a key to postmodernity, so too is the poet, a native-born Nigerian domiciled in London for the greater part of his life, a participant in this micro-narrative 'dream', and in being-towards-death. The antithetical play of what (black) people do and do not want is, not surprisingly, subverted in the erasure of boundaries, as in 'everywhereness' which implies a temporal and spatial remove from the specific.

Pivotal concepts throughout this anthology are lack of limitations, a breaking of boundaries. 'The interplay between perception (or perspective) and reality,' says Van Niekerk, 'is a central concern of postmodernism (the difference between modernism and postmodernism lies in how each *perceives* things – they are different worldviews' (2012: 16; original emphasis). A comparable postmodern reconfiguration of the human condition occurs in Stanzas 1 and 3 of 'The Soul of Nations':

> The soul of nations do not change;
> They merely stretch their hidden range.
> Just as rivers do not sleep,
> The mind of empire still runs deep.
> Into the river many waters flow
> The merging and conquest – history's glow
> ...
> Classes overflow their rigid boundaries
> Slowly stirring dreary quandaries
> Accents diverse ring from its soul,
> A richer music revealing the whole.
>
> (Okri 2012a: 28)

Here, the Sublime is systematized in Claude Lévi-Strauss's semiology of culture. In his theory of Structural Anthropology, Lévi-Strauss argues that language is the system that permits thinking. Thinking is the 'system output' that occurs in the interaction between human subjects (situated within culture) and the environment (Nature) which is the object of thinking. However, the interplay between historical conquest and naturalistic tropes defies the kind of distinction Lévi-Strauss conceives of between Nature (non-human) and culture (human). In the closing couplet, Okri suggests that the demise of imperialism will be brought about by a coalition of the physical and metaphysical: 'History moves and the surface quivers / But the gods are steadfast in the depth of rivers' (ibid.: 28).

Our perceptions are shaped by and, in turn, shape our histories (Van Niekerk 2012: 17). For Leotard (1992) and Lévi-Strauss ([1963] 1972), language is the medium through which this shaping of perception is possible; it is through language that we materialize our ideas. 'At its strongest,' assert Appignanesi and Garratt, 'the anthropic principle suggests that human consciousness is somehow "fitted" to the universe, not only as a component but as an observation necessary to give the universe meaning' (2007: 110). The utopia, here, is not a destination but an evanescent 'noplace' from which to reimagine the African Diaspora and to contest history just as it is in 'Lines *in Potentis*', a poem that invokes an 'axis mundi' to facilitate transformation in

> One of the magic centres of the world;
> One of the world's dreaming places
> Ought to point the way to the world
> For here lives the great music of humanity,
> The harmonization of different
> Histories, cultures, geniuses, and dreams. (Stanza 1: 26)
> ...
> Tomorrow's music sleeps
> In our fingers, in our awakening
> Souls, the blossom of our spirit,
> The suggestive buds of our heart. (Stanza 3: 27)

This poem resonates with subtle allusions to Mircea Eliade's *The Myth of the Eternal Return* (1989) in these stanzas and, likewise, in the final stanza, to Percy Bysshe Shelley's 'Ode to the West Wind' and to John Keats's 'To Autumn' and 'Ode to a Nightingale', shot through with Keats's doctrine of negative capability:[3]

> And while Autumn dallies
> With the West wind
> And the weeping nightingales,
> And Winter clears its sonorous throat
> At the Antipodean banquets, preparing
> For the speech of hoarfrost
> And icicles conjured from living breath,
> I want you to tell everyone
> Through trumpets played
> With the fragrance of roses, that
> A mysterious reason has brought us
> All together,
> Here, now, under the all-seeing
> Eye of the sun.
>
> (Stanza 5: 27)

And, as in Keats's 'Hyperion' where 'One moon with alteration slow, had shed / Her silver seasons four upon the night', in 'Lines ...', the affect is 'flow', reinforced by the cycle of all four seasons: 'Spring waits', 'Summer lingers', 'Autumn dallies' and 'Winter clears its sonorous throat'. The implied shift is 'away from *ideas* in the mind to the *language* in which thinking is expressed' (Appignanesi and Garratt 2007: 56).[4] In this context, one can argue that the Latin, *in potentis*, in the title, has flowed into English, which itself flowed into a global 'lingua franca', the language of travel, the airways and space, like the music of 'undiscovered'/'undefined future orchestras' that transcends borders (cf. Gray 2001). In an evocation of William Blake's aphorism 'without contraries, there is no progress', nightmares are juxtaposed with illumination; boredom with brilliance; slave trading with a dance of souls; division with unity; and chaos with fiestas. By implying that each of the initial concepts is a contrary to be transcended, Okri achieves a dialectic of release. An overarching cosmic dimension, evoked in the omnipresence rather than omnipotence of 'the all-seeing eye of Ra/Sol/the sun' and, by implication, this son of the earth and the skies, informs transfiguration in this poem.

For Okri, heaven and earth constitute a single indivisible unity, which is governed by cosmic law. Okri elucidates: '[T]he metaphysical dimension to my work is something that comes out of the African tradition. There is something about that tradition which, because it doesn't see reality as clearly demarcated as is currently seen in the West, because we have this whole thing about realms of reality, [this] already gives you a metaphysical view of life, even if you are an atheist' (2012b). Boundaries between the supernatural world and that of man do not exist. Like George Gamadmer, Okri considers a person's horizon (his/her historicity and linguistically constituted context) to be 'the production ground of all understanding rather than a negative factor or impediment to be overcome' (Linge 1997: xiv).

Postmodernism in Okri can perhaps be best understood in Jan Szmyd's synopsis of Anna-Teresa Tymieniecka's phenomenology, involving

> a permanent search for new cognitive possibilities for especially metaphysical and anthropological problems, effective avoidance of being locked up in one unchanging intellectual horizon and paradigm, complete openness to new options and cognitive prospects, scientific and philosophical discoveries, far-reaching tolerance for different ideas and intellectual tendencies. (2011: 29)

Okri's third poetry anthology requires the same 'openness'; it begins and ends with poems dedicated to the memory of his late mother and father, respectively, a bookending (to use Okri's own terminology) or sequencing that reflects the postmodern notion of 'being-towards-death'. Martin Heidegger deploys this term in his discussion of understanding and meaning. 'Being-towards-death', Heidegger claims, is pivotal in achieving 'Dasein', already defined.

In the opening poem, 'My Mother Sleeps', for example, Okri recalls both the deprivation of childhood ('sleeping in dark corners', 'Or on wooden chairs in the green / Darkness', or on 'cement platforms near the gutter') and the blessedness of his mother's 'kindly eyes' and 'parted lips' that soothed his 'anxious soul', sitting in a chair, 'watching our / Future become our past' (2012a: 9–10). Then, evocative of the adage 'The child is father to the man', the eulogy closes with '*Now* that she sleeps / In my battered armchair / ... / *I* am watching over her. / *My* turn has come round at last' (ibid.: 10; emphases added). This is a poem 'not about her passing away; it's about her presence', Okri insists, a presence that is continuous, that is indicative of a transcendent awareness of the eternal Now, as in his 'clear lucid stream of everywhereness', with which this chapter began. The implication of the philosophical hermeneutics is that happiness can only be attained if one is attuned to the finitude of existence, aware of one's own historicity, interconnected.

Likewise informed by the nostalgic imperative, but imbued with greater emotive complexity, the penultimate stanza of 'Lion, Roam No More', dedicated to his often estranged, late father, appeals to the lawyer Silver Okri for guidance: 'Into my blood / Plant the secrets of the way / That I may live / More wisely every day. / Imbue me with your myth, / Solid, silvery one, / That I be attuned / With the magic of the sun' (2012a: 96). The heartfelt injunctions here suggest a system to be understood and an uncertainty in which a host of independent memories consort with one another to produce spontaneous self-organization as in the closing lines to Stanza 1: 'Be the invisible warrior / In my life's upward fight / As I strive for more love / And for more light' (ibid.: 95). The eulogy closes with a plea for release for the 'troubled mind' of the son and for eternal rest for his father – for equipoise in the father-son relationship.

So, far from degenerating into elegies or psychodynamic crises of memory and karma, these two poems are full of presences that permeate the volume, seemingly allowing the poet to participate in life: to live his own life more fully or, as West expresses it, '[l]iving while one is alive' (1996: 101–2). 'We don't have a clearly demarcated sense of death in Africa,' Okri explains. 'We have a graded sense of the passing away of people' (2012b). Both poems reflect the postmodern condition of stepping out of time, of experiencing 'a moment / In timelessness' (1999: 3). 'The splendour of the moment,' Russell Dicarlo (2005) muses, 'so dazzles us, our compulsive chattering minds give pause, so as not to mentally whisk us away to a place other than the here-and-now. Bathed in luminescence, a door seems to open to another reality, always present, yet rarely witnessed' (Okri 1999: xv). Dicarlo reminds us that Abraham Maslow called these 'peak experiences' (2005).

It seems apposite to complete the hermeneutic circle by returning to the notion of 'Dasein' or authentic human experience such as the sublime. I, therefore, close with a poem in which Okri invites us to participate in such a 'peak experience'. Stanzas 1–3 of 'Towards the Sublime' are particularly pertinent:

> Have you noticed that in all true
> Transformations what emerges
> Is stranger than before,
> And higher, richer, magical?
> It is as if mass yields
> Light, or pure
> Vision given upward
> Form beyond form –
> Transcending all the laws
> Of its previous condition.
> And so chrysalis into butterfly,
> Water into wine, death
> Into life, weight into
> Flight, burden into illumination,
> Enchantment into the freedom
> Divine.
>
> (2012a: 56)

It becomes evident that Okri's concept of 'magic' inheres in natural transformations as in the marvellous unfoldment of 'chrysalis into butterfly'. Embedded in notions of holism, interconnections, order out of chaos (where chaos signifies a kind of order without periodicity) and the idea of an autonomous, self-governing nature, this complex poem encapsulates Eckart Tolle's proem to *The Power of Now* in which he declares: 'You are here to enable the divine / purpose of the universe to unfold' (2005). In Okri's perception of the Sublime, the successive transformations – both physical and metaphysical – invoke an expansiveness when we 'sneak a peek' into the eternal realm of Being itself, if only for an epiphanic moment, the 'moment / In timelessness' already mentioned, when we come home 'To the sublime within, / Given new being. / Beyond measure. / A joy to the ages' ('Towards the Sublime' (2012a: 56)).

In what, then, does the complexity of Okri's postmodern art inhere? It is perhaps his recognition that 'the lucid stream of everywhereness' is the intaglio of intangibles that embody the hopes and longings of a people, adumbrating a national culture. It is the spirit of the incommensurable that determines the basic issue of cultural experience (Gray 2007). Thus, as in Paul Ricceour's 'no place', the paradoxical connotation of 'everywhereness' is that it is the only space through which the utopian imagination can contest the past and reshape the future – to rewrite 'the space in which [we] slept' (1998: 110). Okri closes *A Time for New Dreams* with

> [a]ll great cultures renew themselves by accepting the challenges of their times, and, like the Biblical David, forge their vision and courage in the secret laboratory of the *wild*, wrestling with their demons and perfecting their character. We must transform ourselves or perish. (2011: 146; original emphasis)

For Okri, renewal lies in and through conscious creativity. In a poem entitled 'The Ruin and the Forest', for example, he writes: 'Creation should be new every time: / New in relation to the chaos that is there / Chaos is new all the time / … / Creation must be reborn / With a new light / With the new dawn. / New every day' (*Wild* 2012a: 44). It is Okri's philosophical thinking, coupled with his groundbreaking literary aesthetics, that makes him one of postmodernity's most profound conceptual artists.

11

Survivalist culture in 'Laughter beneath the Bridge'

Introduction

This prize-winning short story from *Incidents at the Shrine* ([1986] 1993) is a child's eye view of the Nigerian Civil War. The chapter starts by briefly contextualizing Biafra's quest for freedom in the late 1960s. In the broad context of civil war in Africa and the quest for freedom, it is rare indeed to find such a substantial body of literature as is evidenced by Nigerians in their multi-generic representations of the Nigerian Civil War of 1967–70. Reflecting fifty years later on one of the bloodiest wars in modern history, former Leiden Africa Studies Centre fellow Jays Julius-Adeoye observes: 'Some writers have classified the Nigeria-Biafra War as a genocidal response by the Nigerian military government under General Yakubu Gowan to the 30 May 1967 declaration of independence of the Republic of Biafra by Colonel Chukwuemeka Odumegwu Ojukwu' (2017: Introduction). Other writers have sought to justify the war, believing that the Federal government acted wisely in its attempt to prevent 'the splintering of the territory by force' (ibid.). Creative writers, in their fictive, autobiographical reconstructions of wartime existence, belong largely to the former category. One such is acclaimed writer Ben Okri.

A rousing tale of civil war and the curtailment of freedom, 'Laughter beneath the Bridge' alludes to the demise of Igboland in the Biafran war of secession (1967–70), otherwise known as the Nigerian Civil War. This short story explores the impact of civil strife on a nameless Igbo mother and her young son. Freedom, or the lack thereof, is thus considered from both a personal/ethnic perspective and a national viewpoint. A correlative of the girl child narrative voices in Chinua Achebe's *Girls at War and Other Stories* ([1977] 1983), Okri's story is an example of a relatively rare perspective – that of a 10-year-old boy as the narrating, experiencing ingénue. It is nonetheless rich in socio-historical and cultural interest.

Significantly, it can be read as a moving tale that shows the universality of survivalist culture. One of the few Jewish holocaust survivors, Elie Wiesel, attests to this claim when, in his *Souls on Fire*, he asserts: 'Revolt is not a solution, neither is submission. What remains is laughter, metaphysical laughter' (1972).

In an Afterword to his *The Book of Laughter and Forgetting*, Czech-born exile Milan Kundera explains what is meant by 'metaphysical laughter' ([1980] 1983: 232–3).

Drawing attention to the Absurd,[1] as does Okri in 'Laughter beneath the Bridge', Kundera responds to his parable that illustrates metaphysical laughter by pointing to the irony that the devil laughs because God's world seems senseless to him, while the angel laughs, but with joy, because everything in the world has its meaning. Pertinently, he draws a correlation with humankind: '[M]an uses the same physiologic manifestation – laughter – to express the two different metaphysical attitudes' (ibid.: 232). In illustration, Kundera provides the example of someone's hat falling 'on the coffin in a freshly dug grave' (ibid.). Quite obviously, he notes, 'the funeral loses its meaning and laughter is born' (ibid.). Contrary to this type of devil's laughter is that of angels: 'Two lovers race through the meadow, holding hands, laughing. Their laughter has nothing to do with jokes or humor, it is the *serious* laughter of angels expressing their joy of being' (ibid.: 233; original emphasis). He concludes with the philosophical paradox: 'Both kinds of laughter belong to life's pleasures, but when it is carried to extremes it also denotes a dual apocalypse: the enthusiastic laughter of angel-fanatics, who are so convinced of their world's significance that they are ready to hang anyone not sharing their joy. And the other laughter, sounding from the opposite side, which proclaims that everything has become meaningless, that even funerals are ridiculous' (ibid.). Here, the tension between fanaticism and scepticism signifies the kind of comic pantomime that Nigerian-born Londoner Okri writes of in his 'Laughter beneath the Bridge', as well as in his 'The Comic Destiny' from *Tales of Freedom* (2009)[2] or that which Florence-born exile Dante Alighieri elaborated on in his celebrated medieval epic poem, *The Divine Comedy* ([1939] 1975).

While Wiesel and his father were survivors of both Auschwitz and Buchenwald, capturing the horrors of Nazi Germany's extermination of its Jewish citizenry in his stirring yet spiritually uplifting novel about the Second World War entitled *Souls on Fire: Portraits and Legends of Hasidic Masters* (1972), Okri, whose mother was part Igbo and 'de facto' perceived as the enemy of a united Nigeria, is a survivor of the conundrum of internecine warfare. In an interview with Julia Rix in 2010, Okri explains: 'My mother was half Igbo [from the south-east of Nigeria] while my father was Urhobo, from the Delta region, so the war was a family thing. We spent a lot of time hiding Mum – and I nearly got killed, I'm still stunned by what people are able to do to their neighbours' (2010: 7). These facets of reality are incorporated into 'Laughter beneath the Bridge' to horrifying effect.

Although the two historical events (the Nigerian Civil War and the Holocaust) are by no means equivalent, both writers fictionalize the all-too-common experience of 'man's inhumanity to man', to invoke the common dictum; both underscore two intertwined imperatives of the human condition: freedom and laughter. Despite the common tropes as evidence of the indomitable human spirit, the concern here is not with representations of Germany but with that of Nigeria. Four years after the republication of *Incidents at the Shrine*, Okri highlights the paradox of survivalist culture in *A Way of Being Free*, musing: 'It is possible that a sense of beauty, of justice, of the interconnectedness of all things, may yet save the human species from self-annihilation' (1997: 132). Arguing that it should not be left to the 'contemporary victors' to speak (or write) 'for human history', he cites Achebe's dictum that 'suffering should also give rise to something beautiful' (ibid.).[3] Okri has his young narrator wondering why he remembers the war as 'a beautiful time' (1997: 9). Perhaps this explains why Okri asserts that '[w]e are all still learning how to be free. Freedom is the beginning of the greatest possibilities of the human genius. It is not the goal' (ibid.). As conceptual artists, Achebe, Kundera, Okri and Wiesel transmit to close gaps and to create much needed bonds.

The right to benefit from their rich oil reserves was, arguably, a principal factor for the Igbo determination to secede, but power was also a motivating factor. Whatever the causes, the outcome was the tragedy of civil warfare.

The Nigerian Civil War (1967–70) in brief

Rejecting 'subtlety' for uncharacteristic 'ideological zealotry' in his war memoir, *There Was a Country: A Memoir* (2012), as Biodun Jeyifo comments (in Julius-Adeoye 2017), Achebe ascribes the resultant starvation to power broking by a local chief, Obafemi Awolowo, indicting him for his 'overriding ambition' for personal and tribal (Yoruba) power. Recollecting the tragic loss of homeland, Achebe writes: 'In the Biafran case it meant hatching up a diabolical policy to reduce the numbers of his enemies significantly through starvation' (2012: 233).

To reveal the ideological constructedness of both abstract and concrete aspects of wartime existence in Nigeria and the dynamic between them in relation to the trajectory of 'Laughter beneath the Bridge', it is necessary to provide a brief overview of the 30-month-long war, described as 'undeniably the worst in the twentieth century' (Julius-Adeoye 2017). Just as the world is all too familiar with the term 'Holocaust', so too are we familiar with that of 'Biafra'. The very young and the old were among the first to suffer from the famine caused by the fighting in what was known as Biafra. Notwithstanding the severe hardship and widely photographed emaciated children that resulted from the collapse of the breakaway state's 'economy' (read 'starvation into submission') during the civil war, dismissive reconstructions of the war from the early 1980s were published, such as 'Biafra, the name of an abortive Nigerian secessionist state (1967–1970) in the south-east of the country, inhabited principally by Ibo [*sic*] people'. This report goes on to explain the reason for the decision to secede: 'It seceded after mounting antagonism between the eastern region and the western and northern regions, Colonel Ojukwu declaring the east independent. Civil war followed.' The journalist follows with the reaction of Nigeria's immediate neighbours and that of the United Kingdom and Russia, stating that 'Gabon, Ivory Coast, Tanzania, and Zambia recognized Biafra, while Britain and the USSR supported the federal government. When Ojukwu fled to the Ivory Coast, General Effiong capitulated in Lagos in 1970 and Biafra ceased to exist' (1968: 1005).[4]

Pointing to the impact of the conflict on Okri, Sarah Abdullah (2017: 1) unintentionally underestimates it with a bland statement: 'The event gave him first hand exposure to suffering', but then she quickly observes that 'his war experiences very much shaped his consciousness as a writer as they exposed many of the coercive political structures that were operative at the time and sensitized him to issues of ethnic violence in a conflict ridden society' (ibid.). This petro-fiction is testified to in

Okri's Booker Prize-winning novel, *The Famished Road* (1991), his short story under discussion and *The Freedom Artist* (2019).

It is of interest that after the Biafran war, Kundera's Czechoslovakia, which was all too soon to suffer a similar fate of erasure, had joined forces with the Soviet Union to supply the Nigerian victors with jet fighters and transport aircraft (*The Almanac of World Military Power* 1972: 238). Not without pathos, Kundera – jazz pianist turned writer – was later to reflect: 'If someone had told me as a boy: One day you will see your nation vanish from the world, I would have considered it nonsense, something I couldn't possibly imagine.' He adds philosophically: 'A man knows that he is mortal, but he takes it for granted that his nation possesses a kind of eternal life' ([1980] 1983: 229). This remark was precipitated by the recognition that in the previous fifty years, forty million Ukrainians had been 'quietly vanishing from the world without the world paying any heed' (Kundera [1980] 1983: 229–30) – five times as many as the eight million who perished with their country, Biafra. Both Okri/Achebe's Biafra and Kundera's Czechoslovakia have ceased to exist. But not so the lasting impact.

On the aftermath of the Nigerian Civil War, A. M. A. Kirk-Greene (1970: 340) ponders on the deep causes of the civil war – the how and the why – and 'who was to blame'; he predicts that 'all these [are] issues that will arouse many sorts of minds to continuing analysis and argument' (ibid.) and then draws a parallel with the American Civil War that still haunts the American psyche, saying, 'The time-span is unlikely to be less than that covered by the shadows of suffering and suspicion inseparable from the aftermath of any civil war. It may, given the precedence of the American Civil War, last for longer: the rights and wrongs of that tragedy have their ardent advocates a hundred years and more after Gettysburg' (ibid.). Kirk-Greene concludes ominously: '*The wounds of history do not heal quickly; some indeed leave their mark on the nation's soul for ever*' (ibid.; emphasis added). The implication is that shared memory is a survival tactic. Anna-Teresa Tymieniecka interpolates usefully on the abstraction of 'the soul'. She argues, 'The human soul, having the mind, consciousness as its instrument, projects and negotiates with the life horizons' (2011: 11). Believing that the soul is the preeminent vital life force, she adds:

> And so the living agent, with the influx of individualizing life of the specifically human inventive/ creative/ imaginative system through which the human mind operates, projects not only necessary links for the vitally expanded functioning of ontopoietic becoming, but also and foremost unfolds in tandem innumerable morally, aesthetically, emotionally, imaginatively evaluative threads as well as other lines of sense through which the living agent progressively acquires a human mind. (Ibid.)

Mind and soul, she posits, function together; they are complementary and co-supportive: 'The human mind continues the work of the vegetatively-vitally subservient agent now unfolded in a self that imaginatively projects, in a determined, self-selective, and self-decisive human individual' (ibid.). The core of her inaugural lecture, from which this phenomenological excerpt is taken, climaxes with an explanation on how consciousness and, by extension, the intuitive consciousness of writers are linked firmly to transformative powers:

> The intentional system of consciousness directing this entire apparatus of life and compassing its full extent – from primitive sensing, feeling, desiring, evaluating to constituting the world, to esoteric longings to escape all that existentially binds and to transcend it – that is, the living agent, who incorporates the prerogatives of the human mind, amounts to what we call the 'soul', in whose fulgurating *symphony* of life's becoming, the entire course of life resounds into *infinite* realms. (Ibid.; emphases added)

Fellow Nigerian Kole Omotoso (possibly one of the most widely published post-civil war writers) comments, in his 1997 *Woza Africa* (*Come on Africa*): *Music Goes to War*, on the cacophonous 'marks on the soul' of war-torn Africa. His rhetorical question 'What is happening in Africa?' is followed by the lamentation: 'Why are signs of positive gains being overwhelmed by tragedies of sisters and brothers killing one another? Why are children being wasted and men, women and the aged turned into *heaps of corpses* and stragglers on refugee routes through the forests and valleys of Africa? Surely something is wrong with our continent' (1997; emphasis added). Omotoso's rhetorical questions regarding internecine strife invoke a mythic conjunction of Kundera's devil's laughter and Julia Kristeva's notion of abjection. Regarding the chilling symbolism of 'heaps of corpses', Kristeva argues in the *Powers of Horror* that what she terms 'the abject' is a breakdown of meaning caused by the loss of distinction between subject and object or between self and other (1982: 2–3).

'Laughter beneath the Bridge'

An incident in Okri's short story serves to illustrate Kristeva's fracturing abjection. En route to their home village, the lorry carrying the child narrator and his mother is stopped at a checkpoint where the passengers are searched and interrogated. In the course of the interrogation, some passengers are summarily shot, and a young woman is brutally gang raped. Yet the stupefied passengers either turn a blind eye to the violence or, concerned with their own fate, offer no resistance to it (cf. Abdullah 2017: 1). More pertinently, Kristeva explains that the primary example of this breakdown of meaning is the *corpse*, for it traumatically reminds us of our own materiality.[5] This symbolism pertains to 'Laughter beneath the Bridge' where, together with the bridge, it becomes emblematic for lack of freedom and the horror of internecine strife that erodes that freedom.

Okri transports us imaginatively to consider the loss of meaning caused by the insanity of warfare. Here, where the bridge becomes a simulacra for those in power, that is, those with the power to inflict violence, those 'beneath' the bridge are the living dead caught in the fray, together with the bloated corpses in the river below the bridge that can no longer flow because it is choked with 'the swollen bodies that were *laughing*' (Okri 1997: 18) – a dirge of the devil in a symbiosis of Wiesel and Kundera's metaphysical laughter and Kristeva's abjection. In addition to the corpses, Okri picks up on a correlative physiological symbol that, in line with Kristeva, elicits the horror of the abject (i.e. 'shit') and its attendant macabre laughter. Being gruffly interrogated by a soldier with the comical, allusive sobriquet of Frank O'Nero and instructed to 'speak a word of your language' to prove he is his mother's son, the child – choking back his terrified laughter – blurts out the only word he can recall in his father's language. The word is incomprehensible to the inept soldier, so mother quickly interprets 'that he wants to shit' (ibid.: 8). The expletive 'shit' has the same effect as Kundera's example of the hat on the coffin; the bully's authority is completely undone, and '[t]he soldiers passed the joke all the way round the barricade' (ibid.).

The argument shows how the writer's graphic symbolism mediates perceptions of time and place informed by the ideology of power and violence while, at the same time, having singular signifying possibilities and so limitations. These possibilities and limitations are pointed to in a synopsis of Okri's short story, where its title suggests either 'the fusion of the phenomenal and divine worlds in artistic representation', to quote Volynsky's transcendental Platonic view of symbolism in 1900 (Chadwick 1971: 58); or, in terms of human symbolism, where '[t]he Symbolist tries to arouse in the reader by the melody of his verse [or poetic prose] a particular mood' (Bryusov in 1894, in Chadwick 1971: 58), the laughter beneath the bridge conflates both signifier and signified to evoke absurdity and metaphysical laughter.

In terms of setting, the story can be divided into three sections. It begins in an evacuated boarding school where three abandoned children anxiously await the coming of their mothers. Sadly, only the narrator's mother arrives, and she dare not risk implicating the remaining two children in the accident of her own birth. The bitter satire of their alternative, inevitable fate is patent! Then there is the journey in a dilapidated lorry through the forest away from Igboland, involving further trauma at the checkpoints. And, as a prelude to the final setting on the bridge manned by trigger-happy soldiers, there is a brief but important interlude of homecoming and cultural enactments of the Egungun ritual among the young village children. This ritual ultimately brings the innocents, in a fatal final dance, onto the bridge and into the hands of power and violence.

The opening gambit at once draws the reader imaginatively and emotionally into the civil war milieu and its impact on the young left to forage for survival: 'Those were long days as we lay pressed to the prickly grass waiting for the bombs to fall … Three of us were left behind. We all hoped someone would turn up to collect us. We were silent most of the time' (Okri 1997: 1). The backdrop to this dramatic scene is yet more chillingly symbolic with vultures circling the school, 'religious maniacs' screaming about 'the end of the world', 'a wild bunch of people from the city scattered through searching for those of the rebel tribe' (ibid.) and opportunistically looting the chapel. Reminiscent of Wiesel's adage: 'What remains is laughter, metaphysical laughter', life has lost its meaning as underlined by the bathetic images of the Irish priest furiously peddling away on his Raleigh bicycle and ghosts flitting through the ransacked chapel. The transparency of these negative symbols is, however, mediated by positive ones: a multitude of lizards take over the school premises, while the child narrator, as displacement activity, 'dreams' of his childhood sweetheart, Monica. So, what could these two symbols – lizards and dreams of Monica – signify? In what ways can they be read as correlatingly positive?

In Mazizi Kunene's *Anthem of the Decades: A Zulu Epic* (1981), the salamander symbolizes swiftness and an absence of ingenuity. The Zulus of South Africa see it as the opposite of the chameleon, which represents slowness and ingenuity. Sopelekai Maithufi perhaps comes closer to what may be Okri's intention, saying that both animals should not be seen as binary opposites or as standing for them. He explains that it is about harmony and reconciling the thesis with the antithesis. In other words, the solution is synthesis. Illustrative of creative genius with its implication of harmonious coexistence, the ingenuous narrator conceives of a parallel harmony in his escapist thoughts of Monica and the lizards, stating: 'I dreamed of her new-formed breasts when the lizards chased us from the dormitories, and when the noise of the fighter planes drove us to the forests' ([1986] 1993: 3). The narrator's coping mechanisms, here, reveal a growing consciousness in the young child.

Thus, much of the ideological constructedness of wartime existence in Nigeria is embedded in the narrative viewpoint. Drawing attention to creative construction, Okri provides a useful metafictional aphorism: 'The basic prerequisite for literature is freedom', and significantly in terms of the young narrator's awaking dreams, Okri adds: 'The first freedom is mental freedom' (2015: 1042). Abdullah concurs, saying: 'The beauty of the narration lies in the very fact of the child narrator reporting with the utmost objectivity without spelling out things for the reader so that what the reader eventually has is a graphic picture with all its horrors intact' (2017: 3). Despite some factual errors, Abdullah concludes with a pivotal statement about Okri's narrative strategy: 'Hence it is not an event that is built up through a series of images but the images that build up an event thereby developing the narrative in a series of vivid visual shots' (ibid.). Extending the operation of eidetic memory, it is through the child's obsessive preoccupation with Monica that the narrator matures gradually and sufficiently to experience the meaning of civil war in all its ugly reality and to realize that once Monica is unmasked and captured, the soldiers will have their way with her and he will never see her again. 'Tragic fate,' writes Soyinka, 'is the repetitive cycle of the taboo of nature, the karmic act of hubris witting or unwitting, into which demonic will within man constantly compels him' ([1988] 1993: 36).

In his portrayal of Monica, Okri successfully creates the young girl child as a mediating moral force among the Nigerian power brokers and leaders. To borrow loosely from Ezenwa-Ohaeto,[6] Okri goes beyond the sociopolitical level to the deeper, more fundamental level of the myth of origin. 'In the myth, the Almighty sent His daughter, Idemili, to the earth in order to give a moral character to Power, which in the beginning "rampaged our world naked"' ([1986] 1993: 134). As leitmotif, dreaming of Monica serves to unify the three phases of the story.

Forced to abandon his school mates when his Igbo mother collects him, the narrator 'tried to think only of Monica' (Okri [1986] 1993: 4); on board the homeward-bound lorry, 'starving and bored' (6), he again thinks of Monica; clouted by a soldier for mimicking the blowing of his nose onto the lemon grass at a checkpoint, he 'saw one of Monica's masks in the stars' (ibid.); bemused by the brutal raping of a fellow traveller, he 'thought of Monica' (7); and it is her brother, his little friend Ugo, who was shot and tossed into the river, ominously giving a 'face' to one of the corpses 'beneath the bridge'. Prefiguring the final dramatic action in the tale, Monica is captured for belligerently speaking her language – understood to be that of the enemy – after having her Egungun mask torn off her face, itself a cultural sign of ill-omen. Early on, we read that the precocious Monica broke the 'sexual taboos and began dancing our street's Egungun round town, fooling all the men' (ibid.: 2).

In *Myth, Literature and the African World*, Wole Soyinka provides insight into the significance of the Nigerian Egungun ritual and Monica's capture in the context of dramatic depictions of man's attempt to come to terms with the spatial phenomenon of his being: 'The real unvoiced fear is: will this protagonist survive confrontation with forces that exist within the dangerous area of transformation?' ([1976] 1995: 42). The Nigerian Nobel laureate elucidates: 'Entering that *microcosm* involves a loss of individuation, a self-submergence in universal essence. It is an act undertaken on behalf of the community, and the welfare of that protagonist is inseparable from that of the total community' (ibid.; original emphasis).

Even more pertinent for the discussion is the description of Monica's truly harrowing experience – urinating 'down her thighs', shivering 'in her own puddle' and wailing and jabbering 'in her own language' (Okri [1986] 1993: 21). It can be deduced that this is the mother tongue of those 'born (un)free' in the context of the Nigerian Civil War. However involuntary, these actions prefigure Monica's capture and death 'on behalf of the community'. Soyinka concludes that '[t]he transmission is individual. It is no less essential to the sum of fragmented experiences, individual and vicarious' (1995: 42). Thus, Monica's 'insane laughing mask split in the middle of the face' (Okri [1986] 1993: 21) serves not only to evoke a 'consoling metaphysical statement from natural phenomenon' (Soyinka 1995: 42) but also to remind us of Wiesel's maxim on 'metaphysical laughter', of Kundera's explication thereof and of Kristeva's notion of the 'abject'. Multiple allusions to the devil's laughter in 'Laughter beneath the Bridge' weave a linear thread throughout this tragicomedy.

In addition to those already examined, consider, for example, the sight of three grown men 'huddled in a pit' (Okri [1986] 1993: 5) and the child narrator's account: 'One of them had been shot through the teeth. Another one was punctured with gunshots and his face was so contorted it seemed he had died from too much laughing' (ibid.); with '[t]he taste of madness like the water of potent springs, the laughter of war,' the 10-year-old narrator reminisces, 'that is perhaps why I remember it as a beautiful time. And because in the lorry, with corpses drifting past along the road and soldiers noisy in their jeeps, we were all silent' (ibid.: 9). Exacerbating the agony, the young protagonist adds that '[t]he soldiers were laughing above the bridge ... Above on the bridge, one of the soldiers laughed so hard he had to cough and spit at the end of it' (ibid.: 17). And, just prior to the narrator's realization of what was causing the terrible smell from the river and Monica's explanation that she sat under the bridge because that was where Ugo's body had been tossed into the river, we read that 'she started to laugh. I had never heard that sort of twisted laughter before. After a while I couldn't see her clearly and I called her and she laughed and then I thought it was all the swollen corpses that were laughing' (ibid.: 18). These graphic instances conflate in an elegiac fugue. As if commenting on the inevitability of the death that follows the unmasking of the Egungun, a symbol for the transitional deaths of both Monica and Biafra in this story, Kundera writes: 'When a big power wants to deprive a small country of its national consciousness it uses the method of *organized forgetting* ... Politics unmasks the metaphysics of private life, private life unmasks the metaphysics of politics' ([1980] 1983: 235; original emphasis). In *Long Drums and Cannons*, Margaret Laurence and Nora Foster Stoval tellingly observe: 'Masks are a tangible means of connection with the other world.' Elaborating on the metaphysics of the Egungun culture – where dancer and Egungun merge – they add that '[masks] are regarded with reverence and at the same time provide a near-touching of the revered object-god become flesh – for in the act of the possession of the dancer by the spirit of the mask, dancer and mask merge in a union of the mortal and the immortal' (2001: 18).

Of the importance of remembering the past that Okri reconstructs for the country of his birth, Kundera expounds: 'A nation which loses its past gradually loses its self. And so the political situation has brutally illuminated the ordinary metaphysical problem of forgetting that we face all the time, every day, without paying any attention' ([1980]1983: 235). Faced with the 'abject', or with what Kristeva (1982: 3) describes as being 'at the border of my condition as a living being', one can choose to 'expel' oneself, to 'spit' oneself out or to redream the world, as Okri suggests in 'Laughter beneath the Bridge' (1993) and in *A Way of Being Free* (1997). In the latter, non-fictional book, almost in echo of Achebe's notion of the birth of the beautiful via suffering, Okri asserts: 'Whatever resilience has kept wounded people and devastated continents here, alive, can be transfigured to make them strong, confident, and serene. They have to question everything in order to build for the future' (1997: 132). Thus, the key to the thrust of Okri's short story can, arguably, be found in its closing aphorism: 'The young shall grow' ([1986] 1993: 22), for this, too, is the legend painted on the side of the 'old wooden bodywork' (4) of the overcrowded lorry transporting the Igbo mother and her pre-teen son away from Biafra, on their journey through the insect-infested forest where Nigerian soldiers wait to torture, rape and butcher their countryfolk. Recalling his experience in the Biafran army, Achike Udenwa (2011, Chapter 6) highlights the iniquities of rape, prostitution and murder as endemic to the war and the war's deleterious effect on the Igbo community and on society in general. The juxtaposed dichotomy between death and survival is, of course, evocative of the cycle of life.

Conclusion

The key concepts in this chapter are freedom, laughter, the abject, power and literary representation of civil war. I have striven to highlight the ways in which civil war affects the two principal characters in Okri's short story: the young boy narrator, who relies largely on displacement activity as a coping mechanism, obsessing about the lead girl child, Monica; and Monica, the emergent young adult and sacrificial lamb. The argument invokes Wiesel and Kundera's notions of metaphysical laughter to determine the meaning of the term 'laughter' in Okri's title to his short story. Kristeva's notion of the abject is deployed to suggest the impact of power and violence.

In a subsection of her *Powers of Horror*, entitled 'An Exile Who Asks "Where"?' Kristeva argues: 'The one by whom the abject exists is thus a *deject* who places (himself), *separates* (himself), and therefore *strays* instead of getting his bearings, desiring, belonging, of refusing' (1982: 8; original emphases). Significantly, she concedes that this is '[s]ituationist in a sense, and not without laughter – since laughing is a way of placing or displacing abjection' (ibid.). Using her notion of the abject, the discussion has attempted to allude to the fine line between 'laughing with' and 'laughing at', between pleasure and pain. Focusing on the pleasure/pain paradox illuminates how satire works in Okri's story. The freedom to laugh[7] juxtaposed with the curbing of laughter can be explicitly connected with the physical pain and suffering of the characters, particularly that of the young narrator, suggesting how readers are implicated in and redeemed from represented systemic violence.

As if pointing to Okri's motivation for the composition of 'Laughter beneath the Bridge' and the need for its wider dissemination, K. Olu-Ololabi laments the dearth of critical capacity in Nigeria. He attributes the state of regression to this fact and contends that '[a]ll these signs of impending perilous times are products of our unexamined living ... but the good life, an ideal that philosophers have sought since time immemorial, can only be realised by constant rigorous and critical reflection' (2011: 43). This kind of critical rigour is, however, evident in responses to the Nigerian war writings of Achebe, Saro-Wiwa, Amadi, Adichie, Emechetta, Soyinka and Okri, among others. These writings form a coherent body of work that shows that war is no laughing matter.

Foremost among these writers is, of course, Wole Soyinka, detained in 1967 for an article published in the *Daily Sketch* (Gibbs 1983: 3) and later held in solitary confinement. Incarceration resulted in his acclaimed prison notes, *The Man Died* ([1972] 1994) and a collection of poems, *A Shuttle in the Crypt* (1972). A stanza from his poem 'Joseph' from his prison anthology serves to represent the mood among the veritable tapestry of Nigerian war writers: 'A time of evils cries / Renunciation of the saintly vision / Summons instant hands of truth to tear / All painted masks, that poison stains thereon / May join and trace the hidden undertows / In sewers of intrigue.'

Lest we should be tempted to think that the 'hidden undertows / In the sewers of intrigue' are confined to West Africa or even to the African continent, we have only to turn to Soyinka's *Art, Dialogue and Outrage* ([1988] 1993: 17) in which he provides a salutary corrective, saying that '[f]or the situation in Africa today is the same as in the rest of the world, it is not one of the tragedies which come of isolated human failures, but the very collapse of humanity'. In other words, as with Okri's short story, Soyinka seeks recuperation: freedom and dignity for humanity and for literature 'in an epoch of unfreedom and alienation for the vast majority of Africans and the rest of the human race' as Biodun Jeyifo writes in his introduction to Soyinka's powerful critique and indictment of humankind (1993: xi). Power, however, has both negative and positive connotations.

Alluding to the power of creative output in his wartime novel, *Anthills of the Savannah* (1987: 124), Achebe identifies the social and ethical power of story by having one of his characters ask: 'So why do I say the story is chief among his fellows?' The authorial voice intrudes to respond: 'Because it is only the story can continue beyond the war and the warrior. It is the story that outlives the war-drums and the exploits of brave fighters.' He continues: 'It is the story, not others, that saves our progeny from blundering like blind beggars into the spikes of the cactus fence.' The graphic use of simile and metaphor illustrates the power of the pen. In synchronicity with Achebe, Okri stresses the timelessness of story, saying that '[s]tories do not belong to eternity. They belong to time. And out of time they grow' (1997: 113 no. 25). Pointing to the redemptive potential of storytelling, Okri concludes: 'And it is through lives that touch the bedrock of suffering and the fire of the soul, it is through lives, and in time, that stories – relived and redreamed – become timeless' (ibid.: 114).

Crediting the mother country with an innate propensity for storytelling, Okri aphorizes: 'Africa breathes stories' (1997: 115 no. 34). 'In its creation and interpretation of history, Nigerian war literature has enriched the body of historical writing from Africa, especially historical fiction,' opines Ezenwa-Ohaeto (2000: 14). Evaluating the import of this body of Nigerian writing, he notes significantly that '[i]n this way the writers have made literature continue to function as a mirror of society. In the process of mirroring society and criticizing its pitfalls, the war literature also serves as a compass for social redirection.' The quest for freedom, resistance to tyranny, brutalization and alienation are the linear rhetorical tropes running through literary representations of the Nigerian Civil War.

12

The poetic muse of archaeology

Introduction

This discussion explores a triptych of rock poems from Ben Okri's anthology, *Wild* (2012), that serves to (re)vivify geological, anthropological and cultural connections for the westernized psyche. The poems are read, not in the order in which they appear in Okri's third anthology, but in chronological sequence. All three poems are connected by an imagined locus in Olduvai Gorge in Tanzania and stimulated by the discoveries of fossils of the earliest hominids. The exploration situates each of the poems within its Palaeozoic era and African archaeological context. The period between 2 million and 1.2 million years ago was the radiometric dating of the respective stones before the dawn of *Homo sapiens*; this was the era of the earliest tool-making hominid, or man-like primate, the *Australopithecus*, who lived from about five million to one million years ago and who was once wrongly assumed to be man's ancestor. His remains have been found only in eastern and southern Africa and so it seemed likely that, until one million years ago, the presumed predecessors of man were still confined to Africa, also the homeland of the earliest primates. In *A Time for New Dreams*, Okri aphorizes: 'Africa is our dreamland, our spiritual homeland' (2011: 133 no. 5). Thus, the continent is a reminder, and an urgent one for this Nigerian-born poet, of Africa as the motherland of the world. Although Africa came to continental self-consciousness rather late, fellow Nigerian Chinua Achebe intimates in his acclaimed novel that this is the continent that heals and teaches, trains and unites an otherwise potentially rapacious ego, such as that of the unbridled self of his anti-hero, Okonkwo, sent to 'the motherland' for re-education after murdering Ikemefuma in accordance with oracular dictates ([1962] 1976). Okri proposes that 'Africa breathes stories', for '[w]here stories are, struggles have been lived through, fates have been lived out, triumphs have danced with failures, and human destinies have left their imprints: their souls and their stories on the land' (1997: 115 and 117 nos 34 and 35).

This reading suggests that these poems speak to the impulse to 'colonize', a word taken in the broad sense to mean the urge to dominate ('ius dominandi') an environment by force of will. This urge among *Homo sapiens sapiens* is given poetic form as Okri's speaker traces an evolutionary trajectory of humankind.[1] *Homo erectus* and *Homo faber* (man, the maker), the human 'colonizer' of the environment is described in the first of these poems, 'The Crystalline Quartz, Olduvai Gorge,

2 million years ago' (2012: 61) as having 'the power to make' and having 'broken the night'. Okri balances this profoundly worrying insight into the deepest roots of the impulse to 'open the skulls', to 'break the secret / Of the sky in the valley' in the second poem, 'Basalt Stone, Olduvai Gorge, 1.8 million years ago' (ibid.: 80–1), or to 'break the rock', 'bend and crack / And change' the world in the third rock poem, 'Solidified Volcanic Lava, Olduvai Gorge, 1.2 million years ago' (ibid.: 41–2). He places the poems in a collection which is an eloquent suggestion of ways in which (to use Ngugi wa Thiong'o's ([1986] 1994) term) to 'decolonize the mind' but used here in the Okrian sense of redreaming the world, accessing a higher nature and so being able to 'sleep again / Like a child does, and still create' ('Dreaming by the Water of Leith', 2012: 17).

In a collection of essays in *A Time for New Dreams*, Okri contemplates the nature of poetry, concluding that poetry is, at once, cerebral and intensely personal; it is 'an inner dialogue' (2011: 4). Elucidating, he muses: 'It suggests a private journey to one's own truth' (ibid.). In reviewing this assertion, Kathie Birat points out perspicaciously that 'there is no simple way of entering the world of Ben Okri's poetry' (2015: 1066). Acknowledging that this statement is true of the genre in general, Birat points to its complexity in the Okrian oeuvre:

> Okri's multicultural background and his blending of diverse literary, philosophical, and spiritual influences requires an approach that takes these factors into account without allowing them to overshadow the personal encounter between poem and reader which is, for Okri, the heart of the reading experience. (Ibid.)

That Okri is conscious of his meditation on the eternal, evanescent mystery of the poetic is particularly evident in several of the poems in his third collection, *Wild* (2012). Consider, for instance, his invocation of 'the secret harmony / Of the stars and the sun' in 'The Ruin in the Forest' (ibid.: 47). His awareness of a notional reader with whom he is sharing the enigmas of being is evident in his conception of 'wild' as 'our link with the stars', as 'an alternative to the familiar ... where art meets the elemental, where chaos can be honed' and so our link with cosmic harmony.[2]

Although he is mistaken in his supposition that the three rock poems chosen for discussion here emanate from 'a trip to Tanzania's Rift Valley', Chris Ringrose correctly observes that their Olduvai Gorge setting is 'so important in the history of evolution and palaeoanthropology, to consider human history and potential' (2015: 1147) – the thrust of this current discussion as stated at the outset. Olduvai Gorge is of prime importance in the history of humankind for it was here in 1972 that Richard Leakey of the Kenya National Museum made two vital discoveries. Not only were the oldest known stone tools, dating from as long ago as 2.5 million years, discovered near Kenya's Lake Rudolf, but the skull and leg bones of a man-like creature considerably more advanced than the *Australopithecus*, who probably made the tools, were also unearthed. These remains, provisionally dubbed the '1470 Man' in accordance with their catalogue reference, together with fragments of bone of another tool-making creature, discovered at Olduvai Gorge by Richard's father, Dr Louis Leakey, led to a revised picture of the evolutionary chain. The skull of '1470 Man' indicated a relatively large brain size – about double that of the chimpanzee, while the leg bones indicate that he was about 1.5 m (5 ft) tall and could walk upright. Dr Louis Leakey named his parallel find in Olduvai Gorge in Tanzania, *Homo habilis* and claimed that this 'handy man' lived at the same time as *Australopithecus* and represented a more advanced hominid on the direct line to *Homo sapiens* (see *Reader's Digest Library of Modern Knowledge* 1978: 428). Okri's Olduvai Gorge triad of poems are underpinned by this archaeological evidence.

The geological classification of the rocks is symbolically significant, for the three rock forms (crystal (the oldest and hardest rock), basalt (the base of the ocean) and igneous rock (volcanic shaping and reshaping of the earth's crust)) found in Olduvai Gorge are, not coincidentally, the base of planet earth. All three poems are thus connected by an imagined locus in Olduvai Gorge in Tanzania and stimulated by the discoveries of fossils of the earliest hominids. And, as already intimated, I discuss the poems in the order of their dating, rather than in the order in which they appear in Okri's third anthology.

'The Crystalline Quartz, Olduvai Gorge, 2 million years ago' (*Wild* 2012: 61)

'The Crystalline Quartz' is the first to speak to the impulse to 'colonize' or control one's environment, as already intimated. Here, this propensity, exhibited by *Homo erectus* since his earliest technological inventions as hominid, is poeticized in this shortest of the three poems, which features the earlier pre-sapient period. Fear, darkness and hunger are key aspects of Stone Age life, as invoked in the opening quartet: 'Fire in the riverdream / And fear in the valley. / Night and the stone, / And hunger in the sky' (2012: 61; Stanza 1, ll. 1–4). These four, verbless lines illustrate poetry at its most compressed and elusive; its most allusive. The cascade of iconographic, eidetic images at once engages our Higher Consciousness. In the title poem to the collection, 'Wild', Okri points to his symbolist mode: 'Those ancients saw / The world as it is, / A system of cooperation, / Where things are both themselves / And symbols and correspondences' (ibid.: 51).

An interview by Asis De in India sheds light on Okri's symbolist frame of reference. Asked for his views on culture, Okri decodes his complex use of the fire symbol (used in 'The Crystalline Quartz'): 'CULTURE is a secret ingredient in civilization. It is the frozen things we bring with us from the past, transformed by the ever-living *fire* of the mystery of being' (2015: 246–51; emphasis added). This situates 'The Crystalline Quartz' in a mythic zone two million years ago, when 'the gods' listened to our cries 'in silence / And heave the earth with *fire*' (2012: 61, ll. 14–15; emphasis added) as 'Rocks gush with water and lightning' (ll. 11). Underlining the extra-temporal frame, the neologism 'riverdream' likewise transcends time, where the 'ever-living fire of the mystery of being' transforms our past (cf. Asis De 2015: 249 and 251). The river is possibly Okri's most prevalent poetic motif as encountered in his Booker Prize novel, *The Famished Road* (1992), and in his *Wild* poems, 'Heraclitus' Golden River' (2012: 92–4) and 'Dreaming by the Water of Leith' (17), for instance.[3] The river, as symbol from the ancient Wisdom Corpus, signifies the continuity and mutability of all life forms or the inexorable flow of life. Okri extends the image to embrace the imagination and his maternal figure, the Great Mother, Gaia, and so signifying the spirit or divine spark (cf. Asis De 2015: 250). The symbols conjoin to evoke the image of nomads living close to Nature who, like their fellow creatures, are dominated by fear and the natural environment, '[o]n the move in the hills' singing 'songs to the wild heavens' as 'Night rises from the earth'. The poetic persona intrudes in the closing lines with 'Our future, grainy as the sky, / Who can read it, save the gods? / And they are quiet now' (Stanza 3, ll. 20–2)'.

Ringrose usefully contextualizes the era, saying that '"The Crystalline Quartz, Olduvai Gorge, 2 million years ago" … invokes ancestral figures ("Upright walk / The Stone makers") at the very beginning of human existence' (2015: 1148), as discussed in relation to the archaeological discoveries of Richard and Dr Louis Leakey. Okri provides the interpolation: where the inscrutable future is 'grainy as the sky' and is capable of being read only by the gods, who are 'quiet now'. Adumbrating an emergent cognitive trajectory, there is a suggestion of material culture deriving from natural objects; this is driven home in an unexpected rhyming couplet, seemingly at odds with the free verse in the opening quartet, quoted earlier: 'And then *we* make with stones / True items of our homes' (Stanza 3, ll. 18–19; emphasis added).

In the distant past fire, for human nature, remained 'in the riverdream'. Before we learnt to exploit the natural environment to the full, crystalline quartz – a product of 'solidification of minerals from gaseous or liquid states' over time (Read 1956: 53–4) – was present. The poet alludes to its igneous origin, for this was a time when only the gods could 'heave the earth with fire' (Stanza 2, l. 15). The early Greeks, however, presumed that crystal quartz resulted from 'the freezing of water under intense cold' and hence the name 'krustallos', meaning 'clear ice' (ibid.: 53).

Thus, both the trajectory of the poem and its title serve to suggest evolutionary processes: rock formation and humankind's emergent ability to utilize natural objects as tools. In three short stanzas, the poem moves from a distant past prior to the discovery of fire, to alluding to humankind's unique intelligence, skills and knowledge that spring from a brain that has evolved beyond the instinctive responses of his fellow creatures, so hinting at the acquisition of indigenous knowledge in the making of shelters and stone artefacts for our homes.

'Basalt Stone, Olduvai Gorge, 1.8 million years ago' (*Wild* 2012: 80–1)

With the emergence of *Homo habilis* at the close of 'The Crystalline Quartz', the second poem is dominated by the first-person plural, 'we', used only once in the first poem (see emphasis above). This highlights a developing cognitive capacity: 'We hold the secret' (2012: 80); 'We can break the secret / Of the sky in the valley' (Stanza 3, ll. 18–19). Ringrose pertinently observes in his reading of the Okrian poetic oeuvre:

> If there had been any doubt about to whom the 'we' of the poems in *An African Elegy* was addressed, that uncertainty is resolved here: human life begins in Africa, in 'the cradle of mankind', but Okri's soaring vision is addressed to the human race, which will go on to 'break the secret/ Of the sky in the valley'. (2015: 1148)

Significantly, 'The *will* has now risen' (Stanza 2, l. 14; emphasis added), putting the animal kingdom to flight: Animals / Have heard us scratch / From the boiling / Rock this incantation / In stone' (Stanza 2, ll. 10–14).

The poet suggests, however, that moral choice is the flip side of free will: 'We can beat music into bones. / We can heal by breaking' ('Basalt Stone' Stanza 2, ll. 16–17). The dichotomy tempers the frightening irony of human nature. John Alroy (quoted in Kolbert 2014: 234) concurs with the paradox of wilful man as destroyer and healer, when he acknowledges that humans 'are capable of driving any large mammal species extinct, even though they are also capable of going to great lengths to guarantee that they do not'. The opening stanza alerts us to the paradox of the grandiloquent urges of the Anthropocene era that are at the centre of Okri's musings on the family of man: 'This is different. Three fires / In the dark. A world is coming alive; / And all the sky opens / To the coming of a god / With fires all over the sky' (Stanza 1, ll. 1–5).

Prometheus-like, *Homo erectus*'s fire power appropriates that of the sun god's 'skyfire' ('We / Have become the mountain / With skyfire in our veins' (Stanza 3, ll. 21–3)). We can thus not only understand but also use the mountain's 'hidden fire' ('We speak to the mountains / Of their hidden fire' (Stanza 3, ll. 20–1)). The quoted lines 'We / Have become the mountain' arguably allude to humankind's newfound self-deification, underlined by an emergent bravado evoked in 'with wings / In our eyes and fire in our hands' (Stanza 4, ll. 26–7), as we dream of or imagine a fusion with the gods: 'Who can weep now. The god / Has arrived, and power / Is furled into this shape' (Stanza 2, ll. 6–9). The poetic persona is moved to announce 'a new time' (2012: 81) when '[d]reaming is freed' (ibid.), for, as already quoted in part: 'We can break the secret / Of the sky in the valley. / We can speak to the mountains / Of their hidden fire' (Stanza 3, ll. 18–21).

Like crystalline quartz, basalt is the product of the mountain's 'hidden fire'. It too is a sedimentary rock 'derived from pre-existing sedimentary, igneous or metamorphic rock' (Read 1956: 198). These early pyroclastic deposits are 'broken down by the agents of geological denudation – frost, rain, wind, ice, river or sea action' (ibid.). Basalt thus manifests over time, and the poem, too, speaks of transformation: a major breakthrough in the evolution of humankind as the opening words attest: 'This is different. Three fires / In the dark', already quoted. It can be argued that the three fires in this poem are the sun ('skyfire', alluding to the worship of the sun god among the ancient Egyptians and others in north-eastern Africa), the earth's fire (the hidden mountain fire or volcano that 'creates' rock formations) and man's newfound ability to make fire. *Homo erectus* was a full-time hunter-gatherer and this implies cunning, a degree of cooperation and some intellectual capacity. The irony suggested by the poem is, of course, that although our understanding of Nature has grown, our wilfulness blinds us to the fact that we remain forever subservient to it as in the illusion of transformation followed by inevitable reversion in the lines 'Maybe at night we join the gods. / And in the day, at dawn, / When the eagles scream, we become / Humans again, with wings / In our eyes, and fire in our hands / Turned to stone' (Stanza 4, ll. 24–9).

As intimated, the development of *sapiens* is associated with that of free will, satirically 'celebrated' in the final poem that treats another igneous formation: 'Solidified Volcanic Lava, Olduvai Gorge, 1.2 Million Years Ago'.

'Solidified Volcanic Lava, Olduvai Gorge, 1.2 Million Years Ago' (*Wild* 2012: 41–2)

Given Okri's interest in the ancient philosophers of the sixth and fifth centuries BC, coupled with his symbolist mode, especially in the invocation of the sacred eagle and three fires in 'Basalt Stone', it is reasonable too to consider Heraclitus's conception of 'Logos', which as W. K. C. Guthrie notes, 'seems so puzzlingly to be at the same time the word he utters, the truth which it contains, and the external reality which he conceives himself to be describing, and to which he gave the name of fire' ([1950] 1978: 14). This resonates with both Okri's notion of poetry and the content of the Olduvai poems.

The inherent danger for *Homo sapiens*, the direct ancestor of our own subspecies *Homo sapiens sapiens*, is that these poems allude to the potential to auto-destruct, as evoked in the alarming energy of the opening stanza of this last rock poem to be discussed, and contextualized as closest to contemporary life, albeit 1.2 million-years-ago: '*We* break the rock; / The force within it screams. / Now *we* have the *power* to make. / Who knows what the rock knows? / *We* do. *We* know the fire inside' (2012: 41, Stanza 1, ll. 1–5; emphases added). Here, man has wrested agency from the mountain. Okri places this poem in direct conversation with 'Basalt Stone', asking rhetorically: 'Haven't we broken the mountain / And shaped the world in our own hands?' (Stanza 5, ll. 23–4). The archaeological record is more explicit.

Inspired by Okri's handling of a stone-chopping tool from the paleontological collection in the British Museum (Okri 2016: 436), 'Solidified Volcanic Lava' is dedicated to the curator of the British Museum in London, Neil MacGregor (2012: 41). Moreover, Okri reminds us in 'The Muse of Archaeology' that '[a]rchaeology is a noble discipline: it deals, whether it likes it or not, with the big questions, the great enigmas' (quoted in Renfrew et al. 2016: 436). One of the most pressing questions is how to deal with the fact that 'our well-being – even our existence – depends on ecological systems and biodiversity' as Barbier et al. ([1994] 1995) caution. Alan Burdick's (2005) view is that *Homo sapiens* is 'arguably the most successful invader in biological history' (Kolbert 2014: 218).[4] This poem ends with the prophetically sombre lines that could allude to our being authors of our own destruction: 'We have become more than we seem' (Okri 2012: 42). This line stands alone as a tentative 'quod erat demonstrandum' (what was demonstrated) to the conundrum of man's evolutionary journey, explored in the three poems. Just as there are no easy answers to the enigma of human nature, so too is the line tantalizing in its ambiguity.

In an earlier article entitled 'Ben Okri's geo-cosmic consciousness in *Wild* (2012)', I argued along this latter reading: that this cryptic line can be interpreted as suggesting that instead of trying to define the world, we have come to accept the mystery of life as implied in the opening line of the penultimate stanza that reads: 'We are as the gods dream' (Stanza 5, l. 22). Taken with the fourth stanza's exultant lines, 'The night has left the sky / As fire and power in our hands' (Stanza 4, ll. 18–19), the closing line implies that in the distant past (*c.*100,000 years ago), *Homo sapiens* was empowered to focus the inner fire to accord life a deeper meaning. Ringrose concurs, noting that

> [f]rom prehistory to the new Europe, Okri's poetry takes on an inspirational mode to reflect the human journey and urge both the individual and humanity to dream themselves with positivity a future that can hold on to the best of the past, forgive, and pride itself on having 'come through'. (2015: 1148)

This poem describes the autonoetic stage of selfhood: it refers to the process of self-recollection involving a mental reinstatement of past events. The 'ancestors from the sky / ... broke through the broken form' (Okri 2012: 42), provoking the realization, in contrast to my earlier reading, that the urge to dominate extends to everything humans touch: our proclivity to exclude, to crush, to control. A proliferation of violent images underlines the message: 'It's like the skull of war. / Weapon of blood to make / Fire, to make hunger die' (Stanza 3: ll. 12–14); 'Night leaps out from our hands' (through firepower) and 'The world is ours at last' (Stanza 4: l. 21) – a prefiguring of Burdick's view of the 'invader', expressed above.

Okri compounds the gradation of human development – from carving the stone with 'the sharp teeth / Of our dreams' in 'The Crystalline Quartz', to 'scratching the boiling rock' in 'Basalt Stone', to shaping the world in our own hands in 'Solidified Volcanic Lava'. Yet, he confounds the gradation with the linear motif of dreaming (axiomatic to Okrian aesthetics), recalling the numinous opening of the poem's: 'Fire in the riverdream'. The 'sharp teeth of our dreams' (2012: 61), transmuted into 'a new time / When dreaming is freed' (81), is in turn transposed into our becoming 'as the gods dream', as we change the world 'into form and dream' (42). As P. E. Vernon reminds us: 'The essential "ars poetica" lies in the technique of overcoming the feeling of revulsion in us which is undoubtedly connected with the barriers that rise between each single ego and the others' (1970: 134). Vernon elucidates on the operation of creativity or ontopoiesis when he states: 'The writer softens the character of his egoistic day-dreams by altering and disguising it, and he bribes us by the purely formal, that is aesthetic, yield of pleasure he offers us in the presentation of his phantasies' (ibid.).

Conclusion

Although the subject of the three poems selected for discussion is our shared origins as *Homo faber* (man, the maker), Okri is concerned with the relation of poetry to the modern world (to borrow from F. R. Leavis's *New Bearings in English Poetry* [1932] 1950: 5). Leavis's provocative observation that 'poetry matters little to the modern world' and that 'very little of contemporary intelligence concerns itself with poetry' (ibid.) is clearly satiric. Leavis's and my discussion align with Okri's correlative but more direct view, as expressed in *A Time for New Dreams*: 'Heaven knows we need poetry now more than ever. We need the awkward truth of poetry. We need the indirect insistence on the magic of listening' (2011: 3).

The Olduvai Gorge-inspired rock poems reveal the destructive part of the nature of *Homo sapiens sapiens*, while subtly inculcating cosmic accord and natural harmony as the better half of our natural impulses. In the context of the Okrian oeuvre, my readings posit that the latter humanist strand awakens in the individual sympathies for all fellow creatures on planet earth, nurturing a sense of natural community.

In his essay 'The Muse of Archaeology' (quoted in Renfrew et al. 2016: 436), Okri argues that archaeology is a 'living' science, 'because it has to extrapolate, from the beliefs and objects, something of the rich humanity with which, in the darkness of unknowing, we invest our lives'. In Okri's cosmogony, past and present coalesce. Objects are believed to be animated by those who engage with them, so that a two-million-year-old stone from Olduvai Gorge in Tanzania, the womb of our hominoid family, provides the impetus behind a meditation on the noble role of archaeology as well as on the destructive/constructive nature of humankind. Revealing his poetic sensibility, Okri explains the effect of an object upon cognition: 'I have had a stone from 2 million years ago … placed in my hand and have felt from the contact a leap of images, a scream of visions, which have inspired poems' (2011: 3). Impregnated with 'the mute memory of our passing lives' (ibid.), objects – whether man-made or natural – can revivify past lives, so that once lived lives can traverse 'the boundary of death to inform life with humour, with dread, and with grandeur' (Renfrew et al. 2016: 438), as Okri proclaims.

As with the three basic rock forms of earth's crust, the three poems are mutually permeable, serving to drive home their central messages: the gods remain silent – we cannot predict our future ('The Crystalline Quartz'); despite our wannabe-god delusions, at dawn, 'when the eagle screams' like Prometheus, 'we become / Humans again' [bound to the rock, for eagles to peck out our liver!] ('Basalt Stone'); and 'night leaps out of our hands' ('Solidified Volcanic Lava'). By imbuing the rocks with a hieroglyphic aura, these images are etched into the psyche of humankind.

In her essay on ecocritical practice, Serpil Opperman highlights the 'promising hermeneutical horizon in our interpretations and understanding of the natural world and literature', accruing from the growing consciousness of 'the widespread ecological crisis' (2006: n.p.), but stresses the need for the centrality of language. Okri's viewpoint in 'The Muse of Archaeology' dedicated to Colin Renfrew provides a mythic conjunction between his poetically expressed sentiments and Oppermann's materialist ecocriticism that uses literary representations as 'prisms to possibly bring out the predicaments of the more-than-human collectives in which our lives are embedded' (Iovino 2020):

> Maybe we need a metaphysical archaeology, a new kind of *listening* to material culture, that we may not only work with the fruits of excavation, but also *hear* the radiant speech of objects, and the unheard laughter of the dead. (Okri 2016: 437; emphases added)

The veiled literary allusion to Shelley's indictment of Rameses II, whose grand statue lay in ruins on the sand after his death in the poem 'Ozymandias' reminds us of the irony of our own desire for self-aggrandizement and godlike power and the consequent 'unheard laughter of the dead'. In this perspective, as Serenella Iovino notes: 'the matter of the world is read as a "storied matter": an eloquent text emerging from the concurrence of material-discursive forces and expressing the interactions of human and nonhuman actors' (2020).

Such decolonial turns are embedded within a counter-narrative that evinces a remarkable shift in perspectives on the post-colony era. The argument is that a poet from Africa, who has borne witness to what colonizing and being colonized means in real terms, reminds us that we need to transcend our innate will to 'colonize', used metaphorically in the specific sense of our desire to subdue, dominate and destroy. As Kathie Birat (2015: 1069) reminds us, Okri affirms in a chapter in *A Time for New Dreams* entitled 'Healing the Africa Within' (2011: 134) that '[t]here is a realm in everyone that is Africa. We all have an Africa within.' Birat (2015: 1069) insightfully observes: 'It is this interrelation of Africa as both an aesthetic and an emotional experience that can be seen as one of the forces shaping the writer's later poetry.' The argument is that Okri evidently wants to connect his African-origins narrative, potentially uniting all humanity, with poetry as a medium for maximum depth and imaginative connection. Okri speaks from a broader consciousness than the subaltern's. He suggests that through poetry we can leap across a self/other divide and 'spread illumination / through this darkening world' ('Heraclitus' Golden River' 2012: 92–4). This is because the poetic imagination is the furthest from the brute force and cunning described in the three poems. Through the 'Imaginatio Creatrix', we can redream our world, access our higher nature and so 'sleep again / Like a child does, and still create' ('Dreaming by the Water of Leith' 2012: 17).

Arguing for a shared heritage, a synthesis of centre and margin, rather than perceiving the gap as unbridgeable, the chapter has explored the destruction/creation dichotomy in *Homo sapiens sapiens*, attempting to show how a heightened consciousness or ontopoietic self-awareness can offset the will to power. This is because, alone among the animals, humans seek a meaning in life, and we can express our aspirations symbolically through the arts.[5]

Part Four

The wheel of transformation:
The writer as lodestar (guide)

13

Sublime transformative paremiology in *A Way of Being Free*

Introduction

This chapter is informed by the underlying question as to whether the postmodern era has erased the essence of art, where art unifies inner and outer consciousness in its attempt to suggest sublimity. Ben Okri's oeuvre is informed by a conscious desire to provide an 'antispell [*sic*] for the 21st century' (1999) through creative sublimity. The implication is that humankind needs to give serious thought to sublime transformation. This is nowhere more apparent than in a poem, 'Towards the Sublime', from his third anthology of poetry entitled *Wild* (2012: 56), the opening quatrain of which reads: 'Have you noticed that in all true / Transformations what emerges / Is stranger than before / And higher, richer, magical?' (Stanza 1, ll. 1–4) The multivalent rhetorical question at once draws the reader into a contemplation on what is meant by 'all true transformations'. To borrow from G. H. Durrant – albeit it in a different context – 'there is yet no proclamation of any transcendental doctrine; and there seems indeed to be an insistence on the empirical basis of all knowledge and all wisdom' (1969: 18). However, as in all sublime poetry or poetry on the sublime, critical insight reveals that the epithets 'stranger', 'higher', 'richer' and 'magical' are evocative of what 'true transformation' signifies. As if in explication, Okri cites the case of 'chrysalis into butterfly' in Stanza 3 (l. 11), thus providing an 'empirical basis'. Reminding us of nature's sublime alchemy, the butterfly is a prime symbol of immortality. The exemplum of 'death / Into life …' (Stanza 3, ll. 12–13) transposes the customary mental progression of life into death and is thus 'A living testament / To the sublime within' (Stanza 4, ll. 19–20). Aligning his heightened consciousness with Longinus's, Okri's view seems to insist on a clear rejection of theism; the sublime is 'Beyond measure. / A joy to all ages' (Stanza 4, ll. 22–3); it inheres in the 'Divine freedom' of 'This bright new thing / … / Given new being' (Stanza 4, ll. 18 and 21). Enhanced by the anthropomorphism of the butterfly's beingness, the impression is that poetic or true wisdom accrues from careful observation of natural magic and its scientific laws as revealed by a sense of wonder.

This argument finds its correlative in three aphorisms on 'The Joys of Storytelling' from *A Way of Being Free* (1997: 124 and 125). Number 75 alludes to the chaos, madness and nightmare that a 'true storyteller suffers' to resolve, to see clearly and to guide the reader 'through the fragmentation and the shifting world'. The echo of

Plato's *Phaedrus* (2009) – 'If any man come to the gates of poetry without the madness of the Muses ... then shall he and his works of sanity be brought to nought' – seems palpable. Number 76 proceeds to define the particularity of the kind of story Okri has in mind: 'I am not referring to just any story, but only those great ones, rich and rare, that haunt, that elude, that tantalise, that have the effect of poignant melodies lodged deep in barely reachable places of the spirit' (1997: 124).

One is struck by Okri's frequent use of poetic device, such as amplification, as if in tacit acknowledgement of the Platonic source. The recognition of this elementary fact, as T. E. Harty notes in his article on Wordsworth, 'leads to a better understanding of the kind of meaning which characterises poetic utterance' (1968: 61). Okri first helps us to rediscover the world of wisdom literature in Number 75; the next aphorism (1997: 76) slowly draws us into the world of the imagination with its hidden 'poignant melodies' (both just quoted); then, Number 79 implies the triumph of the illusory that defines the tradition of sublime art: 'Magic distracts our attention from the hidden methods, art draws our attention to the hidden revelation' (125).

The idea of art drawing 'our attention' to the 'hidden revelation' suggests the gaining of authentic insight through acceptance of heightened awareness, the 'Imaginatio Creatrix' or intuitive creativity.[1] Embedded in this notion is not factual truth as related to history but poetic truth as contained in art forms, that is, in representations of sublime transformative truths. By apprehending the implications of the complex syntactical organization – the juxtaposition of magic and art – the reader gains intellectual and emotional insights that provoke a reordering of his/her faculties in such a way as to account for the 'ecstasy' or perception of the sublime, noted by Longinus.

Longinus: *The Treatise on the Sublime*

The monograph's introduction intimates what is meant by Okri's sublime transformative paremiology, where paremiology is the study of proverbs, otherwise known as aphorisms, adages or maxims. Paremiology explores the quintessence of oft-repeated, unforgettable nuggets of wisdom which, 'de facto', makes the best of them sublime. But, what is meant by the notion of sublimity? Longinus declares that 'sublimity consists in a certain excellence and distinction in expression' (Dorsch 1974: 100). Eschewing ignoble qualities such as passion for novel ideas, bombast and indiscriminate adornment, and attributing the sublime to 'some innate power' (read intuition), Longinus elucidates: 'a piece is truly great only if it can stand up to repeated examination, and if it is difficult, or, rather impossible to resist its appeal, and it remains firmly and ineffaceably in the memory' (ibid.: 107), as illustrated by the brief overview of Okri's poem on the sublime and the selected aphorisms.

In clarification, Longinus provides five sources of sublimity, all pertinent to this discussion on sublime transformative paremiology. Longinus sees 'the ability to form grand conceptions' as the most important source (see 'chrysalis into butterfly'); the second is 'the stimulus of powerful and inspired emotion' (see the discussion on the four epithets from Okri's poem). These two aspects are, Longinus argues, 'very largely innate'. The next two sources of sublimity 'are the product of art: figures of thought and figures of speech': 'noble diction', understood to involve 'the use of imagery', and elaborate style, where style is seen as the deployment of rhetoric. The last is 'the total effect resulting from dignity and elevation' that encapsulates the other four qualities of sublimity (Dorsch 1974: 108).

A discussion on Longinus's perception of the shortcomings of the *Treatise on the Sublime* suggests the origination of the treatise that has been attributed to Longinus. First, although this is not necessarily a stumbling block, we know little about either the author or the date of composition.[2] A twentieth-century critic and translator, T. E. Dorsch (1974: 24), surmises that the treatise was composed in the first century AD and that it was 'partly a corrective to a lost work on the same subject by a certain Cecilius, who was a friend of Dionysius of Halicarnassus' (ibid.). In a possible error, through association with a third-century critic, Cassius Longinus, the manuscript has, Dorsch notes, been attributed to 'Dionysius or Longinus' (ibid.). Be this hedging of bets as it may, as we have it, the dialogue in the *Treatise on the Sublime* is purportedly between Longinus and one Postumius Terentanus, although the treatise is, paradoxically, a monologue – talking at rather than talking to or with a second party. This begs a couple of questions: given the unlikely name, was 'dear Postumius' a Roman 'Zeitgeist' or an 'alter ego' of the Greek Longinus? And, was Cecilius the initial author of the treatise on the sublime, or was the 'lost' treatise merely a first draft by Longinus, who then revised it in a Socratic dialogue with himself, as we have learnt to expect in Plato's *Republic* ([1909] 1926)? Of course, literary critics who worry about historical facts run the risk of being both bad historians and poor critics.

This preamble points to one of the dilemmas of literary/art criticism, a problem that it evidently shares with philosophy. In his *The Problems with Philosophy*, Bertrand Russell argues that philosophy has little practical utility. Nevertheless, it has a valuable function to perform which is relevant to literary criticism, as Russell sees this purpose as both illumination and liberation:

> Philosophy, though unable to tell us what is the true answer to the doubts it raises, is able to suggest many possibilities which enlarge our thoughts and free them from the *tyranny of custom* … it removes the somewhat arrogant dogmatism of those who have never travelled into the region of *liberating doubt*, and it brings alive our sense of wonder by showing familiar things in an unfamiliar light. (1912: 156–7; emphases added)

The philosopher in Ben Okri seeks the delight, joy and ecstasy of philosophical contemplation; his oeuvre seeks to re-inculcate the pleasure principle of living meaningfully, based on the premise that human life is worth preserving. Coincidentally, this excerpt serves to underline both the problematic nature of criticism and the philosophical underpinnings of aphorisms or proverbs, in general, and those by Okri, in particular. Yet, it also hints at the exhilaration that accrues from the 'liberating doubt' of thoughtful literary critique.

Longinus's theory of the sublime is an obvious critical lens for my analyses of Okri's aphorisms, as intimated in the discussion on his poem 'Towards the Sublime'. In the introduction to his *Treatise on the Sublime*, Longinus highlights the main shortcoming of Cecilius's treatise that he is (purportedly) revising; he sees this as the use of examples in lieu of definition, asserting that '[i]n any systematic treatise two things are essential: first, there must be some definition of the subject; second in order of treatment, but of grander importance, there must be some indication of the methods by which we may ourselves reach the desired goal' (Dorsch 1974: 99). The excerpt highlights the importance of methodology.

The chosen strategy in this reading was to begin with Okri's interest in the sublime to justify my title. A brief outline of the historical context of *The Treatise on the Sublime* is followed by a discussion of select aphorisms on 'The Joys of Storytelling' from *A Way of Being Free* (1997: 109–27), in contrast to my previous paper on Okri's aphorisms that focuses on those in *Birds of Heaven* (1996), *A Time for New Dreams* (2011) and *Callaloo* (2015: 1042–3).[3]

Sublime aphorisms on 'The Joys of Storytelling'

The quintessence of proverbs is their pithy wisdom (Bryant 1951: 134; Trench 1957: 8). I now explore some additional intuitive or ontopoietic aphorisms by this Nigerian-born author that uplift our souls in reflecting on how to transform the essence of our being. It seems to me that one such is the conceit that '[t]ranquillity is the resolution of the tensions and paradoxes of story into something beyond story: into stillness' (1997: 116 no. 37).[4] The rhetorical devices, here, such as the consonance yoking tranquillity and tensions together and synthesizing story and stillness, are what makes the real appeal of these poetic maxims. The ploy brings about a quick rush of warmth, a sudden unrestrained intellectual surrender that is a measure of its worth. The resultant sublimity of aphorisms, such as this, is summarized by Desiderius Erasmus:

> [T]o weave adages deftly and appropriately is to make the language as a whole glitter with sparkles of Antiquity, please us with the colours of the art of rhetoric, gleam with jewel-like words of wisdom, and charm us with titbits of wit and humour. In a word, it will wake interest by its novelty, bring delight by its concision, convince by its decisive power. ([1540] 1982: 17)

The affect is enhanced by Longinus's prescribed route to the sublime: 'It is the imitation and emulation of the great historians and poets of the past' (Dorsch 1974: 119). 'For many authors,' Longinus asserts, 'catch fire from the inspiration of others' (ibid.). He elaborates: '[C]ertain emanations are conveyed from the genius of the men of old into the souls of those who emulate them and, breathing in the influences, even those who show very few signs of inspiration derive some degree of divine enthusiasm from the grandeur of their predecessors' (ibid.). Okri concurs with this kind of mystical afflatus. In an interview with him in 2011, Okri acknowledges that

> [o]ur ancestors cut a path and we cut further paths, building on their foundations. It is as if one receives the baton and carries on. The process is both cyclical and vertical. I have felt the need to take the baton and to carry on. It's a question of

standing on these writers' shoulders, just as they have stood on the shoulders of earlier writers.

The duty of the artist is to extend the boundaries. (Okri in Gray 2012: 8)

The mystical path Okri would lead us along is here understood to be the fruit of a steady and organic growth: an experiential path beyond, one towards sublime consciousness.

Okri's chapter on 'The Joys of Storytelling' bears testimony to this extension of 'the boundaries': it includes 101 aphorisms. It would therefore be a work of many pages to trace all the subtle interconnections by which the strong intellectual structure of these aphorisms is given organizational coherence. By way of comparison, in his study of the New Testament, Crossan (1983: 28, 269–71) estimates that there are between 102 and 103 such sayings in the speeches of Jesus Christ. Okri evidently recognizes this important heritage by saying that '[t]he parables of Jesus are more powerful and persuasive than his miracles' (1997: 109 no. 2). As if to endorse the legacy, aphorism 73 states: 'Only a profound storyteller would say something like "Suffer little children to come unto me"' (ibid.: 123). Although it is difficult to impute tonal quality, the imperative evokes a kind of sublime ecstasy, especially as Christ is here shown to transpose the Old Testament adage of 'spare the rod and spoil the child' as in Prov. 29.15 that declares: 'The rod and reproof give wisdom: but a child left to himself bringeth his mother to shame,' while Prov. 13.24, in similar vein, reads: 'He that spareth his rod hateth his son: but he that loveth him chasteneth him betimes.' Okri is seemingly aware of the sublimity of Christ's teaching in Number 9, too, which states that '[t]he miracles of Jesus came down to us as stories, magical stories. It is the stories, rather than the facts, which still enchant us towards belief' (ibid.: 111).

For its use of periphrasis – further acknowledging the wisdom of the ancients – Fragment 33 is particularly perspicacious: 'It is through their stories that the ancient Greeks so profoundly influence and shape the world. Prometheus, Ixion, Sisyphus, Perseus, the Gorgon's head, Calypso, Odysseus – their stories are eternal metaphors of the partially revealed nature of the human condition' (1997: 115). Such reasoning counters the feebleness of our thinking when it comes to what is essential. The use of periphrasis is pivotal as Longinus attests in stating that 'periphrasis often harmonizes with the direct expression of a thought and greatly embellishes it, especially if it is not bombastic or inelegant, but pleasantly tempered' (Dorsch 1974: 137). In grasping the meaning, we reconstruct the imaginative processes which were at work in the composer and so share in the acuity of his insights.

Reviving the Wisdom Corpus of antiquity, Okri's role as postmodernity's (leading) African paremiologist provides a repository of nodes of knowledge that draws on and flows into his extensive aphoristic, fictional, non-fictional, dramatic, poetic, storytelling, 'stoku', filmic and word/image output. His ability to marry creative impulses from the oral tradition with those within the written tradition puts Okri in the company of such luminaries as Heraclitus, King Solomon, Jesus and his disciples, Confucius, Geoffrey Chaucer, Desiderius Erasmus, William Shakespeare, John Calvin, Lao Tsû, Sir Winston Churchill, Martin Luther King and Nelson Mandela – to mention but a few famous proverbialists.

If Africa is the cradle of mankind, another ancestor upon whose shoulders Okri stands is, of course, Longinus. Reflecting on the nature of sublimity, Longinus states: 'Sublimity is the echo of a noble mind' (Dorsch 1974: 109). Three sequential Okrian aphorisms neatly capture such nobility of mind, while serving to define the requirements demanded of 'true storyteller[s]':

> The infinite interpretability of great stories – and their serenity. (No. 68)
> To see the madness and yet walk a perfect silver line. (No. 69)
> The greatest guide is the clearest spirit and mind. (1997: 122 No. 70)

Taken as a unit, these three aphorisms illustrate the device of polyptoton – accumulation, variation and climax – that Longinus regards as 'very powerful auxiliaries in the production of elegance and of every kind of sublime and emotional effect' (Dorsch 1974: 132). The imagination and senses leap from the general in the serenity of 'great stories', to the particular (the writer in action), to the climactic superlatives of the 'greatest guide' and 'clearest spirit and mind'. In Number 24, Okri links sublime stories to the nature of an author's experience, saying that '[o]nly those who have lived, suffered, thought deeply, loved profoundly, known joy and the tragic penumbra of things tell truly wonderful stories' (1997: 113). Somewhat ironically, this could be perceived as an evaluation of self-worth for an author who grew up in war-torn Nigeria during the Biafran war of secession! More importantly, Number 23 articulates the therapeutic value of storytelling, that is, the ability to transform our consciousness: 'When we started telling stories we gave our lives a new dimension of meaning – apprehension – comprehension' (ibid). Okri seemingly extends the unintended biographical analogy to a more general African epistemology in Fragment 44:

> Where stories are, struggles have been lived through, fates have been lived out, triumphs have danced with failures, and human destinies have left their imprints and their souls and their stories on the land, in the air, and even on the waters. Strangers to these lands can feel the vibrations of the people's forgotten histories and fates in the air. (ibid.: 118)

What is *new* and *relevant* in the essential questions Okri asks of essence, of story, of creativity, of consciousness (themes grand and intimate) in the realization of each work is the poetic intelligence so strongly built into the structures of meaning, feeling, thought, and expression. Consider, for example, his tribute to early storytellers in *A Way of Being Free* (1997: 117): 'The stories of the Egyptians and Greeks, rather than their poems, shaped the world's consciousness and named the stars' (no. 39). This resonates with Ernest Hemingway's 1954 brief Nobel Prize for Literature statement: 'It is because we have had such great writers in the past that a writer is driven far out past where he can go, out to where no one can help him,' and is implicit in an epigram in *The Magic Lamp* (2017: 11): 'All things have been talking to you from the beginning of time … and you've not been listening.'[5] This is at once witty – words spoken by a blue jay – and sublimely profound. As aphorism Number 41 explains: 'The African mind is essentially abstract, and their storytelling is essentially philosophical' (1997: 117).

Two transformative aphoristic correlatives are Numbers 42 and 43: 'In Africa the mood in its music is a poignant golden story of everlasting hope and prayer', and 'The happiness of Africa is in its nostalgia for the future, and in dreams of a golden age' (1997: 117). The paradox in the latter aphorism gives pause for reflection; these pithy maxims are unadorned and lack pretence. It is principally through association that one is able to catch the full import of communal wisdom here; and a summing-up of all the associations stirred by these sublime aphorisms gives the best clue to the emotional direction. 'For by some innate power,' Longinus explains, 'the true sublime uplifts our souls; we are filled with a proud exaltation and a sense of vaunting joy, just as though we ourselves produced what we had heard' (Dorsch 1974: 107).

Okri evidently understands the inscape or true essence of the 'true sublime', for, in paying tribute to another predecessor in the world of storytellers, James Joyce, he imagines that '[a] great challenge for our age, and future ages: to do for storytelling what Joyce did for language – to take it to the highest levels of enchantment and magic; to impact into story infinite richness and convergences; to make story *flow* with serenity, with eternity' (1997: 111 no. 13; emphasis added). To intimate that a statement is imaginative is not to say that it stimulates a *flow* of sensory images but that it affects the thoughts and emotions in a way unparalleled by other kinds of statement. Longinus points to the criteria for a sublime statement, story, concept: it needs to 'outlive a single hearing', provoke a 'sense of wonder', create 'more food for reflection' (Dorsch 1974: 107). Okri's oratorical aphorisms on creativity do just this:

Creativity is a secular infinity. (No. 87)
Creativity is evidence of the transhuman. (No. 88)
Creativity is the highest civilizing faculty. (1997: No. 89)

Becoming more philosophical, he invokes our deepest emotional trigger with '[l]ove is the greatest creativity of them all, and the most blessed' (no. 90). These declamations climax in Number 91: 'Creativity of any valuable kind is one of the fullest expressions of the human and the godlike within us' (1997: 125). The cumulative effect of these five aphorisms on creativity reflects a kind of asyndeton where 'words come gushing out, as it were, set down without connecting links, and almost outstripping the speaker himself', according to Longinus (Dorsch 1974: 129).

Building on the creativity trope and alluding to sublime transformation in story writing, Okri asserts: 'It is in the creation of story, the lifting of story into the realms of art, it is in this that the higher realms of creativity reside' (1997: 119 no. 51). His innovation inheres not only in transdisciplinary and cross-generic insights and modes that flow into his larger body of literary production, as already stated, but also in their accommodation of the poetics of narrative synthesis in which oral and literate forms and styles interfuse.

Two main principles of the African oral tradition infuse Okri's work: authority and association. An idea is given validity by being placed side by side with another idea that bears the stamp of communal approval and by its being linked to the storehouse of collective wisdom. Aphorism Number 34 encapsulates the cultural heritage: 'Africa breathes stories' (1997: 115) and is reinforced by Fragment 35 which avers: 'In Africa everything is a story, everything is a repository of stories' (ibid.). The fragment continues somewhat whimsically: 'Spiders, the wind, a leaf, a tree, the moon silence, a glance, a mysterious old man, an owl at midnight, a sign, a white stone on a branch, a single yellow bird of omen, an inexplicable death, an unprompted laughter, an egg by the river, are all impregnated with stories.' After risking becoming bombastic in an overuse of amplification, the fragment concludes more sedately, more sublimely with: 'In Africa things are stories, and they yield stories at the right moment of dreaming, when we are open to the secret side of objects and moods' (ibid.). 'Sublimity consists in evaluation,' says Longinus, 'amplification in quantity' (Dorsch 1974: 117).

Okri is able to globalize and poeticize his sublime transformative paremiology with such wisdom as evidenced in Number 29 that takes the custom of legends and folktales beyond the African tribal fire circle: 'It is through the fictions and stories we tell ourselves and others that we live the life, hide from it, harmonise it, canalize it, have a relationship with it, shape it, accept it, redeem it, or flow with the life' (1997: 114).

Conclusion

The phenomenon of quintessential aphorisms gives weight to the view that meaning is to be sought not in a simple relationship between words and thoughts but in astute syntactical arrangement and a complex interrelationship between human behaviour and environment (adapted from Harty 1968: 69). Okri's aphorisms reveal and exploit our internal states and tendencies and effectively create new fields of meaning. His sublime transformative paremiology is relevant in demonstrating the pleasure of lucid organization; all these aphorisms form part of a perspicacious unity. His attitudes are synaesthetic – conveyed by the cognitive meaning of the aphorisms and, at the same time, evoking corresponding feelings in the reader. Underlining Okri's poem, 'Towards the Sublime', quoted at the outset, Wordsworth's 'Lines written a few miles above Tintern Abbey' likewise serve to illustrate sublimity: 'While with an eye made quiet by the power / Of harmony, and the deep power of joy / We see into the life of things' (July 13 1798: ll. 48–50).

In these lines, as with Okri's aphorisms chosen for discussion here, the power of revivification comes from the reminder of the powers that are latent in all human souls.

The aphorisms are therefore not just a falsification of the world nor yet merely the private vision of the writer; they provoke reflection and imperceptively lead to inner transformation. More than a statement of the composer's thoughts and attitudes, the aphorisms stimulate a reflection on the quality of the reader's beingness, ameliorating his or her views on the essence of being conditioned by postmodernism's obsessive need for surround sound and hyper-connectivity. As concise emotive and mental utterances, the aphorisms induce sensibility and intellectual responses in the reader; they may even modify the reader's attitudes towards existence in some way, implying a sublime ontology.

14

'The Standeruppers': The frightening irony of the Anthropocene

Introduction

This discussion is predicated on two principal sources: Elizabeth Kolbert's *The Sixth Extinction* (2014) and Ben Okri's 'stoku', 'The Standeruppers' ([2017] 2019: 135–8). It invokes Edward O. Wilson's 2002 argument on the inherent dangers of the human trajectory: the irony of the survival of our own species. Kolbert dubs human(un)kind's predatory proclivity that threatens creation, our 'unnatural history'. Using Okri's rock poems (2012) as allusive side references, the argument draws attention to his understanding of human nature and of humans in Nature. Both his 'stoku' and his Olduvai Gorge-inspired rock poems reveal the destructive nature of *Homo sapiens*, while subtly inculcating cosmic accord and natural harmony.

Palaeontologists John Anderson and Martin de Wit (2016: 5) surmise that the Anthropocene dates from 9,600 BP, whereas environmental writer Elizabeth Kolbert reiterates popular misconceptions that '[t]he Anthropocene is usually said to have begun with the industrial revolution, or perhaps even later, with the explosive growth in population that followed World War II' (2014: 234). The much earlier dating accords with Edward Wilson, who notes that '[t]he human race is a newcomer dwelling among the six-legged masses, less than two million years old, with a tenuous grip on the planet' (1992: 211). Although the inception of the sixth extinction appears to be contestable, writers consider that humankind has initiated 'an unnatural history' (Kolbert 2014).

So, when did humans become 'a world-altering force', ushering in the Anthropocene or Holocene, the catalyst for Okri's 'stoku', 'The Standeruppers', a short fiction set one hundred thousand years ago? It may have been the advent of modern machinery and urbanization, or 'the stone makers' of two million years ago. Okri imagines these Stone Age men of two million years ago, who 'Upright walk' and 'carve these stones / With the sharp teeth / Of our dreams' in his poem 'The Crystalline Quartz, Olduvai Gorge' (2012: 61). The date of inception matters less than the fact, as Okri reminds us in 'The Muse of Archaeology' (2016), that '[a]rchaeology is a noble discipline: it deals, whether it likes it or not, with the big questions, the great enigmas' (Renfrew et al. 2016: 436).

One of the most pressing questions is how to deal with the fact that 'our wellbeing – even our existence – depends on ecological systems and biodiversity' as Barbier et al. ([1994] 1995) warn us. Alan Burdick's (2005) view is that *Homo sapiens* is 'arguably the most successful invader in biological history' (Kolbert 2014: 218). Dubbing the sixth extinction or Anthropocene's process of annihilation the New Pangaea Project, Kolbert aligns the era with 'the period when modern humans first migrated out of Africa' (ibid.: 210). Palaeobiologist John Alroy (2001) has argued that the sixth extinction and, more specifically, that of the demise of the megafauna, is a 'geologically instantaneous ecological catastrophe too gradual to be perceived by the people who unleashed it' (Kolbert 2014: 234), while David Papineau, in his *New York Times Book Review*, asserts that '[t]he central message of Edward O. Wilson's stirring new book (*The Diversity of Life* [1992: ii]) is that "Homo sapiens" is in imminent danger of precipitating a biological disaster to rival anything in evolutionary history'. Tom Jones and Ellen Stofan insist that 'previous mass extinctions were caused by giant impacts or massive volcanic eruptions; this one is primarily caused by humans' (2017: 99). When an entomologist (Wilson) joins hands with a planetary scientist (NASA's veteran astronaut, Jones) and planetary geologist (Stofan), the agreement between their views is difficult to dispute. 'It is clear,' says Jones, 'that loss of habitat and climate change are the biggest threats' (ibid.). The actions of humankind have undoubtedly exacerbated the crisis, but an obvious rebuttal to over-pessimism is Earth's interglacial story: the advances and retreats of the Arctic ice sheet across the northern landmasses during the Pleistocene and the climactic birth of civilization in the Fertile Crescent, as Anderson and De Wit observe (2016: 5). Poets too have long been concerned with Anthropocene's destructive tendencies. John Milton ([1973] 1979), for example, cryptically castigates humankind's foolishness in *Paradise Lost* with 'Into a Limbo large and broad, since called the / Paradise of Fools, to few unknown' (Bk XI). In 'Anatomy of the World', the metaphysical poet, John Donne (1896), laments that '['t]is all in pieces, all coherence gone' (l. 9) before presenting his dramatic view of man with

> For had a man at first in forests stray'd,
> Or shipwreck'd in the sea, one would have laid
> A wager, that an elephant or whale,
> That met him, would not hastily assail
> A thing so equal to him; now alas,
> The faeries, and the pigmies well may pass
> As credible; mankind decays so soon,
> We are scarce our father's shadows cast at noon,
> Only death adds t'our length: nor are we grown
> In stature to be men, till we are none.
>
> (ll. 137–46)

Both Milton and Donne paint a depressingly negative view of humankind's predatory proclivity, while W. B. Yeats is chillingly prophetic in his evocation by the 'Spiritus mundi' of the death of innocence and the birth of the predatory monster (part lion, part man) with 'A gaze blank and pitiless as the sun' ('The Second Coming' Stanza 2, l. 15). Okri is more nuanced, less pessimistic. In his poem, 'Basalt Stone, Olduvai Gorge, 1.8 Million Years Ago', this fellow poet-seer points to the destructive/constructive dichotomy in human nature: 'The will is now risen. / We can open the skulls. / We can beat music into bones. / We can *heal* by breaking' (2012: 80; Stanza 2, ll. 14–17; emphasis added). These lines draw attention to Okri's understanding of human nature and of humans in Nature. Both his 'stoku' and his Olduvai Gorge-inspired rock poems reveal the destructive nature of *Homo sapiens*, while subtly inculcating cosmic accord and natural harmony in the paradox encapsulated in 'We can beat music into bones. / We can heal by breaking'. These lines mitigate the ironic awfulness of the Anthropocene or Holocene era in Yeats's aphorism that 'Things fall apart; the centre cannot hold'. The paradoxical notion of healing by breaking coincidentally prefigures the twenty-first century's breaking of the Berlin Wall to heal the rift, created by Communist politics, between East and West Germany.

Alroy (quoted in Kolbert 2014: 234) concurs with the paradox of wilful man ('The will is now risen') as destroyer and healer, when he acknowledges that humans 'are capable of driving any large mammal species extinct, even though they are also capable of going to great lengths to guarantee that they do not'. The paradox of the animus/anima urges of the Anthropocene era are at the centre of 'The Standeruppers' (2017), commissioned for inclusion in the Africa Alive project, the epic story of our mother continent. Before exploring this 'stoku', it is necessary to define the genre.

The 'stoku'

My article entitled 'Promoting the Poetic Cause in Ben Okri's "Stokus" from His *Tales of Freedom* (2009)', explores the theme of the poetic in Okri's thirteen rhapsodies in prose (Gray 2016: 18–27). Integral to this new, cross-generic literary mode – an amalgam of short story and *haiku* – is its use of serendipity. As argued in that article, 'as a sudden insight, serendipity becomes, in this Nigerian writer's hands, a poetic device equivalent to illumination or an epiphanic moment' (ibid.: 18). The mode of the short story is well known; its defining characteristic is economy, while that of the *haiku* is extreme economy, with its wordless line or the white space Okri alludes to when he muses in *A Time for New Dreams*: 'All our creativity, our innovations, our discovery come from being able to see what is there and not there; to hear what is said and not said ... the art of intuition' (2011: 27).

Illustrative of the wordless line or aporia and 'art of intuition' is Marié Heese's *haiku* 'Facts of Life': 'After a rainstorm / A whole swarm of ants can fly. / But wings do not last.' (1997: 5). This African *haiku* encapsulates the power of poetry: its appeal to the visual (seeing what is there and not there – intuiting wingless flying ants). The implied audible/inaudible (the calm following the storm) invokes the wonder of Nature contrasted with an implicit indictment of the preoccupations of contemporary humankind. The operation of intuitive imagination or Higher Consciousness informs my reading of 'The Standeruppers' ([2017] 2019).

'The Standeruppers'

'The Standeruppers', imagined as occurring one hundred thousand years ago, emulates the aspects/techniques of both short story and *haiku*, inclining towards a poetically rendered moment of insight, a vision or a paradox (Okri 2009: 108). Akin to the Japanese *haiku* form with its seventeen-syllable intuitive insight into Nature, illustrated by Heese's 'Facts of Life', Okri's 'stoku' invokes a dialogue between past and present as he portrays the complex nature of humankind.

In five short paragraphs, Okri transports third-millennium readers back in time, capturing the process of speciation,[1] from crouching hunter-gatherers to the emergence of *Homo erectus*. Around this time, our modern human tree 'began branching and diversifying on the African continent' (Anderson and De Wit n.d.: 50). The divergence saw the inception of a distinct Khoisan lineage in the south and a Bantu lineage in the north, each with distinct ethnic characteristics. A ten-degree Celsius (10° C) warming curve, through ten thousand years (ibid.), is on archaeological record. So, global warming is not a recent phenomenon.

Chapter 8 on the 'stoku' form depicted the writer as poet-philosopher: this one focuses on Okri's role as griot. Unique to West Africa, but no less poetically philosophical, griots are primarily historians and storytellers, as Thomas Hale in his *Griots and Griottes: Masters of Words and Music* (1998) explains. As implied in the title to Hale's book, griots are male or female and fulfil several interrelated functions, some of which are illustrated in 'The Standeruppers'. Here, for example, as genealogist, Okri recounts an early history in the family of man one hundred thousand years ago. As recorder and spokesman for the thoughts and actions of early man, the writer initially adopts a third-person omniscient authorial viewpoint, transitioning swiftly to first-person, narrating experiencing communal selves. The description in he '*had seen them trying to crouch … had seen them reaching for something in the air that was not there*' (135) is quickly transposed into '[*we*] *were dancing in the water of the gods*' (ibid.). The past is integral to the initial actions – '[*f*]*or some time*' (past), both the crouching and the attempts to stand erect had been observed; the ritual of dancing in 'the piss of the gods' brings us into the immediate present. The effect is to draw the reader into the communal ritual as participant; the griot turns praise singer and conveyer of an animistic culture that could *hear* the gods speaking and witness/*see* the earth's response. 'We need ritual, initiation, transcendence of consciousness,' Okri (1994 interview) insists. As millennial spiritualist and custodian of his culture, the persona shares with us the pleasure of the chase: by day, our early crouching carnivores chanted and shouted as they '*followed the wild beast across the grass*' (2019: 135), and, in an echo of Okri's poem, 'The Crystalline Quartz, Olduvai Gorge, 2 million years ago' (2012: 61), which reads: 'We carve these stones / With the sharp teeth / Of our dreams. Upright walk / The stone makers', early hominids 'had sharp stones to stab them with'. The fastest ran '*with our four legs*', and '[*w*]*e had sharp stones to stab them with*' (2019: 135) is suggestive of the inception of blood lust. These troglodytes '*dreamed of [the beasts] all night in the cave*' (ibid.). They had the power of transcendence; they could conjure the image of the beast with their chants and could *see* them in their minds. They had the ability 'to see what is there and not there', quoted earlier, suggestive of the art of intuition. By sleight of hand, shifting the era closer to the third millennium, the narrator informs us that the 'standeruppers', crouching in the '*blackness*' brought upon them by '*the god of night*', went to the place where they could '*do anything. There are many other beings there*' (2019: 135) that they did not know. This dream-time consciousness follows the seeing of '*many things*' in the moonlight, '*on the other side of the dark where the shadow people live*' (136). The moon, poetically rendered as '*the round white in the sky*' (ibid.), has long been an object of mystery and worship, a symbol of cultural mythology.

In 'Amongst the Silent Stones', in *A Way of Being Free*, Okri explains the myth of 'the shadow people', alerting us to the belief in 'the interpenetration of the worlds of the living and the dead' in West Africa, 'drawing death over the living spaces' (1997: 99). This also includes 'a belief in the world of spirits as being conterminous with that of human beings', as Vanessa Guignery (2015: 1000) notes. Okri's writing, she argues, 'therefore aims to reflect several gradations of reality in which the marvellous and the magical, the esoteric and the invisible are other dimensions of quotidian reality, thus running counter to the faith in rationality of Western philosophy' (ibid.).

Several gradations of reality are encapsulated in the 'double entendre' in the proto-rationalist neologism or creolization for *Homo erectus* as 'standeruppers'. The implication of standing up for one's beliefs is evocative of *Homo sapiens sapiens*; their rock paintings record the role of the newly upright cave dwellers as the earliest artists – a subtle slippage between now and then. This points to the mediating role of sculpting in the poem and of rock art in 'The Standeruppers'. Creative discernment is implicit in the term 'standeruppers' and is endorsed in the narrative voice's assertions that '*it was a good day*,' and '[*t*]he *best among us were the crouchers*' (2019: 135 and 136). The white space, characteristic of the *haiku*, prefigures the central serendipity with which the 'stoku' closes: '*I liked it best when the light-god rose over the grass*' (138). Okri is specific: it is *better*, when one lives in harmony with Nature.

As griot, Okri thus serves as interpreter, as evident in '*They were the first standeruppers. We did not know what to do with them. Because of them it was easier to have meat between our teeth and grass under our heads*' (2019: 138). The 'standeruppers' are feared; they laugh at the majority, the 'crouchers' (another creolization), who have difficulty in comprehending changes among themselves and beat the rock paintings with sticks, because they cannot distinguish between the real and the represented. This confusion alludes to both superstition and social stratification in primitive cultures. Fearing what they do not understand, the crouchers contemplate murder: '*At first we wanted to kill those that did not crouch anymore, those on two legs balanced*' (38), even though, paradoxically, the artistic images meant that the crouchers '*knew how to fight [the beasts] now that they were made of stone*' (137). An important consideration here is the conflict between ignorance/superstition and moments of human enlightenment and how we react to that dichotomy. Okri describes one of those epochal moments of intelligence which catapults mankind forward, capturing the agitation and opposition that such a light or insight causes. In '*Changing too fast. With the beasts on the cave walls and not couching anymore, changing too fast*' (138), the reactive reiteration serves to evaluate the epochal speciation (from crouchers to standeruppers).

Spanning three days and two nights such illumination is ushered in by '*the light-god*' and '*the god of night*' (135). This timeframe is evidently Okri's conception of the time it takes for full illumination, as discussed in my essay on *The Age of Magic* (2014).[2] His poetic prose 'stoku' problematizes the notions of chaos, the collapse of order in reference to Yeats's 'The Second Coming' with its sobering opening octet and celebrated aphorism:

> Turning and turning in the widening gyre
> The falcon cannot hear the falconer
> *Things fall apart; the centre cannot hold;*
> Mere anarchy is loosed upon the world,
> The blood-dimmed tide is loosed, and everywhere
> The ceremony of innocence is drowned;
> The best lack all conviction, while the worst
> Are full of passionate intensity.
>
> ([1933] 1955: 210–11; emphasis added)

The 'ceremony of innocence' lost in the 'blood-dimmed tide' is reflected in the Okrian echoes '*Changing too fast … changing too fast*' (138); '[m]*uch redness came from us in that battle with the wall*' (136). The posthumous edition of the *Collected Poems of W. B. Yeats* ([1933] 1955) includes an author's note (: 536) that explains the symbolism of 'the widening gyre'.[3] It alludes to Macrobius's comment on 'Scipio's Dream' (Lib I. Chapter XII. See note 5): 'When the sun is in Aquarius, we sacrifice to the Shades, for it is in the sign inimical to human life; and from thence, the meeting place of Zodiac and Milky Way, the descending soul by its defluction [*sic* for defluxion] is drawn out of the spherical, the sole divine form, into the cone.' Third-millennium quantum physics has since verified the ancient astrologer's mind-changing observations.

Conclusion

Okri's insight into man in Nature in his 'The Standeruppers' 'stoku' is comparably mind-changing. He is considered here as a griot, shaman or socio-cultural seer: the writer speaks through his rock poems and 'stoku' to apprehend an imminent precipice in time. Although this piece is ostensibly about the beginning of man's journey on earth, it is a cautionary tale about our end. This brings the argument back to Burdick's indictment of *Homo sapiens* as 'the most successful invader in biological history' (2014: 210), quoted at the outset, and to Kolbert's sobering comment on mankind's 'modus vivendi' [way of living]: 'no matter how big an animal is, we don't have a constraint on what we can eat' (ibid.: 233). Both Okri's 'stoku' and his Olduvai Gorge rock poems reveal the destructive nature of humankind, while subtly inculcating cosmic accord and natural harmony through poetic symbolism and lacuna. In the context of the Okrian oeuvre, this reading posits that this humanist strand awakens in the individual sympathies for all fellow creatures on planet earth, nurturing a sense of natural community.

Okri foresees the cyclical ending of the gyre of human inhabitation of the planet. His injunction in *A Time for New Dreams* pertains to his poetic prose 'stoku': 'Heaven knows we need poetry now more than ever. We need the awkward truth of poetry. We need the indirect insistence on the magic of listening' (2011: 3). As poet/priest/'vates'/ 'inSanusi' or 'griot', Okri envisions the Anthropocene: self-annihilation of the human species through gross disregard for the ecology and animal inhabitants of our world (be they two-legged or four-legged). In this green philosophy and prediction of the end of our species, Okri adopts a specific position, tone and intertextual association: he tempers the frightening irony of what is endemic to Anthropocene humankind, what Kolbert (2014: 236) calls the 'madness gene', by pointing to our 'animus/anima' urges or the destructive/constructive dichotomy of human nature. Derek Wright's summation of the Okrian approach is useful. Okri, he writes, has

> [n]one of the older writer's faith in the remedial political action and improved leadership. Instead, there is an inward movement away from protest and polemic and toward interior psychic healing; there is also a visionary introjection of the world into the artistic consciousness that places a tremendous emphasis on the redemptive energies of dream, myth and the imagination. (1997: 158)

Okri's writing thus manifests an awareness of the crisis facing our planet as the Holocene bears its poisoned fruits for humankind. His writing subtly paves the way to a better future for all through love, dream, myth and creativity. Lines from his anthology, *Wild* ('The Ruin and the Forest' 2012: 45) are indicative: 'Habit is thus a great / Force of nature. / When used blindly, / Without wisdom, / In the creation of art / It cultivates a fruitful mediocrity. / Hitched to a great new dream / Or vision it is the creation of marvels / And enduring pyramids of creativity.' The arresting metaphor of 'pyramids of creativity', the context of this 'stoku', seems to allude not to the tombs of great Egyptian pharaohs but to the Mayan temple pyramids. As with the ziggurats of Mesopotamia, these temple pyramids represent the Cosmic Mountain: the dwelling place of the gods and the navel of the world, that is, the mythological centre from which all life emanated (Steven 1998: 110). The implication is of seeking knowledge through love of our fellow creatures on planet earth and not through a desire for the power that knowledge accords the human species.[4]

15

Conscious reveries in *The Magic Lamp: Dreams of Our Age*

There is a dream dreaming us.

—Laurens van der Post

Introduction

The contrary images of darkness and light in the Okri–Clunie text-image publication, *The Magic Lamp* (2017), are part of an ancient, continuing and public tradition. The notion of 'conscious reveries' is predicated on the book's subtitle and the heightened consciousness that invests ordinary stuff with metaphysical conjectures. In the ancient philosophy of the East, as Brian Grassom reminds us, dreams take two forms: 'one is illusion, and one is vision' (2016: 59). The reveries in my title refer principally to the latter, which is 'a harbinger of liberation', albeit that both types belong to the larger dream that is 'dreaming in and through us' (ibid.). There are also two basic kinds of consciousness: the first concerns 'the objective study of the brain', while the second has to do with phenomenal consciousness – 'where feelings come from' – according to David Chalmers (1996; in Papineau and Selina 2013: 19 and 21). *The Magic Lamp: Dreams of Our Age* turns on both aspects of consciousness: causal roles (objective/clinical) and physical realizations (sensibilities).

This reading challenges Julia Flynn's review of *Starbook* that appeared in *The Telegraph* of 13 September 2007, partly because the publication of Okri's text-image, *The Magic Lamp*, ranges globally, drawing on psychology and Wisdom philosophy, and partly because it was launched in September 2017, a decade later, giving the lie to Flynn's contention that Okri's 'striving for universality in fey fairy tales is looking more and more like a creative "cul de sac"' (2018: 1).[1] Curiously, the front cover of the 2017 publication and Erica Wagner's review (2018) – perhaps influenced by Flynn's summation of the earlier novel – dubs the new book 'fairy tales for adults'. This falls short of an adequate summation for tales of transcendence and transformation that include 'life philosophies [in the transhumanist mode] that seek the evolution of intelligent life beyond the current human form and limitations' (More 1990: 6–12). Whereas fairy tales generally deal with a simplified imaginary, with a moral pointer to good versus bad, Okri's so-called fairy tales are deeply philosophical and cerebral, bringing one to the cusp of a mythical realm that stretches beyond our earthly existence, a realm that deals with the meaning of life and the human condition. So, if we must have a fairy tale, should we not qualify the term and opt instead for 'Künstmärchen' (art fairy tale) that foregrounds the fantastical? Dreams are not fairy tales either. 'To work with dreams,' comments Anthony Stevens in *Ariadne's Clue*, 'is to understand that we are moved by energies and influenced by structures that we do not control' (1998: 298). In this sense, dreams are a lot like intuitive creativity. While Stevens argues for an essentially religious understanding of reality, in the context of the discussion, the preference would be for a protorationalist or higher-order understanding of reality. Stevens elaborates in defence of the choice of the term 'religious', saying that '[s]uch energies and structures are experienced as "divine" because they come from the biological ground of all being'. Pertinently, he adds that '[w]e do not create them, they create us' (ibid.). This reciprocity coincidentally supports the comparison with intuitive creativity. Stevens distinguishes between public (rites) and private (dreams) rituals. However, both types of ritual 'canalize' the energies and 'activate' the structures, because in rituals 'something *transcendent* to the intentions of the individual takes over, and personal will is sacrificed to the will of the collective' (ibid.; emphasis added). In abstract Jungian terms, 'the ego becomes to the self ... as the moved to the mover' (ibid.).

Okri asserts that '[t]he African mind is essentially abstract, and their storytelling is essentially philosophical', and that '[c]reativity is evidence of the transhuman' (1997: 117 no. 41; 125 no. 88). A core value of transhumanism is that it is 'the destiny of humankind to transcend the human condition' (Seung 2013: 273). Transhumanist philosophy is a contemplation on the meaning of life, and 'only meaning allows ontological continuity because only conscious acts bring out crystallized themes among multiple heterogenous objects and events' (Smith 2011: 17). In the reflective mode, thinking is represented by self-consciousness, an ontopoietic awareness of our role as human beings. Okri demonstrates a deeply conscious awareness of *our age's* concern with the transhuman, when he claims, as quoted, that the transhuman is evinced by the operation of the creative imagination (1997: 125 no. 88). To underline what this signifies, he follows with the aphorism: 'Creativity is the highest civilizing faculty' (ibid. no. 89). In synchronicity with Okri's aphorisms, transhumanism holds that the human condition 'is not unchanging and that it can and should be changed' (Sandberg 2014: 1). The introduction to this word-image collection invites us to '[w]ander round this book as through a world laid out in the prism of words and colours' (2017: 3). In agreement with Anders Sandberg's view on the transhumanist project, Okri surmises: 'If we are going to change the world, we need to understand how it is made, and what dreams find concrete form in the forms of our times' (ibid.). He concludes by revealing the significance of the waking dream and our responsibility to Mother Earth, averring that '[i]t is with dreams that realities are made. We ought to work on the world as it is and on the dreams that daily become concrete in the hard stone and flowers of our times' (ibid.).

For a Homeric scholar, such as Okri, any consideration of transhumanism – be it individual, creative or cosmic – subscribes to the post-Enlightenment critique of reason, raising questions concerning the meaning of life or even 'becoming something akin to a Greek god' (Sandberg 2014: 2). Presumably the invocation is to the original meaning of 'theos' (Greek, a god i.e. a being who rises above the human condition or who strives to being above the norm).² So, in stating that '[c]reativity is evidence of the transhuman', Okri invokes the creative intuition of poetic quest.

Rise like Lions (Okri 2018) tacitly encapsulates transhuman sentiment in the title to this anthology. Consider, for instance, what he says of the power of protest poetry: 'It speaks to the condition before injustice was perceived and it speaks to the condition after we have taken up the arms of our spirit and our voices against the injustice … It reminds us that beneath our differences, beneath our oppositions, something mysterious unites us that is greater than our dissensions and divisions' (ibid.: 181). Providing further food for thought, he adds:

> Sometimes the truth of a condition is not what the mind thinks. Sometimes when the heart is stilled the truth rises up in our souls, and it is beyond words … No laws written by man or woman can legislate this knowledge that rises up in us from the deep roots of our unexpected humanity. (Ibid.: 181–2)

It seems that what is implied here and in Okri's understanding of transhumanism, particularly as alluded to in the subtitle to *The Magic Lamp*, that is, *Dreams of Our Age*, is that we must be alert to the culture of our own day, to our inner humanity, and be able to distinguish between works of art and the vulgarizing influence of the media with its unscrupulous advertising and aesthetically deadening mass production and noise. As critics, we need to concentrate on the work; we must attempt to find out what it means and whether that meaning adds to our understanding of our own lives and forces us, for a moment and after due meditation, to see, hear, touch, taste and in other ways sense more of some aspects of experience than we ordinarily do. Above all, we need to hearken to the delicate and complex stirrings of an awakened intellect and the heightened senses of our reinvigorated waking dreams that aspire towards the marvellous in transhumanism.

Given that *The Magic Lamp* opens up the imagination of the West to an Eastern sense of marvel: with genies emerging from lamps and illustrations of sacred Egyptian ibis and heron flitting across pages and the jackal-headed god, Anubis, weigher of souls against a feather in the afterlife, in a piece entitled 'The Mystic Betrothal' – and even a magic star tree, it seems appropriate to follow Italo Calvino's ([1988] 1992: 49) description of his own brief compositions and refer to Ben Okri's comparably ephemeral legends and images from folk literature that give narrative form to Rosemary Clunie's paintings as 'petits poèmes en prose' (little prose poems). This collection recognizes subtle forces connecting macrocosm and microcosm, ranging from those of ancient Egyptology and Celtic mythologies to 'those of the Neo-Platonic firmament to the spirits of metal transformed in the alchemist's crucible', to loosely appropriate a line from Calvino's *Six Memos for the Next Millennium* (1992: 19).

Classification is always problematic with an experimental author such as Okri whose works defy pigeonholing. 'Like dreams,' Wagner, opting for the illusionary dream, concurs, 'these stories resist interpretation' (2018: 3). One could argue that these pieces extend Okri's own sub-generic category of 'stoku'³ but are more consciously poetic. Wamuwi Mbao insightfully proffers the term 'ambient literature' in its 'defence of magic as the vital energy behind life, an energy that cannot be summoned at will, but which instead appears in introspection' (2018: n.p.). He elaborates, implicitly referring to the transhuman project: 'The stories locate their politics in the realm of feeling; some characters express longings for worlds that have vanished, but a different set of characters in a different story are just as likely to remake a world that seems on the brink of annihilation' (ibid.).[4] The symbolism of both image and text reflects a complementary aesthetics of consciousness of the most delicate natural forces and abstract ideas of space and time as testified in Okri's and Clunie's respective introductions:

> The spirit of playfulness yields lovely inspirations and hillsides of red and yellow flowers. Playfulness is the dreamtime of the spirit. Light forms appear and dance across the stage. But behind them, sometimes faintly heard, mostly not heard at all, a sombre music plays. It may be the music of mortality. It may be the music of transcendence. (2017: 4)

Alluding to the title, Okri elucidates: 'Sometimes when we play mysterious things speak through us, like genies from a magic lamp' (ibid.). Of the paintings, Clunie articulates her mode of sacred alchemical play in 'These paintings were made by experimenting with colours and evanescent forms. The coloured textures came first, and suggested the forms and images. A narrative moment is crystallized into being from the inner world of colours and their geometries' (ibid.). Identifying the central ethos captured in the artworks, Clunie adds that '[a]ll the paintings share the premise that we are an integral part of our landscape' (ibid.: 5). The idea of play is akin to the aesthetic. 'Play here plays with the outer and inner worlds, which art brings together, transmutes, and transposes,' as Grassom (2016: 59) explains. For this pair of creative artists, we may be 'too late for Gods and too early for Being. Being's poem, just begun, is man' (Heidegger [1947] 1962: 4). In this context, a cognate of transhumanism is re-humanization, and the recognition of our being inseparable from 'our landscape'. In literary parlance, it involves 'creating' oneself as Being, a status that gives Being openness to a free play of thinking cosmically. The playfulness that Okri sees as 'the dreamtime of the spirit' is a natural way to demonopolize thinking as an activity that tends to overestimate itself, to drift into self-conceit (cf. Stafecka 1999: 50). In the act of play, one stands still in time against oneself as an onlooker.

Of 'time' and its universal artistic manifestation, Okri states that '[t]ime is a riddle which the writer and artist interpret in their dreams. And their dreams are coded versions of all our dreams, given the tinge and temper of our mood and our spirit' (1997: 3). Then moving to a life-saving Epicurean universal, he adds: 'The spirit reads time through art. The spirit drinks the timeless through art. In that sense, writing is painting in the spirit, and painting is writing in colours and forms. They both point to the same mysterious allegory that is our lives' (ibid.). This brings the discussion to the text-image publication 'per se'.

The Magic Lamp: Dreams of Our Age

Using a time-honoured fable of wish-fulfilment to explain intuitive creativity, Okri has chosen Clunie's etching of an Aladdin's lamp as simulacre for his artistic

Muse. As narrating experiencing self, Okri draws the reader into the lamp legend, first sharing the potency of the phantasmagorical with the reader, saying: 'First a painting appeared, and the morning after that the legend accompanying it wrote itself miraculously, in a clean handwritten script, on the pages of a black notebook' (2017: 8). Then, after hinting at a series of misfortunes that followed the metaphorical rubbing of the lamp, he alludes to the Midas dangers: 'May you never wish for that which only genies can fulfil. Their gifts are always ambiguous' (ibid.: 9). So, when magic is the approach to the supernatural, it will always bring the imagination back to earth again. In contrast to the epigraph to the collection that suggests an expansion of the imagination in Alice's reflection, 'what is the use of a book ... without pictures and conversations' from Lewis Carroll's (1887) 'Alice's Adventures in Wonderland', that seemingly inspired the mode of *The Magic Lamp*, djinns or genies are locked in a limited reality, implying Blake's (1966) notion of 'mind-forg'd manacles' in his poem 'London' (Stanza 2, l. 4).

Of importance is Okri's more sombre statement that '[t]he stories do not illustrate the paintings. They reach to a world from which the paintings came, the understream of our lives' (2017: 1). The 'understream' is thus a metaphor for the collective unconscious where 'our dream shades into a vast sea of being that we all unknowingly share' (ibid.). Text and art are linked firmly to the powers of transformation. As if prefiguring this synthesis of art and mystical prose, Okri aphorizes in *A Way of Being Free* that '[m]agic distracts our attention from the hidden methods, art draws our attention to the hidden revelation' (1997: 124 no. 79). The implication is that artistic creativity, whether text or image, is alchemical; both transport one to the dazzling world of high order cosmic certainties, intimating that everything is possible. A gossamer-like linear thread weaves poetic prose and painting into a fragile spider web in an evanescent weightlessness as evoked in unit headings such as 'A Vanishing World' (2017: 19), 'Artists in the Fading World' (27), 'Gazing into a Dream' (45) and 'Things not There' (53). Random examples serve to illustrate a counter-narrative to the trapped genie, itself a symbol of what Calvino suggests is our entrapment in 'the frantic spectacle of the world, sometimes dramatic and sometimes grotesque' (1992: 4).

'Things not There', purportedly a contemplation on the troubled memory of a yellow rose, and illustrative of Clunie's experimentation 'with colours and evanescent forms', opens with a proliferation of images, gliding seamlessly from the individual to the natural, from the descriptive to the painterly: 'His grin stretched across the landscape, intersecting the altar of the sleeping church. The house sloping on the hillside slid that bit more down towards the sea. The green was encroached upon by the yellow' (2017: 53). As if responding to the colour-washed ideogram, the piece closes equally enigmatically with the grin as agent (the preposition now omitted before the action verb) and the figure as mirage,

> His grin *stretched* the landscape, *altering* the spaces between the house and the church. But he was an outline in our minds, like the indeterminate silver of the horizon. Only the landscape saw him for what he was. The most potent things often appear to be there. All we saw was a fading yellow mist in the air. (ibid.: 56; emphases added)

The suggestion is that the creative process consists of a synthesis of objective and subjective perceptions, that the writer is involved in reconciling the personal values that he projects into Nature with the reality that already exists there. As with the whole, far from being fairy tale, these excerpts tell of a 'cosmo-transcendental positioning of the living being in the universe', to borrow a chapter title from phenomenologist Jadwiga Smith (2011: 17).

And yet, a paragraph from 'A Vanishing World' (2017: 19–22), taken in isolation, may perhaps have led to the sobriquets 'fable' or 'fairy tale':

> Then there comes one riding a horse with a golden saddle. His eyes are blue from a long Atlantean journey. In his saddle-pack a host of stories like genies from lost temples and forgotten pyramids. He comes while our world is on its last page. (19)

However, the final phrase – 'our world is on its last page' – enunciates the theme. This prose poem is a powerful cautionary tale about humankind's blindness to the end of time, to 'the last page of our age' (ibid.: 22). The second paragraph depicts graphic signs of our times:

> There is blood in our eyes and rape in the scent of history. Women are bruised at night across the cities and are abducted in the dry North. Flowers are starved of pollen. There are oil spills in the guts of Dolphins and the fragrance of melted icecaps above the masts of polar ships. (Ibid.)

This exemplum captures a dense and cryptic warning of the Sixth Extinction: from violence against women, to human trafficking, to climate change, to endangered species, to industrial pollution and holes in the ozone layer. Coincidentally, Calvino provides an articulation of the contrasting modes in the two passages quoted, observing that '[w]henever humanity seems condemned to heaviness, I think I should fly like Perseus into a different space. I don't mean escaping into dreams or into the irrational. I mean that I have to change my approach, look at the world from a different perspective, with a different logic and with fresh methods of cognition and verification' (1992: 7). He summarizes the aim of his creative endeavour with '[t]he images of lightness that I seek should not fade away like dreams dissolved by the realities of present and future' (ibid.). Pertinently, *The Magic Lamp* is bookended by two pieces that exemplify just such 'fresh methods of cognition and verification': 'Birdtalk in a Tentative World' (2017: 11–14) and 'Prophecy' (113–14).

'Birdtalk' (2017: 11–14) is about listening to our inner voice or subconscious mind, here conceptualized as the song of a friendly blue jay that conveys Platonic wisdom about reality: 'You walk the face of the earth and do not notice that all things are dreams' (13). This is coupled with metaphysical conceit in ' "All things have been talking to you from the beginning of time," it said, "and you have not been listening" ' (ibid.: 11). One wonders if Clunie's iridescent colour-wash, depicting a young androgynous/'male' figure and a 'bird' on a post in the foreground and three trees in the background was inspired by Rembrandt's justly famous 1643 etching, 'The Three Trees'. David Smith says that this etching 'has a fair claim to being the single most celebrated landscape in Dutch art … which … entails a further distinction between "poetic" and realistic modes of presentation' (2005: 1). Okri imagines Clunie's trees as 'born of song', while Smith sees Rembrandt's etching as a marriage of prosaic reality and the pastoral ideal. As in Rembrandt, Clunie's trees stand apart 'as an attempt to test not just a vocabulary of natural forms, but notions of pictorial genre and literary conventions' (cf. ibid.).

Alluding to the way in which poetic images can become the focal point in encoding dream-like sensations, 'Prophecy' has the same lightness of touch, nourishing visions in which heaviness disappears as in the opening lines:

Once, when I was gazing into the air, a man with a crown, who was seated on a throne of gold, summoned me. He whispered things in my ears which became a green fire in my head. Sometimes out of this fire images take form. (Okri 2017: 113)

Here, the opening adverb of time, 'once', perhaps adds to the fairy tale sobriquet, as in 'once upon a time'. Quite to the contrary, however, the piece points to a voyeuristic ability derived from ontopoietic ways of seeing and a need to recognize the active function of consciousness in perception, the function of interpretation and of interpretation and correction. It alludes to knowledge of events past and present and an awareness of relativity in '[b]y gazing and not gazing into the infinite present, it seems all worlds are here' (ibid.: 114).

Okri's conscious reverie accords with Calvino's observation that '[t]oday every branch of science seems intent on demonstration that the world is supported by the most minute entities, such as the messages of DNA, the impulses of neurons, and quarks, and neutrinos wandering through space since the beginning of time' (1992: 8). The atomizing of things starts in the visible aspects of the world but, like atoms, is ever-changing. In Okri's hands, they transmute into an image from mythic fables: 'The grass stirs, and a heron considers the world with a question in the shape of its beak' (2017: 114). The heron, according to Lewis Spence who details the religious history of ancient Egypt, signifies 'the bennu, a bird of the heron species [that] gave rise to the mythical bird, the phoenix' ([1915] 1922: 196). It is identified with the rising and setting sun, and so is a symbol of the cycle of life but, more particularly mythologically, of rebirth/regeneration, for the phoenix rises again from its ashes. It is, however, the sacred ibis, likewise of the heron species 'a bird of a deep black colour, with legs like a crane' that has the Okrian 'strongly hooked beak' (Spence 1922: 296). The legendary ibis guarded the city of Hermopolis by destroying winged serpents, brought to Egypt by the west wind (ibid.). For the purpose of this discussion, whether heron or ibis, I surmise that 'the question in the shape of its beak' is a metaphysical one, such as, 'What is the "constructive emergence of the world for human consciousness"?' or 'What is its involvement in "the universe of cognition"?'– questions posed by Anna-Teresa Tymieniecka in her study of consciousness (Tymieniecka 2011 quoted by Smith 2011: 18). As Spence observes, among primitive peoples, 'the soul is frequently regarded as possessing the form and attributes of a bird' (1922: 31).[5]

'The Mythic Betrothal' (2017: 15–18), arguably the core story allegorizing a 'hieros gamos' (divine marriage) of spirit and soul/Heaven and earth, also – but more overtly (intentionally or otherwise) – invokes Egyptian mythology. The painting features a bridal couple 'waiting for the moment that will bring them together' (ibid.: 15) in the foreground, set against a city in flames in the background, perhaps a subtle reminder of wanton destruction of the Twin Towers in Manhattan in 9/11. Okri captures the waking dream thus: 'They are the mysterious hope of the kingdom ... He holds the ankh like a weapon against fire. Her bridal dress a panacea against all corruption. Her arms folded in benediction. Time is magical here' (ibid.: 15 and 18). As Wagner observes, 'the woman protected against fire offers hope, a hope that is threaded throughout this bright, mysterious book' (2018: 3). In a hope that invokes the conventions of Petrarchan poetry, Okri writes:

> In this garden they stand and they wait ... The alchemical ceremony takes place under the aegis of unseen masters. There are no witnesses, except our hopes ... The flower blooms again as the syllables renew the air. Something has changed in the heart of the fallen kingdom. The water tastes new in the rivers. (Okri 18)

The illustration carries faint echoes of Rembrandt. However, in contrast to his barely visible lovers in Arcadian attire in 'The Three Trees', hidden in a bower of bliss and conjuring up the literary world of medieval pastoral romance, Clunie's groom is jackal-headed. The painting is evocative of the Egyptian god, Anubis, weigher of hearts or souls in the underworld, portrayed as jackal-headed (cf. Spence [1915] 1922: 30). Whether it is hearts or souls that are weighed in the afterlife is unimportant, for this 'is a mystic betrothal in an age of madness' (Okri 2017: 18). Here, the artwork and legend coalesce creating a sharp distinction between the poetic and the prosaic, bringing together polarities of rural bliss and urban chaos, earth and sky, light and dark, small and large, inside and outside. Graphic imagery of a world run amok with 'churches in green flames' (ibid.: 16–17), suggestive of arson, 'wailing sirens beyond the tower blocks' (a pointer to the Grenfell tower disaster in London, perhaps), vermin-infested 'maisonettes', widespread corruption and cacophonous music coupled with 'the gibbering of the mad, the anxious and the disillusioned' (ibid.: 17), climaxes in a wry observation about contemporary spirituality that '[e]ven atheists have lost their faith' (17). It is doubtful whether even children would disagree that this is hardly the stuff of fairy tales. The purpose may seem to be to convey sublime love as opposed to the worldly profane, but this is an allegory, possibly for a visionary dream that captures an epiphanic moment in intuitive creativity: 'But you are here now in this ring of trees. The turtle dove murmurs yellow melodies. Flute music waters the lavender and honeysuckle. The houses are all symbols with spacious rooms in which the air is pure. Blue clouds create a reality that is like a dream' (ibid.: 17–18).

This brings the argument back to Okri's views on the transhuman project, requoted here: 'It is with dreams that realities are made. We ought to work on the world as it is and on the dreams that daily become concrete in the hard stone and flowers of our times' (2017: 3). The excerpt seems to be a prime example of what Okri means by his aphorisms 'Creativity is evidence of the transhuman' (1997: 125 no. 88) and 'Creativity is the highest civilizing faculty' (ibid., no. 89), cited at the outset.

Okri's conscious reveries resonate with Shamanistic practice as articulated by Calvino: 'Faced with the precarious existence of tribal life – drought, sickness, evil influences – the shaman responded by ridding his body of weight and flying to another world, another level of perception, where he could find the strength to change the face of reality' (1992: 27), as exemplified in 'From the Magic Lamp' (49–52), the last 'petit poème en prose' touched on. Superficially, it comes closest to fairy tale mode in emulating the title to this collection. But it is illustrative of literature that has an existential function, the search for lightness as a reaction to the weight of living (cf. Calvino 1992: 26). As if flying to an entirely illusionary Oriental Bazaar on his magic carpet, the narrator attests to the serious undercurrent: 'If you find your way here it will be because you have at last been overcome by those things which you sought but would not acknowledge' (ibid.: 49). Suggestive of living in the 'now', the narrator's conscious reverie transmutes into the 'axis mundi' in 'I stand now in such a moment. The world pours through these blue empty spaces, dreamers seeking their most secret dreams' (ibid.: 52). As the fleeting vision of lamp, genie and bazaar dissolves, as in 'Things not There', the narrative voice concludes with an enigmatic counting of one's blessings in '[m]aybe I am lucky to have sought the wrong thing, and to have found what makes things true' (ibid.). Here, Okri pictures the 'infinite' as a spiritual state in which all beings exist within the radiance of the Eternal Light.

Conclusion

Deferring to the definable and indefinable reality of the natural world provokes 'conscious reveries', as Coleridge suggests. In his lecture 'On poesy and art', reproduced in *English Essays: Sidney to Macaulay* (1909–14), Coleridge muses: 'In the objects of nature are presented, as in a mirror, all the possible elements, steps, and processes of intellect antecedent to *consciousness*, and therefore to the full development of the intelligential act' (2017: 3; emphasis added). In *The Magic Lamp: Dreams of Our Age*, Nature is transposed into painterly or poetic prose: 'words, images, text, dream, the alchemy of art and literature' (Okri 2017 pers. com.).

This chapter has attempted to show how the 'play' of art 'channels and reflects the nature of life as profound play' (Grassom 2016: 59) and how conscious reveries or visionary dream and semblance can serve to illuminate 'reality'. This notion of 'play', as Grassom observes in a comparable context, points 'to something higher and deeper; and how the play of ambiguity at the heart of art leads not to confusion, but to certain delight' (ibid.). This constitutes literary transhumanism. Seung elucidates: 'The "meaning" of life includes both *universal* and personally dimensions' (2014: 1; emphasis added); in simple terms, this gives rise to the questions: 'Are *we* here for a reason?' and 'Am *I* here for a reason?' (ibid.; emphases added), respectively.

This is a collection that links the internal world of past experiences with the external world of present sensations and, in linking them, produces the imaginative worlds of the poet's mind. Whether text or its complementary image, this is a book shot through with arcane wisdom, transmitted through myths, legends and folktales or via the collective unconscious, that forms the basic cultural resources of all societies. The abstractions of Clunie's paintings, arguably inspired by the parallel worlds in Okri's justly famous *The Famished Road*, coupled with Okri's forever new experimentation, have resulted in a style that is itself even more dialogical in its oppositions than usual and, for that reason, more compellingly experiential, creating a dramatic eidetic visionary effect. To cite the author, 'the book is both an allegory and a discovery; it allegories our times and the creative process, and it discovers a new functionality, a new alchemy' (2018 pers. com.). In all twenty-five poetic prose 'waking dreams', Okri's narrative voices form a chorus of lodestars who seem to have happened upon a synthesis, gathering up the various aspects and degrees of reality into a glorious symphonic unity.

16

'The Incandescence of the Wind' (1982): 'Rain wisdom down upon the earth'

Introduction

A critique of 'The Incandescence of the Wind' necessitates some exploration of the sociopolitical and biographical contexts in which this protest poem was generated. Compatriot thinker and writer Wole Soyinka provides a sobering entrée into Ben Okri's 'The Incandescence of the Wind'. In *The Open Sore of a Continent*, Soyinka points to the 'dirty tricks' and 'covert military operations' that 'instigated an unceasing round of bloodletting' (1996: 5). In fact, massacres by military killer squads in post-Biafran Nigeria[1] simply exacerbated the protracted rapacity, lack of control and accountability that were to guarantee what Soyinka terms 'Nigeria's yet unheralded membership card for the club of practitioners of "ethnic cleaning"' (ibid.: 6).

Rooted in the natural world to expose the unnatural in power politics and man's inhumanity to man, Okri's 'The Incandescence of the Wind' was written in August 1982 – between the 'patently rigged elections' (Soyinka 1996: 7) of 1979 and 1983, when a military junta seized control, and after the decimation of oil-rich Ogoniland that foreshadowed the capture, incarceration and death of fellow poet and activist Ken Saro-Wiwa on 10 November 1995. Coups and countercoups, displacements, expropriation of property, ruthless clampdowns, violence and rape became endemic, and climaxed in the 'arbitrary annulment of the national election on 23 June 1993'[2] that 'violently robbed the Nigerian people of their nationhood' (ibid.: 9). Internecine strife, then, is the broad sociopolitical context for Okri's poem, first published in his *An African Elegy* ([1992] 1997: 35–7) and chosen by the author for his selection of protest poems in *Rise like Lions* (2018b: 89–92).

Whereas Soyinka's 'personal narrative of the Nigerian crisis' is a requiem for the Nigerian nation, Okri conceives of an imaginative redemption of the suffering he so graphically depicts in this early poem. Both writers acknowledge the complexity of contemporary nationhood. Nation status, Soyinka surmises, 'has never been an absolute or a constant … it has ever followed the politics of conflict, interest, alliances, power, and even accident' (1996: 14–15). Like Saro-Wiwa, both Soyinka and Okri are feisty, passionate and celebrated; yet, neither living poet postures as an inimitable authority, although conceptual artists do write with and within a personal experiential authority.

In an interview with Claire Armistead on 6 September 2018, preceding the opening night on 14 September 2018 of Okri's stage adaptation of Albert Camus's (1946) novel, *L'Éstranger* (The Outsider), Okri (2018a) reiterates an incident that he fictionalized in 'Laughter Beneath the Bridge' from *Incidents at the Shrine* ([1986] 1993). Recalling his first-hand knowledge of the Nigerian Civil War and his terrified recollection of the only Urhoba word he could recall, that for 'shit', which saved his life, Okri states matter-of-factly that at six, 'I was nearly shot because I could not speak my dad's language' (2018: n.p.). And language is crucially important to this protest poem. Regarding national justice, that which Okri believes ought to be 'the law that governs the rise and fall of nations', he is moved to assert: 'What does not grow, dies; what does not face its truth, perishes; those without vision deserve the destruction that will fall upon them; those that believe that they can suppress freedom and yet live in freedom are hopelessly deluded' (1997: 108). These are clearly the sentiments of a visionary. Continuing his carrion call to action, he warns: 'Either a nation faces its uncomfortable truths, or it is overwhelmed by them; for there is a prophetic consequence in the perpetuation of lies, just as there is an unavoidable fate for all those who refuse to see' (ibid.). Okri sees truth-telling, however unpalatable, as a moral obligation, and he cautions against 'careless' fictive composition, saying: 'Beware of storytellers who are not fully conscious of the importance of their gifts, and who are irresponsible in their application of their art: they could unwittingly help along the psychic destruction of their people' (1997: 109). This fragment from 'The Joys of Storytelling' in *A Way of Being Free* seemingly provides a mandate for the heightened awareness in 'The Incandescence of the Wind'; it also informs Okri's tribute to Ken Saro-Wiwa in the same book. Appalled by the execution of this mentoring activist, an illegally silenced voice of a nation, aided and abetted by those in power and exploited for commercial gain by a petroleum company, Okri intones: 'If you want to know what is happening for an age or in a nation, find out what is happening to its writers, the town-criers: for they are the seismographs that calibrate impending earthquakes in the spirit of the times' (ibid.: 104).

The writer as barometer of the age: 'The Incandescence of the Wind'

At the early age of 23 with several plays and two published novels under his belt, Okri demonstrates his acute social consciousness and intuitive creativity. His poetic aesthetic is encapsulated in a subsection in *A Way of Being Free* entitled, 'The Human Race is not yet Free'; he writes: 'In a world like ours, where death is increasingly drained of meaning, individual authenticity lies in what we can find that is worth living for' (1997: 56 no. 26). Characteristically, he is specific; he adds: 'And the only thing worth living for is love' (ibid.). In case one is in need of clarification, Okri first prioritizes the biblical maxim, 'Love thy neighbour as thyself', thus articulating the essential meaning of love with 'Love for one another. Love for ourselves'. He elaborates with a guiding catechism on love, embracing a multitude of aspects of humankind's core emotion:

Love of our work. Love of our destiny, whatever it may be. Love for our difficulties. Love of life. The love that could free us from the mysterious cycles of suffering. The love that releases us from our self-imprisonment, from our bitterness, our greed, our madness-engendering competitiveness. The love that can make us breathe again. Love of a great and beautiful cause, a wonderful vision. A great love for another, or for the future. The love that reconciles us to ourselves, to our simple joys, and to our undiscovered repletion. A creative love. A love touched with the sublime. (1997: 56–7)

For this writer, love is, as in Judaeo-Christian mythology, the primary life force; it symbolizes the divine as in 'God is Love'. Such is the ethos that enables the poet to conclude his angry protest against the Nigerian sociopolitical situation with lines illustrating a subliminal turn of the wheel of transformation in the closing stanza:

The graveyards heave
The riverbeds sigh.
And I wake surprised:
   - the incandescence has become
   our own
   - the skeletons have reclaimed
   the lands
   - a new spirit breathing phosphorous
   has grown
   into the blue roots of the times.
([1992] 1997: 92)

The omission of conjunctions (asyndeton) here simultaneously checks and urges the utterance on. The ideogram and highly skilled oratory are indicative that the poet speaker has mastered his rage; the incandescence of the wind that 'bothers' him in the opening lines is transmuted into amazement: he 'wakes surprised' as the incandescence now signifies only that which emits light. The sublimity inheres in the fact that he seems impervious to the powerful emotional impact that his choice of diction has stimulated. As with his short story, 'Laughter beneath the Bridge' (1986), this poem with its characteristic Okrian theme of an imaginative redemption of suffering is thus, at once, protest and promise. Regeneration is suggested by the image of growth, an emergent rebirth in 'the blue roots'. Blue is, as Anthony Stevens explains, 'the colour of the sky and the sea; it therefore shares in their symbolism, their translucency, their vastness, their infinity, and their coolness' (1998: 149); in African cosmogony, it signifies transition into the cycle of death becoming life. Coupled with the image of phosphorous, a chemical element that bursts into spontaneous yellow light when exposed to air, the closing lines allude to that which exceeds the human condition; the four elements in the poem – riverbeds (water), roots (earth), phosphorous (the alchemy of air and fire) conjoin to represent the ultimate and the eternal. Okri is forever the conscious artist and didactic power: he challenges us to open the envelope of two-dimensional existence and stand in awe at the replete universe of three- and four-dimensional life of which we are an intimate part.

In addition to its depiction of the fires of civil strife that Okri witnessed first-hand as a small child, the poem is also arguably informed by personal happenstance: an initial setback in Okri's academic career. A Nigerian government scholarship awarded in 1980 was curtailed in 1982, forcing a promising student to abandon his Bachelor of Arts degree in Comparative Literatures at the University of Essex in England[3] and to live on his wits. One can surmise that this disappointment informs the reflective mood in the poem. This talented young writer was saved only by his creative gifts that had already seen the publication of his first two novels: *Flowers and Shadows* in 1979 and *The Landscapes Within* in 1981, a remarkable achievement.

The poem, a prelude to his famed *The Famished Road* (1991)[4] and *The Freedom Artist* (2019), is both angry and enigmatic, as deduced by the 'double entendre' of the words 'incandescence' and 'wind' in the title. In its noun form, 'incandescence' means that which sheds light; used adjectivally, incandescent means 'very angry' (*Oxford Advanced Learner's Dictionary* 2010); 'wind' is, of course, literally 'air that moves quickly as a result of natural forces' (ibid.). 'Wind' is also a metaphor, 'inter alia', for natural cleansing and is used politically – as in 'the winds of change' – to signify an alteration in nation status. The poem captures the prevailing winds, with its creator as both headwind and tailwind. 'Double meanings, approximations, word-play and homophonies' are, according to legendary alchemist Fulcanelli ([1964] 1971; in Roob 2014: 512), characteristic of the language of alchemists. The nuanced diction frames the poem, yet it is evident that it is an ill wind that 'bothers' the poet in the opening stanza: 'Is there a searing clarity / about the noises / rising daily / from this riverbed we call our own?' 'There are poets,' Okri acknowledges in *Rise like Lions*, 'who believe that poetry should not get mixed up with the sordid stuff of politics and society … But poetry is language and language is part of the fabric of power, of the laws, of the making and unmaking of society' (2018b: 78). Coincidentally, he aligns his point of view with that of Shelley's oft-quoted maxim about poets being the 'unacknowledged legislators of the world' (explained later), he believes that poets can and should protest when things are unacceptable, to effect change, to shift thoughts, because it is they who are able to 'use the finest instrument they have and they sing with delicacy and with power of the ills of society' (ibid.: 77).

This concern with the poet's responsibility and with linguistic exactitude is voiced throughout his multi-generic oeuvre. In *Astonishing the Gods*, for instance, he surmises that the act of naming causes things to disappear: 'names have a way of making things disappear' ([1995] 1999: 6). This is 'why all art aspires to the condition of wordlessness' (1997: 89), Okri states in his lecture at Trinity College, Cambridge – published in *A Way of Being Free* (1997) as 'Beyond Words'. Okri does not mince his words; pointing to the destructive potential of ill-considered words, he suggests that words can describe or misdescribe reality. Like acid, they can kill or cure. 'The highest things,' he insists, 'are beyond words' (ibid.: 89), because literature affects one silently, in dreams, like music and painting. Its aim is to 'enchant', 'transform', 'make life more meaningful or bearable in its own small and mysterious way' (ibid.). Echoing this power of words, the subtitle to this chapter, also taken from Okri's first anthology of poems, occurs in a poem tellingly entitled 'Stammerings on Bedrock' (ibid.: 22–6). While the mood of this latter poem is sustained in 'The Incandescence ...', and its trajectory points to the ameliorative guiding vision underpinning the Okrian corpus, its deployment of 'incandescent' in the injunction to 'Hold us in the palm / Of incandescent understanding' (ibid.: 26, Stanza 11) is more overtly obvious, clearly signifying enlightenment. And yet, 'Stammerings ...' is unequivocally likewise a protest poem, an invocation to cosmic forces against the terminal cancer of lies, terrors and misrule. Stanza 2 exhorts:

> Rain wisdom down upon the earth
> Wash thunder upon us
> And on this landscape smash our beginnings:
> Smash the endings that they foresaw
> Hold us in the palm of incandescent
> Understanding
> Bare us to those birds of madness
> That peck at our false bindings
> And reveal the pulp of flesh
> Our cross of fire.
>
> ([1992] 1997: 22, ll. 9–19)

The persona's desperate anaphoric reiteration in 'smash our beginnings / Smash our endings ...' serves to endorse Okri's avowal that '[b]y the very nature of language the poet, whether they choose to accept it or not, is part of the order of things' (2017: 78).

The setting of 'Incandescence ...', with its tension between biblical and typically African imagery – vineyard and riverbed – is evocative. A landscape that once yielded nature's bounty has become a dry riverbed. It is in this scorched-earth space – 'from this reverbed we call our own' – that the persona asks rhetorically: 'Is there a searing clarity / about the noises / rising daily?' The epithet 'searing' denotes intense/burning/shooting and is normally associated with pain; linked to 'clarity', it calls for responsiveness to the status quo. In his preface to his collected protest poems in *Rise like Lions*, Okri elucidates on that which incites protest writing with 'Sometimes poetry, roused by something intolerable in society, awoken by some injustice, rises to the condition of protest.' Elaborating on the worldly conditions that lead to creative reaction, he avers that '[s]ometimes the poet is so choked by the foulness of the world, or some unacceptable condition of society, that they abandon briefly the woods and flowers and love ditties to sound a powerful note' (2018b: 77). The use of polyptoton (interchange of singular and plural) – 'the poet' ... 'they' – in these lines functions as a powerful auxiliary in the production of emotional effect and is deployed with subtlety in the shifts in personal pronouns from 'I' and 'me' to 'we' throughout 'The Incandescence ...'. That the poem generates protest becomes clear in the shift in mood, tone and number in Stanza 2 where Nature and the citizenry are portrayed as victims of Nigerian power politics; even the staple foodstuff and scavenging birds are subjected to the tyranny: 'The yam-tubers bleed our sorrows / Crows in the fields / scream of despair / Machetes pollute our food / With rust' (Stanza 2). In this erstwhile nation, 'The masters conduct their / plunderings / with quiet murders: / The victims perform maypole dances / around the village shrines' (ibid.). It seems that poetry can barely contain the horrors of wholesale slaughter of any in opposition, as implied in the 'quiet murders', a euphemism for swift and secret killing sprees, as underlined in the 'maypole dances' of those caught in the fray.

Stanzas 3 and 4 pile on the agony in tortuous imagery that transmits a 'danse macabre' and where a heightened auditory sense draws the reader into an experiential hell on earth. In Stanza 3, the persona 'hears' a cold fire 'consume the groins / of heroes / and shrivel the guts / of martyrs'. The sustained oxymoron in 'a cold fire in the air' that consumes and shrivels evokes a state of cold panic, while the alliteration in 'groins' and 'guts' and 'grave stones' quickens the pace heralding the 'collective cowardice' of those complicit in the destruction of life and limb, 'names squeezed from tubers of life' arguably through being unable to withstand torture. No one can escape the mayhem; in Stanza 4, helpless mothers, unable to protect their offspring, whether from the dangers of the 'city fires' or 'neon signs' and 'cellars of madness', 'scream'; the menfolk are even more vulnerable: their identities are 'lost in files' as they are caught in the crossfire or, worse still, doused with petrol and 'barbecued' as elections, riots and coups become the order of the day. The strength of the implicit allusion to cannibalism appals, amplifying the poem's remonstratory resonance.

A mid-poem climax is reached in Stanza 5 for 'The incandescence in the air / burns inward'. The self-devouring rot prompts a profound series of rhetorical questions: 'Is there a name for this fear? / Is there a fearful country / in these fields / where such realities are / manufactured whole?' Echoes of the 'fearful symmetry' in Blake's 'Tiger' and *The Killing Fields* seem patent as the poet questions the very possibility of the existence of nationhood.

Preceding a call to arms in Stanzas 7 and 8, the poet speaker elaborates on the devastating effects of 'the short-sightedness of power' worldwide. The imagery in Stanza 6 becomes more horrifyingly graphic: there are whispers in the wind ('I heard a secret') of the tragic impact on both the animal and human kingdoms with the production of sterile 'eggs of blood' and riverbeds and junkyards choked with 'multiple deaths … polluting our world / with the irascible sense / of failure'. The trajectory of the poem now becomes clear. What 'bothers' the poet speaker in the opening stanza is described with mounting clarity in Stanzas 2–5 in relation to the Nigerian crisis, to become a global problem of what is euphemistically termed 'the short-sightedness of power' in Stanza 6 – the understatement making the indictment even stronger, leading to a poetic rendering of implied prosaic questions – Do we accept our fate? Do we capitulate? Or do we take action in the corridors of power? – seen in 'Shall we join them / or shall we celebrate / the vision of empty offices'. The poem now moves swiftly to its wind-induced awakening – 'And I wake surprised' in the closing stanza (see also note 4) – with two alliterative b's in 'Break the bread / of initiation into / revolt', the onomatopoeic plosives suggesting that it is up to us to stop the rot. The idea of rejoicing in the decision to take action is implicit in the reiteration of the word 'celebration' in Stanzas 6 and 7 that also picks up the word 'incandescence' in 'We shall celebrate with our / emaciated chests.

/ We shall clench and raise our fists / in the wonder of incandescence' against those who feed off the living dead: 'those worms / that ravage our serenity' (Stanza 8). As is characteristic of this lodestar (guide), the underlying interrelated questions are, as noted by Robert Fraser (2002: 24): What does it mean to be a citizen? What are the responsibilities of the artist? What does it mean to be a human being? This returns the discussion to the transformative awakening in the final stanza.

Conclusion

In 'The Incandescence of the Wind', Okri engages in what philosophers call 'higher-order thinking' or HOT consciousness. He asserts that '[p]oets are set against the world because they cannot accept that what there seems to be is all there is' (1997: 3), the syntax here demanding slow reading and even rereading, thus enhancing the emotive affect. Endorsing Shelley's famous maxim about poets being the unacknowledged legislators of the world, because they take the world at face value, as 'a given' (ibid.: 4), Okri explains that poets 'come with no tablets of stone, and they do not speak with God' (ibid.: 3). Poets, unlike the biblical Moses, are not given, nor do they give, commandments. Signifying that it is, instead, the marvel of creation, intuitive creativity, dreams that inspire poets to 'remake the world in words', Okri submits that it is the poets' sharpened sensitivity and keen sensibility to 'human suffering' that raises poetic consciousness. Perhaps more importantly as he posits in *Rise like Lions*, a poet says no when he finds things unacceptable; essentially, he believes that 'something can be changed, that the world can be altered' (2018b: 77). Change for the better is not wrought by politicians but by the poet who 'suffers our agonies ... and combines them with all the forgotten waves of childhood' (1997: 3–4). In a reworking of the age-old adage 'Out of the mouths of babes and sucklings' into 'Out of the mouths of poets speak the yearnings of our lives' (ibid.: 4), Okri intimates that it is not so much childish innocence but rather childlike trust in truth, allied with justice,[5] that enables one to *see* the possibilities of ameliorative transformation. Fortuitously, a fragment from *A Time for New Dreams* encapsulates the tone and mood of 'The Incandescence of the Wind':

> All our myths: they should be reunited in the knowledge that unless we return to the unfragmented truth of the family of humanity, unless we return love back to the centre of our ways, unless the colours return home to light, we will be trapped in our myths, which will then become our prisons. Then eventually will follow our doom, and the twilight of all our stories. (2011: 121 no. 25)

This fictive liberation is an enactment of the human agency that Okri appeals for in his elegiac protest poem. A coincidental assertion of autonomy and of the self subtly shifts our thoughts and feelings about the world, showing 'by indirection, that the world's visage is not fixed' as he opines in *Rise like Lions* (2018b: 79). The horror and terror of killing in the elegy also points to the resurgence of transhuman consciousness and the possibility of renewal in life. The deep wisdom of living without anger or resentment ('sine ira aut studio'), is an alchemical guideline which strategically places Okri way ahead of many peer writers. In this poem, as elsewhere, Okri's closing stanza with the persona's amazed realization that 'the incandescence has become our own', and multiple use of asyndeton in the quoted lines, 'the skeletons have reclaimed / the lands / a new spirit breathing phosphorous / has grown / into the blue roots of the times' (Stanza 9), speaks of an unfolding of a supranational soul, identity and phase of national being.

Part Five

In search of the marvellous: The sacred ziggurat (symbolic celestial mountain)

17

Protean magic in *The Mystery Feast* and *The Magic Lamp*

Introduction

In contradistinction to James Frazer's 'magic, religion, and science' chronology, which he sees as distinct ([1922] 1991: 711), Ben Okri constructs an interlaced magic/science/myth poetics in *The Magic Lamp* (2017). Here, as in *The Mystery Feast* (2015), intuitive creativity and the ever-changing Protean magic of being bring about a synthesis of rational, non-rational and supra-rational domains. This mythic conjunction is seen in lines from his epigraphic poem entitled 'All That We Do' that introduces his discussion on storytelling: 'Like the spider we turn / All things into ourselves. / We bend the light / Of time into fables' (ibid.: 2; Stanza 3, ll. 10–13). What this suggests is that storytelling is inherently timeless in human nature. Then, supra-rationally or paradoxically, personal agency is wrested from us by the enigma of 'reality': 'Beyond our mind, reality moves / Unknowable like the darkness / Before creation' (ibid.; Stanza 4, ll. 14–16). The arachnid simile in Stanza 3 conjoins with unfathomable cosmic reality in Stanza 4 to reveal the kind of natural magic Okri conceives of as governing a story-making beingness. An experiential scientific aphorism from the same book underlines this subconscious activity: 'We incubate stories like maggots in rotting meat. We incubate stories like spores' (2015: 32 no. 15). The countless metamorphoses of the microorganisms – maggots and mushrooms – hidden from normal sight allude to the Protean magic, the mystery behind the cosmos that, in turn, parallels the uncanny reversed reciprocity implied in 'In every moment we are part of the infinite stories that the universe is telling us, and that we are telling the universe' (ibid.: 8). Okri's aesthetic of Protean magic thus seems to be an intriguing, if unstable, admixture of Western magical innovations and indigenous African Shamanistic realities as indicated in his response to the contemporary dominance of/reverence for science and technology: 'At the heart of all science – its experiments, the theories, its mathematics, its discoveries, its interpretations – is the story instinct' (ibid.). To reveal the truth of our times, Okri builds on a socially conscious objectivity, arguing that '[t]he scientific mind would be impossible without the story DNA, without the story-seeing brain cells' (ibid.), the workings of which are, of course, invisible. Invoking an African philosophical truism, he states that '[e]very human being immersed in the cyclorama of reality is implicated in the cosmic story-making quality of reality' (ibid.). More tentatively, he suggests first that '[m]aybe this story-making quality of reality is what constitutes the heart of our existence' (ibid.). Just as the delicate web woven by the spider is temporary in its fragility yet lethal, so too is the storytelling quality of being both temporal and potent. 'Maybe this story-making quality of being,' Okri muses, 'is the principle magic as well as the principle illusion of our lives' (ibid.: 9).

That the art of magic is virtually inseparable from human curiosity is widely evident in cultural mores and religious beliefs throughout the world. Aligning himself with Shamanistic spiritual transformations, Okri reminds us that '[i]n ancient Africa, in Celtic lands, storytellers were magicians. They were initiates' (2015: 24). The opening gambit in Lewis Spence's *The Magic Arts in Celtic Britain*, mirrors this view: 'The tradition of the arcane and the mysterious cleaves to certain races so naturally as to make it seem an inherent and inalienable possession' ([1945] 1999: 11).[1] The writers of antiquity, Okri explains, 'understood the underlying nature of reality, its hidden forces' (2015: 24). H. A. Reyburn (1936: 135) likewise argues for the ubiquity of the practice of magic despite 'the derision cast upon it' by science and 'the condemnation it receives' from religion. The irony is that natural magic is inseparable from science, while religions everywhere are predicated upon belief in the magical. Echoing Gerardus van der Leeuw's *Phänomenologie der Religion* (1933: 349ff.), Mircea Eliade argues that world mythologies hold that 'all religious acts have been founded by gods, civilizing heroes, or mythical ancestors' (1954: 22). And there exists a symbiosis of religious myth and natural scientific magic. Consider Christ's miracles, transubstantiation, immortality, belief in the divinity of kings, popes and other leaders[2] on the one hand, and the natural magical transformation of chrysalis into butterfly, the tiny acorn becoming a giant oak tree, speciation,[3] fractals, DNA and cosmic reality, on the other. The adage, 'quod ubique, semper, et ab omnibus creditus' (what (is) everywhere, (what is) always, (is) believed by everyone), seems to pertain.

Although Okri does not seem to see African art in terms of 'magic', it can be argued that all fields of human endeavour involve magic or aspects of magic, where the principles of thought upon which magic is based – to use James Frazer's science-based classification – are those in which 'like produces like', or where 'an effect resembles its causes'. And then there are those principles in which 'things which have once been in contact with each other continue to act on each other at a distance after the physical contact has been severed' ([1922] 1991: 11). In accordance with mathematical processes of combinational analysis, Frazer calls this first principle the 'Law of Similarity', which is imitative or mimetic; the second principle is the 'Law of Contact and Contagion', reflected as 'homeopathic magic' and 'contagious magic', respectively. Brian Copenhaver reminds us not only that Frazer famously linked 'magic, religion, and science' in *The Golden Bough* (2015: 10) but also that Frazer described his acclaimed study as 'comparative mythology', thus universalizing it.

In terms of religious festivals and cultural rituals, Eliade (1954: 22) proposes that their effectiveness accrues from acts exactly repeated in accordance with mythical models 'performed at the beginning of time by a god, a hero, or an ancestor' – an instance of the Law of Similarity. If magic is interpreted in the context of that which the magician or medicine-man practices, and both the Laws of Similarity and Contact have universal application, that is, if they apply equally to human actions and inanimate

Nature, then 'magic', Frazer states, 'is a spurious system of natural law', if a 'fallacious guide of conduct'. In other words, the notion of 'magic' – and, by extension, myth – is, at once, a 'false science' and 'an abortive art' ([1922] 1991: 11).

If one's interpretation of magic is limited to magicians or sorcerers as practitioners, as that of Reyburn and others seems to be, and little distinction is made between the conjurer or illusionist, and the necromancer or wizard, this begs the question: Where do the seekers after the power to *know* fit in? What of the lovers of truth such as the philosopher, the poet, the mystic, the scientist and followers of the world's many religious mythologies? Frazer makes a useful distinction between 'theoretical' magic based on a system of natural law that governs the sequence of events, practised by the scientist, and the 'practical' magic of the magician, illusionist or primitive sorcerer that involves a set of precepts which human beings observe (and repeat) to 'compass their ends' ([1922] 1991: 11). As Frazer maintains, the latter is always an art and never a science.

The impulse behind the quest of the mythmaker – whether creative artist, philosopher or theologian – is contemplative knowledge, inspired by love, the laudable purpose of which, as Bertrand Russell attests, is 'delight or joy or ecstasy' (Lenz 2017: 9). In this context, Susan Greenwood (2009) proffers a theory of magical consciousness, and this pertains to writers like Ben Okri. For Okri and Greenwood, magic has to do with the workings of the human mind in terms of an expanded awareness, or what the late Anna-Teresa Tymieniecka calls 'ontopoiesis', rather than with sociocultural explanations, such as 'magical realism'.[4] Expanded consciousness/ontopoiesis embraces the self-creative activity of consciousness. This resonates with the brand of magic encountered in Okri's works, particularly in *The Magic Lamp* (2017). This querant reveals himself to belong to the class of seekers after a higher order: the ecstasy of contemplative knowledge transmuted into ekphrastic prose-poems. Akin to the Augustan concept of 'curiositas' (quality of being inquisitive, curious or fastidious) each piece is a codification of 'naturalia' and 'mirabilia' (the natural and the wonderful). Each suggests ways in which we might recover the primordial 'substantia vitae', to appropriate William Eamon's terminology. Each prose-poem is a subtle philosophical statement on natural magic that Eamon defines as 'the science that attempt[s] to give rational, naturalistic explanations of the occult forces of [N]ature' (1994: 9). For Eamon, as for Okri, 'the basic assumption of natural magic [is] that [N]ature teem[s] with hidden forces and powers that could be imitated, improved upon, and exploited for human gain'. One could claim then that the quintessence, separated off from the dross through distillation, functions as a metaphor for the reformation of clamorous postmodern society. Okri's alchemical poetic prose, fused with Rosemary Clunie's paintings, help to redefine 'magic' and portend the possibility of a palliative to restore human vitality.

The thrust of this discussion, therefore, is not on the black arts of wizards and witches, or the Ovidian metamorphoses that herbal and other concoctions and incantations are believed to bring about, although the latter does feature; it concerns the magical interrelationship among (natural) magic, experiential science and myth, be it religious or sociocultural. Exempla abound; we perpetuate the magical myth of the sun rising and setting, yet the scientific fact is that the earth rotates on its axis, while the sun remains static. The transformation of chrysalis into butterfly and snakes shedding their skins are overt examples of natural magic, observable by scientific methods and leading to myths of transcendental symbolism across cultures and belief systems. Okri describes the butterfly as 'A living testament / To the sublime within' ('Towards the Sublime' 2012: 56).[5] He cites this as an example of 'true/Transformation' that is 'higher, richer, *magical*' (ibid.; emphasis added). In contrast to Reyburn who focuses on the 'pretended art' which 'seeks to control the course of events' (2012: 136) and who states that science and religion are 'competitors' of magic, I take my cue from Okri's intuitive creativity, seeing magic, science and myth as a triad, as braided together, or as akin to a Pythagorean triangle in sacred geometry. Transformation, Okri asserts, is itself at once 'magical' and 'Divine'; as he observes, the birthing of the butterfly transcends 'all the laws' of its 'previous condition' (2012: 56). This magical science, in turn, lends credence to the religious myths of Jesus turning water into wine at the wedding feast and of the promise of eternal life. The focus now turns to the ways in which this theoretical argument can be used as a lens to interpret selected extracts from *The Magic Lamp* (2017).

Selections from *The Magic Lamp*

In the poetic prose illustrative of the nature of magic, selected for discussion in this chapter, Okri resuscitates the Italian renaissance's attitude to curiosity that affirmed the value of inquisitiveness about Nature.[6] This is an attitude that is perhaps more familiar in the poetry of Gerard Manley Hopkins that seeks to reveal the inner essence or inscape,[7] that is, the medieval cultural ideal of virtuosity ('virtuositas') of nature. It is also reflected in post-expressionism/magical realism of art critic Franz Roh (1925), which Sarah Lincoln astutely aligns with modernity's 'self-regard of modern subjects, their attempt to make sense of their often confusing and alienating circumstances' (2012: 250).

In his 'L'Époque Magique', a re-publication of the poem 'The Age of Magic' from *Wild* (2012: 72–3), Okri raises the cultivation of 'virtue'[8] to a high art. Set beside the river Thames that intersects the city of London, the piece enumerates a multitude of wondrous occurrences in a time zone that brings to an end 'the dark age of iron' (2017: 31), presumably symbolizing the contemporary era of mechanistic materialism. Mysteriously transported across 'a magic line in time', the third-person narrative voice can see beyond the veil, where the stars in the firmament appear 'brighter', colours have 'fragrance' and, as morning breaks, the children of the poor see 'blinding flashes of a yellow angel's wings'. In this higher-order thinking or HOT consciousness with the sensibilities of the narrator and his companion at their peak, Nature is stylized into hyperreality: feet tingle, a mermaid sings, a beggar levitates and, satirically evoking Dante's mode in his *Divine Comedy*, a dead poet recites 'forgotten terza rimas in reverse'. Invoking the myths of River Styx and the philosopher's stone, we witness an alchemist 'on a barge', whose incantations and 'black powder' (ibid.) turn a dead pigeon into gold in a parodic allusion to Ovidian metamorphosis. Predicated on origination, ingenuity and a magical consciousness, the prose-poem concludes the following afternoon with an amazed Romany child's vision of a woman 'laced with blues and reds' sprouting 'beautiful wings' (2017: 33). This, we are told, brings the seemingly interminable 'dark age of iron' to an end and ushers in the 'age of magic'. The closing exhortation of an intrusive authorial voice is to '[u]nveil your eyes' (ibid.), an evocation the magic revealed via an expanded awareness. The concept of unveiling one's eyes or concern with occlusion and exclusion – be it physical, social or symbolic – is one given wide credence; the idea is captured in one of Okri's aphorisms: 'All our creativity, our innovations, our discovery, come from being able first to see what is there, and not there; to hear what is said, and not said. Above all to think clearly; to be nourished by silence. And – beyond that – the art of intuition' (2011: 27). By extension, this recalls the distinction between the perceiver and the perceived that was of concern to Maurice Merleau-Ponty (1908–1961), as Robert Fraser (2002: 88) points out in his study of Okri's works. In *Le Visible et l'invisible* (1968), published posthumously, Merleau-Ponty articulates his realization that data received via our (five) senses cannot ordinarily account for everything our brains register. By implication, and as illustrated in the proem just discussed, to 'unveil' our eyes signifies Greenwood's magical consciousness, in other words, the heightened awareness of our sixth sense. Merleau-Ponty observes that there are unseen attributes that are included in the way in which we construct reality: 'Meaning,' he asserts, 'is *invisible*, but the *invisible* is not the contradictory of the *visible*: the visible itself has an invisible inner framework ['membrure'], and the invisible is the hidden counterpart of the visible, it appears within it.' Thus, his proposition is that the invisible appears within the visible; 'one cannot see it and every effort to *see it there* makes it disappear, but it is *in the line of* the visible, it is its virtual focus' (original emphases). Merleau-Ponty deduces therefore that the invisible 'is inscribed within' the visible '[in filigree]' (1968: 215).

With the sixth sense alert after crossing the 'magic line in time' (Okri 2017: 31), a rite that has suspended profane time and duration, the narrator, somewhat paradoxically, enumerates the five-stage timeline in this piece – evening, dawn, morning, dusk and the following afternoon – that seemingly mimics that of world beliefs in the five days of cosmic creation.[9] Globally, humankind, as Eliade states, 'only repeats the act of the Creation' (1954: 22) in year-long religious calendars that commemorate, by re-enactment, 'all the cosmogonic phases which took place "ab origine" [from the beginning]'. Even more significantly, via this sacred repetition, human beings exist 'ex tempore' or are transported beyond time and are 'contemporary with the cosmogony and with the anthropogony because ritual projects him [or her] into the mythical epoch of the beginning' (ibid.), into the age of magic that the narrating magus captures in 'L'Époque Magique'.

The operation of natural magic is even more patent in 'Dimensions of a Storm'. As Eamon observes: 'Natural magic does not work against [N]ature but is a minister of magic, supplying by artificial means what [N]ature wants' (1994: 16). Marriage rites, for example, like those in the annual calendar, are a re-enactment of natural magic and likewise have a divine model. Human marriage, as in the prose-poem 'Betrothal',[10] reproduces the archetypal hierogamy symbolizing the marriage of heaven and earth, an archetype that forms the undercurrent to 'Dimensions of a Storm' and can be found in Indian and Roman mythologies. In the Hindu procreation ritual, 'the generative act becomes a hierogamy of cosmic proportions, mobilizing a whole group of gods'

(Eliade 1954: 24). In Virgil's *Aeneid* (1990: Book VI, l. 160), Dido celebrates her nuptials with Aeneas 'in the midst of a violent storm'; their union, as Eliade notes, 'coincides with that of the elements; heaven embraces its bride, dispensing fertilizing rain' (1954: 24). This then appears to be the primordial myth that underpins and interpenetrates 'Dimensions of a Storm'. Here, the cosmic union of the elements is manifest in the omniscient narrator's vibrant and all-encompassing depiction of a violent thunderstorm:

> It's all there: the swelling and the heaving, the magnificent roll of the *invisible*, heaving and pushing out against the air as if beyond the membrane of the world. Great hulking *invisible* beings blowing a sustaining storm above the trees. (2017: 23; emphases added)

This excerpt replicates Merleau-Ponty's theory of the visible and invisible. It is pregnant with allusion and meaning; and the modernist preoccupation[11] with the seen and the unseen is clearly integral to Okri's aesthetics in *The Magic Lamp*, where true meaning is secret and hidden. Evocative of the myth of Olympian gods, whose 'infinite breathing' is not only the impetus or the prevailing spirit of the wind behind the storm, 'blowing a sustaining storm above the trees', but is also the cause of the 'hieros gamos' that unites the heavens with the earth, as intimated in '[t]he blue was dense up there above the green' (2017: 23). Colours are characteristically significant for Okri. Serendipitously, there is the natural magic of primary colours: a red bird, yellow lightning and blue sky; and yellow mixed with blue magically produces green.

In 'Dimensions of a Storm', a streak of lightning, depicted obliquely as 'a point of yellow', is the prelude to the thunderstorm. Then, in a painterly simile, the lightning is likened to 'a [red] bird inscribing a spiral' (2017: 23). Abruptly, the storm itself is metaphorized into a huge bird, 'swell[ing] in the air and falling like the beating of giant hurricane wings', the sound of which is described as '[m]usic on the wings of a soaring bird' (ibid.) ingeniously expressive of the science of cosmic rhythms.

The prose-poem is characterized by verbal alchemy and Keatsian negative capability. The *invisible* is transmuted into 'a blue world *barely seen*', while the ominous 'breathing' behind this planetary storm '*obscures*' all. And yet, the omniscient teller 'senses' that the tree tops 'house' or embrace the storm with exuberant songs of praise ('shrieking hallelujahs') as if in celebration of this re-enactment of the archetypal ritual union that bears fruit so to speak as a stunted tree growing in a stone wall, illustrative of the tantalizing tenacity of Nature (2017: 25). Suggestive of alchemical magic, the vivid depiction of the storm (the rhetorical device of diatyposis) unifies the four basic elements – earth, air, fire and water – adding the oriental fifth element, wood. Little wonder then that human beingness is portrayed as a microcosmic cypher, 'a walking line on the landscape', the meaning of which, in an echo of the Merleau-Ponty extract cited above, 'only those hidden eyes know' (ibid.). This notion of privileged sight is prefigured by a typical Okrian neo-Platonic maxim: 'To see is not to see' (ibid.). This cryptic oxymoron elevates the reader's consciousness in its evocation of the 'real' and the 'really real' of Plato's cave, a notion that infuses 'The Blue Crusade'.

Inspired by the spirit of inventiveness, 'The Blue Crusade' serves as a metonymic antidote to the potent unease and (dis)ease of contemporary politics. In terms of sympathetic magic, Okri sees 'our unease with the world' as the impetus behind 'our hidden desire to change it' (2018: 37). Lord Byron's couplet, quoted as the epigraph to Percy Bysshe Shelley's 'Ode to Liberty' (2018), provides a mythic conjunction between 'Dimensions of a Storm' and 'The Blue Crusade': 'Yet, Freedom, yet, thy banner, torn but flying, / Streams like a thunder-storm against the wind' (Okri 2018: 147). In this context, this ekphrastic prose-poem becomes an ode to freedom. If one looks and listens carefully, one can almost hear and envision a St John's band marching to 'Onward Christian Soldiers' evoked by both the proem's title and Clunie's artwork, with its large blue cross embedded above the text. Redolent of the 'torn but flying' flag is the narrator's paradoxical summation of progress in our postmodern age: 'We acquired more knowledge of the world and less knowledge of ourselves. We knew more, but somehow we knew less' (2017: 69).

Whereas 'Dimensions of a Storm' unifies the basic elements of earth, air, fire and water, the linear progression in 'The Blue Crusade' traces the three mythical stages, archetypally reflecting the triad: heaven, earth and hell. It begins in a paradisal state with many discoveries 'in the unseen realm', the most important of which 'was the colour blue' (2017: 67). This is followed by the loss of paradise; over time, 'this blue wisdom was lost'. Finally, the 'silent ones' and the 'listening ones' seek out 'the forgotten mages' (ibid.: 69) and take up the banner of the 'underground [blue] crusade' to regain paradise. In an astute use of the rhetorical figure of hyperbaton or inversion, it is suggested that perhaps 'the forgotten beauty of blue … took us up as a crusade' so that 'the cause could well be the effect, and the effect the cause' (ibid.: 71). This implies a conflation of Frazer's homeopathic and contagious magic, so that 'The Blue Crusade' becomes a blueprint for the recovery of paradise, for an end to the interminable darkness of the 'age of iron' mooted in 'L'Époque Magique' and here mutated into 'the age of realism' (ibid.: 69). The 'cause' of realism is humankind's mastery 'of the forces of [N]ature and the power of the machine' (ibid.) with an attendant loss of self-knowledge.

The colour blue dominates the prose-poem. 'The capacity of the brain and eye to perceive the different colours of the spectrum,' says Anthony Stevens in his *Ariadne's Clue*, 'is phylogenetically very ancient, and each colour is linked to a web of cognitive and affective association' (1998: 146). Blue is of course the perceived colour of both the sky and the sea. Even though this is not technically true, for the sky is more black than blue and the sea is more green and white than blue, the colour blue shares the symbolism of sky and sea – 'their translucency, their vastness, their infinity, and their coolness' (ibid.: 149). 'Because their extent so far exceeds the human condition, their colour represents both the ultimate and the eternal, the Beyond and Fate' (ibid.). In his contemplation of blue, Okri features 'this mystic colour' as a magical 'potion' used by sages to create 'protective spells' that can destroy evil, perhaps alluding to Ovid's *Metamorphoses* (2004). Not only can we 'travel in this colour' – a scientific fact owing to advancements in air transport and space travel, but we could also 'pass through a certain tone of blue into the world beyond thought' (ibid.: 67). Stevens lends scientific credence to this seemingly hyperbolical notion by explaining the workings of synaesthesia: it 'lends a certain felt meaning to each colour or can give different days of the week, different musical tones, etc. a different hue in the minds of susceptible individuals' (1998: 146).

Underlining the title of *The Magic Lamp: Dreams of Our Age*, the teller of the tale expands on the mysterious possibilities of blue: it is a cure-all for the blues, be these mental, subconscious or wish-fulfilment in Nature: 'no darkness of mind but can be soothed and dissolved by its ministrations'; 'We dreamed in blue'; and some 'made magic carpets of blue on which we visited our friends in remote constellations' (2017: 67). Melding the advanced science of intergalactic travel and religious myth, blue becomes a portal into 'the immeasurable world where the gods dwell' (ibid.: 69) and, in an intimation of drug-like-induced ritual renewal, '[i]n our ecstasies we went through portals of blue to the source of our highest joys' (67).

Given such powerful potentialities of blue, its loss[12] is keenly felt and a catalogue of esoteric loss is listed: loss of the art of 'wonder-working', the art of 'the magic of the beyond', the art of 'blue', 'the paths of the lost tradition' and 'the lost dream' (2017: 69). The mission of 'the blue crusade' is thus, not surprisingly, 'to awaken it in all those who secretly quivered to the music of the spheres' (ibid.: 71) through the alchemy of magic, that is, through symbols and rituals, guided 'through death into life' (69),[13] recalling the natural magic of chrysalis into butterfly discussed at the outset but here wrought by the wisdom of the mages. Ultimately, blue, like the gods in the heavens, illuminates with *visible* life, first itself, then all the *invisible* celestial and mundane bodies (to borrow loosely from Merleau-Ponty). This new enlightenment sets the scene for a discussion of the final prose-poem chosen for discussion, the last in the collection.

Illustrative of the powerful force of the imagination and myth, the opening lines in 'Prophecy' bring us face-to-face with the anthropomorphized godhead of Judaeo-Christian pictorial mythology: 'Once, when I was gazing into the air, a man with a crown, who was seated on a throne of gold, summoned me. He whispered things in my ear which became a green fire in my head' (2017: 113). Although one could be forgiven for imagining that this is to be a child's fairy tale, given the conjunction 'Once' as in 'once upon a time', the final sentence in this paragraph – 'Sometimes out of this fire images take form' – seems to me to acknowledge with childlike wonder (deduced by the verdant 'green fire') that creativity is divinely inspired. The allusion to the Celtic iconographic Green Man's metamorphosis seems patent. This points to the inner or *invisible* meaning of 'prophecy'. Prophecy for Okri is not Yeats's Rosicrucian spectral or occult seeing but a Blakean impetus for (Protean) change, where 'change is a making visible, a making real' (2018: 129), born not by 'seeing into the future but seeing into higher states of being *in* the world' (37; emphasis added) or what Soyinka terms 'self-apprehension' ([1976] 1995). In his collection of poetry, *Rise like Lions*, Okri confesses that poetic vision seeks to 'alter the world' (2018: 129). It is not innocent but political because 'it posits an alternative reality to the one we know'. This, he believes, is 'one of the most mysterious functions of poetry'. It is transformative and, in envisioning the possibility of another, different reality; 'it already begins to put the reality we know in doubt' (ibid.). Prophecy is thus true vision as opposed to voyeurism; it partially equates with 'intensity'. Citing the biblical adage that for want of vision a people perish, Okri laments the dearth of 'far-seers' and 'clear seers' (2018: 37).

This prose-poem is not about the mythical imaginary of belief or leaps of faith. The cascade of exempla that follows the first person narrator's tacit realization that 'I had always been gazing into realms of prophecy right in front of me and not known it' (2018: 113) are not flights of fancy but examples of an ability to *see* 'what is there and not there' (Okri 2011: 27); this equates with an ontopoietic perception of a composite reality of cosmic dimensions that encompasses the past, present and future of historical time but goes beyond profane time and duration to sacred time, to what lies 'au dehors de la réalité historique' (outside historical reality). The 'glimpses' of 'lost wars, future births, the fall of empires, the changing fields, the dwindling river' (2018: 113) hint at a lunar consciousness. The moon, as Stevens notes, is 'our primordial clock' (1998: 136). It symbolizes cyclic time: 'it governs tides, rains, floods, and the menstrual cycle'. The light of the moon illuminates 'the darkness of night, and thus represents the consciousness that comes to us in dreams' (ibid.) as made apparent in Okri's subtitle to *The Magic Lamp*, 'Dreams of Our Age'.

Cautioning against the black arts, the speaker says: 'I have witnessed lands devasted because the people brought to the surface that which should have been left in the deep' (2018: 113), an admonitory allusion to the myth of Proteus, The Old Man of the Sea. In illustration, nightmare visions of the elders, as boys and girls undergoing initiation rites 'in the dark blue forest' (ibid.: 115) are alluded to. The antidote is to be detected in the closing image of a heron, an archetypal symbol of freedom as well as a traditional symbol of the natural magic of bird talk, considering 'the world with a question in the shape of its beak' (ibid.). It is not therefore coincidental that this collection is bookended by a blue jay in conversation with the narrator, in 'Bird Talk' and a bird of the same genus, a philosophical heron contemplating existence in 'Prophecy'. This suggests that Okri conceives of natural magic as an empirical, even experimental science and inseparable from myth. The goal of natural magic is to reveal the hidden or *invisible* enigmas of Nature, and to render them *visible* for those of us who are 'at sea' and cannot 'see'.

An intrusive authorial voice shares with us his intuition that '[i]t is as if everything is here, if we know how to see it'. As the closing sentence attests – 'By gazing and not gazing into the infinite present, it seems all worlds are here' – the proem, as a meditation on the 'infinite present', is a climactic synopsis of the meaning of Merleau-Ponty's *Le Visible et l'invisible*. 'There is a seeing so intense,' says Okri, 'that it reveals unseen aspects of the world' (2018: 37). This is what constitutes natural magic, be it homeopathic or contagious.

Conclusion

Reminiscent of Merleau-Ponty's proposal that the elusive invisible lies within the visible, 'one cannot see it and every effort to *see it there* makes it disappear, but it is *in the line of* the visible, it is its virtual focus', and that the invisible 'is inscribed within' the visible, '[in filigree]' (1968: 215), Okri coincidentally articulates his visionary aesthetic of ontopoiesis in the ekphrastic pieces discussed here with 'Poetry is susceptible to vision. And vision in poetry is both seeing clearly what is there and seeing what will be, what might be, a deeper seeing into the reality of things' (2018: 37). The implication is that the 'Imaginatio Creatrix' in the stillness of time is akin to lunar consciousness or inner *gnosis*. This is the knowledge 'revealed by the reflected light of the divine sun mirrored in the soul' (Stevens 1998: 136–7), and what we refer to as the waxing and waning of the moon or the rising and setting of the sun – an illusion of magic – 'links us inevitably with archetypal notions of death, rebirth, and eternity' (ibid.)

These prose-poems reveal an impulse to reject concrete, historical time and return to the mythological time at the beginning of time itself ('ab origine'), reinstating the magic of traditional and archaic mythology 'in illo tempore' (then). As native Africans, nurtured in the cradle of mankind, the link between us, the cosmos and cosmic rhythms is the unsevered umbilical cord of the motherland. This runs counter to modernity's creation of and insistence upon historical time, a notion itself disproven by scientific evidence of space travel. Encapsulating Soyinka's explanation of the origin of myth, 'For let it always be recalled that myths arise from man's attempt to externalise and communicate his inner intuitions' ([1976] 1995: 3), Eliade avers that an account is mythic in so far as 'it reveals something as having been fully manifested and this manifestation is at the same time creative and exemplary since it is a foundation … of a kind of behaviour' (1954: 18).

In illustration of Protean magic, Okri ponders '[h]ow to make those intuitive leaps that can transform humanity, how to make this mysterious faculty available to all – this will be the true turning point in the future history of civilisation' (2011: 27).[14]

'An Interval in the Enchantment of Living':
The Age of Magic

Introduction

In Ben Okri's novel, *The Age of Magic* (2014), the text – following in the tradition of Thomas Mann's *The Magic Mountain* ([1924] 1980) – is an examination of abstractions: three fundamental, interrelated, closely interwoven abstractions viz. the idea of Arcadia, the ideal of happiness and the self. As with all phenomenological discourse, Okri provides no pat answers; the abstractions remain enigmas – as they must – despite careful discursive consideration. Explaining the need for such consideration, Mann has his protagonist declare that, '[f]or himself, it was precisely because he did not know the answers that he put the questions' (1924: 345). 'Abstractions, are central, whether in the study of literature or in the study of the brain,' Douglas Hofstadter (2007: 26) says.[1] 'Sans' (without) abstractions, the study of literature, he reminds us, would focus on page size, paper, bookbinding and other tangible aspects, rather than exploring '"the high abstractions" "at the heart of literature" – "plot and character, style and point of view ... allusion and metaphor"' (ibid.) and so on. Analogously, 'we don't want to focus on the trees (or their leaves) at the expense of the forest' (ibid.).

The literary text and its abstractions

The novel is a sequel to Okri's *In Arcadia* (2002) with the same cast of characters, but in the earlier novel, they stop in Paris while here they stop in Switzerland. They are en route to Greece. Foregrounding his mode, Okri prefaces his new work with Camus's '[a] work of art that retraced the conquest of happiness would be a revolutionary one' (*Noces* [1939] 1959). This first epigraph is amplified in the discussion in the novel of three abstractions – Arcadia, happiness and the discovery of authentic self as being the purpose of the journey of this life (2014: 13, 14, 24). His second epigraph, 'The age of magic has begun, / Unveil your eyes', from the medieval 'Pensero Il Camino' (lit. contemplate the path), prefigures the novel's mystical journey of transformation and enlightenment. These two key ideas conjoin to inform the narrative thrust that turns on the collocation of a happiness that accrues from being at home in three dimensions: this world, the imaginal world and the metaphysical world. In the imaginal world, which is that of enhanced consciousness, Okri invites us to share his insights. The omniscient narrator's ontopoietic declaration is that the film crew were making a journey 'to a place', but 'in truth' it was 'a journey to an idea', a journey that 'began as a documentary' but became 'one in which against their wills, they were being changed' (2014: 13). This delineates the narrative trajectory and the alchemy of change within the minds of the characters.

The journey Okri uses in which to embed his discussion of transformation and enlightenment is the second stage of a journey from London, via Paris and Basel to the original Arcady in the Peloponnese. And it is in Switzerland, as in Thomas Mann's *The Magic Mountain*,[2] in a 'seemingly sleeveless speculation' (1924: 344) on being-towards-death that insight dawns. Early in the narrative, Okri's lead character points to the inexorability of the 'death' that must perforce precede human re-formation. Mann's Hans Castorp puts it thus: 'death is the *spiritual* principle, the "res bina" [dual matter], the "lapis philosophorum" [philosopher's stone], and the pedagogic principle, too, for love of it leads to love of life and love of humanity' (1924: 596; original emphasis). Lao muses that 'the old self must die' (Okri 2014: 59) as he recalls an African agrarian cultivation metaphor: 'The seed must die before it can grow' (ibid.). This truism is reminiscent of Anna-Teresa Tymieniecka's observation that there is but one 'logos' that, as a living ontopoietic metamorphic force, induces and regulates the becoming and development of being in its internality (1988; 2000: 5). Much of Okri's thinking thus resonates with global thinkers; he is luminously aware of world mythologies and this novel embodies many cultural cultivation myths.

This novel, then, as a sequel to his 2002 neglected masterpiece, *In Arcadia* (2002),[3] itself a three-part novel that culminates in a visit by the characters to the Louvre in Paris and centres on an ekphrasis (a description with great visual content, where art is complementary to literature),[4] is quite appropriate for the pastoral implications of an Arcadian story. In that story, he foregrounds his labyrinthine reading of the symbolism in Nicolas Poussin's painting, *Les Bergers d'Arcadie*, as the climax to the novel's motif of Akashic still points[5] or intervals of silent contemplation that 'help one organize and integrate what one already knows, thus leading to fresh and creative insights' (Gray 2009a: 47).[6] Okri defines Akashic still points as 'the resting point(s) of an idea that has travelled thousands of years in the mind of humanity' ([2002] 2003: 204).

In an interview with Madeleine Wilson, Okri underlines the importance of moments of quiet in contemporaneity, saying: 'There are moments in the book where I want the mind to stop, to stop thinking, to stop trying to make sense of – just to stop, for a moment' (2015: 1). This chapter attempts to show how this novel of ideas or dialectic novel, as does its precursor, counters the contemporary obsession with hyper connectivity – 'inter alia' the Internet, smartphones, social media – by describing how to slow down, to sense the magic of a moment of timelessness[7] and the invisible: to recapture the numinous elements of our lives.

Okri's rhetorical decoding of Poussin's painting continues in *The Age of Magic* focusing on the idea of Arcadia, and develops the painting's enigmatic inscription, 'Et in Arcadia ego' (I too have lived in Arcadia) (2014: 48, 50, 51). But this aspect is not discussed here as it warrants a paper of its own.

Interestingly, Mann's rhetorical questions on the conundrum of beingness and immanence of death also feature a peasant from Arcadia (see 2014: 345). Philosophy, as Maurice Merleau-Ponty notes, 'does not raise questions and does not provide answers that would little by little fill in the blanks'; 'The questions are within our life, within our history: they are born there, they die there, if they have found a response, more often than not, they are transformed there; in any case, it is a part of experience and of knowledge that one day ends up at this open wondering' (1968: 105). Both Okri, in this novel, and eco-phenomenologist, Tymieniecka (1988; 2000: 5), explore this 'open wondering' or evolutive ontological conception. But, whereas Tymieniecka's phenomenological approach finds that the immediate intuition of the constructivism of life coincides with our own creative constructivism in the cultivation of the virtualities of being, Okri's key characters reverse the historicist priority of time over space, stepping into mythic time, mythic space. On encountering an 'Abiku' musician, called Nothung, for example, who is mesmerized by Lao's companion, Mistletoe, who sends him on a quest for the Holy Grail, Lao 'found himself thinking about the silent watchers of the human drama who are fascinated by what each person chooses to become. He had the notion of being in the same drama, over and over again, actors in an infinite play' (2014: 236). Here, thought is not something extrinsic to the thinker; it is an expression of a mode of being, a mode of presence in 'an infinite play'. Okri is engaged in reawakening our archaic potential for the archetypal, transhistorical experience. This stepping out of secular, linear temporality requires a relation to eternity (Mann 1924: 542; Cheetham 2003: 11) encapsulated in the chapter's title phrase, 'An Interval in the Enchantment of Living', from Okri's telling subheading to Section 3, Book 7; its narratological placement emphasizes primal infinitude, because prime numbers are indivisible and so simulacra for the eternal, a pivotal instance of stepping out of time. With its focal word, 'interval' – an evocation of sacred geometry – this points both to an expanded sense of presence and to the 'when' we might cultivate being, which is 'the enchantment of living'. Okri suggests through the experiences of the characters in *The Age of Magic* that perpetual human re-formation is possible through epiphanic insights despite living in a world of nihilistic materialism. A train journey to an idyllic family hotel in an unnamed town on the edges of Lake Lucerne (2014: 64), beneath the majestic Rigi (70) Mountains in the Swiss Alps is 'where' we are invited to ruminate.

As noted, the themes are principally Arcadia, happiness and selfhood, but there is also much to be said about relativity and evil, an inversion of which is, for Okri, a modified palindrome of live. At the hotel, the *seven* weary film crew break their onward journey that began in London in the prequel, for *two* days (and *three* nights). Unsurprisingly, Lao – the tellingly named black poet and film presenter[8] – chooses an auspicious[9] Room number *7* at the hotel for himself and his companion, Mistletoe – a fey artist and the *eighth*[10] person in this intriguing group of hitherto out-of-work social misfits.

Damning with faint praise, an anonymous reviewer in the *Irish Times*[11] dubs the novel 'a novel that's not a novel', declaring: 'Whimsically dealing in ideas, assertions and abstractions that are a hotchpotch of religions and pop psychologies, *The Age of Magic* is more fable or allegory than novel' (2014: 2). By contrast, a more perceptive Wilson notes that 'the strength of the novel, as in much of Okri's fiction, is its luminous ruminative quality and its ability to manipulate the reader's understanding and experience of time through the unorthodox narrative structure' (2015: 2).

'The hotchpotch of religions and pop psychologies' damned in the *Irish Times* reveals, with a little more investigation, the work to be steeped in a Sufi mysticism, which is itself coherent. From the mysterious green Nature spirit, the Quylph (2014: 271 and 274), to the description of the imaginal world, perhaps our virtual world, through which Lao and Mistletoe walk, and then to the mountain, not of Qaf but ordinary Rigi, the narrative tenor suggests that the pair are enchanted and experience happiness at first hand; the work constantly references esoteric oriental ideas of the virtual. It transpires that the mountains function as an objective correlative for the power of timelessness that Wilson by implication detects, of transcending chronological time and being mystically transformed by Nature as in

> [t]hey made [Lao] want to change his life, to become more, to be more alive …
> The mountains gave him a sense of things greater than history. They didn't make him feel humble; they made him feel imperfectly developed. They made him ache for an unrealized grandeur. (2014: 219)

But the mountain is also a classical symbol of the sacred ziggurat, a symbolic portal to the spiritual domain, an aspect that permeates Lao's consciousness. Pertinently, Hofstadter cites Gödel's (1931) discovery in his *Principia Mathematica* that 'thanks to mapping, full-fledged meaning can suddenly appear in a spot where it was entirely unsuspected' (2007: 148). Okri advises the reader at the outset to '[r]ead slowly' (cf. 2014: 50), suggesting that, in a book about magic, the enchantment must be approached with due attention (cf. the Quylph's early warning to '[b]e more awake next time' (10)).

The story is not, however, of magic, which is sleight of hand, but the magic of being that can be developed to embrace an expanded experience of time and existence. Henry Corbin (1903–1978) explains the worldview of the esoteric, encapsulated in Sufi mysticism:

> There is the *physical*, sensible world encompassing both our terrestrial world (governed by the human souls) and the sidereal universe (governed by the Souls of the Spheres). The sensible world is the world of the phenomenon (*molk*). There is also the *supersensible* world of the Soul or Angel Souls, the Malakût … which starts at the 'convex surface of the ninth Sphere'. And there is *the world of pure archangelic Intelligences*. Each of these *three* worlds has its organ of perception: the senses, imagination, and the intellect, corresponding with the triad: body, soul and mind. (1972: 5; emphases added)

The world of the imagination, the 'mundus imaginalis' (imaginal world), is not a world of fantasy in the sense imagination has had since the eighteenth century. Corbin explains this most persuasively in his writings on Islamic mysticism. His reading of Heidegger's critique of Western philosophy in *Being and Time* (1927) led him through his studies of Arabic mysticism to an equally radical critique of the secular, rationalist view of history.

Okri uses the device of the imaginal world to describe how Lao and Mistletoe's characters feel the spell of Arcadia working in them. They experience the imaginal world in their wanderings through the Swiss village and countryside. The syncretism of suggesting that Arcadia, the pastoral paradisal world of classical antiquity, is a synonym of the imaginal world is in keeping with a long tradition of conflating vastly different cultural responses to nihilistic materialism. What Cheetham says of Corbin is that 'the way to step out of [the current of history] is by means of gnosis: transformative knowledge that changes the mode of presence of the knower and which is synonymous with esotericism' (2003: 9). This describes the omniscient narrator in the novel. Okri's lead characters have a different mode of presence during (and after) their stay from that which they had on first arrival, through transformative knowledge expressed through Lao and apparently known instinctively by the artist, Mistletoe. Okri subtly embeds examples of such gnostic principles. For instance, he sustains Sufi primality throughout his counter-narrative, structuring the novel into seven books with subsections. This mimics the novel's key *seven* letter word, *Arcadia*. Okri is even more specific about his novelistic innovation, his ability 'to find myth in life and life in myth'. Through his protagonist, a thinly disguised authorial self, Okri notes that the word *Arcadia* 'began and ended with the first letter of the alphabet' (2014: 18). Highlighting the narratological technique, Lao adds: 'Begin at the beginning; at the mid-point begin again; and at the end return to the beginning' (ibid.). This implies that the journey towards transformation is circular. If one wishes to talk about the properties of a word (such as Arcadia), Hofstadter suggests that 'one must use its *name*' (2007: 58; original emphasis).

The significance of circularity for understanding is a well-researched but tricky idea. The act of naming accords with the paradoxical way in which talking about language elides language talking about itself, where metalanguage imperceptibly becomes a self-reflective loop. Such an example is provided by the anecdote Hofstadter recounts. Reflecting on trying to fathom, at a very young age, why $2\times2=4$, while $3\times3=9$ rather than six if one counted dots placed in a square, Hofstadter concludes: 'The point is that among my earliest memories is a relishing of loopy structures, of self-applied operations, of circularity, of paradoxical acts, of implied infinities. This, for me, was the cat's meow and the bee's knees rolled into one' (2007: 60). It is precisely such a loopy structure that Okri uses to highlight the strange effects of meditating on being. The first movement in the novel leads up to a 'hieros gamos' (divine marriage of body and soul (part of alchemical mysticism)), building up to events which completely transform the human substance. A mysterious alchemy is clearly at work.

It is therefore no surprise that Okri adapts Sufi cosmogony with its *three* levels of existence: this world concretized in the here and now of the train journey; the imaginal world represented by the Alpine retreat deplete of other people and affording an opportunity to gain knowledge; and the metaphysical world of the gods and angels. These *three* levels are here highlighted by two other triads: first, the Quylph (possibly derived from the Persian Nature spirit, Khidr), Malasso (a figment of the imagination or the operation of the superego for he is 'attired like a dark magician' (2014: 34)) and the fey artist, Mistletoe; and second, by Lao's formulaic intuition that '[t]o live is to love, evolve, create' (29).

Okri ends his novel with a naked immersion episode and what that signifies. So, invoking symbolism common to many religions, Lao comes to the surface of the waters and imagines that 'with any luck ... like fishes we will be hooked and eaten by the universe, as holy food' (2014: 286). The closing lines return to mystic colour symbolism as Lao's sense perception is altered and he observes 'that the earth was blue' (ibid.).

To develop the idea of Persian and Islamic allusions, colours are given importance in the novel. Colour may be defined as 'the attempt of light to become visible'.[12] Colours act as a kind of veil through which the colourless light can be perceived. Hence, colours have always played a symbolic role in religions, poetry, daily life and human understanding. Okri gives expression to the 'spirit' of colours in *The Age of Magic*, combining allusions to and descriptions of various colours. At the very outset in a literal but also figurative sense, Lao notices the world beyond the train changes from white to green (2014: 10). And, there are mystical allusions to variegated colours – Husk is 'neurotically beautiful' in her 'floral dress' (ibid.: 15); Lao 'slept in a shining orb' (11), then 'fell into a stained glass reverie' (25); the poor inhabitants stare at the passing train 'with pale [read unseeing] eyes' (28); while Jim, echoing biblical lore, describes the Devil as 'simply dazzling' (65). The pendulum continues to swing from real to surreal: there are references to the golden river of the Garden of Eden (ibid.: 18); 'fields of yellow flowers'; a countryside with 'blue flowers ... and an ochre church' (34); the train seat covers are red (ibid.); and the Quylph is 'long and thin and green' (271).

So, what do colours signify? Lao explains to Mistletoe that the generally invisible green Quylph, akin to the Green Man icon on Baroque cathedrals, symbolic guardian of creativity, is 'a [N]ature spirit, a guardian of treasures' (2014: 274). In Sufism, green is the colour of life-giving water and the plants that appear as signs of life. It can therefore relate to resurrection or paradise, where the blessed rest on green pillows and wear green silk. 'The ones who wear the green' ('sabzpūš') are either the inhabitants of paradise and the spiritual world or the angelic spirits that convey good tidings to human beings (read Quylph). In Sufi lore, green is the colour that appears on higher stages of the mystical path. The symbolism is extended in Semnānī's Sufism: it is the colour that is reached once the Sufi has passed through the 'black light' and emerges at the emerald mountain, the symbol of divine proximity and eternal duration.[13] This association is all the more fitting as the green emerald was considered to have healing powers that could blind the eyes of serpents and dragons. The mystical guide was sometimes associated with a wondrous emerald. In what could also be construed as a veiled literary allusion to *Sir Gawain and the Green Knight*, Lao has one such a guide, the Quylph, in addition to his companion, the evergreen Mistletoe – with its classical allusiveness to Virgil's guide in the underworld in Dante's epic.

The argument returns to that other singular thread in *The Age of Magic* – numerological symbols, as related to the symbolism of colour. Through these touches once again Okri references esotericism. On disembarking at Basel station and offloading their luggage, both Lao and the film producer, Jim, seem to be seeing things. In light-hearted social commentary, Lao sees 'monsters' in animated conversation (2014: 41), symbols of the evils the *seven* film-crew had brought with them in addition to their twenty-two pieces of luggage. The compulsive artist, Mistletoe, alone has a 'sprite', a flashback to her being described as the daughter of Pan in *In Arcadia* and here as dryad-like (a female spirit who lives in a tree) (ibid.: 74).

This vision, evocative of hell and heaven, respectively, leads to what Lao terms 'the theme-note that was being played in him' (2014: 42) and an insight about micro- and macro-experiences. The micro-experience signifies 'the experience of the moment as it is lived', the macro - 'the experience of it afterwards when the whole is sensed' (ibid.), a mythic conjunction that leads to Lao becoming conscious of other such conjunctions: the synchronicity of the twenty-two pieces of luggage (twice the prime number eleven) being driven away, with the 'twenty-two letters of the Jewish alphabet, twenty-two cards in the major arcana of Tarot, and twenty-two paths on the tree of life' (2014: 42–3), the insight signifying a braiding of the quotidian, with Christian and Kabbalistic mythologies.

Less obviously but interlinked, Okri synchronizes his play on numbers and letters in the Quylph, his imaginary spirit guide, who is in conversation with a dozing Lao, lulled by the soporific sound of the train's wheels, at the outset of the novel. This elusive mystical creature chastises Lao to '[b]e more awake next time' (2014: 10), clearly an injunction for heightened awareness. Completing the structural circularity of the text, yet another loop, in the penultimate chapter – a final **Chapter 7** in Section **5** (both prime numbers) – the reader is informed in capital letters that 'LAO WROTE ANOTHER POEM' (ibid.: 285). As if to prod the recondite reader, it declares: *The Quylph / Came from / Aleph* (cf. Hebrew 'alef' air, one of the 'Tria Prima', the three fundamental alchemical symbols). The magic of the naming is that it has already occurred; it has already been voiced/written, as intimated earlier. In what appears to be a play of art and life, Okri not only mimics the stated trajectory of his narrative, inspired by the word Arcadia but, in context, Lao's so-called poem also suggests an etymological link between the first letter of the Semitic abjabs, 'alep' in the Phoenician alphabet meaning 'ox' (sacred in Oriental mythology), and his spirit of illumination, the *Quylph*. But *aleph* also represents the numeral ONE; both are symbols that precede everything that is said or communicated, 'ever exceeding the intentions of those who speak' (Stables 2016: 133).

Interestingly, if one accepts that 'P' is the 'Great last Prime in the Sky', Hofstadter imagines the number 'Q' as the product of all prime numbers and that is paradoxically itself 'divisible by 2 and also by 3, 5, 7, 11' and so on (2007: 118–19) 'ad infinitum'. In *The Greek Qabalah: Alphabetic Mysticism and Numerology*, Kieren Barry reminds us that '[i]n recent times, numerology, Hebrew Qabalah, enneagrams, divination, and similar topics have experienced a renaissance as part of the esoteric doctrines of interest to the so-called New Age movement' (1999: xiv). Circling back to the significance of the novel's title, *The Age of* Magic, in illustration, Lao pronounces: 'Never move far from the alpha of life. Replenish yourself in the aleph. Renew the core with the alf. In A we begin and to A we return' (2014: 18). These three sentences typify Okri's narrative strategy, revealing as they do a juxtaposition of worldly feelings and mystical or metaphysical sensations, a technique that encapsulates Merleau-Ponty's observation on spatial relations and hermeneutic time or eternal return:

> Every ideation, because it is an ideation is formed in a space of existence, under the guarantee of my duration which must turn back into itself in order to find there again the same idea I thought an instant ago and must pass into the others in order to rejoin it also in them. Every ideation is borne by this tree of my duration and other durations, this unknown sap nourishes the transparency of the idea; behind the idea, there is the unity, the simultaneity of all the real and possible durations, the cohesion of one sole Being from one end to the other. (1968: 11)

Okri marks, for the reader who reads slowly to perceive and be enchanted by the loopy nature of being, pointers on how to understand his writing. In the second chapter of the final part of this novel (Book 7), the narrator provides an analogous juxtaposition of timelessness and perceptivity at the close of day *two* when Lao and Mistletoe

> lingered on the shore of the lake, no longer looking at the mountains, the lake, the clouds. They let the mountain, sky and lake act on them. They let go. They surrendered themselves, and vanished into the eternal present.
>
> It's impossible to say how long they were gone. Mystics say a moment in eternity is a lifetime in history. It's possible that in the margins of their immersion is inscribed the history and future of the human race. (2014: 279)

This is the unknowable world of mythic time, mythic space:

> Such moments have no name. They leave no recollections in the mind. It's a moment's freedom made real and then forgotten: an angel's kiss that alters nothing except the total shape of one's destiny. Altered but not known. (Ibid.)

Okri closes his novel in a brief but significantly numbered chapter 8 in which, at the end of their interval in the enchantment of living and their sojourn in the Alps, Lao and Mistletoe strip naked and take a midnight dip in the cold, dark waters of Lake Lucerne (2014: 286).[14] Such golden moments recall Okri's reference to the fifth river that flows from Eden to Arcadia. The omniscient narrator explains:

> Four rivers flow into the Garden of Eden. In one of them, as an old commentary says, *the gold of the land is good*. A fifth river can be said to flow from Eden to Arcadia, and its allegories are wonderful, its gold good. When we are young we set out with dreams. In the middle of the journey of our lives we find perhaps that we have lost our way. At the end we find the origin and we begin again.[15] (Ibid.: 18; original emphasis)

In literary symbolism, both Eden and Arcadia, here closely linked by living waters, signify an earthly paradise, in turn, reflecting back to the significance of the inscription on the tomb in Poussin's painting: 'Et in Arcadia ego' in *In Arcadia* and adumbrating its resuscitation in *The Age of Magic* (more loops within loops!).

The experience of the imaginal world is described paradoxically. Okri's sentences are a blue print of the way in which, or 'how', we can cultivate the innate virtualities of the force of life, lost through time. This involves recalling Heidegger's notion of the hermeneutics of 'being-towards-death' or 'Dasein', as well as the centrality of dream time as a further example of stepping out of the current of historical causality (Cheetham 2003: 11–12).

Of course, Freud and Jung had much to say on oneiric experiences, and Okri has always shown a fascination with dreams as discussed in my reading of his second novel, *The Landscapes Within* (1981), as an unfinished symphony,[16] and in which oneiric records provide the catalyst for the tale. *The Age of Magic* opens with both lead characters asleep. While Lao 'slept in a shining orb' (2014: 11) in conversation with an imaginary spirit guide, 'Mistletoe was asleep with a smile on her face' (ibid.), both suggestive of dreamtime. Later in the narrative, the cameraman, Sam, 'stole' the faces of the fellow passengers 'while they dreamt', which leads to Lao attempting to profile character from the 'faces in sleep' and pondering whether sleeping faces betray 'the mind's construction' thus revealing the 'criminality' of criminals (ibid.: 32–3). This again alludes to the Sufi idea of 'correspondences' (what is inside shows on the outside). Jim's acrostic poem on his obsessive desire to '[k]ill Malasso' begins with '*[k]ings do not dream at night*' (ibid.: 54; original emphasis), a hegemonic discourse on the effect of power. Then, in an extended, more sinister incident, the producer (Jim) confides in Lao about his dream (ibid.: 61) of a Faustian attempt to sell his soul to the devil in return for an at last successful documentary. Unlike Goethe's Mephistopheles, however, this time in an all but bathetic loop, we learn that Jim's soul is rejected, because he 'didn't have enough potential for good or evil'; his 'middling soul' is like that of 'an English sheep' (ibid.: 63)!

The thoughts in these episodes are the climax of Lao's earlier realization that the word *live* in reverse spells *evil*, implying that what constitutes evil is 'to die in life' (2014: 29) by not 'living in the present moment' (28). In an allusive cross-reference to Mann's *The Magic Mountain* (1924), set in a sanatorium high in the Swiss Alps, and where the characters are there for a rest cure, Lao stumbles upon the paradox that one of 'the benefits of illness' is that it gives 'people time to catch up with themselves, to arrive at where they are in life's fast-moving story' (Okri 2014: 28) – in other words, to dream or to daydream – and that '[t]o live is to love, evolve, create … to be replenished by the origins' (ibid.: 29), already alluded to. By extension, 'evil is exile from the living waters' and 'Arcadia is the place where life is renewed, where evil is turned around' (ibid.).

Conclusion

In the creative act, word and thought are indivisible and the mind at once recoils from and rejoices in the inherent wizardry, where an imaginary train journey provides an 'interval' for profound reflection about our life journey and illusion as evoked in Lao's intuition that '[m]aybe true travel is not the transportation of the body, but a change of perception, renewing of the mind' (Okri 2014: 35). Thus, the narrator suggests that trains are 'a bridge between two realities' (ibid.: 39), affording space 'to take stock, to dream, to muse. It gives a sense of freedom' (ibid.). Continuing this train of thought, the narrator states that 'Arcadia is a dream, and dreams infect reality with their truth' (ibid.: 71). This recalls the epiphany that occurs immediately prior to arrival in Basel, couched in a brief but important interchange between Lao and Mistletoe, a meeting of minds that prefigures the 'hieros gamos' mentioned earlier: 'He shrugged, "Just when I'm beginning to understand something, we always arrive." / "I know," Mistletoe said, "Journeys are perverse. We arrive at our destination before we arrive at our revelation"' (ibid.: 36). Later, too, in an authorial intrusion that highlights the contemplative nature of this narrative and having happened upon the neo-Platonic notion that '[a]ll things are ideas' (ibid.: 198), Lao states that Arcadia too is an idea, one that has its inception 'inside us' (ibid.: 199). Then, in metanarrative self-reflection, Lao asserts that '[a]bstractions defeat us'. We need 'real and visible things' (ibid.), because of the perception that 'solid things are condensations of primal energy' (2014: 198).

Discussing the inadequacy of scientific knowledge, Merleau-Ponty argues that 'in it truths of fact and truths of reason overlap' (1968: 108). This is because 'the carving out of the facts, like the elaboration of the essences, is there conducted under presuppositions that remain to be interrogated' (ibid.). In an effort to comprehend what Nature, history, the world and Being *are*, 'to think himself in the essences, to think the world in himself, to unravel the jumbled essences to form finally the significant "Being," he encounters doubt,' says Merleau-Ponty, whereas philosophy finds beneath the doubt an 'a priori' knowledge, 'a horizon' that encompasses both 'our negations as our affirmations', penetrating that horizon to define 'anew this new something' (1968: 109). Okri, in turn, argues that the necessary 'higher instrument' of complete vision is 'poetry, the organ of intuition' that can 'supply to consciousness the highest data' (2014: 199). This is the imaginal world in this poetic novel. The idea is captured in the pure poetry of Lao and Mistletoe's dreamlike interlude on their final day in Switzerland that ends 'their Arcadian days within their Arcadian journey' (ibid.: 279). Auspiciously, at the close of day *two*, the two lead characters experience what appears to define a sublime, but necessarily fleeting, happiness, cited earlier:

> They lingered on the shore of the lake, no longer looking at the mountains, the lake, the clouds. They let the mountains, sky, and the lake act on them. They let go. They surrendered themselves, and vanished into the eternal present. (Ibid.)

Early in the novel, the narrator had linked the travellers' 'idea of Arcadia' with their 'ideal of happiness' (2014: 13). Later, one of the more reticent passengers, the globe-trotting New Yorker, Emily, provides an exegesis on happiness and home, concluding that 'basically most of us are happiest wherever we feel at home' (ibid.: 24). These words summarize Okri's cultivation paradigm, climaxing in his definition of an interval in the enchantment of Being, of a supernatural consciousness of at once 'being watched' and of 'watching ourselves' (ibid.: 227), while wandering through an 'empty' and 'silent' Swiss town, that seemed like 'a stage upon which an arcane ritual was to be enacted' (ibid.): 'If they knew how, they could have walked through the mirror of beauty into a shining world. In that moment, between strides, they could have seen that nothing was meant to be, but only what they made it. They could have rewritten their lives in the margins of the book of life' (2014: 228). This not only recalls Lao's Miltonic assertion that '[t]he idea behind Arcadia … is the suspicion that we have lost something: the feeling that we tend to lose our best dreams' but also encapsulates the historical transition from the fatalistic notion that 'happiness is what happens to us, and over which we have no control' (McMahan 2006: 19) to the modern Western perspective on happiness in which at its most basic level, 'humans might hope to influence their fate by their own actions' (ibid.: 20).[17]

Appositely for Okri's novel, Socrates argued that the lover of wisdom could ascend the ladder in 'search of the pure form of beauty' (in McMahan 2006: 36). In other words, happiness and harmony – the highest good – could be attained by the lover of wisdom when 'the better elements of the mind prevailed' (ibid.) through self-control. This brings my argument full circle, returning to the 'high abstractions' of both neuroscience and literature, but which, of necessity have only been touched upon.

Colours are, for Sufi thinkers, veils or vessels (which colour the water according to their own hue), and that to change colour meant also to change one's character. The changing colour of the mountain, at the beginning of the narrative, and the changing sky, at the close, appear to allude to this view. In ancient Persia, the divine essence is compared to a dyer who finally dyes everything in his own colour, that is, the invisible, radiant light, and, once this state has been reached, colour distinctions are bound to disappear. Little wonder then that axiomatic to the tale are Lao's two early epiphanies: 'Arcadia is the place where life is renewed, where evil is turned around' (Okri 2014: 29), and '[m]aybe true travel is not transportation of the body, but a change in perception, renewing the mind' (ibid.: 35), which accord with the theme of cultivation as a paradigm for sustainable production and human formation. Okri's work can be seen as an attempt to safeguard human spiritual diversity against the ravages of narrow-minded dogmatisms, whether spiritual or scientific. More than reading and thinking, he cultivates a deeper understanding of Nature and holism. He gives back in reciprocity indicative of generosity of spirit. For him, the virtualities inhere in three abstractions: Arcadia, happiness and an ontopoietic consciousness of self.

19

When chaos is the god of an era: Rediscovering an 'axis mundi' in *Starbook*

Introduction

Ben Okri's metafiction is itself an attempt to reveal how best to read *Starbook* (2007) and to understand life, as contingent upon the author's inner, most intense view of reality,[1] embodying both chaos and consolation. He redefines 'reality' in terms of an animistic celebration of life, symbolized in 'a full keyboard of life' (the black and the white keys). Reminiscent of Lewis Carroll's *Looking Glass* (1887), Okri conceives of texts as simulacra: erasing the boundaries between author and reader that may exist where symbols obscure essence through the gauze of correspondences. 'Don't just read the words. Go into the *mirror*,' urges Okri. He exhorts readers to step 'Through the Looking Glass' for '[t]hat is where the *real* secrets are. Inside. Behind. That's where the gods dream, where realities are born' (2011: 83 no. 10; emphasis added). This injunction transports the reader into a world of alchemy.

Key concepts, evoked in my opening paragraph, suggest what Okri perceives as meaningful reading: 'simulacra', or mirrored images, and 'reality', respectively. In contrast to Samuel Taylor Coleridge's (1909–14) reconciliation of opposites, Gilles Deleuze (1983: 5) views simulacra as 'dissimilitude' or 'disparateness', which is closer to Charles Baudelaire's questioning of correspondences between art and life. Texts, for Okri, are divinatory simulacra; the 'real secrets' in the mirror are synechdochic traces, simultaneously encoding and decoding signification. In *Starbook*, reality is conferred through participation in the 'symbolism of the centre', or through what Mircea Eliade in *The Myth of Eternal Return* ([1954] 1989: 5) terms an 'axis mundi', a sacred geophysical space or ziggurat where the temporal (the earth) and the divine (heaven and hell) coalesce.

Pertinently, 'reconstitution' lies at the heart of Okri's pre- and postcolonial aesthetic because simulacra offer ceaseless mutations and a series of variations that violate the hierarchies and, importantly, the stasis and unity of colonial aesthetics. In *A Way of Being Free* (1997: 2), Okri argues that writers (read 'poetic' writers) sometimes cut 'tangentially across the morning waves of humanity' moving against the 'great tidal waves of everyday events' (ibid.). This cross-cutting highlights his project of dreaming into reality a better future for mankind through imaginative endeavours and a lively re-visioning of re-humanized living. The role of the storyteller (poet/artist) is, he insists, 'to redream our world' (ibid.: 49).

In an interview with Okri (16 February 2011), I proffered my perception that his view of reality was innately optimistic encapsulated in his non-fiction and *Songs of Enchantment* (1993; *The Famished Road* trilogy), particularly. From the silence of 'unblindedness', Azaro's father in conversation with his son, a 'spirit-child'/an 'Abiku', is moved to muse that '[t]he light comes out of the darkness' (1993: 287). My observation elicited the telling response: 'No, I wouldn't call it optimism so much as realism.' He cautioned against defining terminology, especially terms as inherently fraught as 'reality'. For an African, reality embraces not only the five senses but also the sixth sense, 'what is unknown and unseen', as Okri asserted in our discussion. To this mix must be added embedded sociocultural wisdom: 'The primordial African spirit views reality from a wider spectrum [than the Western one]. It is informed by the metaphysical sense embedded in all the great traditions, but particularly in the African tradition. The African world view takes in the hierarchy of metaphysical beings.' This led to an exchange of rhetorical questions regarding perceptions of reality: What constitutes one's reality? Is one's reality true only for that individual? Isn't our reality limited to what we are taught to see?[1] (See Chapter 20 of this monograph.) This discourse tries to address these, first, by elaborating upon Okri's inimitable aesthetics.

Outlining Okri's aesthetics

Writing against the exclusive concentration on one aspect of validity, Okri asserts that poets – and, by extension, poetic writers – 'seem to be set against the world because we need them to show us the falseness of our limitations' (1997: 2). Adopting a kind of aesthetics of resistance, Okri seeks to illuminate a metaphysical-historical African moment, a moment related to life problems but transcending and transforming them through a higher order of consciousness. Criticism has been less concerned to establish the organic unity of literary works and more open to such works as 'occasions for the jostling of orthodox and subversive impulses', to cite Stephen Greenblat (2001: 254).

Whether there are layers of reality or not as in Plato's theory of the 'double remove' is open to conjecture, but Okri's basic assumption can be construed as one 'of a world of wholeness that is obscured with illusion as a result of dualistic thinking'.[2] In conversation with Okri, he elaborated on his perception of reality with an 'a priori' musicology analogy, one which manifests a very specific consciousness of reality:

> A piano with only five keys is a reality. But, if we include all the keys, the white keys and the black keys, this is a different reality. So *reality depends on our cultural perception of the keyboard of life*. Using the full keyboard, Azaro's father discovered a new perception of fundamental questions, especially the question of what constitutes the nature of reality. Is it outside oneself or fatally linked to human sensibilities? How does one construct reality? (Gray 2012: 5; emphasis added)

Such a comprehensive, polyphonic view constitutes a field of force, an Okrian existential defence of life. He followed matter-of-factly with the truism: 'One cannot truthfully tell an African tale according to Jane Austen's reality,' or, I interjected, 'an early nineteenth-century English tale according to an African reality.' 'Dialogue with the West,' he asserted, 'is thus difficult, because the concept of reality is not universal' (Gray 2012).

These excerpts highlight Okri's tendency to cut 'across the morning waves of humanity', his interest in difference rather than commonality. His premise entails defining the 'universal' (if such a term retains an application) from within a given cultural framework, 'which dissolves reality into multiple and multivalent reflections of consciousness' (White 1973: 551). Okri's reality equates with a melody, a simulacrum for the marvellous, an 'axis mundi' or ziggurat. Just as the notes on the keyboard are incapable of creating harmony singly, so 'reality' is what it is owing to its spacio-temporal and metaphysical relationship; its melody is dependent upon interrelationships. His point about Austen – that her reality differs essentially from his African one – is thus the really important point and the one that sheds light on *Starbook*'s non-dualistic, allegorical form of realism.

With regard to the symbiosis of the kind of allegory one encounters in the prose and poetic *Edda* intertexts and the kind of African realism seen in *Starbook*, Anthony Chennells provides a useful argument: 'Allegory is often used to present this ideal Africa and, although in Western literary theory allegory is traditionally seen as opposed to realism, in the African novels ... the allegorical becomes a form of realism because Africa's diverse realities are displaced by an idea of Africa that allegory can contain' (2006: 49).[3] Okri's poetics begs the question of literary belonging.

Literary belonging?

The paradigm shift from socialist realist modes to more Africanized forms of representation epitomizes the trajectory of West and East African writing: from Ousmane Sembene (*God's Bits of Wood* [1962] 1970) to Ayi Kwei Armah (*Two Thousand Seasons* 1978; see Gray 1997), and from Ngugi wa Thiong'o (*A Grain of Wheat* [1967] 1986) to Okot p'Bitek (*Song of Lawina* and *Song of Ocol* [1966] 1967; see Gray 2000) or Margaret Ogolo (*The River and the Source* 1994). It has been argued that Okri's writing has, from the start, traced a single trajectory, that of non-realism or magical realism. In an article entitled 'Esoteric Webwork as Nervous System: Reading the Fantastic in Ben Okri's Writing', Ato Quayson (Gurnah 1995: 144), for instance, makes a plausible case for what he calls the author's 'non-realist' form of representation, claiming that Okri's writing is particularly relevant for assessing non-realist narrative modes in African writing 'because he focalizes several aspects of narrative through a prism of indigenous beliefs ... it manages a careful balance between fantasy and reality'.[4] More characteristic and prompted by Okri's Booker Prize novel *The Famished Road* (1991), other critics prefer the term 'magical realism' to non-realism. Angelique Serrao's estimation of *Starbook* is typical: 'Okri mixes a range of styles which successfully weaves a story of magical realism with African myth to develop a novel that is truly unique' (2010: 2). If magical realism defines the shift away from a linear perspective of reality towards a worldview that undercuts traditional empirical, rational tenets and embraces holistic patterns of reality, chaotic and unexpected manifestations of human experience, one can hardly quarrel with this all but canonical reading. However, non-realism and magical realism are terms that Okri tacitly refuted in our conversation in London in 2011. As the opening excerpts show, his refutation of the positivism implied in 'magical realism' in favour of simply 'realism' has to do with his perception of reality, which is closer to the Platonic, but also to 'obstinate questionings / Of sense and outward things' ('Mental Fight', ll. 145–6). Asked if there was an element of the Platonic notion of the 'real' and the 'really real', he responded: 'Yes, but also the Scandinavian concept of reality.' There is a reality in Okri's *Starbook*, but it is a transcendent reality that deliberately exceeds the confines of Western concepts of reality. To appropriate William Ready's insight, for the Scandinavian, reality expresses 'more profoundly the truth that lies hidden behind realism, and it takes some getting used to' ([1969] 1973: 82).

Pertinently, in the *Prose Edda of Snorri*, a representative philosophic introduction to Norse cosmogony, the seeress is summoned from her grave in a piece entitled 'Vøluspá' ('The Prophecy of the Seeress'). She tells the assembled gods of the first-created things: 'In the beginning how the heavens and earth / Rose out of Chaos' (Hollander [1962] 2008: 1).[5] And in 'The Lay of Rig' (from the *Poetic Edda*), 'the god Heimdall [Rig] was the progenitor of the three human estates: slaves, freemen, and nobles'. 'This mythological, gnomic poem celebrates the institution of monarchy, the princely races of the motherland. Heimdall, "the One shining above the world" is the warder of the gods' (2008: 2 no. 2). *Starbook* – its title (echoing the One shining above the world / 'the book of life among the stars' (2008: 3)), its epic qualities (an extended fable of the survival and regeneration of the kingdom of a dying African prince) and parallel estates (slaves, freemen and nobles) – reflects an intertextual synthesis of both these skaldic verses. 'The most important element of the Norse myth lies in Courage' (Ready 1973: 82) and Okri invokes courage time and time again. The novel's speculations, however, on pre-existence, the unborn and the implied 'benediction of our heavenly home' is perhaps also and more reminiscent of Wordworth's 'Imitations of Immortality'.[6]

Okri's writing evidences his conscious assimilation and unconscious apprehension of many intertextual nuggets. The author has emphasized the realistic dimensions of his work,[7] and his concept of realism must be seen to embrace cosmic harmony: the medieval music of the spheres, the ancestors and Urhoba myths and legends are an integral part of the real world, of urban life and of rural life and of life beyond life. Local beliefs are part of his real world, not parallel to it. Robert Bennett coincidentally summarizes this aspect; he remarks on Okri's eschewing of the simplistic appellation of magical realism: Okri emphasizes that 'he is not trying to create a world of magic and myth that exists next to the real world as much as he is trying to extend our sense of the real world itself to include myths and magical events within it' (1998: 2). This is precisely what the double thrust of my chosen title seeks to encapsulate: 'When chaos is the god of an era: Rediscovering an "axis mundi" in … *Starbook*.'

Elucidating the title

Elsewhere, I have referred to Okri's spirit-in-life beings as leading sentient double lives.[8] Pointing to the framing theme of redemptive living in *Starbook* and reflecting back to the *Prose Edda*, Okri states: 'Only in light can truth be found ... Beyond is where it really begins' (2007: 118). This effectively summarizes what he writes in *Birds of Heaven* about true inspiration and the most sublime ideas of living 'that have come down to humanity come from a higher realm, a happier realm, a place of pure dreams, a heaven of blessed notions. Ideas and infinite possibilities dwell in absolute tranquillity' (ibid.: 12–13). It also resonates with the *Poetic Edda*'s 'golden age of innocence' before the 'coming of the Norms [the Fates], who wreak havoc upon the world' (no. 5), as Okri makes clear in his use of the adversative: 'Before these ideas came to us they were pure, they were silent, and their life-giving possibilities were splendid. *But* when they come to our earthly realm they acquire weight and words. They become less' (ibid.: 13; emphasis added).

The discussion now moves to the dichotomy between the 'pure', 'silent' esemplastic ideas and the tarnished earth inherent in Okri's representation of reality in *Starbook*, or the possibility of harmony rising from chaos in Scandinavia's 'Prophecy of the Seeress', and in my title. An early descriptive passage in *Starbook* captures this possibility: 'Gifted children often said that they could hear the trees [of the dense forest] singing charmed melodies. On certain nights, when the moon was full and white like the perfect egg at the beginning of creation, the wise ones claimed that the trees whispered stories in the abundant darkness' (2007: 3–4). Early in the novel, we read: 'Long ago, in the time when the imagination ruled the world, there was a prince in this kingdom who grew up in the serenity of all things' (ibid.: 4). But the soothsayers predicted a conflicting life: 'He will be a king and a slave ... He will be sold like a goat, treated like an animal, ... he will suffer like a great sinner, he will live like a god, and will know freedom more than the freest of men' (ibid.). Evoking such contiguous contraries, a couple of decades before *Starbook* – and, coincidentally, the inspiration behind my title – is Okri's 'when chaos is the god of an era, clamorous music is the deity's chief instrument. [Ede] didn't fully understand the thought, but it illuminated why he felt drawn to music that had clear, burning melodic lines like forces of [N]ature' (1988: 165). Immanence and transcendence coexist; these abstractions are integral. Okri's melodious reality is transcendent within the embodied perceiver. Taken from his tellingly entitled short story 'When the Lights Return' in *Stars of the New Curfew* (1988), the extract reflects cosmic consciousness exemplified in the author's spirit-in-life fictional characters, where the professional singer, Ede, is making his way through the detritus of fly-infested slums (possibly Lagos) to his mortally ill lover. In a moment of contrite self-reflection and remorse, leading to the realization of how profligate he has been in his love for Maria, a fragile, fey beauty, songwriter Ede experiences a partially understood attraction to music emanating from a nearby record store, to the 'burning melodic lines like forces of [N]ature' (ibid.). This illumination points to an indissoluble connection with the cosmos and cosmic rhythms, a connection to a certain 'valorization' of human existence – to borrow a term from Eliade ([1954] 1989: vii).

This short story, like *Starbook*, is indicative of the author's desire to expand notions of the real beyond the material and historical. In the former text, such notions parallel the spiritual aspirations of Okri's lovers which catapult them out of the narrowed world of their poverty. By contrast, *Starbook*'s 'star-crossed' lovers are, respectively, from the monarchical and freeman/professional strata of society.

Starbook

As in 'When the Lights Return', *Starbook* features a love relationship: this time between a dying prince and an ethereal maiden from an ephemeral tribe of artists, whom he secretly watches as she dances with a handful of close girlfriends, communing with Nature beside an unspoilt river somewhere in Africa, where 'a haunting barely audible music could be heard from its earth' (2007: 3). This mythic[9] relationship ultimately leads to a numinous coupling that bears fruit to ensure the continuation of the prince's royal line despite his flight, and death, shortly thereafter. (The lovers had been spied upon by jealous suitors for the maiden's hand.) His was an 'enchanted illness' (ibid.: 25), a 'fatal happiness' (5); hers the 'tragic happiness' (79) of a lost ingénue. Describing the ecstasy of their eventual lovemaking as the couple lie on the shore near a bank of flowers, Okri encapsulates the cyclical moment by celebrating the purity and metaphysical dynamism of the meeting of two souls. 'They caught glimpses of what they had been to one another in time past beyond memory and what they would be to one another in the beautiful time to come beyond death, in another life, where the true story of their love would seem to begin ... slightly frightened by the depth of love they saw deep within the other' (ibid.: 394). But a foreboding of 'where the real secrets are' is at once evoked, heralded by the all but emblematic mirror image: 'It seemed a love too strong for mortal life, a love that would make itself the sole purpose of living, a love that was like eternity gazing into the *mirror* of eternity; a love that would do nothing but simply exist in the blissful light of the other as in the light of the sun after the darkest night' (ibid.; emphasis added).

The lovers' first kiss is described as a kiss of many lives – the 'unimaginable dissolving of one soul into another' (Okri 2007: 397). Stuart Holroyd explains the operation of such transpersonal experience and its resultant epiphany:

> Intellectually, it is an experience of illumination or revelation, a visionary insight into 'the meaning and drift of the universe', and understanding 'that the life which is in man is eternal; that the soul of man is as immortal as God is; that the universe is so built and ordered that without any peradventure all things work together for the good of each and all; that the foundation principle of the world is what we call love; and that the happiness of every individual is in the long run absolutely certain.' (1989: 84–5)

In contrast to the short story, this novel, like the Norse 'Lay of Rig', focuses more nearly upon 'the princely races of the motherland', albeit transmuted to Okri's own motherland, an Africa yet to be healed but whose future 'bristles with possibilities'

(2011: 62). In contradistinction with Ede and Maria, neither the prince nor his dusky maiden is named. Their story is closer to the 'Künstmärchen' (art fairy tale) mode; the archetypal lovers lack the realist traits of Okri's more Nigerian characters, despite Okri's protestations. Arguably, what Okri is striving for is neither the Englishness of an Austen world nor the Nigerianness of an Achebe world, but rather an imaginative link between an Old Norse and an old African cosmology (as he suggested in my 2011 interview).

Despite the differences between the two pairs of lovers, what these characters share is nostalgia for a salutary recollection of an Edenic universal (a periodic return to a mythical time at the beginning of things beyond life). Theirs is a sacred history, transmitted through mythology. Their cultural reality embraces the ebony and the ivory of Okri's full keyboard of life. The prince, like Azaro in *The Famished Road* trilogy, is an 'Abiku', who understands good and evil: 'He was very handsome and fair and bright and the elders suspected that he was a child of heaven, one of those children from another place, who was not destined to live long' (2007: 4). She, likewise, 'was not a child from here ... She is from a star no one has seen yet' (ibid.: 101). In an earlier act of 'self-healing' (ibid.: 125) following her initiation into womanhood, the love-sick maiden had voyeuristically created 'an inexplicable sculpture of a dying prince' (211). What this suggests, is that the sensitized human being and the world are so intertwined that each defines the other. 'The crude product of [N]ature, the object fashioned by the industry of man, acquire their reality, their identity, only to the extent of their participation in a transcendent reality' (Eliade [1954] 1989: 5). The life of the prince evinces a reciprocity between a 'real' or lived life and the precious stone carving. His life acquires or is raised to a spiritual dimension, revealing an original ontology. Killam and Rowe observe: 'Okri translates his remarkable knowledge of African cultures into a rich array of images and symbols. His interest in the relationship between the natural and the supernatural worlds leads to a negotiation between the two paradigms that characterize his approach to the discussion of human existence' (2000: 198). In clarification for those unfamiliar with the oeuvre, the authors proffer an illustration: 'the image of the "Abiku," the spirit child that dies soon after birth only to be reborn again and again, recurs in Okri's work. Although the "abiku" image has been used by Wole Soyinka and J. P. Clark ... [Okri] subverts its ordinary connotations to posit contemporary meanings and an extension of its semantic implications' (ibid.). The prince and his beloved in *Starbook*, as with Azaro in *The Famished Road* trilogy, are 'Abikus' who 'are continually aware of spirit companions demanding [their] return to the spirit world'. They flit 'among worlds of the living, the dead, and the unborn, a *trinity* that is unique in the African world' (ibid.; emphasis added), just as Okri flies narratologically between extant and primordial cultural worlds.

Early in *Starbook*, the hidden prince poses three life questions to the maiden and her answers provide a comparable cosmogonic *trinity*:

'First,' he said, 'where does the river end?'
'In the wisdom of God,' she replied humbly ...
'Second ... where does all our suffering end?'

'In the happiness that lies beyond all things,' she replied, as if in a trance …
'And finally, what are we all seeking?'
'The kingdom,' she replied, 'which we are in already, which we have got, and which is our home'. (Okri 2007: 10–11)

And, in *Mental Fight*, the injunction in a section called 'Turn on your light' is to recapture the subliminally real: 'The most authentic thing about us / Is our capacity to create, to overcome, / To endure, to transform, to love, / And to be greater than our suffering. / We are best defined by the mystery' (1999: 61). The next lines seemingly provide precise guidance on just how to seek 'the kingdom' of God, experienced epiphanically as an 'axis mundi': 'That we are still here, and can still rise / Upwards, still create better civilizations, / That we can face our raw realities, / And that we will survive / The greater despair / That the greater future might bring' (ibid.). Here, the cumulative effect of infinitives – 'to create, to overcome, / To endure, to transform, to love, /And to be greater than our suffering' – foreshadow the dialectic of the greater the despair, the greater the promise. Surely this testifies to an innate optimism that Okri prefers to call 'the full keyboard' of life. Okri's valorization of human existence is thus metaphysical, subscribing to the notion that the cardinal problems of metaphysics could be 'renewed through a knowledge of archaic ontology' (Eliade [1954] 1989: viii), as in the Scandinavian *Edda* intertexts. Eliade explains: 'For the man of the traditional and archaic societies, the models for his institutions are believed to have been "revealed" at the beginning of time, that, consequently, they are regarded as having a superhuman and "transcendental" origin' (ibid.: xii).

The contest of the individual to gain and enjoy integrity is celebrated in a kaleidoscope of spiritual colours and forms in Okri's works. At its first level, this contest in *Starbook* seems to be a struggle to rise above the shadows of the governors general who tried to cow the bodies and minds of so many 'primitive' Africans through the slave trade. Higher up, this fight/flight for inner illumination takes us to a more universal level of existential truth: to the archaic ideology of ritual repetition which, as the opening extracts show, and as Okri[10] himself confirms is, at once, cyclical and vertical. If life is understood as an organic whole, constituting a lived connective with its surroundings, lived experience is at once horizontal and vertical. The repetition of such experience(s), as of life itself, is – certainly for the 'Abiku' – as cyclical as the seasons. Unsought and without warning, the flight is ecstatic and consoling; accompanied by an inner sense of belonging to and participating in an abundant living reality of cosmic dimensions beyond 'logos' as witnessed in the consummation of love, already discussed. In *Birds of Heaven*, Okri elucidates: 'Yes, the highest things are beyond words' (1996: 5). He explains why this is especially so in for art:

That is probably why all art aspires to the condition of wordlessness. When literature works on you, it does so in silence, in your dreams, in your wordless moments. Good words enter you and become moods, become that quiet fabric of your being. (Ibid.)

And this encompasses all art forms:

Like music, like painting, literature too wants to transcend its primary condition and become something higher. Art wants to move into silence, into the emotional and spiritual conditions of the world. Statues become melodies, melodies become yearnings, yearning become actions. (Ibid.)

As with Okri's earlier novels, *Starbook* is couched in mythopoeic tropes of art, sculpture, dreams, silence and music. These function as potent symbolic markers in his books and, more particularly, in *Starbook*. They are magic, mental, psychic and moral images, awakening new notions, ideas, sentiments and aspirations. They 'require an activity more profound than that of study and intellectual explanation' to borrow from an anonymous writer (1993: 4). Consider, for example, the statue of a dying prince, mentioned earlier, and the maiden's people, whom the prince intuits as 'a tribe of artists', 'an underground tribe, who lived and created invisibly, not disdaining others, but knowing that the only way they could serve the land was to live their own way, with their own freedom, following their own magical and fluid laws, guided by constant intuitions and directives of the spirit, in accordance with the needs of the times' (2007: 41). In a later synoptic passage illustrative of true living, Okri views art itself as an 'axis mundi': 'All things came from art and fed back into it, as far as the tribe was concerned' (ibid.: 94). This correlates with an aesthetic of life lived at the meeting point of heaven, earth and hell (the sacred ziggurat):

Art was their religion, science, dream, temptation, seduction, recreation. Art was their hell and their heaven. Every cataclysm or disaster, every crisis, came out of art or was absorbed into it. Plagues were seen as a failure of their art in some way, a failure to listen, to see, to dream, to interpret, to prophesy, to envision, to be silent at the oracles. (Ibid.)

In order to access our essence, Okri suggests here that it is necessary to balance the apparent paradoxes, oppositions or polarities within our nature.

Dreams, too, mirror the eternal dialectic of living, dying, conception, corruption: 'It was a dream about a golden heron lost in its own dream' (2007: 130). As in the 'dream' of lived life, dreams signify unfathomability:

Not all things glimpsed in a dream are clear. All dreams retain an enigma. Not all events glimpsed in the great book of life among the stars are clear. Only while dreaming does the dream make sense. When one awakes, that which made sense suddenly becomes strange, tinged with mystery. (Ibid.: 346)

Then, on his deathbed, silently listening 'in the sublime fire of the centre of the golden circle' (ibid.: 354), the prince is accorded a revelation in a dream which, at once, illustrates the pivotal tropes (art, dreams, silence and music) collectively and functions as an encapsulation of living the full keyboard of life, the reality of the mercurial unfoldment[11] of the Spirit in this novel. It is illuminating to quote the rem-time musings of Okri's dying prince at some length as they are axiomatic to a fuller understanding of *Starbook* and its implied injunction for synergy:

> If he were to sum up the paradox of his being, in those moments in the forest, under the tree where he rested, and passed into the *blue gaps*, and saw distant revelations, he would say this: How do you survive the worst with the highest? What is the music of this paradox? What is its song? And can you show anyone its *shadow*, so that they can see the spirit of such a conjunction of the *sublime* and the *horror*? And yet, for all time, in the present and future story, the prince found within him the unquenchable mood of an immeasurable laughter. And all this was born on the night when, unknown to him, a father [the king] gazed with love on the form of his sleeping son. (Ibid.: 355; emphases added)

Typical of the postmodernist deployment of the notion of simulacrum, the images, picture, reproduction in this excerpt are diffused reflections ('somnium imago' (dream image, mirage, shadow)). But their synthesis lies in the archetypal image of a father's love for his son. Concomitant with the notion of the sublime (a correlative for 'the centre of the golden circle') is that of the horror of chaos of the earthly realm (symbolized in this novel by a grotesque masquerade, a disturbing sculpture, the suitor, Mambo's malicious rumours of the maiden's coupling with a unicorn and the 'white wind' of slavery). The 'blue gaps' through which the prince passes evoke the archaic belief in celestial archetypes of geophysical spaces (an 'axis mundi').

As if in endorsement and in response to the maiden's answers to his three quoted questions, the prince 'caught his breath. For the first time in his life he knew that deep inside agony there is a sweetness that is beyond compare. Only those who venture into such a dark abyss find such a light. Deep in the pain is beauty from *the high mountains of the sublime*' (2007: 10; emphasis added), an evocation of the sacred ziggurat. These extracts echo the 'infinite possibilities [that] dwell in absolute tranquillity' (1996: 13).

Eliade provides an elaboration on the architectonic symbolism of the Centre: first, the 'Sacred Mountain – where heaven and earth meet – is situated at the center of the world'; second, every 'temple or palace – and, by extension, every sacred city or royal residence – is a Sacred Mountain, thus becoming a Center'; and being 'an "axis mundi"', the sacred city or temple is regarded as the meeting point of heaven, earth and hell' (1996: 12).[12] There is a single setting in Okri's *Starbook*: a landscape of the Edenic sublime that resonates with Eliade's notion of an 'axis mundi': a sacred city with its shrinehouse, palace, and village: 'an oasis of huts and good harvests in the midst of an enveloping world of trees' (2007: 3).

> In the heart of the kingdom there was a place where the earth was dark and sweet to taste. Anything that was planted grew in rich profusion. The village was built in the shape of a magnificent circle. And in the centre of the circle stood the palace of the king. Four rivers met in the forest around the village. The shrinehouse was at the edge of the village and the path that ran past it led to the outside world. The forest was dense about the village, and it seemed that those in the heart of the kingdom lived in a magic dream. (Ibid.)

Starbook's landscape of a primordial Edenic sublime reverberates with the triadic elements of integration, synthesis and synergy/mercury, sulphur and salt.

The action shifts between the evanescent village, where the maiden lives, and the king's palace: 'at the centre of the circle' or alchemical 'quincunx' (the Physic Compass). In the village, echoing chivalric romance,[13] the prince becomes an invisible apprentice to the maiden's father, the master craftsman or 'magus of the tribe' (2007: 82) and later duels with the maiden's most monstrous suitor (Mambo); in the palace, he is confounded by 'the many slaves', the 'numerous servants', the 'many wives' (ibid.: 11) of his father, the king – a benevolent despot – given to raucous laughter[14] in his intuitive recognition of the paradoxes of life (of his corrupt and scheming councillors amid plenty). Okri, however, quickly disabuses the Western reader of life being an idyllic medieval romance. Reminiscent of Blake's 'Tiger', Okri highlights the contraries of life embedded in my title and integral to his perception of reality in a meta-narratorial statement: 'Chaos was a deep law, applied judiciously. Order was its obvious counterpart. Asymmetry was a great law, if used with a sense of great balance' (ibid.: 95). As if striving to make sense of the chaos and the stable patterns in Nature from which a heightened consciousness can emerge, yet remaining at once integral to and overlapping with these paradoxical life forces, the now omniscient author declares:

> The tribe did not favour such simple things in its art as order, balance, harmony. These were easy, and had been fully explored for generations. The tribe had advanced to the higher harmony of broken cadences, discord as beauty, warring elements, violent storms flashing pure lightning of fleeting beauty that cracks the soul asunder till one glimpses illumination. It favoured tactical rawness, indirection, eyes where the navel should be, for the navel is a kind of eye, and the eye is a *kind of navel* linking us to the known world. It favoured disjointed metaphorical thinking; fusion of unthinkable elements. The greater the discord, the greater the artistry required to bring forth the highest beauty and, paradoxically, the greatest simplicity. (Ibid.: 95–6; emphasis added)

Metaphorically speaking, the narrative of *Starbook* is thus suggestive of ritual repetition linking us to the world's navel. This is an ancient trope, which recites a legendary story; it is an old story within a new story. *Starbook* opens unequivocally with '[t]his is a story my mother began to tell me when I was a child. The rest I gleaned from the book of life among the stars, in which all things are known' (ibid.: 3). Towards the end of the final part of the novel – chapters 15 and 16 of this four-part novel in a mock authorial intrusion – Okri poses the question: 'How did this tale come down to my mother, this tale that she began to tell me when I was a child?' (ibid.: 415). Michel de Certeau suggests a triangulated rejoinder: 'Our society has become a recited society, in three senses: it is defined by stories, by citations of stories, and by the interminable recitation of stories' (1984: 186).

However, *Starbook* is far more than a recitation of a cultural legend learnt on a mother's knee. Okri entices his readers into the centre of the story by inviting them to participate in 'a new kind of drama' (2007: 415), devised by the maiden's father, tribal griot and sculptor, now on the verge of death. This inward drama marks 'the swan song of the tribe in its elegiac stage' (ibid.: 416). The injunction raises the reader's horizons of expectation: 'Listen wisely with your souls, not with your eyes or ears,' urges the principal actor, '[i]f you enter through the magic gate, if you walk through the encampment of the tribe' (ibid.). Here, to cite Douglas Low, albeit in a different context, 'the opening of the personal, situated, embodied perceiver upon the world crosses into and partially blends with it, forming a union more real than its parts' (2011: 81), while the reader is invited to pass through 'the blue gaps', discussed earlier. A short meta-narratorial comment from *A Way of Being Free* serves to elucidate the ellipsis in the invitation articulated in *Starbook*: 'Even when it is tragic, storytelling is always beautiful ... It wraps up our lives with the magic which we only see long afterwards. Storytelling reconnects us to the great sea of human destiny, human suffering, and human transcendence' (1997: 47).

The core story itself is as pithy as it is brief.[15] Perhaps alluding to the famed Kingdom of Benin, the narrative voice intones:

> You will find a place alive with art in every corner, art in the square, art all around the shrines. You will find a place alive with constant creativity. Such was the place the prince encountered as he entered the encampment of the tribe, disguised as a humble man, according to his principle of the heron, in quest of a maiden. (Okri 2007: 417)

Embedded in the dramatic plot of the lovers' eventual meeting, coupling and the birth of their son (notwithstanding the death of the prince) is the allegory of the rebirth of 'mother' Africa, itself a mythical return to a matriarchal society. Book 4, the last in *Starbook*, significantly entitled 'The Alchemy of All Things', concludes by reiterating the myth of eternal return coupled with the dichotomy of fragmentation, disjointedness, and a lack of centre, of earthly chaos:

> What more is there to tell? Just fragments in the book of life. All stories lead to infinity. There is no end to them, as there is no beginning. Just an epic sensed in the unheard laughter of things. Just fragments seen in the murky mirror of mortality, when bright things shine momentarily in the brief dream of living. (Ibid.: 422)

This suggests that the 'Alchemy of All Things' in the story of *Starbook* has always existed; it has been excogitated within the collective unconscious of an elect minority and perpetuated in secrecy from one consciousness to another. This 'book of life' returns us to the tree of life: the octagonal symbol crucial to alchemy, the Jewish Kabbala, Norse myth and the Knights Templar.

This, then, is a perennial tale that melds African legend with postmodernist traits; it shows that freedom – such as that experienced by the prince and quoted at the beginning of the discussion of the paradoxical prophecies pertaining to his life – is not a destination, a stasis to be reached, but an ongoing cyclical and vertical journey. Gerald Larue reveals the complexity inherent in the workings of this braiding of the chaotic with the theophanic and cultural mythology that underpins this novel:

> For the most part, the mythic antecedents of what we inherit are lost in complex patterns of the past. We cannot always know what persons or groups become

catalysts of change or stabilizing influences. Historical lines are broken; the lacunae are enormous ... people [in yesteryears] ... did not consider the world from the point view of 'I – it' relationships. But rather on 'I – thou' terms ... All life was seen in terms of relationships. (1975: 10–11)

Invoking the natural cycle of life, which coincidentally *mirrors* Okri's retelling of this ancient story, Larue concludes: 'Seasons came and went because ancient mythic patterns were repeated in a cyclic rhythm. As seasonal gods had risen and fallen in power and influence "*in the beginning*" that rise and fall was cyclically and seasonally reflected' (ibid.: 11; emphasis added to recall the Norse 'Prophecy of the Seerer').

In this novel, as elsewhere in Okri's works, silence and love are the keys to enlightenment. Ben Brown sagely observes: 'This is a vision of a paradise both found and lost ... *Starbook* is a novel at "the mercy of ultimate mysteries"' (2007: 2). Okri does not wish to solve these mysteries; he reveres them too much for that, and instead he seduces the reader with a rapt recounting of the infinite, within the particular. And, as he notes in *Birds of Heaven*, '[a]t best our cry for meaning, for serenity, is answered by a greater silence, the silence that makes us seek higher reconciliation'. He adds: 'I think we need more of the wordless in our lives. We need more stillness, more of a sense of wonder, a feeling of the mystery of life. More love, more silence, more deep listening, more deep giving' (2007: 2). Anita Sethi's review in *The Independent* (Sunday, 26 August 2007) perceptively points to the central message: 'Okri deliberates on how one ought best to read and interpret life'.[16]

Conclusion

In contrast to socialist realist novels that ask the reader to think more clearly, Okri aims to educate both the mind *and* the spirit. He prompts us to look at ourselves honestly and critically, to examine our inner motives, to be self-reflective, to go beyond. However, as with an Austen novel, 'the "text" initiates and controls – but partially, never wholly – the response in the 'reader'; and the 'reader', in responding to the 'text', produces an 'interaction' that is more than the 'text', or at least in some respects different from it' (Williams 1986: 3).

Although Okri disclaims the possibility of universal experience, his articulation of African mind, heart and soul is so trenchant that he does in fact allow a greater degree of universality. He allows more Westerners to hear the music of the full keyboard, with its major and minor keys, to experience – albeit vicariously – the marvellous. And, as with much contemporary writing, Okri's novel should be read in the context of the mythologies in which it is grounded. In *Ancient Myth and Modern Man*, Larue explains why, tracing the common origin of myth, coincidentally pointing to the origin of storytelling itself: 'Because man was not prepared to live with the absurd, he developed myths. Because he did not know how to live with the absurd, he canonized his myths. The myths echoed human hopes and dreams, repeating time and again in ritual drama and cultic ceremonies that the world had meaning, order, and purpose, and that man had meaning, direction, and purpose' (1975: 211). In *Starbook*, as in Okri's earlier novels, the leading characters are querents in search of regenerative wholeness, reflecting Larue's explication of the canonization of myths.[17] Okri looks to Africa to produce a literature that '*mirrors*, reveals, liberates' (2011: 62; emphasis added). With Africa's 'weird resilience', he argues, as if endorsing my charge of optimism: '[S]he will flower and bear fruit as the Nile once flowered into the Pyramids, or like the savannahs after the rains' (ibid.).

The central narrative of *Starbook* is one that suggests the way in which narrative can recreate idealized cultural norms and expectations.[18] It is the story of the community's reverence for art and for life, as much as it is that of a utopian coupling to ensure the continuity of the best that a well-ordered, hierarchical society can produce. Here, narrative discourse posits a single story, as a continuation of an earlier story, another 'text', of (an)other tradition. This is a Protean meta-narrative, always in process, creating a lacertine pattern of mythological intertexts, of pre-existing socio-religious and cultural resonances that engender the story and extend it. My aim has been to show that this is fiction doubling back on itself, and so offering a metaphor for its own origins. Through its link to Norse and African cosmogony – its own 'in the beginning' presupposes both the chaos and the sacred 'music' of an 'axis mundi'.

20

In conversation with Ben Okri

First, let me express my deep gratitude to you for taking time out of your busy schedule and the public demands made upon so celebrated a writer to talk to a reader who finds your works – be they poetic, dramatic or prose – intriguing and compelling.[1] I can well understand why the International Pen Club has you as their vice president. Second, I must tell you that I would like to use this interview as the opening piece in a monograph of your works that I hope to publish shortly, containing articles by myself and perhaps those by my postgraduate students at the University of Pretoria in South Africa.

R.G. I'd like to begin by asking you to respond to my perception that throughout your oeuvre, there seems to be a single guiding principle, a deeply embedded philosophical credo, if you like. Of course, I could be mistaken, being driven in my reading of your work by my own horizons of expectation (to borrow a term from Robert Jauss). In other words, I may be being misled by my own reception aesthetics. The principle I refer to is, I believe, nowhere better expressed than towards the end of *Songs of Enchantment* when, from the silence of 'unblindedness', Azaro's father, in conversation with his son, a 'spirit-child', an 'Abiku', is moved to muse that '[t]he light comes out of the darkness' (1993: 287).

This is a catalyst for two other questions and for a request I should like to make, but perhaps you'd like to respond to my contention about your guiding principle before I pose the two questions that arise out of this one. Am I on the right track in attributing an innate optimism to you?

B.O. No, I wouldn't call it optimism so much as realism. But, it is important how one defines realism. Realism takes in what is seen, felt, touched; what is unknown and unseen. The primordial African spirit views reality from a wider spectrum (than the Western one). It is informed by the metaphysical sense embedded in all the great traditions but particularly in the African tradition. The African world view takes in the hierarchy of metaphysical beings which, in turn, leads to a number of essential questions: What constitutes one's reality? Is one's reality true only for that individual? Isn't our reality limited to what we are taught to see? A piano with only five keys is a reality. But, if we include all the keys, the white keys and the black keys, this is a different reality. So, reality depends on our cultural perception of the keyboard of life. Using the full keyboard, Azaro's father discovered a new perception of fundamental questions, especially the question of what constitutes the nature of reality. Is it outside oneself or fatally linked to human sensibilities? How does one construct reality? One cannot truthfully tell an African tale according to Jane Austen's reality or an early nineteenth-century English tale according to an African reality. Dialogue with the West is thus difficult because reality is not universal.

Comment by R.G.: Is there an element of the Platonic notion of the 'real' and the 'really real' here?

B.O. Yes, but also the Scandinavian concept of reality. I can draw it for you. (This Okri did in my copy of *Starbook*; I later discussed the *Edda* in two articles. [See Chapter 19, for instance.])

Comment by R.G.: Although the author has himself emphasized the realistic dimensions of his work, this realism must be seen to embrace the ancestors, myths and legends, which are an integral part of the real world, of urban life and of rural life. Local beliefs are thus part of the real world, not parallel with, but contiguous to it. Elsewhere, I have referred to Okri's spirit-in-life beings as leading sentient double lives (see Chapters 5 and 19). In *Starbook*, Okri states: 'Only in light can truth be found … Beyond is where it really begins' (2007: 118), which is itself an effective synopsis of what he writes in *Birds of Heaven*:

> The greatest inspiration, the most sublime ideas of living that have come down to humanity come from a higher realm, a happier realm, a place of pure dreams, a heaven of blessed notions. Ideas and infinite possibilities dwell in absolute tranquillity.
>
> Before these ideas came to us they were pure, they were silent, and their life-giving possibilities were splendid. But when they come to our earthly realm they acquire weight and words. They become less. (1996: 12–13)

R.G. The bond between father and son is so tragically wanting in Achebe's seminal African text – *Things Fall Apart*. In your novels, especially in the *Famished Road* trilogy, this relationship is robust. I am wondering if this Telemachian aspect speaks of a healed or healing lineage in the postcolonial consciousness. Would you care to comment?

B.O. That is a very difficult question. The reflection of the father/son relationship is a mirror of the degree or presence of freedom in society. It reflects the extent to which the parental relationship, whether this be that of the child(ren) to the father or to the mother, mirrors society. This becomes a microcosm of the strategies for self-definition and emotional sensitivity. In a brutalized society, the father/son relationship is naturally distorted.

Comment by R.G.: Yes, of course. Maya Angelou deals extensively with this aspect in her novels, doesn't she, especially in *I Know Why the Caged Bird Sings*? Damaged souls lead to a cyclic pattern of disaster.

B.O. Yes, the family is the intimate theatre of society. Novelists have sensed that this micro-theatre reflects the larger societal tensions. *The Famished Road* shows the extent to which a transition has taken place; so, the relationship unfolds according to our own microcosm.

R.G. Also arising from my personal reception aesthetics is the question of an interrelationship between what the 'abiku' child perceives as the wisdom emanating from the silence of his dad's regaining of his sight, his 'unblindedness' – an Akashic still point. Is there a symbiosis between these two moments of enlightenment? Does such enlightenment spring from what Jung has termed the collective unconscious, or what Taoism calls the Akashic record, or am I yoking two disparate notions together by violence (to borrow loosely from Alexander Pope)?

B.O. A thread runs through all cultures. Every now and then for individuals, whether caught in tragic revelation or great suffering, all traditions lead to experience outside common perception into some higher space. In Scandinavian sagas, for example, whatever it is, it is going on outside the dome. All the traditions have this, but it is the breaking out that is the grandeur of tragedy.

R.G. Its cathartic potential?

B.O. Quite! Suffering leads to enlightenment, and they both interconnect. We are defined by the depth in the hermeneutic.

*

R.G. To return to my request. I am currently compiling a thirty-three-year history of Expo for Young Scientists in South Africa, an apolitical, a-racial youth science fair begun by my late husband at the height of apartheid when we moved to South Africa in 1979 and now one of the largest such fairs in the world. I should like to use 'The light comes out of the darkness' as the prefatory title to this book as I believe that it defines quite precisely my husband's vision. Would you have any objection to my doing so? I hope to go to print soon after my return to South Africa.

B.O. Tell me more about this Expo.

R.G. We held the first Expo for Young Scientists in 1980 in Pretoria Boys' High with 180 'kiddies' and their projects. Although most people saw a non-racial event as an impossibility in a country under the National Government, Expo continued to grow and to thrive under Derek's determination and careful guidance. At his death in 1998, there were twenty-six regional Expos and one National Finals with approximately twenty-six thousand participants nationwide, and we had, by then, participated in several international Youth Science Fairs. There are still twenty-six regions with anything between 26,000 and 35,000 participants. It is, as I have said, one of the largest such fairs in the world. Your 'light' truism embraces Derek's enlightened, if then, unorthodox vision. My British-born husband simply refused to acknowledge any connection between youth science and politics.

B.O. Yes, your choice of title seems appropriate.

*

R.G. Staying with political issues, a prevalent argument (supported by historical evidence) holds that white colonial thieves stole African land by force and then imposed both Western civilization and the Christian religion upon the peoples. Works by several black Africans (Achebe, Armah, Emechetta, Ngugi, Marachera et al.) understandably write back to the imperial centre. Your works and those of Wole Soyinka, in contradistinction, seem to go a step further in pushing aside any attempts to colonize either the mind or the heart of Africa. Would you like to comment on this 'newer' creative approach?

B.O. The poetic axis is there. To chew over the imperial or the colonial is not what I feel or what Soyinka thinks. I sense that it is well dealt with by others. Too much of it would allow it to define the narrative, but there is a need to show aspects of the continuum. We are not defined by history. The human spirit is limitless and our job as writers is to unveil. It's not just the pistol shots! Of course, colonizing the mind is implied as a sort of backdrop, but this does not define the text. Soyinka and I are not side-stepping the issue. We have taken the punch and then carried on. There is a profound responsibility of writer and readers: what you produce and what you examine eventually becomes defining. There have only been a hundred or so years of oppression in the life history of humankind. The redemption of the human spirit occurs when we throw light on the depredation of history.

Comment by R.G. Yes, some critics seem to have misread Alex la Guma's *A Stone Country* as a simple indictment of apartheid rather than a depredation of history's defining role. It's a tour de force of the best way to follow (see Gray 1999: 87–93).

B.O. I haven't read that, but I should like to do so.

*

R.G. In an extension of the previous question, Achebe's *Things Fall Apart*, Coetzee's *Waiting for the Barbarians* and Conrad's *Heart of Darkness* seem to be three pillars of the stage on which the revelation of colonial savagery is based. Your work, however, appears to fly above these concerns while, at the same time, being predicated upon such truths. To what extent is this part of a conscious artistic strategy?

B.O. The music of an artistic tradition! Our ancestors cut a path and we cut further paths, building on their foundations. It is as if one receives the baton and carries on. The process is both cyclical and vertical. I have felt the need to take the baton and to carry on. It's a question of standing on these writers' shoulders, just as they have stood on the shoulders of earlier writers. The duty of the artist is to extend the boundaries.

*

R.G. In his acceptance speech, Mario Vargas Llosa (7 December 2010: 11) points to the inherent paradox of storytelling. This then most recent recipient of the Nobel Prize for Literature asserts that

> [l]iterature is a false representation of life that nevertheless helps us to understand life better, to orient ourselves in the labyrinth where we were born, pass by, and die. It compensates for the reverses and frustrations real life inflicts on us, and because of it we can decipher, at least partially, the hieroglyphic that existence tends to be for the great majority of human beings, principally those of us who generate more doubts than certainties and confess our perplexity before subjects like transcendence, individual and collective destiny, the soul, the sense or senselessness of history, the to-and-fro of rational knowledge.

Would you please respond to this view of fiction-making?

B.O. I don't know about 'false'. Perhaps the word was lost in translation from the Spanish. It is not false; it is not a lie. There is a paradox. It is both. Art is a lie that tells the truth. Life is imponderable, so one cannot tell the whole truth. A reproduction on a stage, for instance, at once demarcates a new dimension. Literature is an abstract and it is a guise. We bring it into being by our being, our infinite permutation. This is the magic of literature. How you perceived this magical transformation is central to writing. Literature creates a parallel mirror, a parallel reality. We only see things through reflection. We perceive by translation, by reflection. Literature is one further step in this translation. What we trust is the aggregate of science (knowledge). It is a triple transaction.

*

R.G. In the now famous documentary on the Congo entitled *Leopold's Ghost*, young Congolese children have their hands amputated for not collecting full buckets of latex. Likewise, in Zimbabwe, unspeakable horrors are committed in the Vumba Mountains near Mutari by Korean trained 'askaris' to 'protect' the gold from the local inhabitants. The rapacious materialism of the neocolonialist mind is glancingly dismissed in your works, with the possible exception of its treatment in the demise of Madam Koto in your earlier novels and, then, in the stories in *Tales of Freedom* (2009). Do you perhaps think that the emotional and imaginative indigence of the 'Western' and neocolonial mind has deepened irretrievably, or is there a way out, a way on?

B.O. It comes back to metaphysics; to epistemology, to the theogony of reading.

*

R.G. Your writing celebrates the mythic and spiritual dimensions of the eternal African soul. Is this a reflection of an abiding interest in Taoist philosophy or is this attributable to your own Urhoba/Igbo consciousness, or perhaps to Perennial theology or what Mircea Eliade calls 'the myth of eternal return'? To what extent am I correct in the supposition that what you propound in your non-fictional writings and, essentially, in the novels *Astonishing the Gods* ([1995] 1999) and *Starbook* (2007) is a freeing of the fetters of the past and a visualization of universal justice 'through careful spiritual and social evolution' (*Astonishing the Gods* [1995] 1999: 72)? Is the frame of reference eclectic?

B.O. I am very cross-cultural. This is not eclecticism. I am fascinated by similar threads that run throughout philosophy that appear to come from the primordial tradition. For example, visits to the underworld and trickster gods occur in literature from very many parts of the world. This is not because human nature is similar; it is more profound. These threads running through so many cultures give me a sense not of diversity but of one source, a unity. Myths tell parallel stories. They enrich one another, and the future of the race depends on paying more attention to these streams that fascinate me and enrich the quality of life.

*

R.G. In one of your books, you use the unusual word 'pullulating' twice. It struck me that this heavily onomatopoeic word speaks for an insistence for liberty and a unique urgency not only to live but also to dream. To what extent is this so?

Comment by R.G. The word occurs in *Starbook* (2007: 336). Having reread *Starbook* just prior to this interview and conscious of time constraints, I decided against posing this question, for in this novel Okri provides the clearest of answers to the injunction to dream, which I quote in full:

> The prince sat under the tree, rested on its trunk, and was borne off to sleep. But it was not a normal sleep, nor was it a long one. And during that sleep many things happened to him that he would only remember in fragments of dreams over the many years of the suffering to come. He dreamt the beginning of all things, and their end. He dreamt all the stories of humanity. He dreamt of the answer to the greatest question, told him by a being in space unlimited inside a kingdom of silence. All that he was, all that he would be; and the solution to death; the answer of immortality; he dreamt them all in a brief moment of sleep. Then he awoke refreshed and found himself in a different place. The tree was in flower. The birds had awoken and were singing. Nine maidens in white drifted past him smiling. The forest was gone. The gap he sought stood before him like a ring of enchanted fire. He stepped into the fire and found himself on the other side, near the river of his village.

R.G. The contest of the individual to gain and enjoy integrity is celebrated in a kaleidoscope of spiritual colours and forms in your work. At its first level, this contest seems to be the struggle to rise above the shadow of the governors general who tried to cow the bodies and minds of so many Africans. Higher up, this fight or flight for inner illumination takes us to a universal level of existential truth. How far would you agree with this estimation?

B.O. In many ways, this is a misperception. One work cannot define my work. I have journeyed through the reality of life in my early novels to a spiritual dimension. So, this does not reflect the full dimension of my work. I would prefer to say that I fly with, not above. Life is a crucible. My quest is to attempt to touch all points: man in love, man in crisis, woman in society, suffering, becoming, freedom and so on. Sometimes I try to use the whole keyboard and to touch all in one novel. It is necessary to point to another aspect, to adopt a circular approach.

*

R.G. I have argued that your project is how to turn spiritual exhaustion into spiritual energy, how to distil human experience, how to 'domesticate infinity' (to use your own words from *Mental Fight*) (see Chapter 6). The guiding spirit seems to be a universalist one in that you at once conflate the intellectual currents of German philosophy (with its will to transgress the boundary between the human and the divine) with the Judaeo-Christian tendency to confront almost without mediation the problems of the absolute and its promises, and to move beyond this to a return to Arcadia, to a Blakean song of innocence. Please comment on this view.

B.O. African literature has a preponderance of the historical and the social, because of its history. But it is also necessary to draw attention to *The Divine Comedy*. There should always be a hint of an attempt to tease out all dimensions. Writers must remind people of this – must enrich the interpretation of the hieroglyphics.

*

R.G. Many of your novels track self-development in the path of the traditional 'Bildungsroman', but straightaway one pulls back from that conclusion to consider whether you have not brought into being a unique genre of the novel – the *enlightenment novel*. Developing or becoming is not enough. 'To be', we need light from within. We need, like your Azaro's dad and the classical Tiresias, to be blind in order to see! To what extent would you agree or disagree with this estimation, this attempt to pinpoint an emergent genre?

B.O. Yes, I accept the term. It's interesting. *Astonishing the Gods* and *Starbook* are essentially books that aim at the enlightenment of the human spirit. The conclusion to all novels must come full cycle. It has been done in poetry – to ask questions in a non-religious sense – about the evolution of the human spirit: Is there something in all the myths? Is something going on? Myths and philosophy need to be part of the novel – not in a stream of consciousness sense but marrying the synchronic and the circular.

R.G. As well as the diachronic?

B.O. Yes, it has to do with ways of seeing. (There followed a short discussion on John Berger's *Ways of Seeing* which both interviewer and interviewee had read and enjoyed.) Is it possible that the human spirit can take a leap, become enriched? What will the implications for this be for the novel? If we strive for some transcendence, would we not be better writers, better teachers?

*

R.G. Talking of ways of seeing brings me to my last question. The Peruvian laureate, mentioned earlier, asserts that

> fiction is more than entertainment, more than an intellectual exercise that sharpens one's sensibility and awakens a critical spirit. It is an absolute necessity so that civilization continues to exist, renewing and preserving in us the best of what is human. So we do not retreat into the savagery of isolation, and life is not reduced to the pragmatism of specialists who see things profoundly but ignore what surrounds, precedes, and continues those things. (2010:11)

In fact, singing the praises of writing, in general, and of fiction, in particular, Llosa goes so far as to attribute the transition from barbarism to civilization to storytellers:

> From the time they began to dream collectively, to share their dreams, instigated by storytellers, they ceased to be tied to the treadmill of survival, a vortex of brutalizing tasks, and their life became dream, pleasure, fantasy, and a revolutionary plan: to break out of confinement and change and improve, a struggle to appease the desires and ambitions and that stirred imagined lives in them, and the curiosity to clear away the mysteries that filled their surroundings. (Ibid.)

I have quoted Llosa at some length because in your own *A Way of Being Free* (1997), you also credit creative artists with this same civilizing capability, asserting that

[p]oets seem to be set against the world because we need them to show us the falseness of our limitation, the true extent of our kingdom.

The poet turns the earth into mother, the sky becomes a shelter, the sun an inscrutable god, and the pragmatists are irritated ... The problem is with those who are frightened of the rather limitless validity of the imagination, frightened of people who continually extend the boundaries of the possible, people who ceaselessly reinvent existence; frontiers people of the unknown and the uncharted.

Please respond.

B.O. Literature at its best leads to civilization. The novel should not just be a pot boiler. Reading is an act of making (in the medieval sense of creating), not of the writer but of the reader. Making is visualization, prevision – then civilization becomes unstoppable. We either return to blindness or make a leap to a now. There are only two options: retreat to the cave or leap. This is primal. We have inherited from the ancestors. This must take us forward, not back!

Literature and civilization are different but not different. The society that gave rise to *The Divine Comedy* flowered as a renaissance; the society that gave rise to Shakespeare led to a greater civilization. Literature does not create it, but there is an inspirational link like mercury and the alchemist's stone. Literature shows the presence and reveals and enhances a psychic strength, pulls it out to reflect a greater civilization.

Comment by R.G. Okri argued in *The Guardian* (January 2003) that the decline of nations begins with the decline of its writers, stating that '[b]ecause writers represent the unconscious vigour and fighting spirit of a land[,] [w]riters are the very sign of the psychic health of a people: they are the barometer of the vitality of the spirit of the nation'.

*

R.G. Thank you for your time, Ben. I am blown away by your generosity of spirit and cannot thank you enough for giving me such quality time with you.

Further comment: For this interview, I deliberately kept my questions general, if somewhat philosophical in the hopes that it will inspire others to join the voyage of discovery into Okri's oeuvre. Apprised of the authorial comment in *Starbook*, quoted below, I did not pose direct questions about the interpretation of specific works, for unravelling meaning is the task and joy of the critic.

> The greatest masters say nothing about their works because there is nothing to say, save that it was done, it was seen, it was unseen, it was rendered, it was remembered, carried across, brought here, imperfectly. The less one makes, the more is made. (2007: 98)

(Ben Okri was invited to Cape Town in 2012 to present the annual Steve Biko Memorial Lecture; he received a doctorate *Honoris Causa* in 2014 at the University of Pretoria and returned in 2015 to present a public lecture entitled 'Whither the African Renaissance' for the Institute for African Renaissance Studies at Unisa's Little Theatre during my post-retirement tenure there.)

Figure 3 Ben Okri

Courtesy of Matt Bray.

Notes

Preface

1 The views expressed here are mine alone. Terminology, where deemed necessary, is glossed within the chapters.
2 See, e.g., Jennifer Wenzel (2006), 'Petro-Magic-Realism: Toward a Political Ecology of Nigerian Literature', *Postcolonial Studies* 9 (4): 449–64; and Sarah Lincoln (2012), 'Petro-Magic Realism: Ben Okri's Inflationary Modernism', in Mark A. Wollaeger and Matt Eatough (eds), *The Oxford Book of Global Modernisms*, 249–66, London: Routledge. Both are well substantiated; they are recommended for readings of *Stars of the New Curfew* and *The Famished Road*. Wentzel provides an important insight in the context of Nigerian 'boom' and 'bust' international economy of the 1980s:

> If the publishing industry, like the palm or petroleum industries, exerts different kinds of pressures within and outside Nigeria as it circulates commodities, then the concept of *petro-magic-realism* offers a way of understanding the relationships between the fantastic and material elements of these stories, linking formal, intertextual, sociological, and economic questions about literature to questions of political ecology. (2006: 450; original emphasis)

3 Alexander Roob (2014), *Alchemy and Mysticism*, 23–6, Los Angeles, CA: Taschen.
4 Ben Okri's 'A Ruin in the Forest' (2012: 44–7) in *Wild* (London: Random House).
5 Ben Okri's 'Lines *in Potentis*' (2012: 26–7) in *Wild* (London: Random House).
6 Rosemary Gray (2012). 'Interview with Ben Okri'. *Journal of Literary Studies*, 28 (4): 4–13.
7 Ben Okri's 'Heraclitus' Golden River' (2012: 92–4) in *Wild* (London: Random House).

1 Ben Okri's aphorisms: 'Music on the wings of a soaring bird'

1 See *Birds of Heaven* (1996: 41 no. 87) and Gray (2017).
2 Synaesthesia signifies an experience of two or more kinds of sensation when only one sense is being stimulated (Abrams 1999: 315).
3 According to the philosophy of Anna-Teresa Tymieniecka, 'Imaginatio Creatrix' liberates the human spirit from one-sided dependence on nature and opens it to the acts of interpretation of organic processes. 'The creative act is an act of self-individualization ... the evolution of the universe is to be seen as being fundamentally connected to the process of seeing' (in Smith 2011: 17).
4 Themes in the book of Proverbs, attributed to King Solomon, encapsulate almost all aspects of what constitutes the good or upright life: from generosity, helpfulness and

humility; through work ethic, teamwork and wealth creation, the law, prudence and governance; to the benefits of knowledge/understanding/wisdom and to the dangers of evil and the need to fear God – where God's ontology, as asserted in Genesis, is that God is all attributes and all attributes are God ('Logos').

5   'Originally the hospice or hostel (< L. "hospes" a guest) for the reception of pilgrims.' The word 'hospital' 'later applied to a charitable institution for the aged or infirm' or to charitable institutions for the education of children (Brewer 1970: 549). Cf. the Knights of St John's in Jerusalem and the Knights Hospitalliers at Rhodes and in Malta, dating back to the Middle Ages. For the ancient Greeks, hospitality provided an opportunity for gift-giving and storytelling, with the host protected by Zeus.

6   See, for instance, Prov. 29.15: 'The rod and reproof give wisdom: but a child left to himself bringeth his mother to shame,' while 13.24, in similar vein, reads: 'He that spareth his rod hateth his son: but he that loveth him chasteneth him betimes.' Prov. 10.11 states: 'A wise son maketh a glad father: but a foolish son *is* the heaviness of his mother.'

7   Cf. Tymieniecka (1966) and Gray (2017).

8   An example of the 'mysterious animating element' that turns a work of art into a classic is, of course, Shakespeare's (1936) *Henry IV* Part 1, particularly when Falstaff initiates the wordplay by affecting a melancholy (one of the four humors) disposition:

> *Falstaff* I am as Melancholy as a Gyb-Cat, or a lugg'd Beare.
> *Prince* Or an old Lyon, or a Louver's Lute.
> *Falstaff* Yea, or the Drone of a Lincolnshire Bagpipe.
> *Prince* What says't thou to a Hare, or the Melancholly [*sic*] of Moore Ditch?

Martin Orkin (1982: 3) explains: 'Falstaff and the Prince allude, in turn, to the proverbial phrases: *As melancholy as a gibbed cat* 1592 (Tilley C129), *Lincolnshire bagpipes c.*1545 (Tilley B35), *As melancholy as Moorditch* 1608 (Tilley M1134), and to the proverb *Hare is melancholy meat* 1558 (Tilley H151). Hal's ability to meet proverb with proverb leads Falstaff to compliment him for his "most unsauory similes," and for being "the most comparative rascalliest sweet young Prince" (I. ii. 70–71).'

9   P. D. Miller explains that the original Hebrew phrase is 'copy of the law' (1990: 2). Deuteronomy is where one can find the Ten Commandments.

10 Bauckham's selection is, understandably, somewhat limited.

2 Epistemic ecology and 'diminishing boundaries of a shrinking world' in 'Heraclitus' Golden River' from *Wild*

1   Heraclitus (*c.*535–475 BC) lived during the so-called Archaic Period usually from *c.*700 to 494 BC. He was not a philosopher but a sage and cosmologist.

2   As Nicoletta Ghigi argues, pointing to the anguish and disease that characterize our generation and the need to re-humanize, to re-appropriate one's own life and one's own telos: 'To constitute a metaphysics as a science that makes this telos its own object or to think of a philosophical reflection that is completely turned toward life and its meaning offers us the possibility of rethinking the human and to rethink her existence as a true return to authentic existence … as the being to which we are and

in which we participate insofar as we are single personalities endowed with our own interiority and, above all, our own telos that gives form to life' (2014: 9).
3 See Gray (2009).
4 Graham (2014).
5 'Heraclitus' (2015).
    Compare: 'No man even steps in the same river twice, for it's not the same river and he's not the same man' (Aquileana 2015: 3).
6 Heidegger calls this 'Dasein'.
7 Compare Wole Soyinka's drama, *The Road*: 'Samson: May we never walk when the road waits, famished' (60). The allusion is to the myth of Ogun, the Yoruba god of the road, who feeds off the remains of road accidents, causing such accidents when he is hungry. And the insights into the inevitability of death encapsulated in:

> 'Prof.: But there is this other joke of the fisherman, slapping a loaded net against the sandbank. [Looks around him.] When the road is dry it runs into the river. But the river? When the river is parched what choice is this? Still it is a pleasant trickle–reddening somewhat–between barren thighs of an ever patient rock. The rock is a woman you understand, so is the road. They know how to lie and wait.' (1965: 58)

8 In this play, the Professor is a well-to-do forger of driver's licences and so an accessory to road accidents. His quest is for the meaning of 'the word', 'which may be found companion not to life but Death' (11), a veiled indictment of the church as 'the final gate to the Word' (93) and of the elusiveness of complete knowing.
    Homer's invocation to the muse was already ancient in the eighth century BC.
9 See Baym (1965: 713–32). She argues that what Frost uncovers in his investigation of Nature is a sombre truth, the law of 'change and decay'.
10 Phokaia, Chios, Erythrai, Klazomenai, Teos, Lebedos, Kolophon, Ephesos, Samos, Priene, Myous, and Miletos (Hdt. 1.142).
11 Robert Frost's (1874–1963) iconic Nature poetry appears to correlate with that of Okri. His message in 'Mending Wall' (1914) – that something is amiss in a world of walls – is endorsed in Okri's 'Heraclitus' Golden River'.
12 Quoted in Peter Straus (2012: 20). The reference to stone smiths is probably to the late Anglo-Saxon building with stone rather than wood – a legacy from the Roman occupation of Briton/Britain.
13 Wood (2016).
14 In Virgil's *Eclogues*, Tityras is beneath a beech tree that comes to symbolize the wisdom of rural restraint and peace as in much seventeenth-century poetry and discussed later in terms of *sophrosyne*.
15 This legacy can be seen in the Christian marriage rites.
16 Kamwangamalu (1999: 25–6) argues that 'Ubuntu' is integral to pan-African philosophy, and he shows that it has multiple phonological variants, e.g., 'umundu' in Kikuyu (Kenya), 'bumuntu' in KiSuma and KiHaya (Tanzania) and 'gimuntu' in KiKongo and giKwezi (DRC). Ramose (2001: 3) however, while acknowledging that 'Ubuntu' is a fundamental ontological and epistemological category of thought, delimits its significance to the Bantu-speakers of South Africa. The relevance of the term to the present discussion is that, morphologically, the prefix ubu- indicates a general state of being, whereas -ntu means 'a person'. The composite word thus signifies two aspects of being, encapsulating both self and other, that is, an indivisible interrelatedness.

17 Compare Okri's self-reflexive comment (Essakow 2016: 3) on *The Famished Road* trilogy:

> Dancers' limbs twist and thread / In this highly atmospheric / Conclusion to an elemental / Trilogy that veers between the / Airy and the grounded.

3 Ontopoiesis in Okri's poetic oeuvre and *A Time for New Dreams*

1 See Gray (2012c).
2 The poem is dedicated to R.C. – Okri's companion, Rosemary Clunie.
3 See Aristotle's *Metaphysics* (A,2,982). In Tymieniecka's words: 'Aristotle emphasizes that philosophy does not aim at realizing anything. It proceeds not from a desire to solve any life difficulties or arguments but from marvelling about the simplest of things, whose reasons escape us at first' (2004).
4 See Gray (2012b).
5 A.-T. Tymieniecka explains in 'Logos and Life' (2000: 1): 'Thus "logos" hitherto hidden in our commerce with earth is revealed in its intertwinings with the cosmos through the trajectories of the phenomenological ontopoiesis of life. The crucial link between the soul and the cosmos, in the new geo-cosmic horizon, is thus being retrieved.' http://www.springer.com/philosophy/philosophical+traditions/book/978-94-007-1690-2 (accessed 6 November 2011).

4 Recovering our true state of being in 'The Comic Destiny'

1 An allusion to both Okri's *Starbook* (2007) and Maya Angelou's *I Know Why the Caged Bird Sings* (1993). See also Koyana and Gray (2002).
2 Okri acknowledges that he was profoundly affected by first-hand experiences of the Nigerian Civil War and its wanton slaughter of innocent bystanders. He explains to Caroline Jowett: 'These people who were killed left a huge impression on me. In a way that's the core of almost everything I do and think about; the mysteries of life, justice' (Jowett 1995: 28). These are key themes in 'The Comic Destiny'.
3 As the Ionian philosopher, Ion Soteropoulos (pers. com.), and the Nigerian symbolist, Ben Okri, believe with Chadwick that symbolism can be defined as 'the art of expressing ideas and emotions not by describing them directly, nor by defining them through overt comparisons with concrete images, but by suggesting what these ideas and emotions are, by re-creating them in the mind of the reader through the use of unexplained symbols' ([1971] 1973: 2–3).
4 It denotes 'dike' – in Greek literature, literally 'the way or path', as in the way the various classes customarily behaved. Compare the modern phrase 'as one would expect', rather than the right way. 'Virtue' from the Greek 'arête' was vocational, and as Guthrie affirms, '"arête" then meant first of all skill or efficiency at a particular job, and ... such efficiency depends on a proper understanding or knowledge of the job in hand' ([1950] 1978: 9).

5 There is an escaped murderer and a young argumentative couple who have forgotten how to love and who end up in leg irons, whereas the mad murderer ultimately runs towards his recapture – so the siren signifies literal policing but also alludes, figuratively, to the cacophony of the living dead (read exhausted) and the leitmotif of slavery.
6 Jay Panini's (2009) observation is that Pinprop 'combines elements of Lucky and Pozzo from *Waiting for Godot*', but although suggesting that the setting could be Africa, he damns 'The Comic Destiny': 'But this is Beckett on hallucinogens'. In contrast to my reading, Nisha Obano (n.d.) states categorically that ' "The Comic Destiny" employs a series of absurd dialogues and dramatic situations that are reminiscent of Beckett's *Waiting for Godot*'.
7 Aesop was a legendary Greek slave and composer of moralistic animal fables of the sixth century BC. The most well known of these in English literature was the Cock and the Fox in Chaucer's 'The Nun's Priest's Tale'.
8 This is encapsulated in Okri's neologism, 'eviling', where 'evil' is a palindrome for 'live'. The slave, Pinprop, who delights in obfuscation rather than revelation, suggests this interpretation by asserting: 'The final destination of the goose is when it can become an egg; and with the trap it is when it ends up as a mouse' (2009: 6–7). The wordplay points to the need for a careful rereading of both legendary examples and, coincidentally, of Okri's fable and *Starbook*.

5 Apologia pro *In Arcadia*: A neglected masterpiece?

1 All references in this chapter are to the 2003 Phoenix edition.
2 See Rosemary Gray (2007a and b).
3 In *Beyond Death*, Charles Casey explains of Edgar Casey's belief: '[E]very action and thought of every individual makes an impression upon the Universal Consciousness, an impression that can be psychically read. He correlated this with the Hindu concept of an Akashic Record, which is an ethereal, fourth-dimensional film upon which actions and thoughts are recorded and can be read at any time' (2007: x).
4 Harrison's progression is a typical Western developmental linear construct. He terms the third stage 'breakout', whereas I have chosen 'emergence', which, in line with Okri's Urhobo mythology, would be followed by a re-emergence. The pattern is cyclical: philosophically, the argument supports the notion of reincarnation and assumes that one learns so little in the flesh form however many times the soul is reborn.
5 Treglown cites, as example, 'the invidious irritability that specialists in psychosomatic creativity identify as preceding unusual irradiations of perceptivity' (2002: 68).
6 Of the former, Okri writes: 'Procous being the name of this imaginary semi-deity of disasters, mischief, local catastrophes, lost things, improbable thefts, and unlikely rumours'; and of the latter, 'this malign Prospero figure who would have such dreadful power over our lives' (2003: 25).
7 The inscription on the lid of the virginal, MUSICA LETITIAE CO[ME]S MEDICINA DOLORIS[IS], means 'Music is a companion in pleasure and a balm in sorrow' (Gowing n.d.: 2).
8 At the still point of the turning world. Neither flesh nor fleshless; / Neither from nor towards; at the still point, there the dance is, / But neither arrest nor movement.

And do not call it fixity, / Where past and future are gathered. Neither movement from nor towards, / Neither ascent nor decline. Except for the point, the still point, / There would be no dance, and there is only the dance, / I cannot say, how long, for that is to place it in time. / The inner freedom from the practical desire, / The release from action and suffering, release from the inner / And the outer compulsion, yet surrounded / By a grace of sense, a white light still and moving.

9 Andrew Gough's 'Arcadia'.
10 Hoodwin (n.d.).
11 Soyinka (1973).

6 'Domesticating infinity' in *Mental Fight* and *Astonishing the Gods*

1 Al-Hujwiri defines perennial as 'enduring for an indefinite or infinite time; lasting, permanent, never failing, continual, perpetual, everlasting, eternal'. A Perennialist refers 'to teachings, activities, and teachers having to do with the Perennial Tradition' (1055 CE; 15).

2 These are spirit children who frequently cross from this world into the chthonic realm. In *The Famished Road*, Okri explains:

> There are many reasons why babies cry when they are born, and one of them is the sudden separation from the world of pure dreams, and where there is no suffering.
>
> The happier we were, the closer was our birth. As we approached another incarnation we made packs that we would return to the spirit world at the first opportunity. We made these vows in fields of intense flowers and in the sweet-tasting moonlight of that world. Those of us who made such vows were known among the living as 'abiki', spirit-children. (1991: 4)

3 Cf. William Blake's poem 'Jerusalem the Golden': 'I will not cease from Mental Fight / Nor will my sword sleep in my hand / Till we have built Jerusalem / On England's green and pleasant land.'

4 The extract is also resonant with Nietzsche's myth of eternal recurrence. Cf. T. S. Eliot's *Four Quartets* (1978), 'Burnt Norton' (1935), for a coincidental echo:

> Time present and time past
> Are both perhaps present in time future
> And time future contained in time past,
> If all time is eternally present
> All time is unredeemable.
> What might have been is an abstraction
> Remaining a perpetual possibility
> Only in a world of speculation.
> What might have been and what has been
> Point to one end, which is always present.

5 Cf. $v = s/t$ [velocity equals space divided by time]. In other words, the theory is that 'space and time were but abstractions and shadows, and the reality behind them was space-time' and that 'motion or velocity depends on the time taken to cover the

distance travelled' (Smuts 1932: 4–5). Einstein's theory of relativity thus extended Newton's discovery of the mutuality rather than the separateness of time and space.

6   A querent is both one who asks questions and one whose questions relate to astrology.
7   Deleuze's (2001) rhizome theory was renamed 'ecosophy' (Leitch 2001: 1596) by fellow critic Guattari. Thomas Berry's (1996: 1–9) Harvard address on environmental ethics is pertinent to the argument.
8   Here, the dichotomy is also that between the world of concrete fact and the world of abstract symbolism in which both mathematician and creative artists like Okri live. Cf. Robert Louis Stevenson's (c.1881) 'Pulvis et umbra' (literally 'dust' in which the early mathematicians drew their diagrams and 'shade' (metonymic for pleasant rest)):

> Of the Kosmos in the last resort, Science reports many doubtful things. And all of them appalling. There seems to be no substance on which we stamp; nothing but symbols and ratios ... that way madness lies; Science carries us into zones of speculation where there is no habitable city for the mind of man.
>   But take the kosmos with a grosser faith, as our senses give it to us. We behold space sown with rotatory islands, suns and worlds and the shards and wrecks of systems; some, like the Sun, still blazing; some rotating like the Earth; others, like the Moon, stable in desolation. All these we take to be made of something we call Matter, a thing which no analysis can help us to conceive, to whose incredible properties no familiarity can reconcile our minds. (Raikes 1932: 17)

Italo Calvino also explores this notion in his novel *Invisible Cities* (1969).

9   Ben Okri was born in 1959 in Minna, northern Nigeria, to an Igbo mother and Urhobo father. Jules Smith's (2002) critique corroborates the claim of this chapter when he notes that 'an animating conception within Okri's writing is that "the world is full of riddles that only the dead can answer" ... His fiction also harks back several decades to the immediate pre-independence era ... [to] a traditional society with its herbalists and native medicine, animal sacrifices and magic'.
10 This is not unlike the physicists' theory of everything.
11 At the 'Mad [Hatter's] Tea-Party' (Carroll [1865] n.d.: 76–7), Alice remarks on the Hatter's 'funny watch' that 'tells the day of the month' but not 'what o'clock it is'. He retorts that hers does not tell 'what year it is'. Ultimately, although Lewis Carroll was a scholar of mathematics at Oxford, the question of time is left as an unsolved 'riddle', probably because time was not as fully understood scientifically as it is today but was clearly a preoccupation among mathematicians. Coincidentally, this discussion reflects what was later to be formulated as the relativity of time. Stephen Hawking ([1988] 1997: 12–13) provides a succinct explanation of relativity and its relation to quantum mechanics: 'The general theory of relativity describes the force of gravity and the large-scale structure of the universe, that is, the structure on scales from only a few miles to as large as a million million million million (1 with twenty-four zeros after it) miles, the size of the observable universe. Quantum mechanics, on the other hand, deals with phenomena on extremely small scales, such as a millionth of a millionth of an inch.'
12 In *Ways of Seeing*, John Berger explains this ever-present gap between perception and knowledge more simply:

> It is seeing which establishes our place in the surrounding world; we explain that world with words, but words can never undo the fact that we are

surrounded by it. The relation between what we see and what we know is never settled. Each evening we *see* the sun set. We *know* that the earth is turning away from it. Yet the knowledge, the explanation, never quite fits the sight. (1972; original emphases)

Perception is essentially personalized: 'The way we see things is affected by what we know and what we believe' (1972: 7–8).

13 I am indebted to Smuts, who explains:

The attempt to fix the position of an atom has altered its velocity and momentum. The measure affects the body to be measured and *vice versa*, and a certain unavoidable uncertainty arises in the determination ... This uncertainty involves that it is impossible to determine both the exact position and the velocity of a particle at any particular moment. The more accurately we locate a particle *here*, the more its velocity is altered, and it becomes uncertain whether it is here *now*, and not rather in the immediate past or the immediate future. (1932: 6; original emphases)

14 Fortuitously, in a chapter entitled 'Cybernetics and Ghosts', Italo Calvino helps us to understand, in terms of our mental processes, the significance of the graphic chessboard patterning of Okri's galactic city, of Quantum mechanics and of entropic time:

In the place of the ever-changing cloud that we carried in our heads until the other day, the condensing and dispersal of which we attempted to understand by describing impalpable psychological states and shadowy landscapes of the soul – in the place of all this we now feel the rapid passage of signals on the intricate circuits that connect the relays, the diodes, the transistors with which our skulls are crammed. Just as no chess player will ever live long enough to exhaust all the combinations of possible moves for the thirty-two pieces on the chessboard, so we know (given the fact that our minds are chessboards with hundreds of billions of pieces) that not even in a lifetime lasting as long as the universe would one ever manage to make all possible plays ...

[E]very analytical process, every division into parts, tends to provide an image of the world that is ever more complicated, just as Zeno of Elea, by refusing to accept space as continuous, ended up by separating Achilles from the tortoise by an infinite number of intermediate points.

The process going on today is the triumph of discontinuity, divisibility, and combination over all that is flux, or a series of minute nuances flowing one upon the other. ([1980] 1997: 8–9)

15 Cf. T. S. Eliot's 'Ash Wednesday' (1930) with its 'jewelled unicorns' who 'draw by the gilded hearse'.
16 This is reminiscent of Arthurian legend, although the sword of the Lady of the Lake is not associated with justice 'per se'. It does, nonetheless, mark the era of King Arthur, who – as king – metes out justice.
17 The lesson echoes that of Kahlil Gibran's prophet:

Of time you would make a stream upon whose bank
You would sit and watch its flowing.
Yet the timeless in you is aware of life's timelessness,
And knows that yesterday is but tomorrow's memory

And tomorrow is today's dream.
And that that which sings and contemplates in you
Is still dwelling within the bounds of that first
Moment which scattered the stars into space.

(2004: 83)

18 The quest for divine grace in Okri's text transliterates those of the central figures of the Anglo-Saxon elegiac poems *The Wanderer* and *The Seafarer*. This quest is in line with the Perennial Tradition. This can be compared with Csilla Bertha's (1999: 119–35) reading of Brian Friel's *Wonderful Tennessee* for this insight.

7 Redreaming ways of seeing: Intuitive creativity in *The Landscapes Within*

1 In *Phenomenology of Space and Time*, Tymieniecka explains:

It is only by isolating from the self-ordering of beingness, cosmic and living, the nature of beingness as such – its ontopoietic-ontic status – that is, by rooting ontopoietic ordering within its originary condition, thus entering into 'linea entis', that we may bring out the central conduit of existential becoming, the conduit of the 'logos' of life that proceeds from the unfathomable part and leads towards an open-ended future and which situates and explains the essential status of concrete existence in the space of the present. This conduit of becoming I appropriately call the ontopoiesis of life (1992: 13).

2 Tolle states: 'Zen masters use the word *satori* to describe a flash of insight, a moment of no-mind and total presence ... Presence is needed to become aware of the beauty, the majesty, the sacredness of [N]ature' (2005: 79).

3 Ted Hughes's poem reads:

I imagine this midnight moment's forest: / Something else is alive / Beside the clock's loneliness / And this blank page where my fingers move. // Through the window I see no star: / Something more near / Though deeper within darkness / Is entering the loneliness: // Cold, delicately as the dark snow / A fox's nose touches twig, leaf; / Two eyes serve a movement, that now / And again now, and now, and now // Sets neat prints into the snow / Between trees, and warily a lame / Shadow lags by stump and in hollow / Of a body that is bold to come // Across clearings, an eye, / A widening deepening greenness, / Brilliantly, concentratedly, / Coming about its own business // Till, with a sudden sharp hot stink of fox / It enters the dark hole of the head. / The window is starless still; the clock ticks, / The page is printed.

4 Elsewhere, Okri calls this 'an Akashic Still Point'. See Gray (2007: 41–52).
5 Omovo's painting and, by extension, his dreams, we are told 'was part of his personal prism' (Okri 1981: 85). Significantly, the phrase is altered in the 're-writing and expansion' (Jowitt 1996: 62–3) to 'a personal and public prism' (Okri 1996: 69).
6 'Polyphony in music is the simultaneous presentation of two or more voices (melodic lines that are perfectly bound together but still keep their relative independence)' (Kundera [1986] 1988: 73–4).

7 In addition to multiple losses of life (the girl; Omovo's mother; Ife's brother drowns; she is shot, Keme's sister goes missing; Omovo's stepmother loses an unborn child; his dad kills Tuwo for cuckolding him), Okri includes loss of fathers (Ayo's and Omovo's imprisoned father loses himself, becoming 'a shrivelled presence' (Okri 1981: 282)), of jobs, fortunes, dignity, sanity, innocence, art works and of country (Dele escapes to America, to freedom, but, ironically, he runs, because he has impregnated his Nigerian girlfriend, and, paradoxically, because he cannot wait to experience sex with a white woman!).
8 A theme in the novel, which becomes more apparent in its rewriting as *Dangerous Love* is the artist's 'responsibilities' (Okri 1981: 278).
9 Cf. Smith (2000: 4).

8 Promoting the poetic cause in 'stokus' from *Tales of Freedom*

1 Viewed 2 June 2015, from http://www.scotsman.com.
2 Viewed 2 June 2015, from http://www.encyclopediaofafroeuropeanstudies.
3 The Japanese *haiku* poet, Basho, explains:

> In the waka of Saigyo, the renga of Sogi, the paintings of Sesshu, and the tea ceremony of Rikyu, the fundamental principle is the same. Those who pursue art follow the 'zōka' and have the four seasons as their companion. Nothing they see is not a flower and nothing they imagine is not a moon … follow 'zōka' and return to 'zōka (Ross 2012: Preface).

It is interesting to note that, serendipitously, the seventeenth-century Japanese *haiku* poet, Basho, who like Okri celebrated 'both the joys and sufferings of life's brief journey' (Lowenstein 2006: 58), had devised his own style of poetic prose composition, to which he gave the name 'haibun'. However, whereas Basho alternated sections of prose and poetry in capturing his many journeys on foot, Okri synthesizes the two modes, as well as placing greater emphasis on the brevity of the telling. But, as with Okri, in his brief poetic prose writings or 'stokus', Basho too considered the nature of his own humanity, while questioning 'the nature of the "windswept spirit" that inhabit[ed] his body' (ibid.), as evoked in the two Basho *haiku* quoted later.

4 This is possibly a reflection on the Nigerian Civil War in Biafra to which Okri was not only exposed as a child but in which he also nearly got killed hiding his Igbo mother in the internecine strife between the Yoruba and Igbo, a conflict in which the Urhobo minority group to which his father belonged became implicated, dwelling as they did in the delta region which lay between the warring factions (Rix 2010).

Cf. 'Laughter beneath the Bridge' (1986) and 'In the Shadows of War' (1988) in *Stars of the New Curfew* (1988) where 'the narrative gaze contemplates the grotesque spectacle of a corpse-littered landscape' (Obano n.d.: 23) as well as *The Landscapes Within* (1981).

5 Cf. Gray (2013: 21–30).
6 Cf. Gray (2007: 85–101).
7 Lewis Carroll's conflation of 'lithe' and 'slimy'. Cf. Lewis's neologism, 'jabberwocky'.
8 Imraam Coovadia (2012: 74) explains this:

In 1947, ... the *Bulletin of the Atomic Scientists*, a public-interest magazine founded by veterans of the Manhattan Project who built the atomic weapons for the Unites States, created the Doomsday Clock and set it at seven minutes to midnight. It was an ingenious attempt to raise public understanding of the possibility of the world ending in an exchange of atomic bombs. The clock still exists, going backwards and forwards depending on the Bulletin editors' assessment of global threats from nuclear warfare to pandemic disease and global warming.

9 Okri urges us to live in the moment, which he expresses succinctly and with urgency in his Blakean *Mental Fight* as an injunction to live with

> A quality of enlightenment / A sense of the limited time we have / Here on earth to live magnificently / To explore our potential to the fullest / And to lose our fear of death / Having gained a greater love / And reverence for life / And its incommensurable golden brevity.

10 Nisha Obano (n.d.: 2) likens Okri's mode to that of Christopher Okigbo, who 'rejected reductive models of African cultural nationalism in favour of a complex transformation of Modernist poetry that could explore indigenous poetic and rhetorical conventions'.

9 Sowing 'a quilt of harmony': Eco-phenomenology in 'Lines *in Potentis*'

1 Aristotle (1941: 251).
2 The poem was commissioned by Ivor Guest, the 4th Viscount Wimborne, a friend of Ben Okri, for his marriage to Latvian beauty Ieva Imsa. Their daughter, Greta, was born in 2011.
3 'Lines ...' was commissioned by the then Lord Mayor of London, Ken Livingstone. It was read by the poet at the memorial of the bombing of London (Rosemary Clunie, pers. com.).
4 Rev. 21.1.
5 Douglas Bush explains Keats's doctrine of negative capability or intuitive empathy in the poet's own words: 'The setting sun always sets me to rights – or if a Sparrow come before my Window I take part in its existence and pick about the Gravel' (1967: 58).
6 Phil. 4.8: 'whatsoever things are true, ... whatsoever things *are* pure, whatsoever things *are* lovely ... Think on these things' (original emphases).
7 The hymn 'Jerusalem' by Parry and Blake obviously informs Okri's vision; his second anthology of poetry is entitled *Mental Fight*. Blake's well-known verse reads: 'I shall not cease from mental fight / Nor shall my sword sleep in my hand / Till we have built Jerusalem / On England's green and pleasant land.' Blake's epic poem, 'Jerusalem', seems, in turn, to have been inspired by *Apocrypha 21*: 'I saw the holy city, the new Jerusalem, coming down from God, prepared as a bride adorned for her husband.' For Blake, Jerusalem (the True Church) was the Bride and Emanation of Albion (the Eternal Man) and of Jesus in Eternity.
8 See Mafeje (2000).

10 'A clear lucid stream of everywhereness' in *Wild*: A postmodern perspective

1. Anna-Teresa Tymieniecka's doctrine of ontopoiesis is, essentially, conscious heightened awareness. It is the path of consecrated action enabling the management of one's life through spirituality and making it possible to make responsible human choices and to find one's way within the axiological complexity of contemporary existence.
2. Heraclitus was born in Ephesus, Ionia, Greece, in 534 BC and died in 474 BC. 'A Greek philosopher of Ephesus (near modern Kuşadası, Turkey) who was active around 500 BCE, Heraclitus propounded a distinctive theory which he expressed in oracular language. He is best known for his doctrines that things are constantly changing (universal flux), that opposites coincide (unity of opposites), and that fire is the basic material of the world. The exact interpretation of these doctrines is controversial, as is the inference often drawn from this theory that in the world as Heraclitus conceives it contradictory propositions must be true.' Available online: http://www.plato.stanford.edu/entries/heraclitus/ (accessed 7 July 2013).
3. Douglas Bush explains Keats's doctrine of negative capability or intuitive empathy in the poet's own words: 'The setting sun always sets me to rights – or if a Sparrow come before my Window I take part in its existence and pick about the Gravel' (1967: 58).
4. Twentieth-century philosophers, such as Bertrand Russell, Ludwig Wittgenstein and Martin Heidegger, following Ferdinand de Sausseur (1857–1913), endorsed this semiological focus on the structure of language as in the formal school of Structuralism, making a distinction between 'La Langue' (language – the synchronic system) and 'La Parole' (the word and its usage – diachronic).

11 Survivalist culture in 'Laughter beneath the Bridge'

1. What would be the point of living if you thought that life was absurd, that it could never have meaning? This is the question that Camus asks in *The Myth of Sisyphus*. He says: 'There is only one really serious philosophical problem, and that is suicide.' Camus and Absurdity | Philosophy Talk. Available online: https://www.philosophytalk.org/blog/camus-and-absurdity/ (accessed 18 March 2018).
2. Cf. Gray (2017: 35–50).
3. See also Achebe (1999).
4. Quote from *The Europa Year Book 1968*, Vol. II, Africa, The Americas, Asia, Australia, p. 1005. London: Europa. Although not a leading figure in the Council of War, Colonel Philip Effiong was the first Vice President of Biafra.
5. Julia Kristeva elaborates: 'The corpse (or cadaver: "cadere," to fall), that which has irremediably come a cropper, is cesspool and death; it upsets even more violently the one who confronts it as fragile and fallacious chance. A wound with blood and puss, or a sickly, acrid smell of sweat, of decay, does not signify death. In the presence of signified death – a flat encephalograph, for instance – I would understand, react or accept' (1982: 3).
6. See Ehling (1993) and Odun Balogun (1993: 133–4).
7. Anca Parvulescu explores the highly complex and ambivalent historical relation to laughter in 'Laughter and Literature' (2017: 2), tracing the rhetorical invocations of the tradition to show that 'literature is a site where various anxieties about laughter

become legible. Literature offers us chronotopes [*sic*] of laughter in need of extended description'.

12 The poetic muse of archaeology

1 In a chapter section entitled, 'Cognitive Archaeology' in *Ariadne's Clue*, Anthony Stevens provides a synopsis of humankind's development: 'Act 1 begins in Africa'; in broad summary – 4.5 million years ago, *Australopithecus ramidus*; 300,000 years later, *Australopithecus amanuensis*; 3.5 million years ago, 'Lucy' (*Australopithecus afarensis*); 2.5 million years ago, *Australopithecus africanus*; 2 million years ago, *Homo habilis* (handy man, capable of using stone tools and catching animals); 1.8 million years ago, *Homo erectus*, maker of stone hand-axes; 150,000 years ago, Neanderthal man; 100,000 years ago, *Homo sapiens* buries his dead and adds animal carcasses to graves; 60,000 years ago, *Homo sapiens sapiens* builds boats and travels from South East Asia to Australia; 35,000 years ago, Neanderthal man disappears and *Homo sapiens sapiens* remains, plants crops and domesticates animals (1998: 163–4).
2 Writing in November 2012, shortly after the publication of *Wild* and with this informing credo in mind, Okri inscribed my copy of the anthology with a cherished correlative: 'To the family of cosmic connections, to the spirit of poetry, wildness, joy and the smile in the face of life's mysteries and fire.'
3 See Gray (2020: 12 pp.).
4 See Gray (2018: 1–12).
5 See Gray (2019: 95–110).

13 Sublime transformative paremiology in *A Way of Being Free*

1 Cf. Gray (2018b: 74–91).
2 T. E. Dorsch ([1965] 1974: 24) explains: 'Of the author of the famous treatise *On the Sublime* nothing is known, not even his name. The nature and treatment of the subject-matter of the work suggest that it was written in the first century AD.'
3 Gray (2018a: 17–24) and Chapter 1.
4 In his exploration of *Tintern Abbey*, Durrant (1969: 19) argues pertinently that Wordsworth too seems to have felt that 'even the motion of an Angel's wing / Would interrupt the intense tranquillity / Of silent hills and more than silent sky' (Wordsworth 'A Volant Tribe of Bards on Earth Are Found', 1823: ll. 12–14).
5 'Bird talk in a Tentative World' from *The Magic Lamp* (2017: 11–14), a word/image text with Rosemary Clunie.

14 'The Standeruppers': The frightening irony of the Anthropocene

1 Speciation is the word given to Darwin's concept of natural selection in his much misunderstood and oft-misquoted *The Origin of Species*. Wilson explains speciation

as 'the process of species formation: the full sequence of events leading to the splitting of one population of organisms into two or more populations reproductively isolated from one another' ([1992] 1993: 405). 'The origin of species is therefore simply the evolution of some difference – any difference at all – that prevents the production of fertile hybrids between populations under natural conditions' (ibid.: 55).
2 See Chapter 18, 'An Interval in the Enchantment of Living: *The Age of Magic*'.
3 The note is on Yeats's poem entitled 'Chosen' and its allusion to the 'learned astrologer' (1955: 311).
4 See Gray (2018): 1–12.

15 Conscious reveries in *The Magic Lamp: Dreams of Our Age*

1 Those who know or are in the know, know that Okri's many publications, public lectures, interviews, special issues of international journals dedicated to the Okrian oeuvre and dramatic readings around the globe in the past decade that show no sign of abating testify to a contrary view to that of reviewers such as Flynn. For Okri's prolific output, we need critique not fantasy.
2 Cf. Guthrie ([1967] 1978: 5–10).
3 Cf. Gray (2016: 18–27).
4 Cf. Gray (2018: 1–12).
5 Spence elaborates: 'The ability of the bird to make passage for itself across the great ocean of air, the incomprehensibility of its gift of flight, the mystery of its song, its connexion with "heaven," render it a being at once strange and enviable. Such freedom, argues primitive man, must have the liberated soul, untrammelled by the hindering flesh' (1922: 31–2).

16 'The Incandescence of the Wind' (1982): 'Rain wisdom down upon the earth'

1 The Nigerian Civil War (1967–70) that saw the erasure of Biafra set the trend for internecine strife that dogged West Africa and especially Nigeria for decades to come. See Part Three, Chapter 11, on 'Laughter beneath the Bridge'.
2 Chinua Achebe cites this date as the effective death of Ken Saro-Wiwa, owing to his long and brutal incarceration without trial.
3 See Fraser (2002).
4 A comparable effect of the incandescence of the wind is seen in a passage where the 'Abiku' child protagonist, Azaro, trying to find shelter from the wind, finds himself under the eaves of the blind old man's house: 'The wind rose again and hurled a fine spray of rain at us. After a while, I felt myself moving. Something in me moved, I resisted. But the wind was stronger. The blind old man laughed as I struggled. I discovered that the wind had divided me, had separated me from myself. I felt an inner self floating towards the blind old man. Or was it that the blind old man was floating into me, invading my consciousness? I wasn't sure' (Okri [1991] 1992: 313).

5 'It is when we begin to protest that we begin to rise to our human potential to shake the foundations of the world, so that justice may prevail. Poetry is most human when it allies itself with justice' (Okri 2018b: 79).

17 Protean magic in *The Mystery Feast* and *The Magic Lamp*

1. Lewis Spence (1999: 11) observes that the writers of antiquity acknowledged the 'native superiority' of the Celtic mind in the science of magic, citing the Wisdom Corpus of Pliny, Siculus, Timagenes, Hippolytus and Clement of Alexander as revealing the belief that Pythagoras was schooled in his mystical philosophy by the Celtic priests in Gaul. Okri states that the bards of old 'could breathe life into a dying civilization with the magic of a story … they could bring transformation with the potency of a myth' (2015: 24).
2. Fraser notes that in Homeric times, Greek heads of state 'were spoken of as sacred or divine'; this included their dwelling places and their 'chariots'. It was believed that good kings could influence the fructification of grain crops and fruit trees and even the seas' catch, a notion widely perpetuated in both political and religious circles throughout the ages ([1922] 1991: 89).
3. Speciation is the word given to Darwin's concept of natural selection in his much misunderstood and oft-misquoted *The Origin of Species*. Wilson explains speciation as 'the process of species formation: the full sequence of events leading to the splitting of one population of organisms into two or more populations reproductively isolated from one another' ([1992] 1993: 405). 'The origin of species is therefore simply the evolution of some difference – any difference at all – that prevents the production of fertile hybrids between populations under natural conditions' (ibid.: 55).
4. See *Wild* (2012: 56), 'Towards the Sublime': 'Have you ever noticed that in all true / Transformations what emerges / Is stranger than before, / And higher, richer, magical? // It is as if mass yields / Light, or pure power, pure / Vision given upward / Form beyond form – / Transcending all the laws / Of its previous condition. // And so chrysalis into butterfly, / Water into wine, death / Into life, weight into / Flight, burden into freedom / Divine.'
5. Appropriated from German art critic Franz Roh's notion of what constitutes the artistic movement of post-expressionism, magical realism is given as a descriptive synonym for the diachronic 'post' and is defined as offering us 'the miracle of *existence in its imperturbable duration*: the unending miracle of eternally mobile and vibrating modules' (1925, in Zamora and Faris [1995] 2005: 22; original emphasis). As Roh explains of what we now know as quantum physics: 'This miracle of an apparent persistence and duration in the midst of general becoming, of universal dissolution: this is what Post-Expressionism admires and highlights' (ibid.).
6. See Chapter 15.
7. E.g., in 'The Wreck of the *Deutschland*', Hopkins (1996) captures the inner essence of 'caritas' as: 'Our hearts charity's hearth's fire, our thoughts chivalry's throng's Lord.'
8. 'Virtue' from the Greek 'arête' was vocational, and as Guthrie affirms: ' "Arête" then meant first of all skill or efficiency at a particular job, and … such efficiency depends on a proper understanding or knowledge of the job in hand' ([1950] 1978: 9).

9 Eliade provides two exempla: the Egyptian god Thoth, who created the world 'by force of his word'; and Iranian tradition in which Ormazd instituted the commemoration of cosmic creation – sky, the waters, the earth, plants, animals and man – after which he rested for five days (1955: 22).
10 See note 6.
11 Cf. Wells ([1897] 2011), Calvino ([1972] 1997) and Okri ([1995] 2002).
12 Loss is a characteristic theme in Okri's oeuvre. See Gray (2013).
13 The literary intertexts are Virgil's *Aeneid* (1990) and Dante's *Divine Comedy* ([1939] 1975).
14 See Gray (2019).

18 'An Interval in the Enchantment of Living': *The Age of Magic*

1 Douglas Hofstadter (2007), who cautions against too narrow a view or the limiting of the study of the brain to physical entities like amino acids, DNA and RNA, synapses and neurons, suggests expanding the discussion of abstractions to additional aspects such as 'the associative link between "dog" and "bark" or "long-term memory and short-term memory"' (ibid.).
2 Thomas Mann ([1924] 1980). The novel won the Nobel Prize for literature in 1929.
3 Cf. Gray (2009a: 41–52).
4 Manuel João Ramos (2000: 147–8) explains that the word 'ekphrasis' was originally used by Greek classical rhetoricians to qualify a description with great visual content. Its use in the European history of art relates to the 'ekphrasein' of ancient Greek paintings of sculptures that have since disappeared (Krieger 1992; Heffernan 1993; Hochmann 1994). A more recent meaning of 'ekphrasis' reflects both a stress on the intricate relation between the visual arts and literature, and on the possibility of using the imagistic capacity of literature as a methodological lever to analyse art. A derivative use of the expression can be found in the study of the complementarities between travel literature and travel iconography (ibid.).
5 Akashic is a Sanskrit word for 'sky', 'space', 'aether'; and in a gradation of elemental essences in the vegetable and animal kingdom, Johnson points out that 'in man, and man alone, all the five essences [aether, earth, water, fire and air] are present and active' ([1962] 1965: 128). In *Science and the Akashic Field: An Integral Theory of Everything*, Ervin László states: 'The Akashic records are to be understood to be a collection of mystical knowledge that is encoded in the aether, i.e. on a non-physical plane of existence' (2004: 9). Shepherd Hoodwin (n.d.: 1) explains that 'the core of the akashic records is the akashic plane, the neutral plane' and it is 'the overall record of the universe'.
6 See note 3.
7 Cf. Gray (2007: 85–101; 2009b: 23–35).
8 Lao is clearly a reincarnation of the Chinese philosopher and founder of Taoism, Lao Tsû.
9 One thinks of the seven colours of the rainbow replicated in the seven colours of the chakras.
10 Eight is the Chinese symbol for infinitude or the eternal. Cf. Max Escher's famous ant painting of the Mobius strip, captured in Soyinka's 'Modius': 'multiform / Evolution

of the self-devouring snake to spatials. / New in symbol, banked loop of the "Modius Strip" / And interlock of re-creative rings, one surface / Yet full comb of angles, uniplane, yet sensuous / Complexities of mind and motion' (1973: 8).
11 'The Age of Magic Review: Giving Substance to the Abstract' (2014: 2). The reviewer concedes that 'like the best fairy tales it has lines of smoothly lyrical beauty' (ibid.).
12 See Corbin (1971a).
13 See Corbin (1971b). The green parrot, too, is associated with heavenly intelligence, contrary to the black crow, in Sufi mythology.
14 In Sufi mythology, surrounding Mount Qaf is the green sea. Not only does this evoke the idea of the biblical baptismal waters, signifying purification, but it could also be an allusion to the ancient Sanskrit story of 'Sinbad the Sailor', in which the protagonist falls into a bowl of water. In that immersion, he lives another lifetime.
15 The key spiritual symbols in the excerpt warrant further exploration.
16 Cf. Gray (2016: 73–83).
17 The first viewpoint is derived from the etymology of the Old Norse and Middle English 'happ' (c.6–15 centuries AD) meaning chance, fortune, what happens in the world, sustained in words such as 'happenchance', 'haphazard', 'hapless' and even 'perhaps' (McMahan 2006: 11); while the second invokes the ladder metaphor.

19 When chaos is the god of an era: Rediscovering an 'axis mundi' in *Starbook*

1 Jerry Fodor remarks: 'The long and the short is: one sees what one believes at least as much as the other way around. One views the world from the perspective of the "paradigms" to which one is antecedently committed' (2011: 24).
2 Cf. Milstead's definition of Zen Buddhism based on holism, a non-dualistic premise that perceives of mindfulness as embracing both intellect and experience and is thus transformative (1998: 5–6).
3 Anthony Chennells observes: 'The first coups of the 1960s and the uneasy slide into dictatorship and rule by corrupt elites in so many African countries made it even more important that the possibility of an ideal Africa should be represented as the real Africa ... Behind the clamour proclaiming and demanding new national loyalties that have replaced the competition of empires, the calmer, more authoritative voice of a united continent can be sounded, a sort of immanence that African fiction, which often uses allegory to further its polemic, can represent' (2006: 49).
4 Quayson continues: 'His ghostly writing raises fundamental questions about narrativity as well as about the relationship between literature and what it purports to represent ... not only is it highly poetic and surreal ... it manages a careful balance between fantasy and reality' (Gurnah 1995: 144).
5 Hollander elaborates: '[the goddess also] tells how man is given the breath of life, how a golden age of innocence (among the gods) ends with the coming of the Norms (the Fates), who wreak havoc upon the world' ([1962] 2008: 1). See also Indian mythology's corresponding myth of the Veda. Like 'The Edda', the Veda (knowledge) is a collection of mythological poems composed in pre-classical Sanskrit during the second century BC (Knappert [1991] 1995: 260).
6 'Our birth is but a sleep and a forgetting; / The soul that rises with us, one life's star, / Hath had elsewhere its setting. / And cometh from afar; / Not in entire forgetfulness,

/ And not in utter nakedness / But trailing clouds of glory do we come / From God, who is our home.' 'Imitations of Immortality' (ll. 62–9).
7. Killam and Rowe provide a useful insight into social realism: 'Okri, one of the most important new voices in contemporary African literature in English, is very conscious of the post-independence realities of African societies; hence his works are often satirical and critical of the various political and economic crises that have plagued African countries since the end of the colonial period' (2000: 198).
8. See Gray (2009: 45).
9. Gerald Larue explains: 'Myth may be understood as the human effort to discriminate between an understanding of life, not as bare existence, but as the relationship between the totality of body, mind, spirit, and the world – the effort to achieve harmonious relationships (peace) within the totality of one's environment ... Myth can also be understood in terms of man's response to or awareness of power outside and beyond himself – to the wholly "other," to ... the "numinous experience" or ... the "religious experience."' (1975: 9–10).
10. Interview with Ben Okri, 16 February 2011, London, by Rosemary Gray.
11. As noted, Ernest Holmes, in the context of Heaven (the result of correct thinking) and Hell (the atmosphere of false thinking), defines 'unfoldment' as 'the birth of ideas coming forth from Mind' ([1919] 1938: 8).
12. In terms of this triadic conjunction, Eliade cites the examples of India's Mount Meru, Siam's Mount Zinnalo, Mesopotamia's Mount of the Lands, Palestine's Mount Tabor and the Christian Golgotha.
13. M. H. Abrams notes: 'Its standard plot is that of a quest undertaken by a single knight in order to gain a lady's favour; frequently its central interest is *courtly love*, together with tournaments fought and dragons and monsters slain for the damsel's sake; it stresses the chivalric ideals of courage, loyalty, honour, mercifulness to an opponent, and elaborate manners, and it delights in wonders and marvels. Supernatural events in the epic had their causes in the will and actions of the gods; romance shifts the supernatural to this world, and makes much of the mysterious effect of magic, spells, and enchantments' ([1957] 1999: 35).
14. In an interesting elucidation of laughter as a survival tactic, Ingrid Betancourt asserts: 'I had to change – not to adapt, which would have seemed like a betrayal to me – but to rise above this morass of petty, base behaviour in which we had begun to wallow. I needed wings, I needed to fly far away above this fiendish jungle that sought to transform us into cockroaches. I didn't know how to go about it. I knew of no instruction manual for teaching a higher level of humanity and a greater wisdom. But I felt instinctively that laughter was the *beginning* of wisdom, as it was indispensable for survival' (2010: 261).
15. As if to explain the 422 pages of this novel, which some bloggers have found tedious, Serrao hyperbolizes: 'Every page, every paragraph and every sentence contains a separate metaphor, which can become tiresome to read. Simplicity is clearly not something Okri is trying to achieve – instead he jam-packs adjectives into every line, just like an epic poem, forming an absolutely beautiful piece of writing' (2010: 2).
16. Jan Carew's tribute to fellow African voyeur, Alex La Guma, seems apposite to this starbook of life: 'For you, art and literature were the lightning rods catching the incandescent glare of truth and transmitting it not only to your own people but to people all over the world who are struggling to make the world a better place to live in' (1985: 180).
17. See Gray (2001: 853–96).

18 See Gray (2007: 71–84 and 2013: 128–45).

20 In conversation with Ben Okri

1 Rosemary Gray (2012), 'In Conversation with Ben Okri'. *Journal of Literary Studies*, 28 (4): 4–13, reused with permission from the publisher. The interview took place at the Marsh Agency, 50 Albermarle Street, London at 14:00 on Wednesday, 16 February 2011.

Bibliography

1 Ben Okri's aphorisms: 'Music on the wings of a soaring bird'

Abrams, M. H. (1999). *A Glossary of Literary Terms*. Fort Worth, TX: Harcourt Brace College.
Addison, Joseph. (1672–1719). 'Criticisms on Paradise Lost'. In Edmund D. Jones (ed.), *English Critical Essays*, 240–60. London: Oxford University Press.
Bauckham, Richard. (2002). *James*. London: Routledge.
Cobham Brewer. ([1952] 1970). *Brewer's Dictionary of Phrase and Fable*. Revised by Ivor H. Evans. London: Folio Society.
Alexander Cruden. ([1949] 1971). *Cruden's Complete Concordance*, A. D. Adams, C. H. Irwin and S. A. Waters (eds.). Grand Rapids, MI: Zondervan.
Erasmus, Desiderius. ([1540] 1982). *Collected Works of Erasmus, Adages*, trans. M. M. Phillips. Toronto: University of Toronto.
Fowler, Roger. (1973). *A Dictionary of Modern Critical Terms*. London: Routledge and Kegan Paul.
Grace, Ronald. (n.d.). 'Benchmarking: The Paremiological Exemplar in Accounting', unpublished.
Gray, Rosemary. (2017). 'Recovering Our True State of Being in Ben Okri's Fable *The Comic Destiny*'. *English Academy Review: Journal of English Studies*, 34 (2): 35–50.
Gray, Rosemary Alice. (2018). 'Ben Okri's Aphorisms: "Music on the Wings of a Soaring Bird"'. *Academic Journal of Interdisciplinary Studies*, 7 (2): 17–24. Reused with permission.
Jones, Edmund D. ([1922] 1963). *English Critical Essays*. London: Oxford University Press.
Miller, P. D. (1990). *Interpretations – Deuteronomy*. Louisville, KY: John Knox Press.
Obiechina, Emmanuel. (1995). 'Narrative Proverbs in the African Novel'. *Research in African Literatures*, 24 (4): 123–40.
Okri, Ben. ([1989] 1997). *A Way of Being Free*. London: Phoenix.
Okri, Ben. (1991). *The Famished Road*. London: Random House.
Okri, Ben. (1996). *Birds of Heaven*. London: Phoenix.
Okri, Ben. (2009). *Tales of Freedom*. London: Random House.
Okri, Ben. (2011). *A Time for New Dreams*. Chatham: Random House.
Okri, Ben. (2015). 'Aphorisms'. *Callaloo*, 38 (5): 1042–3.
Okri, Ben. (2019). *The Freedom Artist*. London: Head of Zeus.
Orkin, Martin. (1982). 'Everyday Is Not a Holiday – Proverb Idiom in *Henry IV* Part 1'. *Unisa English Studies*, XXI (2): 1–5.
Sandberg, Anders. (2014). 'Transhumanism and the Meaning of Life'. In Tracey Trothen and Calvin Mercer (eds), *Transhumanism and Religion: Moving into an Unknown Future*. New York: Praeger.
Seung, Sebastian. (2013). *Connectome: How the Brain's Wiring Makes Us Who We Are*. New York: Mariner Books.

Shakespeare, William. (1936). *Henry IV, Part 1*, S. B. Hemingway (ed.), 154 fn. London: New Valorum Edition.
Smith, Jadwiga S. (2011). 'The Cosmo-Transcendental Positioning of the Living Being in the Universe in Anna-Teresa Tymieniecka's New Enlightenment'. *Phenomenological Inquiry*, XXXV: 14–24.
Soyinka, Wole. ([1976] 1995). *Myth, Literature and the African World*. Cambridge: Cambridge University Press.
The Holy Bible. (1611). *King James Version*. London: Oxford University Press.
The New Oxford Dictionary of English. (1998). Judy Pearsall (ed.). New York: Oxford University Press.
Tymieniecka, Anna-Teresa. (1966). *Is There Something Rather Than Nothing? Prolegomena to the Phenomenology of Cosmic Creation*. Assen: von Gorgum.
Tymieniecka, Anna-Teresa. (2008). 'The New Enlightenment'. *Phenomenological Inquiry*, XXXII: 3–14.

2 Epistemic ecology and 'diminishing boundaries of a shrinking world' in 'Heraclitus' Golden River' from *Wild*

Adorno, Theodor. (2002). 'On the Contemporary Relation between Philosophy and Music'. In Richard Leppert (ed.), *Essays on Music*. Berkeley: University of California Press.
Aquileana. (2015). 'Heraclitus of Ephesus: "The Doctrine of Flux and the Unity of Opposites"', 31 October. Available online: https://aquileana.files.wordpress.com/2014/02/guarda5.png/ (accessed 30 May 2016).
Baym, Nina. (1965). 'Robert Frost's Nature Poetry: An Approach to Robert Frost's Nature Poetry'. *American Quarterly*, 17 (1): 713–32.
Estés, Clarissa. (1998). *Women Who Run with the Wolves: Contacting the Power of the Wild Woman*. Johannesburg: Random House.
Essakow, Hubert. (2016). 'Terra Review – New Ben Okri'. *Guardian*, 15 March: 1–3.
Frost, Robert. (1914). *North of Boston*. Cambridge, MA: David Nutt.
Ghigi, Nicoletta. (2014). 'Towards a New Enlightenment: Metaphysics as Philosophy of Life'. In Anna-Teresa Tymieniecka (ed.), *Phenomenology of Space and Time. Analecta Husserliana*, 3–10. Dordrecht: Springer.
Graham, Daniel W. (2014). 'Heraclitus'. *Internet Encyclopedia of Philosophy*, 31 October: 1–6. Available online: http://www.iep.utm.edu/heraclit/print/ (accessed 8 March 2016).
Gray, Rosemary. (2009). 'Apologia pro Ben Okri's In Arcadia: A Neglected Masterpiece?' *English Academy Review: Southern African Journal of English Studies*, 26 (1): 65–71.
Gray, Rosemary. (2013). 'When Chaos Is the God of an Era: Rediscovering an *Axis Mundi* in Ben Okri's *Starbook* (2007)'. *Research in African Literatures*, 44 (1): 128–45.
Greaves, A. (2010). *The Land of Ionia: Society Recovery in the Archaic Period*. Oxford: Wiley Blackwell.
Heidegger, Martin. (2008). *Basic Writings: Martin Heidegger*, David Farrell Krell (ed.). New York: Harper and Row.
'Heraclitus'. (2015). *Stanford Encyclopedia of Philosophy*. Web. 1 October: 1–6. Available online: http://www.iep.utm.edu/heraclit/print/ (accessed 8 March 2016).
Husserl, E. (1970). 'Cartesianische Meditationen und Pariser Vortäges'. In B. Strasser (ed.), *Husserliana I*. Den Haag: Martinus Nijhoff.

Kahn, C. ed. (1979). *The Art and Thought of Heraclitus: An Edition of the Fragments with Translation and Commentary*. Cambridge: Cambridge University Press.
Kamwangamalu, N. M. (1999). 'Ubuntu in South Africa: A Sociolinguistic Perspective to a Pan-African Concept'. *Critical Arts*, 13 (2): 24–41.
Lazaridis, N. (2007). *Wisdom in Loose Form: The Language of Egyptian and Greek Proverbs in Collections of the Hellenistic and Roman Period*. Leiden: Brille.
Okri, Ben. ([1991] 1997). *The Famished Road*. London: Vintage.
Okri, Ben. ([1989] 1997). *A Way of Being Free*. London: Phoenix.
Okri, Ben. (2002). *In Arcadia*. London: Phoenix.
Okri, Ben. (2007). *Starbook*. Chatham: Random House.
Okri, Ben. (2011). *A Time for New Dreams*. Chatham: Random House.
Okri, Ben. (2012). *Wild*. Croydon: Random House.
Prier, A. (1976). *Archaic Logic: Symbol and Structure in Heraclitus, Parmenides and Empedocles*. The Hague: Mouton.
Ramose, M. B. (2001). 'An African Perspective on Justice and Race'. *Forum for Philosophizing*, 2: 1–27.
Soyinka, Wole. (1965). *The Road*. Oxford: Oxford University Press.
Soyinka, Wole. ([1976] 1995). *Myth, Literature and the African World*. New York: Cambridge University Press.
Spence, Louis. ([1915] 1925). *The Myths of Ancient Egypt*. London: George G. Harris.
Straus, Peter. (2012). *From Beowulf to Prufrock: One Thousand Years of English Writing*. Cowies Hill, KwaZulu-Natal: Solo Collective.
Wood, Bryant. (2016). 'The Walls of Jericho'. 22 May: 1–17. Available online: http://biblearcheology.org/post/2008/06/The-Walls-of-Jericho.aspx (accessed 8 March 2016).

3 Ontopoiesis in Okri's poetic oeuvre and *A Time for New Dreams*

Adonis. (1992). *An Introduction to Arab Poetics*. Cairo, Egypt: American University Press.
Aristotle. (2004). *Metaphysics* (A,2,982). In A.-T. Tymieniecka. 2004. 'The Pragmatic Test of the Ontopoiesis of Life'. *Phenomenological Inquiry*, XXVIII: 5–35.
Gray, Rosemary. (2012a). 'Interview with Ben Okri'. *Journal of Literary Studies*, 28 (4): 4–13.
Gray, Rosemary. (2012b). 'Mythic Conjunctions in Transit: Ontopoiesis in Ben Okri's *An African Elegy* (1992) and *Mental Fight* (1999) and Wole Soyinka's *A Shuttle in the Crypt*'. *Journal of Literary Criticism*, 28 (4): 25–37.
Gray, Rosemary. (2012c). 'When Chaos Is the God of an Era: Rediscovering an "Axis Mundi" in Ben Okri's *Starbook* (2007)'. *Research in African Literatures*, 44 (1): 128–45.
Llosa, Mario Vargas. n.d. 'Nobel Acceptance Speech'. 7 December 2010, p. 11, unpublished.
Low, D. (2011). 'Merleau-Ponty's Enchanted Nature'. *Phenomenological Inquiry*, 35: 49–90.
Okri, Ben. ([1992] 1997). *An African Elegy*. London: Vintage.
Okri, Ben. (1993). *Songs of Enchantment*. London: Jonathan Cape.
Okri, Ben. (1997). *A Way of Being Free*. London: Phoenix.
Okri, Ben. (1999). *Mental Fight*. London: Phoenix.
Okri, Ben. (2011). *A Time for New Dreams*. Chatham: Random House.
Singer, A., and A. Dunn. (2000). *Literary Aesthetics: A Reader*. Oxford: Blackwell.
Soyinka, Wole. ([1976] 1995). *Myth, Literature and the African World*. New York: Cambridge University Press.

Stevens, Anthony. (1998). *Ariadne's Clue*. London: Penguin.
Tymieniecka, Anna-Teresa, ed. (2000). 'Logos and Life', Book 4: *Impetus and Equipoise in the Life-Strategies of Reason*. Dordrecht: Springer Academic.
Tymieniecka, Anna-Teresa, ed. (2004). 'The Pragmatic Test of the Ontopoiesis of Life'. *Phenomenological Inquiry*, XXVIII: 5–35.
Tymieniecka, Anna-Teresa, ed. (2011a). 'Astronomy and Civilization in the New Enlightenment'. *Analecta Husserliana*, CV11: 8.
Tymieniecka, Anna-Teresa, ed. (2011b). 'Phenomenology/Ontopoiesis Retrieving Geo-cosmic Horizons of Antiquity'. *Analecta Husserliana*, 110. Available online: http://www.springer.com/philosophy/philosophical+traditions/book/978-94-007-1690-2 (accessed 6 November 2011).
The Shambhala Dictionary of Buddhism and Zen. (1991). Boston, MA: Shambhala.

4 Recovering our true state of being in 'The Comic Destiny'

Angelou, Maya. (1993). *I Know Why the Caged Bird Sings*. New York: Bantam Books.
Beckett, Samuel. (1931). *Proust and the Three Dialogues*. New York: Riverrun Press.
Beckett, Samuel. (1958). *Endgame*. Kalamazoo, MI: Grove Press.
Beckett, Samuel. (1964). *Play and Two Short Pieces for Radio*. London: Faber and Faber.
Beckett, Samuel. (1966). *Comédie* (film adaptation of *Play*).
Bhabha, Homi. (1994). *The Location of Culture*. New York: Routledge Classics.
Brown, Verna. (2009). 'Separate Dynamisms: The Impasse in Communication in Three of Beckett's Plays'. *English Academy Review*, 26 (1): 62–71.
Chadwick, Charles. ([1971] 1973). *Symbolism*. London: Methuen.
Christie, Agatha. ([1952] 1965). *The Mousetrap*. New York: Dell.
Costantini, M. (2015). 'Transcending Historical Violence: Uses of Myth and Fable in Ben Okri's *Starbook*'. *Callaloo*, 38 (5): 1118–34.
Coundouriotis, Eleni. (2015). 'Things of Poverty and War: Ben Okri and Thing Theory'. *Callaloo*, 38 (5): 1089–99.
Dante Alighieri. (1909–14). *The Divine Comedy*, 'Introductory Note'. The Harvard Classics. Available online: http://www. bartleby.com/20/1001.html (accessed 14 February 2017).
Dante Alighieri. ([1939] 1975). *The Divine Comedy I: Inferno*, John D. Sinclair (trans.). London: Oxford University Press.
De, Asis. (2015). 'In Conversation with Ben Okri: A Personal Interview'. *Global Colloquies*, 1 (1): 246–51.
Gascoigne, Bamber. ([1962] 1990). *Twentieth Century Drama*. London: Hutchinson University Library.
Gray, Rosemary. (2017). 'Recovering Our True State of Being: Ben Okri's Fable, "The Comic Destiny"'. *English Academy Review: A Journal of English Studies*, 34 (2): 35–50.
Guignery, Vanessa. (2015). 'An Interview with Ben Okri'. *Callaloo*, 38 (5): 1053–63.
Guthrie, W. K. C. ([1950] 1978). *The Greek Philosophers from Thales to Aristotle*. London: Methuen.
Hertel, Johannes. (1915). *The Panchatantra: A Collection of Ancient Hindu Tales in Its Oldest Recension, the Kashmirian, Entitled Tantrakhyayika*, Harvard Oriental Series, 14. Cambridge, MA: Harvard University Press.

Irwin, W. R. (1961). 'The Romances of Williams, Lewis and Tolkien'. *The Sewanee Review*, 69 (4): 566–78.
Jowett, Caroline. (1995). 'Writes of Passage: Interview with Ben Okri'. *Sojourn*, October: 26–31.
Keats, John. (2009). *Bright Star: The Complete Poems and Selected Letters of John Keats*, Jane Campion (ed.). London: Vintage.
Koyana, Siphokazi, and Rosemary Gray. (2002). 'Growing Up with Maya Angelou and Sindiwe Magona: A Comparison'. In Andrew Offenbach, Scott Rosenberg and Christopher Saunders (eds), *Safundi: A South African and American Comparative Reader*, 215–36. Nashville, TN: Safundi.
Lawley, Paul. (1984). 'Beckett's Dramatic Counterpoint: A Reading of Play'. *Journal of Beckett Studies*, 9: 25–41.
Lawley, Paul. (1988). 'The Difficult Birth: An Image of Utterance in Beckett'. In Robin J. Davis and Lance St. John Butler (eds), *'Make Sense Who May': Essays on Samuel Beckett's Later Works*, 1–10. Gerrards Cross: Colin Smythe.
Lefkowitz, Jeremy. (2014). *The Oxford Book of Animals in Classical Thought and Life*, Gordon and Campbell (eds). Oxford: Oxford University Press.
Mathuray, Mark. (2015). 'The Famished Road after Postmodernism: African Modernism and the Politics of Subalterity'. *Callaloo*, 38 (5): 1100–17.
Ngugi wa Thiong'o. (1986). *Decolonizing the Mind*. London: Heinemann Educational Books.
Obano, Nisha. (2009). 'Ben Okri'. Available online: http://www.encyclopediaofafroeuropennstudies.en/encyclopedia/ben-okri/ (accessed 1 April 2016).
Okri, Ben. (1981). *The Landscapes Within*. Harlow: Longman.
Okri, Ben. ([1989] 1997). *A Way of Being Free*. London: Penguin.
Okri, Ben. (1992). *An African Elegy*. London: Vintage.
Okri, Ben. (2007). *Starbook*. London: Rider.
Okri, Ben. (2009). *Tales of Freedom*. London: Random House.
Okri, Ben. (2012). *Wild*. London: Random House.
Okri, Ben. (2014). *The Age of Magic*. London: Head of Zeus.
Okri, Ben. (2015). *The Mystery Feast*. West Hoathly: Clairview Books.
Panini, Jay. (2009). 'Okri's Tales of Freedom'. *The Guardian*, 25 April: 1.
Quayson, Ato. (1999). 'Looking Away: Tropes of Disability in Post-Colonial Writing'. In Rod Maughan (ed.), *An Introduction to Contemporary Fiction: International Writing in English since 1970*, 53–68. Cambridge: Polity Press; Maldon: Blackwell.
Tolkien, J. R. R. ([1937] 1995). *The Hobbit*. London: Harper Collins.
Wilson, Edward O. (1992). *The Diversity of Life*. New York: Norton.
•The original article – reused with permission – published in *The English Academy Review: Journal of English Studies*, 2017, 34 (2): 35–50, won the Thomas Pringle award for best scholarly article published in 2016 and 2017.

5 Apologia pro *In Arcadia*: A neglected masterpiece?

Abell, Stephen. (2002). 'Scratcher of Sores'. *Times Literary Supplement*, 5191 (27 September): 23.
Anon. (2008). Peer review report. English Academy of Southern Africa, p. 1.

Bruce, Keith. (2003). 'In Arcadia'. *The Glasgow Herald*, September: 7–10.
Gough, Andrew. (n.d.). 'Arcadia'. Available online: http://www.templaricavalier.it/images/rennes_le_chateau_i_pastori (accessed 26 June 2007).
Gowing. (n.d.). The Royal Collection. Available online: http://www.royalcollection.org.uk/eGallery/object.asp?maker=VERMEER&object=4/ (accessed 5 May 2008).
Gray, Rosemary. (2007a). '"A Moment in Timelessness": Ben Okri's *Astonishing the Gods*'. *Analecta Husserliana: Temporality in Life as Seen through Literature*, LXXXVI: 23–36.
Gray, Rosemary. (2007b). ' "Domesticating Infinity" in Ben Okri's *Mental Fight* and *Astonishing the Gods*'. *English Academy Review: Southern African Journal of English Studies*, 24 (1): 85–101.
Gray, Rosemary. (2009). 'Apologia Pro Ben Okri's *In Arcadia*: A Neglected Masterpiece?' *English Academy Review*, 26 (1): 41–52.
Harrison, Steven. (2005). *What's Next after Now: Post-Spirituality and the Creative Life?* Boulder, CO: Sentient.
Hodgson, Phyllis. (1967). *Three 14th Century Mystics*. London: Longman, Green.
Hoodwin, Shepherd. (n.d.). *The Journey of Your Soul*. Available online: http://209.85.135.104/search?q=cache:Ntj5kTT30cJ:www.michaelteachings.com/akashic_record/ (accessed 5 June 2007).
James, Henry. (1963). *Selected Literary Criticism*, Morris Shapira (ed.). Harmondsworth: Penguin.
Jones, Eldred D. (1973). *The Writings of Wole Soyinka*. London: Heinemann.
King, Bruce. (2003). 'Review of *In Arcadia* by Ben Okri'. *World Literature Today*, 77 (1) April–June: 86–7.
László, Ervin. (2004). *Science and the Akashic Field: An Integral Theory of Everything*. Rochester, VT: Inner Traditions.
Okri, Ben. (1991). *The Famished Road*. London: Random House.
Okri, Ben. (1996). *Birds of Heaven*. London: Phoenix.
Okri, Ben. (1998). *A Way of Being Free*. London: Phoenix.
Okri, Ben. (2003). *In Arcadia*. London: Phoenix.
Okri, Ben. (2007). *Starbook*. Chapham: Rider.
Robbe-Grillet, Alain. (1963). *Pour un nouveau roman*. Paris: Les Éditions de Minuit.
Rowley, George. (1947). *Principles of Chinese Painting*. Princeton, NJ: Princeton University Press.
Soyinka, Wole. (1973). 'Idanre and Other Poems'. In Eldred Durosimi Jones (ed.), *The Writings of Wole Soyinka*, 8. London: Heinemann.
The Royal Collection. A lady at the virginals with a gentleman ('The Music Lesson'). See Gowing.
Treglown, Jeremy. (2002). 'Past Glories Prove Illusive'. *Spectator*, 290 (9086), 28 September: 68–9.

6 'Domesticating infinity' in *Mental Fight* and *Astonishing the Gods*

Al-Hujwiri. (1055 CE). *Kashf Al-Mahjub (The Revelation of the Veiled)*. Available online: http//:www.hermes-press.com/Perennial_Tradition/PTintroduction.htm/ (accessed 21 January 2007).

Bennett, Robert. (1998). 'Ben Okri (1959–)'. In Puspa Naidu and Fatima Joane Sigma (eds), *Postcolonial African Writers: A Bio-Bibliographical Critical Sources Book*, 364–73. Westport, CT: Greenwood Press.
Berger, John. (1972). *Ways of Seeing*. London: Penguin.
Berry, Thomas. (1996). 'The University: Its Response to the Ecological Crisis', Paper delivered at Harvard Divinity School (11 April): 1–9.
Bertha, Csilla. (1999). 'Six Characters in Search of a Faith: The Mythic and the Mundane in *Wonderful Tennessee*'. *Irish University Review*, 29 (1): 119–35.
Bradbury, Dominic. (1999). 'Review of Ben Okri's *Mental Fight*'. *The Times*, 16 January, n.p.
Bunyan, John. ([1678] 1960). *The Pilgrim's Progress*. London: Collins.
Calvino, Italo. (1969). *Invisible Cities*. London: Picador.
Calvino, Italo. ([1980] 1997). *The Literature Machine*. London: Random House.
Carroll, Lewis. ([1865] n.d.). *Alice's Adventures in Wonderland*. London: Collins.
Chopra, Deepak. (2006). *Life after Death*. London: Rider.
Cooper, Brenda. (2003). 'Okri, Ben'. In Simon Gikandi (ed.), *Encyclopaedia of African Literature*, 412–13. New York: Routledge.
Deleuze, Gilles. (2001). 'Cinéma 2: L'image-temps, *The Time-Image*'. In Vincent C. Leitch (ed.), *The Norton Anthology of Theory and Criticism*, 1593–7. London: Norton.
Deleuze, Gilles, and Félix Guattari. (2001). 'Gilles Deleuze and Félix Guattari'. In Vincent C. Leitch (ed.), *The Norton Anthology of Theory and Criticism*, 1593–7. London: Norton.
Doležel, Lubomir. ([1998] 2000). *Heterocosmica: Fiction and Possible Worlds*. Baltimore, MD: Johns Hopkins University Press.
Eliot, T. S. (1978). '*Four Quartets,* "Burnt Norton" 1935 and "Ash-Wednesday" 1930'. In Valerie Eliot (ed.), *The Complete Poems and Plays of TS Eliot*. London: Faber and Faber.
Gibran, Kahlil. (2004). *The Prophet*. New Delhi: Rupa.
Gunn, Alexander. (1929). *The Problem of Time*. London: Allen and Unwin.
Hawking, Stephen. ([1988] 1997). *A Brief History of Time*. London: Transworld.
Holroyd, Stuart. (1989). *The Arkana Dictionary of New Perspectives*. London: Penguin.
Lacan, Jacques. (2001). 'Jacques Lacan'. In Vincent C. Leitch (ed.), *The Norton Anthology of Theory and Criticism*, 1278–310. London: Norton.
Leitch, Vincent C., ed. (2001). *The Norton Anthology of Theory and Criticism*. London: Norton.
Livergood, Norman D. (n.d.). *Esoteric Christianity*. London: Hermes Press. Available online: http://www.hermespress.com/Perennial_Tradition/esoteric_christianity.htm (accessed 12 March 2005).
Mbembe, Achile. (2004). 'African Modes of Self-Writing'. *Chimurenga*, 10–19. Johannesburg: The Sibling.
Okri, Ben. (1991). *The Famished Road*. London: Cape.
Okri, Ben. (1992). *An African Elegy*. London: Jonathan Cape.
Okri, Ben. (1993). *Songs of Enchantment*. London: Cape.
Okri, Ben. ([1995] 1999). *Astonishing the Gods*. London: Orion.
Okri, Ben. (1997). *A Way of Being Free*. London: Phoenix.
Okri, Ben. (1999). *Mental Fight*. London: Orion.
Okri, Ben. (2015). *The Mystery Feast*. West Hoathly: Clairview Books.
Plato. ([*c*.380–367] 1994). *Republic*, Robin Waterfield (trans.). Oxford: Oxford University Press.

Quayson, Ato. (1995). 'Esoteric Webwork as Nervous System: Reading the Fantastic in Ben Okri's Writing'. In Abdulraza Gurna (ed.), *Essays on African Writing*, 144–59. London: Heinemann.
Raikes, H. R. (1932). *Our Changing Worldview*. Johannesburg: University of the Witwatersrand Press.
Smith, Jules. (2002). 'Ben Okri'. Available online: http://www.contemporarywriters.com/BenOkri.htm (accessed 20 January 2007).
Smuts, Jan Christiaan. (1932). 'Recent Advances in Science and Philosophy'. In H. R. Raikes (ed.), *Our Changing Worldview*, 3–16. Johannesburg: University of the Witwatersrand Press.
Stalnaker, Robert. (1979). 'Possible Worlds'. *Nous*, 10: 65–75.
Stevenson, Robert Louis. ([c.1881] 1932), 'Pulvis et umbra'. In H. R. Raikes (ed.), *Our Changing Worldview*, 17. Johannesburg: University of the Witwatersrand Press.

7 Redreaming ways of seeing: Intuitive creativity in *The Landscapes Within*

Bargna, Ivan. (2000). *African Art*. Texas: Jaca Books.
Barthes, Roland. (1977). *Image, Music, Text*. New York: Hill and Wang.
Berger, John. ([1972] 2008). *Ways of Seeing*. London: Penguin Modern Classics.
Camus, Alfred. ([1955] 1983). *The Myth of Sisyphus and Other Essays*, Justin O'Brien (trans.). London: Random House.
Chadwick, Charles. ([1971] 1973). *Symbolism*. London: Methuen.
Coleridge, Samuel Taylor. (1840). *Aids to Reflection*. In Henry Nelson Coleridge (ed.), 'Aphorism LX', 161–210. London: Chauncey Goodrich.
Gray, Rosemary. (2000). 'Divinatory Simulacra in the Novels of Margaret Atwood'. In Jeff Barnard and Gloria Withalm (eds), *Myths, Rites, Simulacra: Semiotic Viewpoints*, 853–6. Vienna: Die Deutschen Bibliothek.
Gray, Rosemary. (2009). 'Apologia Pro Ben Okri's *In Arcadia*: A Neglected Masterpiece?' *English Academy Review*, 26 (1): 41–52.
Gray, Rosemary. (2013a). 'The Creative Imagination in Ben Okri's *The Landscapes Within* (1981)'. *English Academy Review: Southern African Journal of English Studies*, 30 (2): 21–31.
Gray, Rosemary. (2013b). 'When Chaos Is the God of an Era: Rediscovering an "Axis Mundi" in Ben Okri's *Starbook* (2007)'. *Research in African Literatures*, 44 (1): 128–45.
Hughes, Ted. [1970] 1996. *The Norton Anthology of Poetry*, 4th edition, Margaret Ferguson, Mary Jo Salter and Jon Stallworthy (eds), 1697. New York: WWW Norton.
Jowitt, David. (1996). 'Review of *Dangerous Love*'. *Wasifiri*, 24: 62–3.
Jung, Carl Gustav. (2018). 'Letter to Fanny Bowditch, 22 October 1916'. Available online: http://www.carljungdepthpsychologysite.blog/2018/02/08/carl-jung-i-am-afraid-that-the-mere-fact-of-my-presencetakes-you-away-from-yourself/ (accessed 18 May 2018).
Kundera, Milan. ([1986] 1988). *The Art of the Novel*. London: Faber and Faber.
Maithufi, Sopelekai. (2015). 'The Inward and Outward Projections of the Shaman's Journeys: Meditation in Ben Okri's *Dangerous Love* and Zakes Mda's *The Sculptors of Mapungubwe*'. *Journal of Literary Studies*, 32 (2): 81–93.
Maya-Pearce, Adewole. (1992). *A Mask Dancing*. London: Hans Zell.

Mooney, Bel. (2002). 'Review of *In Arcadia*'. *The Times*. 28 September.
Ntuli, Pitika. (2010). *Pitika Ntuli: Scent of Invisible Footprints*. Pretoria: Unisa Press.
Okri, Ben. (1981). *The Landscapes Within*. London: Longman.
Okri, Ben. (1996). *Dangerous Love*. Johannesburg: A. D. Donker.
Okri, Ben. (1997). *A Way of Being Free*. London: Phoenix.
Okri, Ben. (2002). *In Arcadia*. London: Phoenix.
Okri, Ben. (2011). *A Time for New Dreams*. London: Random House.
Okri, Ben. (2012). *Wild*. London: Random House.
Okri, Ben. (2014). *The Age of Magic*. London: Head of Zeus.
Okri, Ben. (2015). *The Mystery Feast*. London: Clairview Books.
Richards, I. A. ([1966] 1972). *Plato's Republic*. Cambridge: Cambridge University Press.
Ross, Jean. (1993). 'Contemporary Authors Interview (with Ben Okri)'. In Donna Olendorf (ed.), *Contemporary Author 138*, 337–8. Detroit, MI: Gale Research.
Rowley, George. (1947). *Principles of Chinese Painting*. Princeton, NJ: Princeton University Press.
Schama, Simon. (1995). *Landscapes and Memory*. London: Harper Collins.
Severac, Alain. (1999). '*Dangerous Love*: Okri's Metafiction'. In Jean-Pierre Durix (ed.), *Theory and Literary Creation*, 175–85. Dijon: Editions Universitaires de Dijon.
Smith, Anna. (2000). 'Dreams of Cultural Violence: Ben Okri and the Politics of the Imagination'. *World Literature Written in English*, 38 (2): 44–54.
Stevens, Anthony. (1998). *Ariadne's Clue*. London: Penguin.
Sylvester, David. (1992). *Magritte*. London: Thames and Hudson.
Tolle, Eckart. (2005). *The Power of Now*. London: Hodder and Stoughton.
Tunca, Darla. (2004). 'Ben Okri's *The Landscapes Within* and *Dangerous Love*: Vision and Revision'. *Belgium Journal of English Language and Literatures*, 2: 85–101.
Tymieniecka, A.-T., ed. (1992). *Phenomenology of Space and Time, Analecta Husserliana* CXVI: 3–36.
Tymieniecka, A.-T., ed. (2004). 'Aesthetic Expression of the Moral Sentiment'. *Phenomenological Inquiry*, 28: 5–35.
Tymieniecka, A.-T., ed. (2011). 'Inspirations of Heraclitus from Ephesus Fulfilled in Our New Enlightenment'. *Analecta Husserliana* CX: 3–12.
Wilkinson, Jane. (1992). *Talking to African Writers*. London: James Currey.
Wright, Derek. (1997). *New Directions in African Fiction*. New York: Twayne.
• The author acknowledges her earlier readings: (2013), 'The Creative Imagination in Ben Okri's *The Landscapes Within* (1981)', presented at Harvard in June 2012 and published in the *English Academy Review: Southern African Journal of English Studies*, 30 (2), 21–31; and (2016), 'Ben Okri's *The Landscapes Within* (1981): The Unfinished Story'. In A.-T. Tymieniecka (ed.), *The Cosmos and the Creative Imagination, Analecta Husserliana* 119, 73–83. Switzerland: Springer International. Reused with permission from the publishers.

8 Promoting the poetic cause in 'stokus' from *Tales of Freedom*

Anon. (2009). 'Interview: Ben Okri – Booker Prize-Winning Novelist and Poet'. *The Scotsman*.
Anon. (1973). 'Eucatastrophe'. *Time*, 17 September: 22.

Astle, D. (2009). 'Ben Okri's *Tales of Freedom* (Review)'. ABC Radio, 16 May. Available online: http://www.abc.net.au/radionational/programs/bookshow/ben-okris'tales-of-freedom-review/ (accessed 4 June 2015).
Burgess, A. (1984). 'On the Short Story'. *Les Cahiers de la Nouvelle: Journal of the Short Story in English*, 2: 31–47.
Cambridge Advanced Learner's Dictionary, 3rd ed. (2008). Cambridge: Cambridge University Press.
Coovadia, I. (2012). *Transformations*. Cape Town: Umuzi, an imprint of Random House Struik.
Daniel, L. (2009). 'Comment'. *The Telegraph*, 30 April. Available online: http://www.telegraph.co.uk/culture/books/bookreviews/5251547/Tales-of-freedom/ (accessed 4 June 2015).
Gillie, C., ed. (1972). *Longman Companion to English Literature*. London: Longman.
Gray, Rosemary. (2007). '"Domesticating Infinity" in Ben Okri's *Mental Fight* and *Astonishing the Gods*'. *English Academy Review*, 24 (1): 85–101.
Gray, Rosemary. (2013). 'The Creative Imagination in Ben Okri's *The Landscapes Within* (1981)'. *The English Academy Review: Southern African Journal of English Studies*, 30 (2): 21–30.
Gray, Rosemary. (2014). 'Ontopoiesis in Ben Okri's Poetic Oeuvre and *A Time for New Dreams* (2011)'. In A.-T. Tymieniecka (ed.), *Phenomenology of Space and Time: The Forces of the Cosmos and the Ontopoietic Genesis of Life: Book One, Analecta Husserliana* 116, 49–59. Switzerland: Springer.
Head, D. (1992). *The Modernist Short Story*. Cambridge: Cambridge University Press.
Heese, M. (1997). *Haiku for Africa*. Pretoria: Unisa Press.
Hodgson, Phyllis. (1967). *Three 14th Century Mystics*. London: Longman, Green.
Lewis, C. S. ([1961] 1995). *An Experiment in Criticism*. Cambridge: Cambridge University Press.
Lowenstein, T. (2006). *Haiku Inspirations*. London: Duncan Baird.
Madden, D., and V. Scott. (1984). *Studies in the Short Story*. New York: Holt, Rinehart and Winston.
Northover, R. A. (2014). 'The Archaeology of Rock Art and Western Philosophy'. *Journal of Literary Studies*, 30 (3): 101–23.
Obano, Nisha. (n.d.). 'Ben Okri (1959–)'. Available online: http://www.encyclopaediaofafroeuropeanstudies.eu.encylopedia/ben-okri/ (accessed 4 June 2015).
Okri, Ben. ([1995] 2014). *Astonishing the Gods*. London: Zeus.
Okri, Ben. (1996). *Birds of Heaven*. London: Phoenix.
Okri, Ben. (1997). *A Way of Being Free*. London: Phoenix.
Okri, Ben. ([2002] 2003). *In Arcadia*. Phoenix, London.
Okri, Ben. (2009). *Tales of Freedom*. London: Rider.
Okri, Ben. (2011). *A Time for New Dreams*. Chatham: Random House.
Parini, J. (2009). 'Introducing the Stoku'. *The Guardian*, 25 April. Available online: http://www.theguardian.com/books/2009/apr/25/tales-of-freedom-ben-okri/ (accessed 2 June 2015).
Pratt, M. (1981). 'The Short Story: The Long and the Short of It'. *Poetics*, 10: 175–94.
Rix, J. (2010). 'Ben Okri: My Family Values, Life and Style'. *The Guardian*, 26 June: 1.
Ross, B. (2012). *Spring Clouds Haiku*. Bangor: Tancho Press.
Said, A. A. (1992). *Introduction to Arab Poetics*. Egypt: American University of Cairo Press.
Soyinka, Wole. ([1976] 1995). *Myth, Literature and the African World*.
    New York: Cambridge University Press.

Tymieniecka, A.-T. (2004). 'The Pragmatic Test of the Ontopoiesis of Life'. *Phenomenological Inquiry XXV*: 5–35.

9 Sowing 'a quilt of harmony': Eco-phenomenology in 'Lines *in Potentis*'

Aristotle. (1941). *Physica* II 8 199B27–31. In Richard McKoen (ed.), *The Basic Works of Aristotle*. New York: Random House.
Campbell, Joseph. ([1962] 2011). *The Masks of God: Oriental Mythology*. London: Souvenir Press.
Fanon, Franz. (1972). *Black Skins, White Masks*. New York: Grove Press.
Keynes, Geoffrey. (1966). *Blake: Complete Writings*. Oxford: Oxford University Press.
Lenz, John R. (2017). 'Bertrand Russell on the Value of Philosophy for Life'. *Philosophy Now*, 120, June/July: 9–11.
Mafeje, Archie. (2000). 'Africanity: A Combative Ontology'. *Codesria*, Bulletin 1: 1–19.
Mbembe, J.-A. (2002). 'African Modes of Self-Writing'. *Public Culture*, 14 (1): 239–73.
Moorey, Teresa. (1997). *The Goddess*. London: Hodder and Stoughton.
Anon. (2012). 'Interview with Ben Okri'. *New Statesman*, 29 March.
Okri, Ben. ([1989] 1997). *A Way of Being Free*. London: Phoenix.
Okri, Ben. (2011). *A Time for New Dreams*. London: Random House.
Okri, Ben. (2012). *Wild*. London: Random House.
Pearsall, Judy and Patrick Hanks, eds. (1998) 2001. *The New Oxford Dictionary of English*. Oxford: Oxford University Press.
Tolle, Eckhart. (2005). *A New Earth*. London: Penguin.
Russel, Bertrand. [1931] 2001. *The Scientific Outlook*. London: Routledge and Psychology Press.
Torjussen, L. P., J. Servan and S. Andersen. (2008). 'An Interview with Anna-Teresa Tymieniecka. The Pragmatic Test of Phenomenology'. Available online: http://www.phenomenology.org/Bergen-Interview.htm/(accessed 26 March 2014).
Tymieniecka, Anna-Teresa. (1997), 'The Theme/the Esoteric Passion for Place'. In A.-T. Tymieniecka (ed.), *Passion for Place,* Book II. *Analecta Husserliana* LI, ix–xiv. Boston, MA: Kluwer Academic.
Tymieniecka, Anna-Teresa. (2008a). 'Interview'. Conducted by L. P. Torjussen, J. Servan and S. Andersen. Available online: http://www.phenomenology.org/Bergen-Interview.htm/(accessed 26 March 2014).
Tymieniecka, Anna-Teresa. (2008b). *The Passions of the Earth: In Human Existence, Creativity, and Literature, Analecta Husserliana* LXXI, 6. Boston, MA: Kluwer Academic.

10 'A clear lucid stream of everywhereness' in *Wild*: A postmodern perspective

Appignanesi, Richard, and Chris Garratt. ([1995] 2007). *Introducing Postmodernism*. Lanham, MD: Totem Books.

Arthur, Brian. ([2008] 2012). *Introducing Chaos*, Z. Sardar and I. Abrams (eds), 165–7. London: Icon.
Bush, Douglas, ed. (1967). *John Keats*. New York: MacMillan.
Delahunty, Andrew, Sheila Dignan and Penny Stock (eds). (2007). *The Oxford Dictionary of Allusions*. Oxford: Oxford University Press.
Dicarlo, Russell E. (2005). 'Foreword'. In Eckhart Tolle (ed.), *The Power of Now*, x–xix. London: Hodder and Stoughton.
Eliade, Mircea. (1989). *The Myth of the Eternal Return*. London: Penguin.
Gray, Rosemary. (2001). 'The Music under the Stone: Alex La Guma's *The Stone Country*'. *Commonwealth*, 23 (2): 47–54.
Gray, Rosemary. (2007). 'Spirit of Place: Mungoshi's Rolling World'. In Mbongeni Malaba and Geoffrey Davis (eds), *Zimbabwean Transitions*, 192–204. Amsterdam: Rodopi.
Gray, Rosemary. (2013). 'When Chaos Is the God of an Era: Rediscovering an "Axis Mundi" in Ben Okri's *Starbook* (2007)'. *Research in African Literatures*, 44 (1): 128–45.
Leotard, Jean-Francois. (1992). *The Postmodern Condition: A Report on Knowledge (1979)*. Manchester: Manchester University Press.
Lévi-Straus, Claude. ([1963] 1972). *Structural Anthropology*, Claire Jacobson and Brooke Schoepf (trans.). New York: Basic Books.
Linge, D. (1997). 'Introduction'. In H.-G. Gadamer (ed.), *Philosophical Hermeneutics*, xi–lvi. Berkeley: Crossroads.
Okri, Ben. (1981). *The Landscapes Within*. London: Phoenix.
Okri, Ben. (1998). *Infinite Riches*. London: Phoenix.
Okri, Ben. (1999). *Mental Fight*. London: Phoenix.
Okri, Ben. (2011). *A Time for New Dreams*. London: Random House.
Okri, Ben. (2012a). *Wild*. London: Random House.
Okri, Ben. (2012b). 'Interview by Sophie Elmhirst'. *New Statesman*, 29 March.
Sardar, Ziauddin, and Iwona Abrams. ([2008] 2012). *Introducing Chaos*. London: Icon.
Swanepoel, A. C. (2007). 'Irregular Regularity: A Chaos-Theory Reading of the Ecology Presented in Coleridge's "Frost at Midnight"'. *Journal of Literary Studies*, 23 (4): 444–58.
Szmyd, Jan. (2011). 'The Role of Anna-Teresa Tymieniecka's Philosophy in the Postmodern World: Cognitive Optimism, Innovativeness and Creativity'. *Phenomenological Inquiry*, 35: 25–48.
Tolle, Eckhart. ([1999] 2005). *The Power of Now*. London: Hodder and Stoughton.
Van Niekerk, L. (2012). 'Postmodernisms Pitstops en Route to Utopia: Language, History and Death in Ben Okri's *In Arcadia*'. *Journal of Literary Studies*, 28 (4): 14–24.
West, G. (1996). *An Introduction to Continental Philosophy*. Cambridge: Polity.

11 Survivalist culture in 'Laughter beneath the Bridge'

Abdullah, Sarah. (2017). '"The Young Shall Grow": Violence, Conflict and Coming of Age in Ben Okri's Laughter beneath the Bridge'. *Journal of Literature, Languages and Linguistics*, 37: 1–6.
Achebe, Chinua. ([1977] 1983). *Girls at War and Other Stories*. London: Heinemann.
Achebe, Chinua. (1987). *Anthills of the Savannah*. London: Heinemann.
Achebe, Chinua. (1999). 'Imagined Commonwealths'. In T. J. Giles (ed.), *Imagined Commonwealths: Cambridge Essays on Commonwealth and International Literature in English*, 167. Dordrecht: Springer.

Achebe, Chinua. (2012). *There Was a Country: A Memoir*. London: Penguin.
Chadwick, Charles. (1971). *Symbolism*. London: Methuen.
Dante Alighieri. ([1939] 1975). *The Divine Comedy I: Inferno*, John D. Sinclair (trans.). London: Oxford University Press.
Dupuy, Col. T. N., and Col. Wendell Blanchard. (1972). *The Almanac of World Military Power*. New York: RR Bowker.
Ehling, Holga G., ed. (1993). *Critical Approaches in Anthills of the Savanah, Matatu* 8. Amsterdam: Rodopi, 155 pp.
The Europa Year Book. 1968. Africa, The Americas, Asia, Australia. London: Europa. Vol. II, 1005.
Ezenwa-Ohaeto. (2000). 'Review'. *A Harvest of Tragedy: Critical Perspectives on Nigerian Civil War Literature, Research in African Literatures*, 31(3): 173–5.
Gibbs, James. (1983). 'Tear the Painted Masks, Join the Poison Stains: A Preliminary Study of Wole Soyinka's Writings for the Nigerian Press'. *Research in African Literatures*, 14 (1): 3–45.
Gray, Rosemary. (2017). 'Recovering Our True State of Being: Ben Okri's Fable, "The Comic Destiny" (2009)'. *English Academy Review: Journal of English Studies*, 34 (2): 35–50.
Julius-Adeoye, Jays. (2017). 'The Nigeria-Biafra War, Popular Culture and Agitation for Sovereignty of Biafra Nation'. African Studies Centre in Leiden (ASCL), Working paper series.
Kirk-Greene, A. M. A. (1970). *Crisis and Conflict in Nigeria: A Documentary Sourcebook 1966–70*, Part 1. London: Oxford University Press.
Kristeva, Julia. (1982). *Powers of Horror*, Leon S. Roudiez (trans.). New York: Columbia University Press.
Kundera, Milan. ([1980] 1983). *The Book of Laughter and Forgetting*, Michael Henry Heim (trans.). Harmondsworth: Penguin.
Kunene, Mazizi. (1981). *Anthem of the Decades: A Zulu Epic*. London: Heinemann.
Laurence, Margaret, and Nora Foster Stoval. (2001). *Long Drums and Cannons*. Canada: University of Alberta Press.
Maguire, Laura. 2015. 'Camus and Absurdity' | *Philosophy Talk*, 27 February. Available online: https://www.philosophytalk.org/blog/camus-and-absurdity/ (accessed 18 March 2018).
Odun Balogun, F. (1993). 'Review of *Anthills of the Savanah*'. *Research in African Literatures*, 24 (2): 133–4.
Okri, Ben. ([1986] 1993). *Incidents at the Shrine*. London: Vintage.
Okri, Ben. ([1991] 1992). *The Famished Road*. London: Vintage.
Okri, Ben. (1997). *A Way of Being Free*. London: Phoenix.
Okri, Ben. (2009). *Tales of Freedom*. Chatham: Random House.
Okri, Ben. (2010). 'Interview by Julia Rix, "Ben Okri: My Family Values"'. *The Guardian*, June 2.
Okri, Ben. (2015). 'Some Aphorisms'. *Callaloo* 38 (5): 1042–3.
Okri, Ben. (2019). *The Freedom Artist*. London: Head of Zeus.
Olu-Ololabi, K. (2011). 'My People Perish for Lack of Philosophy', Inaugural Lecture. Nigeria: University of Ibadan.
Omotoso, Kole. (1997). *Woza Africa: Music Goes to War*. Cape Town: Jonathan Ball.
Parvulescu, Anca. (2017). 'Literature and Laughter'. *Interdisciplinary Approaches to Literary Studies, Literary Theory and Cultural Studies*. Available online: DOI:10.1093/acrefore/9980190201098.013.43 (accessed 2 March 2018).

Soyinka, Wole. (1972). *A Shuttle in the Crypt*. London: Rex Collins; Eyre: Methuen.
Soyinka, Wole. ([1972] 1994). *The Man Died*. London: Vintage.
Soyinka, Wole. ([1976] 1995). *Myth, Literature and the African World*. Cambridge: Cambridge University Press.
Soyinka, Wole. ([1988] 1993). *Art, Dialogue and Outrage*. London: Methuen.
Tymieniecka, Anna-Teresa. (2011). 'Inspirations of Heraclitus from Ephesus Fulfilled in Our New Enlightenment'. *Analecta Husserliana*, CX: 3–12. Dordrecht: Springer.
Udenwa, Achike. (2011). *Nigeria/Biafra Civil War: My Experience*. Ibadan: Spectrum Books.
Wiesel, Elie. (1972). *Souls on Fire: Portraits and Legends of Hasidic Masters*. New York: Barnes and Noble.
•An earlier reading was Rosemary Gray's (2019). 'Ben Okri's "Laughter beneath the Bridge": Born (un)free'. *International Journal of Literary Humanities*, 17 (1): 70–81. https://doi.org/10.188848/2327-7912/CG/vli01/71-81, reused with paid permission.

12 The poetic muse of archaeology

Achebe, Chinua. ([1962] 1976). *Things Fall Apart*. London: Heinemann Educational Books.
Alroy, John. (2014). 'A Multispecies Overkill Simulation of the End-Pleistocene Megafaunal Mass Extinction'. *Science*, 292: 1893–96. In Elizabeth Kolbert (ed.), *The Sixth Extinction: An Unnatural History*, 234. London: Bloomsbury.
Barbier, E. B., J. C. Burgess and C. Floke. ([1994] 1995). *Paradise Lost? The Ecological Economics of Biodiversity*. London: Earthscan.
Birat, Kathie. (2015). 'The Dialogue of the Big and the Small: The Poetry of Ben Okri'. *Callaloo*, 38 (5): 1065–86.
Burdick, Alan. (2005). *Out of Eden: An Odyssey of Ecological Invasion*. New York: Farrar, Straus and Giroux.
De, Asis. (2015). 'In Conversation with Ben Okri: A Personal Interview'. *Global Colloquies*, 1 (1): 246–51.
Gray, Rosemary. (2014). 'Ben Okri's Geo-Cosmic Consciousness in *Wild* (2012)'. Paper delivered at Harvard, Massachusetts on 5 June.
Gray, Rosemary. (2018). 'Ben Okri's Stoku, "The Standeruppers" (2017): The Frightening Irony of the Anthropocene'. *Journal of Literary Studies*, 34 (2): 1–12.
Gray, Rosemary. (2019). 'Ben Okri's *Wild* (2012): The Muse of Archaeology'. *English in Africa*, 46 (1): 95–110. Reused with permission from the publisher.
Gray, Rosemary. (2020). 'Epistemic Ecology and Ben Okri's "Diminishing Boundaries of a Shrinking World" in "Heraclitus' Golden River" (*Wild* 2012)'. In William S. Smith, Jadwiga S. Smith and Daniela Verducci (eds), *Eco-Phenomenology: Life, Human Life, Post-Human Life in the Harmony of the Cosmos, Analecta Husserliana*, 12 pp. Dordrecht: Springer (in press).
Guthrie, W. K. C. ([1950] 1978). *The Greek Philosophers*. Norwich: Fletcher.
Iovino, Serenella. (2020). '(Material) Ecocriticism'. In Rosi Braidotti and Maria Hlavajova (eds), *Posthuman Glossary*. London: Bloomsbury (in press).
Kolbert, Elizabeth. (2014). *The Sixth Extinction: An Unnatural History*. London: Bloomsbury.
Leavis, F. R. ([1932] 1950). *New Bearings in English Poetry*. London: Chatto and Windus.

Ngugi wa Thiong'o. ([1986] 1994). *Decolonising the Mind: The Politics of Language in African Literature*. London: James Gurney; Nairobi: Heinemann.
Okri, Ben. (1992). *The Famished Road*. New York: Doubleday.
Okri, Ben. (1997). *A Way of Being Free*. London: Phoenix House.
Okri, Ben. (2011). *A Time for New Dreams*. Chatham: Random House.
Okri, Ben. (2012). *Wild*. London: Random House.
Okri, Ben. (2016). 'The Muse of Archaeology'. In Colin Renfrew, Michael Boyd and Iain Morley (eds), *Death Rituals, Social Order and the Archaeology of Immortality in the Ancient World*, 436–8. Cambridge: Cambridge University Press.
Opperman, Serpil. (2006). 'Theorizing Ecocriticism: Towards a Postmodern Ecocritical Practice'. *Interdisciplinary Studies in Literature and Environment*, 13 (2): n.p.
Read, H. H. (1956). *Rutley's Elements of Mineralogy*, 24th ed. London: Thomas Morley.
Anon. (1978). *Reader's Digest Library of Modern Knowledge*. London: Reader's Digest Association.
Renfrew, Colin, Michael Boyd and Iain Morley. (2016). *Death Rituals, Social Order and the Archaeology of Immortality in the Ancient World*. Cambridge: Cambridge University Press.
Ringrose, Chris. (2015). 'Redreaming the World: The Poetry of Ben Okri'. *Callaloo*, 38 (5): 1135–50.
Stevens, Anthony. (1998). *Ariadne's Clue*. London: Penguin.
Vernon, P. E. (1970). *Creativity*. Harmondsworth: Penguin.

13 Sublime transformative paremiology in *A Way of Being Free*

Bryant, M. M. (1951). 'Proverbial Lore in American Life and Speech'. *Western Folklore*, 10 (2): 134–42.
Crossan, J. S. D. (1983). *Fragments: The Aphorisms of Jesus*. San Francisco, CA: Harper and Row.
Dorsch, T. E. ([1965] 1974). *Aristotle, Horace, Longinus: Classical Literary Criticism*. Harmondsworth: Penguin.
Durrant, G. H. (1969). '"Tintern Abbey" and "The Life of Things"'. *Unisa English Studies*, 3–21.
Erasmus, Desiderius. ([1540] 1982). *Collected Works of Erasmus: Adages I i 1 to I v 100*, M. M. Phillips (trans.). Toronto: Toronto University Press.
Gray, Rosemary. (2012). 'Interview with Ben Okri'. *Journal of Literary Studies*, 28 (4): 4–13.
Gray, Rosemary. (2018a), 'Ben Okri's Aphorisms: "Music on the Wings of a Soaring Bird"'. *Academic Journal of Interdisciplinary Studies*, 7 (2): 17–24.
Gray, Rosemary. (2018b). 'Redreaming Ways of Seeing: Ben Okri's Intuitive Creativity'. *Tydskrif vir letterkunde*, 55 (2): 74–91. Reused with permission.
Harty, T. E. (1968). 'Meaning and Imagination'. *Unisa English Studies*, 2: 59–69.
Hemingway, Ernest. (1954). Nobel Prize for Literature Acceptance Speech. Available online: https://www.jfklibrary.org/Asset-Viewer/rwLCItn6ZUOCy3TUFl7Oew.aspx/ (accessed 27 January 2018).
Longinus. ([1965] 1973). 'LONGINUS: On the Sublime'. In T. E. Dorsch (ed. and trans.), *Aristotle, Horace, Longinus: Classical Literary Criticism*, 99–158. Harmondsworth: Penguin.

Okri, Ben. (1996). *Birds of Heaven*. London: Phoenix.
Okri, Ben. (1997). *A Way of Being Free*. London: Phoenix.
Okri, Ben. (1999). *Mental Fight: An Anti-Spell for the Twenty-First Century*. London: Phoenix.
Okri, Ben. (2011). *A Time for New Dreams*. London: Random House.
Okri, Ben. (2012). *Wild*. London: Phoenix.
Okri, Ben. (2015). 'Some Aphorisms'. *Callaloo*, 38 (5): 1042–3.
Okri, Ben. (2017). *The Magic Lamp*. London: Apollo.
Plato. ([1909] 1926). *The Republic of Plato*, Ernest Rhys (ed.). London: Dent.
Plato. (2009). *Phaedrus*, Robin Waterfield (trans.). Oxford: Oxford University Press.
Rossetti, William Michael, ed. (n.d.). *The Poetical Works of William Wordsworth*. London: William Collins.
Russell, Bertrand. (1912). *The Problems of Philosophy*. Oxford: Home University Library.
Trench, R. C. (1957). *Proverbs and Their Lessons*. London: Routledge.
Wordsworth, William. (n.d.). 'Lines, Composed a Few Miles above Tintern Abbey'. In W. M. Rossetti (ed.), *The Poetical Works of William Wordsworth*. London: Collins.

14 'The Standeruppers': The frightening irony of the Anthropocene

Alroy, John. (2001). 'A Multispecies Overkill Simulation of the End-Pleistocene Megafaunal Mass Extinction'. *Science*, 292: 1893–6.
Anderson, John, and Martin de Wit. (2020). 'Africa Alive Corridors: Autobiography of the Continent Told along 20 Corridors' (in press).
Barbier, E. B., J. C. Burgess and C. Floke. ([1994] 1995). *Paradise Lost? The Ecological Economics of Biodiversity*. London: Earthscan.
Burdick, Alan. (2005). *Out of Eden: An Odyssey of Ecological Invasion*. New York: Farrar, Straus and Giroux (qtd. in Elizabeth Kolbert, 2014: 218).
Donne, John. (1896). 'An Anatomy of the World'. *The Poems of John Donne*. Available online: https://www.google.co.za/search?q=Donne+An+Anatomy+of+the+World&rlz=1C1ASUM_enZA730ZA730&oq=Donne+An+Anatomy+of+the+World&aqs=chrome.69i57j0l4j69i60.38463j0j8&sourceid=chrome&ie=UTF-8/ (accessed 19 August 2017).
Gray, Rosemary. (2016). 'Promoting the Poetic Cause in Ben Okri's *Stokus* from *Tales of Freedom* (2009)'. *Literator*, 37 (1): 18–27. Reused with permission.
Gray, Rosemary (2018). 'Ben Okri's Stoku, "The Standeruppers" (2017): The Frightening Irony of the Anthropocene'. *Journal of Literary Studies*, 34 (2): 1–12. Reused with permission.
Guignery, Vanessa. (2015). 'Ben Okri: A Man of Many Arts'. *Callaloo*, 38 (5): 997–1003.
Hale, Thomas. (1998). *Griots and Griottes: Masters of Words and Music*. Bloomington: Indiana University Press.
Heese, Marié. (1997). *Haiku for Africa*. Pretoria: Unisa Press.
Jones, Tom, and Ellen Stofan. (2017). 'The Next Earth: What Our World Can Teach Us about Other Planets'. *National Geographic*. New York: Time Inc. Books.
Kolbert, Elizabeth. (2014). *The Sixth Extinction: An Unnatural History*. London: Bloomsbury.

Milton, John. ([1973] 1979). *Paradise Lost*, A. E. Dyson and Julian Lovelock (eds.). London: MacMillan Casebook Series.
Okri, Ben. (1997). *A Way of Being Free*. London: Phoenix House.
Okri, Ben. (2009). *Tales of Freedom*. London: Rider.
Okri, Ben. (2011). *A Time for New Dreams*. Chatham: Random House.
Okri, Ben. (2012). *Wild*. London: Random House.
Okri, Ben. (2016). 'The Muse of Archaeology'. In C. Renfrew, M. Boyd and I. Morley (eds), *Death Rituals, Social Order and the Archaeology Immortality in the Ancient World*, 436–8. Cambridge: Cambridge University Press.
Okri, Ben. ([2017] 2019). 'The Standeruppers'. *Prayer for the Living*, 135–8. London: Head of Zeus.
Renfrew, C., M. Boyd and I. Morley, eds. (2016). *Death Rituals, Social Order and the Archaeology Immortality in the Ancient World*. Cambridge: Cambridge University Press.
Stevens, Anthony. (1998). *Ariadne's Clue*. London: Penguin.
Wilson, Edward O. (1992). *The Diversity of Life*. New York: W. W. Norton.
Wright, Derek. (1997). *New Directions in African Fiction*. New York: Twayne.
Yeats, William Butler. ([1933] 1955). *The Collected Poems of W. B. Yeats*. London: MacMillan.

15 Conscious reveries in *The Magic Lamp: Dreams of Our Age*

Anon. (2017). 'Review of *The Magic Lamp: Dreams of our Age*'. *The Times Literary Supplement*, 19 December.
Blake, William. (1966). 'London'. In Geoffrey Keynes (ed.), *The Complete Writings of William Blake*, 216. London: Oxford University Press.
Calvino, Italo. ([1988] 1992). *Six Memos for the Next Millennium*. London: Jonathan Cape.
Carroll, Lewis. (1887). 'Alice's Adventures in Wonderland'. *Alice in Wonderland and through the Looking Glass*, illustrated by Harry Rowntree. London: Collin's Clear-Type Press.
Chalmers, David. (1996). *The Conscious Mind*. London: Oxford University Press.
Coleridge, Samuel Taylor. (1909–14). 'On Poesy or Art'. In Charles W. Eliot (ed.), *English Essays: Sydney to Macaulay*. Howard Classics. Available online: https://www.bartleby.com/27/17.html/ (accessed 22 June 2018).
Flynn, Julia. (2018). 'Julia Flynn Reviews Starbook by Ben Okri'. *The Telegraph* 13 September 2007, n.p.
Grassom, Brian. (2016). 'Dream and Semblance: The Play of Art and Life'. *Analecta Husserliana: The Cosmic and the Creative Imagination*, CX1X: 59–71.
Gray, Rosemary. (2016). 'Promoting the Poetic Cause in Ben Okri's *Stokus* from *Tales of Freedom* (2009)'. *Literator*, 37 (1): 18–27.
Gray, Rosemary. (2018). 'Ben Okri's Stoku: "The Standeruppers" (2017): The Frightening Irony of the Anthropocene'. *Journal of Literary Studies*, 34 (2): 1–12.
Guthrie, W. K. C. ([1967] 1978). *The Greek Philosophers*. New York: Methuen.
Heidegger, Martin. ([1947] 1962). *Poetry, Language, Thought*. New York: Harper.
Mbao, Wamuvi. (2018). 'The Magic Lamp: Dream of Our Age Ben Okri, illustrated by Rosemary Clunie, 2017'. *Johannesburg Review of Books*, 20 March: 3 pp.

More, Max. (1990). 'Transhumanism: Towards a Futurist Philosophy'. *Entropy*, 6: 6–12.
Okri, Ben. (1991). *The Famished Road*. London: Jonathan Cape.
Okri, Ben. (1997). *A Way of Being Free*. London: Phoenix House.
Okri, Ben. (2017). *The Magic Lamp: Dreams of Our Age*. London: Head of Zeus.
Okri, Ben. (2018). *Rise like Lions*. London: Hodder and Stoughton.
Papineau, David, and Howard Selina. (2013). *Consciousness*. London: Icon Books.
Sandberg, Anders. (2014). 'Transhumanism and the Meaning of Life'. In Tracy Trothen and Calvin Mercer (eds), *Transhumanism and Religion: Moving into the Unknown Future*. Santa Barbara, CA: Praeger.
Seung, Sebastian. (2013). *Connectome: How the Brain's Wiring Makes Us Who We Are*, New York: Mariner Books.
Smith, David R. (2005). 'Rembrandt's Metaphysical Wit: *The Three Trees* and *The Omval*'. *Word [and] Image*, 21 (1): 1–21.
Smith, Jadwiga. (2011). 'The Cosmo-Transcendental Positioning of the Living Being in the Universe in Anna-Teresa Tymieniecka's New Enlightenment'. *Phenomenological Inquiry: Towards the Skies*, 35: 17–24.
Spence, Lewis. ([1915] 1922). *The Myths of Ancient Egypt*. London: George G. Harrap.
Stafecka, Mara. (1999). 'The Thinker as a Poet and the Poet as a Thinker: Heidegger and Pasternak'. In Anna-Teresa Tymieniecka (ed.), *Phenomenological Inquiry: The Range of Phenomenology on the Verge of the Third Millennium*, 49–57. Belmont, MA: World Institute for Phenomenological Research and Learning.
Stevens, Anthony. (1998). *Ariadne's Clue*. London: Penguin.
Tymieniecka, Anna-Teresa. (2011). *Transcendentalism Overturned: From Absolute Power of Consciousness until the Forces of Cosmic Architectonics*. Dordrecht: Springer.
Van der Post, Laurens. (1983). *A Mantis Carol*. Washington, DC: Island Press.
Wagner, Erica. (2018). 'The Magic Lamp by Ben Okri – after the Dream'. *Financial Times*, 20 March: 4 pp.

16 'The Incandescence of the Wind' (1982): 'Rain wisdom down upon this earth'

Camus, Albert. (1946). *L'Éstranger* (The Outsider), Stuart Gilbert (trans.). London: Hamish Hamilton.
Fraser, Robert. (2002). *Ben Okri: Towards the Invisible City*. Tavistock, Devon: Northcote House.
Fulcanelli. ([1964] 1971). *Les Mystère des Cathédrals*. London: Neville Spearman.
Okri, Ben. ([1979] 1989). *Flowers and Shadows*. Harlow: Longmans.
Okri, Ben. (1981). *The Landscapes Within*. Harlow: Longman.
Okri, Ben. (1982). 'The Incandescence of the Wind'. *An African Elegy* [1992] 1997: 35–7; and *Rise like Lions* 2018: 89–92.
Okri, Ben. ([1986] 1993). *Incidents at the Shrine*. London: Vintage.
Okri, Ben. ([1991] 1992). *The Famished Road*. London: Random House.
Okri, Ben. ([1992] 1997). *An African Elegy*. London: Vintage.
Okri, Ben. (1995). *Astonishing the Gods*. London: Phoenix House.
Okri, Ben. (1997). *A Way of Being Free*. London: Phoenix House.
Okri, Ben. (2011). *A Time for New Dreams*. Chatham: Random House.
Okri, Ben. (2018a). *The Outsider* (A dramatic adaptation of Camus' *L'Éstranger*).

Okri, Ben. (2018b). *Rise like Lions*. London: Hodder and Stoughton.
Okri, Ben. (2019). *The Freedom Artist*. London: Head of Zeus.
Roob, Alexander. (2014). *Alchemy and Mysticism*. Los Angeles, CA: Taschen.
Soyinka, Wole. (1996). *The Open Sore of a Continent*. New York: Oxford.
Stevens, Anthony. (1998). *Ariadne's Clue*. London: Penguin.
Turnbull, Joanna, ed. (2010). *Oxford Advanced Learner's Dictionary*, 8th ed. Oxford: Oxford University Press.

17 Protean magic in *The Mystery Feast* and *The Magic Lamp*

Calvino, Italo. ([1972] 1997). *Invisible Cities*. London: Vintage.
Copenhaver, Brian P. (2015). *Magic in Western Culture: From Antiquity to the Enlightenment*. New York: Cambridge University Press.
Dante, Alighieri. ([1939] 1975). *The Divine Comedy I: Inferno*, John D. Sinclair (trans.). London: Oxford University Press.
Eamon, William. (1994). 'Natural Magic and the Secrets of Nature'. In William Eamon (ed.), *Science and the Secrets of Nature*. Princeton, NJ: Princeton University Press.
Eliade, Mircea. (1954). *The Myth of Eternal Return*. London: Arkana.
Fraser, Robert. (2002). *Ben Okri: Towards the Invisible City*. Tavistock: Northcote House.
Frazer, James George. ([1922] 1991). *The Golden Bough*. London: Macmillan.
Gray, Rosemary. (2013). 'Ben Okri's *The Landscapes Within* (1981): The *Imaginatio Creatrix*'. *English Academy Review*, 30 (2): 21–31.
Gray, Rosemary. (2019). 'Of Magic: Ben Okri's *The Mystery Feast* and *The Magic Lamp*'. *Imbizo*, 10 (1): 1–15. Reused with permission.
Greenwood, Susan. (2009). *The Nature of Magic: An Anthology of Consciousness*. London: Berg.
Guthrie, W. K. C. ([1950] 1978). *The Greek Philosophers*. Norwich: Fletcher.
Hopkins, Gerard Manley. (1996). 'The Wreck of the *Deutschland*'. London: Phoenix.
Lenz, John R. (2017). 'Bertrand Russell on the Value of Philosophy for Life'. *Philosophy Now*, 120: 9–11.
Lincoln, Sarah. (2012). 'Petro-Magic Realism: Ben Okri's Inflationary Modernism'. In Mark A. Wollaeger and Matt Eatough (eds), *The Oxford Book of Global Modernisms*, 249–66. London: Routledge.
Merleau-Ponty, Maurice. (1968). *The Visible and the Invisible*, Alphonse Lingis (trans.). Evanston, IL: Northwestern University Press.
Okri, Ben. ([1995] 2002). *Astonishing the Gods*. London: Phoenix.
Okri, Ben. (2011). *A Time for New Dreams*. London: Random House.
Okri, Ben. (2012). *Wild*. London: Random House.
Okri, Ben. (2015). *The Mystery Feast*. West Hoathly: Clairview Press.
Okri, Ben. (2017). *The Magic Lamp*. London: Head of Zeus.
Okri, Ben. (2018). *Rise like Lions*. London: Hodder and Stoughton.
Ovid. (2004). *Metamorphoses*, Elaine Fantham (trans.). London: Penguin.
Reyburn, M. A. (1936). 'The Nature of Magic'. *The Critic*, IV (8): 135–42.
Roh, Franz. (1925). *Magical Realism: Post-Expressionism*, Wendy B. Faris (trans.), *Nach Expressionismus, Magischer Realismus: Probleme der neuesten Europäischen Malerei*. Leipzig: Klinkhardt and Biermann.

Shelley, Percy Bysshe. (2018). 'Ode to Liberty'. In Ben Okri (ed.), *Rise like Lions*, 147. London: Hodder & Stoughton.
Soyinka, Wole. ([1976] 1995). *Myth, Literature and the African World*. Cambridge: Cambridge University Press.
Spence, Lewis. ([1945] 1999). *The Magic Arts of Celtic Britain*. New York: Dover.
Stevens, Anthony. (1998). *Ariadne's Clue*. London: Penguin.
Van der Leeuw, Gerardus. (1933). *Phänomenologie der Religion*. Baden Württemberg: Tübingen University Press.
Virgil. (1990). *Aeneid*. London: Vintage.
Wells, H. G. ([1897] 2011). *The Invisible Man*. Harmondsworth: Penguin.
Wilson, Edward O. ([1992] 1993). *The Diversity of Life*. New York: Norton.
Zamora, Lois Parkinson, and Wendy B. Faris, eds. ([1995] 2005). *Magical Realism: Theory, History, Community*. Durham, NC: Duke University Press.

18 'An Interval in the Enchantment of Living': *The Age of Magic*

Anon. (2014). 'The Age of Magic Review: Giving Substance to the Abstract'. Available online: http://www.irishtimes.com/culture/books/the-age-of-magic-review-giving-substance-to-the-abstract/ (accessed 29 July 2016).
Barry, K. (1999). *The Greek Qabalah: Alphabetic Mysticism and Numerology*. Hong Kong: Samuel Weiser.
Camus, Albert. ([1939] 1959). *Noces suivi de l'été*. Paris: Gallimand.
Cheetham, T. (2003). *The World Turned Inside Out: Henry Corbin's and Islamic Mysticism*, Woodstock: Spring.
Corbin, H. (1971a). 'Color'. *Encylopaedia Iranica* XIV.2: n.p. Available online: http://www.iranicaonline.org/articles/color-persrang/ (accessed 22 October 2016).
Corbin, H. (1971b). *L'homme de lumière dans le soufisme iranien*, 2nd ed. Paris: Librairie de Medicis.
Corbin, H. (1972). *History of Islamic Philosophy*. London: Kegan Paul.
Gödel, Kurt. (1931). 'Über formal unentscheidbare Sätze der *Principia Mathematica* und verwandter Systeme, I'. *Monatshefte für Mathematik und Physik*, 38: 173–98.
Gray, R. (2007). 'Domesticating Infinity in Ben Okri's *Mental Fight* and *Astonishing the Gods*'. *English Academy Review: Southern African Journal of English Studies*, 24 (1): 85–101.
Gray, R. (2009a). 'Apologia Pro Ben Okri's *In Arcadia*: A Neglected Masterpiece'. *English Academy Review*, 26 (1): 41–52.
Gray, R. (2009b). 'A Moment in Timelessness: Ben Okri's *Astonishing the Gods* ([1995] 1999)'. In Anna-Teresa Tymieniecka (ed.), *Analecta Husserliana – Temporality in Life as Seen through Literature*, 41–52. Boston, MA: Springer.
Gray, R. (2016). 'Ben Okri's *The Landscapes Within* (1981): The Unfinished Story'. In A.-T. Tymieniecka (ed.), *The Cosmos and the Creative Imagination, Analecta Husserliana* 119, 73–83. Switzerland: Springer International.
Heidegger, M. (1927). *Being and Time*, Joan Staubaugh (trans.). New York: State University of New York Press.
Hofstadter, D. (2007). *I Am a Strange Loop*. New York: Basic Books.

Hoodwin, S. (n.d.). *The Journey of Your Soul*. Available online: http://209.85.135.104/search?q=cache:Ntj5kTT30cJ:www.michaelteachings.com/akashic_record/ (accessed 5 June 2007).
Johnson, J. P. ([1962] 1965). *The Path of the Masters*. Delhi: Radha Soami Satsung Beas.
Jones, E. D. (1973). *Idanre and Other Poems, the Writings of Wole Soyinka*. London: Heinemann.
László, E. (2004). *Science and the Akashic Field: An Integral Theory of Everything*. Rochester, VT: Inner Traditions.
Mann, T. ([1924] 1980). *The Magic Mountain*, H. T. Lowe-Porter (trans.). Harmondsworth: Penguin.
McMahan, D. (2006). *The Pursuit of Happiness*. London: Penguin.
Merleau-Ponty, M. (1968). *The Visible and the Invisible*. Evanston, IL: Northwestern University Press.
Okri, Ben. (1981). *The Landscapes Within*. London: Longman.
Okri, Ben. (2002). *In Arcadia*. London: Phoenix.
Okri, Ben. (2014). *The Age of Magic*. London: Head of Zeus.
Ramos, Manuel João. (2000). 'Introdução (excerto) do livro "Histórias Etíopes: Diário de Viagem" de M. J. Ramos'. Available online: http://diariografico.com/htm/outrosautores/Ramos/Ramos03.htm/ (accessed 2 November 2016).
Soyinka, Wole. (1973). *Idanre and Other Poems, the Writings of Wole Soyinka*. E. D. Jones ed. London: Heinemann.
Stables, W. (2016). 'Nothing Imperative: Late Beckett'. *Journal of Literary Studies*, 32 (2): 121–42.
Tymieniecka, A.-T. (1988). 'Logos and Life'. *Creative Experience and the Critique of Reason, Analecta Husserliana* XXIV. Dordrecht: Springer.
Tymieniecka, A.-T. (2000). 'Logos and Life'. In *Phenomenology of Life and the Human Creative Condition – Book IV, Analecta Husserliana* LV. Dordrecht: Springer.
Wilson, M. (2015). 'The "magic of moments": Ben Okri Slow Reading and His New Novel'. *The Conversation*, 27 May: 1. Available online: https://theconversation.com/the-magic-of-moments-ben-okri-on-slow-reading-and-his-new-novel-42399 (accessed 29 July 2016).

19 When chaos is the god of an era: Rediscovering an 'axis mundi' in *Starbook*

Abrams, M. H. ([1957] 1999). *A Glossary of Literary Terms*. Fort Worth: Harcourt Brace College.
Armah, Ayi Kwei. ([1978] 1979). *Two Thousand Seasons*. Oxford: Heinemann.
Bennet, Robert. (1998). 'Ben Okri (1959–)'. In Puspa Naidu and Jayne Sigma Fatima (eds), *Postcolonial African Writers: A Bio-Biographical Critical Sourcebook*, 1–3. Available online: https://trove.nla.gov.au/work/22668337 (accessed 10 December 2006).
Betancourt, Ingrid. (2010). *Even Silence Has an End*. London: Virago.
Brown, Ben. (2007). 'Some Day Her Prince Will Come'. *The Observer*, 19 August: 2.
Carew, Jan. (1985). 'In Memorium: Alex La Guma'. *Mail & Guardian*.
Carroll, Lewis. (1887). 'Alice's Adventures in Wonderland'. *Alice in Wonderland and through the Looking Glass*. Illustrated by Harry Rountree (ed.). London: Collin's Clear-Type Press.

Coleridge, Samuel Taylor. (1909–14). 'On Poesy or Art'. In Charles W. Eliot (ed.), *English Essays: Sydney to Macaulay*, Howard Classics. Available online: https://www.bertleby.com/27/17.html/ (accessed 22 June 2018).
Chennells, Anthony. (2006). 'Representing Africa: Revisiting African Realism of the 1960s and 1970s'. *The English Academy Review: Southern African Journal of English Studies*, 23: 48–58.
de Certeau, Michel. (1984). *The Practice of Everyday Life*. Berkeley: University of California Press.
Deleuze, Gilles, and Rosalind Kraus. (1983). 'Plato and the Simulacrum'. *October*, 27: 45–56. Available online: http://www.jstor.org/stable/778495 (accessed 3 April 2020).
Eliade, Mircea. ([1954] 1989). *The Myth of Eternal Return*. London: Penguin.
Fodor, Jerry. (2011). 'Fire the Press Secretary'. *London Review of Books*, 24, 28 April.
Gray, Rosemary. (1997). 'Ayi Kwei Armah's *Two Thousand Seasons*: From Idea to Idealism.' In A.-T. Tymieniecka (ed.), *Analecta Husserliana*. 'Passion of Place' Book ll, Vol. LI, 161–71. Dortrecht: Kluwer Academic.
Gray, Rosemary. (2000). 'Counterpoint in Print: Okot p'Bitek's *Song of Lawino* and *Song of Ocol*.' In A.-T. Tymieniecka (ed.), *Analecta Husserliana: The Aesthetic Discourse of the Arts*, Vol. 61, 87–102. Dordrecht: Kluwer Academic.
Gray, Rosemary. (2001). 'Divinatory Simulacra in the Novels of Margaret Atwood'. In Jeff Barnard and Gloria Withalm (eds), *Myths, Rites, Simulacra: Semiotic Viewpoints*, 2: 853–96. Wein: Die Deutche Bibliothek.
Gray, Rosemary. (2007). '"Domesticating Infinity" in Ben Okri's *Mental Fight* and *Astonishing the Gods*', *The English Academy Review: Southern African Journal of English Studies*, 24 (1): 71–84.
Gray, Rosemary. (2009). 'Apologia Pro Ben Okri's *In Arcadia*'. *The English Academy Review: Southern African Journal of English Studies*, 26 (1): 41–52.
Gray, Rosemary. (2012). 'Interview with Ben Okri', 11 February 2011, London'. *Journal of Literary Studies*, 28 (4): 4–13.
Gray, Rosemary. (2013). 'When Chaos Is the God of an Era: Rediscovering an *Axis Mundi* in Ben Okri's *Starbook* (2007)'. *Research in African Literatures*, 44 (1): 128–45. Reused and revised with permission.
Greenblat, Stephen, ed. (2001). 'The Power of Forms in the English Renaissance'. In Vincent B. Leitch (ed.), *The Norton Anthology of Literature and Criticism*. New York: Norton.
Gurnah, Abdulrazah, ed. (1995). *Essays on African Writing 2: Contemporary Literature*. Oxford: Heinemann.
Hollander, Lee M., trans. ([1962] 2008). *The Poetic Edda*, Austin: University of Texas Press.
Holmes, Ernest S. ([1919] 1938). *Creative Mind*. New York: McBride.
Holroyd, Stuart. (1989). *The Arkana Dictionary of New Perspectives*. London: Penguin.
Killam, D., and R. Rowe. (2000). *The Companion to African Literatures*. Oxford: James Curry.
Knappert, Jan. ([1991] 1995). *Enclopaedia of Myth and Legend: Indian Mythology*. London: Diamond Books.
Larue, Gerald A. (1975). *Ancient Myth and Modern Man*. Englewood Cliffs, NJ: Prentice Hall.
Low, Douglas. (2011). 'Merleau-Ponty's Enchanted Nature'. *Phenomenological Inquiry*, 35: 49–90.
Milstead, C. (1998). 'The Zen of Modern Poetry: Reading Eliot, Stevens, and Williams in a Zen Context', Unpublished doctoral thesis. Knoxville: University of Tennessee.

Ngugi wa Thiong'o. ([1967] 1986). *A Grain of Wheat*. London: Heinemann.
Ogola, Margaret. (1994). *The River and the Source*. Nairobi: Focus Books.
Okri, Ben. (1988). *Stars of the New Curfew*. London: Penguin.
Okri, Ben. (1991). *The Famished Road*. London: Jonathan Cape.
Okri, Ben. (1993). *Songs of Enchantment*. London: Random House.
Okri, Ben. (1996). *Birds of Heaven*. London: Phoenix.
Okri, Ben. (1997). *A Way of Being Free*. London: Phoenix.
Okri, Ben. (1998). *Infinite Riches*. London: Phoenix.
Okri, Ben. (1999). *Mental Fight*. London: Phoenix.
Okri, Ben. (2007). *Starbook*. Chatham: Random House.
Okri, Ben. (2011). *A Time for New Dreams*. Chatham: Random House.
Ousmane, Sembene. ([1962] 1970). *God's Bits of Wood*, Francis Price (trans.). Oxford: Heinemann Educational.
P'Bitek, Okot. ([1966] 1967). *Song of Lawino and Song of Ocol*. Oxford: Heinemann.
Quayson, Ato. (1995). 'Esoteric Webwork as Nervous System: Reading the Fantastic in Ben Okri's Writing'. In Abdulrazah Gurnah (ed.), *Essays on African Writing 2: Contemporary Literature*, 144–58. Oxford: Heinemann.
Ready, William. ([1969] 1973). *Understanding Tolkien and the Lord of the Rings*. New York: Warner.
Serrao, Angelique. (2010). 'A Sense of Self Based on Books'. Available online: https://farafinabooks.wordpress.com/2010/06/ (accessed 31 March 2007).
Sethi, Anita. (2007). 'Starbook: A Magical Tale of Love and Regeneration'. *The Independent*, 26 August.
White, Hayden. (1973). *Metahistory: The Historical Imagination in Nineteenth-Century Europe*. Baltimore, MD: Johns Hopkins University Press.
Williams, Michael. (1986). *Jane Austen: Six Novels and Their Methods*. Basingstoke: MacMillan.
•Originally published in 2013. 'When Chaos Is the God of an Era: Rediscovering an "Axis Mundi" in Ben Okri's *Starbook* (2007)'. *Research in African Literatures*, 44 (1): 128–45. Reused with permission from the publisher.

20 In conversation with Ben Okri

Achebe, Chinua. ([1962] 1976). *Things Fall Apart*. London: Heinemann Educational Books.
Angelou, Maya. (1993). *I Know Why the Caged Bird Sings*. New York: Bantam Books.
Armah, Ayi Kwei. ([1978] 1979). *Two Thousand Seasons*. Oxford: Heinemann.
Coetzee, J. M.(1981). *Waiting for the Barbarians*. Johannesburg: Ravan Press.
Emechetta, Buchi. ([1982] 1984). *Double Yoke*. London: Fontana.
Gray, R. A. (1999). 'The Music under the Stone: A Reading of Alex la Guma's *The Stone Country*'. In Andrew Foley (ed.), *English at the Turn of the Millennium*, 87–93. Randburg: English Academy of Southern Africa.
Gray, Rosemary. (2007). 'Domesticating Infinity'. In Ben Okri's *Mental flight* and *Astonishing the Gods*. *The English Academy Review*, 24 (1) May: 85–101.
Gray, Rosemary. (2009). 'Apologia Pro Ben Okri's *In Arcadia*: A Neglected Masterpiece?' *English Academy Review: Southern African Journal of English Studies*, 26 (1): 65–71.

Gray, Rosemary. (2012). 'Interview with Ben Okri.' 11 Feb. 2011, London. *Journal of Literary Studies*, 28 (4): 4–13.
Jauss, Hans Robert. (1997). 'Hans Robert Jauss: Literary Theory as a Challenge to Literary Theory.' In K. M. Newton (ed.), *Twentieth Century Literary Theory*, 189–94. London: Palgrave.
La Guma, A. (1991). *The Stone Country*. Cape Town: David Philip.
Llosa, Mario Vargas. (2010). 'In Praise of Reading and Fiction.' Nobel Lecture, 7 December. Unpublished.
Marachera, Dambudzo. (1980). *Black Sunlight*. Oxford: Heinemenn.
Ngugi wa Thiong'o. ([1967] 1986). *A Grain of Wheat*. London: Heinemann.
Okri, Ben. (1991). *The Famished Road*. London: Jonathan Cape.
Okri, Ben. (1993). *Songs of Enchantment*. London: Random House.
Okri, Ben. (1996). *Birds of Heaven*. London: Phoenix.
Okri, Ben. (1997). *A Way of Being Free*. London: Phoenix.
Okri, Ben. (1998). *Infinite Riches*. London: Phoenix.
Okri, Ben. (1999). *Mental Fight*. London: Phoenix.
Okri, Ben. ([1995] 1999). *Astonishing the Gods*. London: Phoenix House.
Okri, Ben. (2003). 'The New Dark Age.' *The Guardian* 19 April, p. 1.
Okri, Ben. (2007). *Starbook*. Chatham: Random House.
Okri, Ben. (2009). *Tales of Freedom*. London: Rider.
Okri, Ben. (2012). 'Biko and the Tough Alchemy of Africa.' *UCT News* 13 September.
Pope, Alexander. ([1711] 1977). 'Essay on Criticism.' In John Butt (ed.), *The Poems of Alexander Pope*, 143–68. London: Methuen.
Soyinka, Wole. (1965). *The Road*. Oxford: Oxford University Press.
Soyinka, Wole. (1988). *Art, Dialogue and Outrage: Essays on Literature and Culture*. Ibadan: New Horn.

Index

'Akibu', defined xv, 10, 28, 50, 58, 74, 189, 200, 205–6, 213–14, 236
Achebe, Chinua (1930–2013) 117–20, 125–7, 129, 205, 214–16, 234, 236, 254–6, 265
Adichie, Chimamanda 126
Adonis *see* Said, Ali Ahmed
Aesop/ic 40–1, 227
Akashic, still points/records 47, 49–55, 188, 214–15, 227, 231, 238, 248, 263
alchemy/ical i, iii, vii, xi, xiii, xiv, 1, 3, 6–7, 10, 17–18, 20, 27, 57, 62, 73, 141, 160–1, 164–6, 169–70, 174, 179, 182, 184, 188, 191, 193, 199, 209–10, 223, 261, 266
allegory xi, 26, 36, 50, 89, 160, 164, 166, 189, 194, 201, 210, 239
Amadi, Elechi 126
Angelou, Maya (1928–2014) 214, 226, 246–7, 265
Anthropocene iii, 133, 149–51, 154–5, 235, 256, 258–9
aphorism/s vii, xii–xiv, xxi, 3–11, 15, 21, 28, 70, 77, 103, 113, 123, 125, 141–8, 151, 153, 158, 164, 177, 181, 223, 243, 250, 255, 257–8
Apollo (Greek god) 105–6
Arcadia/n vii, xiii, 15, 20, 48–9, 51–5, 164, 187–9, 191, 193–8, 228, 248
Ariadne xxi, 158, 183, 235, 246, 251, 257, 259–62
Aristotle (B.C. 384–322) 16, 101, 106, 226, 233, 245–6, 253, 257
Austen, Jane (1775–1817) 201, 205, 211, 214, 265
'axis mundi' viii, 72, 103, 111–12, 165, 199, 201–2, 206–8, 212, 239, 244–5, 250, 254, 263–5

Bargna, Ivan 77, 250
Barthes, Roland (1915–1980) 74, 77, 79, 82, 250

Bashō, Matsuo (1644–1694) 91, 232
Bauckham, Richard 10, 224, 243
Baudelaire, Charles (1821–1867) 199
Beckett, Samuel (1906–1989) 39, 43, 87, 227, 247, 263
  Comédie 33, 246
  Endgame 40, 246
  Play 33, 37, 39–42, 246
  Waiting for Godot 39, 227
Bellow, Saul (1915–2005) 63
Benin 38, 74, 210
Berger, John (1926–2017) 73–4, 77, 219, 229, 249–50
Berkeley, George (1685–1753) Philosophical Idealism 65
Bhabha, Homi (1909–1966) xvi, 36, 246
Bible 4, 63, 184, 244
  Deut. 4, 224, 243
  Jas 10
  Jos. 20
  Lev. 7
  Phil. 106
  Prov. 4, 8, 223
  Rev. 27, 63, 103, 106
Blake, William (1757–1827) xiii, 28, 30, 47, 60, 92, 103, 106, 113, 143, 161, 172, 184, 209, 218, 228, 233, 259
Buddhism 29, 239, 246
Bunyan, John (1628–1688) 249
  The Pilgrim's Progress 67, 89–90, 249
Burgess, Anthony (1917–1993) 90, 252
Byron, (Lord) George G. (1788–1824) 183

Calvino, Italo 159, 161–5, 229–30, 238, 249, 259, 261
Campbell, Joseph (1904–1987) 104, 253
Camus, Albert (1913–1960) 74, 79, 234, 250, 255, 260, 262
  L'Éstranger 168, 260

Noces 187
The Myth of Sisyphus xv, 145, 234, 250
Carroll, Lewis (Charles Ludwig Dodgson) (1832–1898) 94, 161, 199, 229, 232, 249, 259, 263
  Alice in Wonderland 65, 161
Chaos/Chaos theory viii, 18, 20–2, 58, 64, 103–4, 109, 111, 113, 115–16, 130, 141, 153, 164, 199, 202–3, 208–10, 212, 239, 244–5, 250, 254, 263–5
Chaucer, Geoffrey (c. 1345–1400) 145
  The Nun's Priest's Tale 227
Chopra, Deepak 57, 249
Christian/ity, xiv 4, 8, 19–20, 27, 39, 42, 51, 59, 63, 79, 183–4, 193, 215, 218, 225, 240, 249
Christie, Agatha (1890–1976) 246
  The Mousetrap 42, 246
civilization xv, 18–19, 28, 31, 36, 64–5, 67–8, 104, 107, 131, 150, 215, 219–20, 237, 246
civil war/internecine strife xii, 20, 33–5, 71–3, 78, 96, 117–25, 127, 167–8, 170, 226, 232, 236, 255–6
Clunie, Rosemary ii, xxiii, 4, 157, 159–65, 179, 183, 226, 233, 235, 259
Coleridge, Samuel Taylor (1772–1834) 79–80, 165, 199, 250, 254, 259, 264
  Aids to Reflection 79
consciousness xi, xv, xvi–vii, 3, 7, 13, 15, 18, 20–1, 25–6, 28–30, 51–2, 58, 60, 62, 65, 69, 71, 73–5, 79–82, 85–7, 93, 95, 101–4, 106, 109, 112, 119–21, 123, 125, 129–31, 134, 136–7, 141, 145–6, 151–2, 155, 157–65, 168–9, 173, 177, 179–82, 185–6, 188, 190, 196–7, 200–1, 203, 209–10, 214, 217, 219, 227, 236, 256, 260–1
Corbin, Henry (1903–1978) 190–1, 239, 262
Covid-19 pandemic, xv

Dante, Alighieri (1265–1321) 40, 42, 192
  The Divine Comedy 31, 33, 34–6, 118, 180, 218, 220, 238, 246, 255, 261
Darwin, Charles (1809–1882) 235, 237
decolonial/ity xii, xv–vi, 130, 137
Deleuze, Gilles (1925–1995) 63–6, 199
demiurge, defined 99

De Sausseur, Ferdinand (1857–1913) 234
Dolêzel, Lubomir 62–3, 66, 249
Donne, John (1573–1631) 150, 258
Dorsch, T. E. (1926–1998) 142–8, 235, 257
dream/s xv, xvi, xxi, 3, 4, 7, 16, 20, 22, 26, 27, 29, 37, 40, 43
  dream logic 41, 43, 50–2, 54, 59, 61–2, 65–9
  re-dreaming 69–73, 76–82, 89, 101–3, 106–7, 109, 110–12, 122–3, 130–5, 137, 147–9, 152, 154–5, 157–9, 161, 163–5, 194–6, 199, 207–8, 210, 217–19, 231, 259–60
dreamtime 71, 78, 160, 195

eco-phenomenology xi, 14–18, 97, 101–2, 104, 106–7, 188, 233, 253, 256
Eden/ic xii, 35–8, 40–1, 48, 50–2, 192, 194, 205, 208, 256, 258
Egungun 122, 124–5
Eliade, Mircea (1907–1986) 113, 178, 181–2, 186, 203, 205–6, 208, 217, 238, 240, 254, 261, 264
  The Myth of Eternal Return 113, 199
Eliot T. S. (1888–1965) xiii, 52, 228, 230, 249, 264
Emechetta, Buchi 126, 215, 265
Ephesus 13, 18, 20, 234, 244, 251, 256
epiphanic moment/s/epiphanies 3, 38, 63, 85, 91, 96, 98, 115, 151, 164, 196–7, 204
Erasmus, Desiderius (1466–1536) 3–5, 144–5, 243, 257
Escher, Max (1898–1972) 55, 238

fable 4, 7, 16, 33–8, 40–3, 64, 106, 160, 162–3, 177, 189, 202, 227, 243, 246, 255
fairy tale 7, 89, 93, 157–8, 162–5, 184, 205, 239
Fanon, Franz (1925–1961) 106, 253
feminism xix, 16–17
Fowler, Roger 5–6, 243
fractals/'metagage' 36, 109–10, 178
Fraser, Robert 173, 181, 236–7, 260–1
Frazer (Sir) James (1854–1941) 177–9, 183
  The Golden Bough 178, 261
freedom 9, 18, 30, 33, 51, 85–91, 95–6, 104, 111, 115, 117–19, 121, 123, 125–7,

141, 168, 183, 185, 194–5, 203, 207, 210, 214, 217–18, 228, 232, 236–7
Frost, Robert (1874–1963) 18–19, 225, 244

Gadamer, Hans-Georg (1900–2002) 113, 254
genre studies xvi
Gibran, Kahil 59, 230, 249
Gödel, Kurt (1906–1978) 190, 262
Goethe, Johann Wolfgang (1749–1837) 195
Green Man icon 184, 192
Griot *see* shaman
Guattari, Félix (1930–1992) 63–6, 229, 249
Gunn, Alexander 57, 249

'haiku' xvi, 85–91, 93–4, 97, 151–3, 232, 252
Handel, George Frederick (1685–1759) 26
Hawking, Stephen (1942–2018) 229, 249
Heese, Marie 85, 87–9, 91, 93, 151–2, 252, 258
Hegel, Georg Wilhelm Fredrich (1770–1831) 17, 20
Heidegger, Martin (1889–1976) 5, 16, 97, 114, 160, 190, 195, 225, 234, 244, 259–60, 262
  'Dasein' 5, 97, 109, 114–15, 195, 225
Hemingway, Ernest (1899–1961) 146, 257
Heraclitus (6th century B.C.E.) xvii, 13–16, 18–22, 35, 38, 109–10, 131, 137, 145, 223–5, 234, 244–5, 251, 256
hermetic/ism 29, 58, 65, 67
hermeneutics xxi, 16, 114, 136, 195, 254
Herodotus (5th century B.C.E.) 18
heterocosmica 63, 249
history xii, xv, xvii, xxv, 27–8, 33–5, 39, 53, 64, 66, 68, 70, 78, 80, 102–4, 106, 110, 112, 117–18, 120, 127, 130, 134, 142, 149–50, 152, 154, 162–3, 181–91, 194, 196, 205, 215–16, 218, 238, 249, 254, 256, 258, 262
Hofstadter, Douglas 187, 190–1, 193, 238, 262
holocaust 117–19
Homer/ic (9th century B.C.E.) xix, xv, 18, 21, 36, 158, 225, 237

Hopkins, Gerard Manley (1841–1889) 180, 237, 261
Hughes, Ted (1930–1998) 77, 231, 250
humanism 21
Husserl, Edmund (1859–1938) 16, 26, 29, 244

Igbo 64, 71, 117–19, 123, 125, 217, 229, 232
illumination xvii, 15, 21–2, 30, 35–6, 38, 40, 59, 61, 67, 72, 78, 85, 87, 89, 98, 106, 110, 113, 115, 137, 143, 151, 153, 193, 203–4, 206, 209, 218
'Imaginatio Creatix' [creative imagination/ heightened creativity], defined xi, 3, 35, 137, 142, 186, 223, 261
indigenous/knowledge systems xv, 7, 19, 58, 64, 132, 177, 201, 233
initiation 47, 57–8, 61, 65–7, 152, 172, 185, 205
intuition/intuitive/ly vii, xi, xv–vi, xix, 3, 14, 28, 31, 47, 50–2, 55, 67, 69–70, 72–4, 76, 78–9, 81–2, 87, 92–3, 101, 121, 142, 144, 151–2, 158–60, 164, 168, 173, 177, 180–1, 185–6, 189–91, 195–6, 207, 209, 231, 233–4, 250, 257
intuitive imaginary 17
invisible/invisibility/visible/visibility xiv, 5, 8, 49, 51, 53, 57, 59, 61–6, 68–9, 73–4, 79, 87–8, 101, 114, 153, 163–4, 177, 181–2 184–5, 188, 192, 196–7, 209, 229, 249, 251, 260–3

Jauss, Hans Robert (1921–1997) 213, 266
Jesus 10, 145, 180, 233, 257
Jeyifo, Biodun 119, 126
Joyce, James (1882–1941) 47, 147
Jung, Carl Gustav (1875–1961) 69, 79, 82–3, 158, 195, 215, 250
justice xx, 9, 21, 33, 35–7 43, 60, 66, 90, 118, 168, 173, 217, 226, 230, 237, 245

Kamwangamalu, N. H. 225, 245
Kant, Immanuel (1724–1804) 29
Keats, John (1795–1821) 43, 65, 103–5
  negative capability 113, 182, 233–4, 247, 254
King, Martin Luther (1929–1968) 111, 145
Kolbert, Elizabeth 133–4, 149, 150–1, 154–5, 256, 258

Kristeva, Julia 121-2, 122, 124-6, 234, 255
Kundera, Milan 80, 82, 117-22, 124-5, 231, 250, 255
Kunene, Mazizi 123, 255

Lacan, Jacques (1901-1981) 59, 249
La Guma, Alex (1924-1985) 240, 266
Langland, William (c. 1332-c.1400)
  Piers Plowman 89-90
Lao Tzû 7, 55, 145, 238
László Ervin 53, 238, 248, 263
laughter/metaphysical laughter 76, 102, 117-19, 121-2, 124-6, 136, 143, 168-9, 208-10, 232, 234-6, 240, 254-6
Leakey, (Dr) Louis (1903-1972) 130-2
Leakey, (Sir) Richard 130, 132
Leavis, F. R. (1895-1978) 135, 256
Lévi-Straus, Claude (1908-2009) 112, 254
Lewis, C. S. (1898-1963) 89, 247, 252
Llosa, Mario Vargas 31, 216, 219, 245, 266
lodestar, defined 139, 166, 173
Logos 7, 14-16, 21-2, 26, 28, 41, 105, 134, 188, 206, 226, 231, defined 234, 246, 263
Longinus, Casius (213-273) 142-8, 257
loss v, xv, 27, 63, 73-4, 77-8, 81-2, 92, 111, 119, 121, 124, 150, 183-4, 232, 238
love xv, xvi, 4-6, 8-9, 15, 17, 19, 28, 36, 38, 40-1, 43, 50-1, 63, 68, 70-1, 80, 97, 102-3, 111, 114, 155, 164, 168-9, 171, 173, 179, 188, 191, 195, 203-6, 208, 211, 218, 227, 232-3, 240, 250-1, 265
Lyotard, Jean-Francois (1925-1998) 112, 254

Mafeje, Archie 233, 253
magic viii, xvii, 21, 30, 37, 47, 64, 85, 94, 96, 102-4, 106, 112, 114-15, 135, 141-2, 147, 153-4, 159-65, 177-88, 190, 193, 202, 207-8, 210, 217, 229, 237, 240, 261-3
magical realism/t xi, 62, 179-80, 201-2, 237, 262
Magritte, René (1898-1967) xxiii, 75-7, 79, 80
Mann, Thomas (1875-1955) 187-9, 189, 233, 238
  The Magic Mountain 187-8, 195, 263

Marx, Karl (1818-1883), Marxism/t 20, 104, 111
Maslow, Abraham 115
Maya-Pearce, Adewole 78, 250
Mbembe, Achile 59, 62, 106, 249, 253
Merleau-Ponty, Maurice (1908-1961) 181-2, 184-5, 189, 193, 196, 245, 261, 263-4
Milton, John (1608-1674) 150, 196, 259
modernity/modernism xi, xii-iii, xv, 34-5, 48, 180, 186, 223, 247, 261
music vii, xv, 3-4, 16, 21-2, 25-7, 50, 52, 68, 77-9, 86, 92-3 , Mozart effect 96, 101-2, 105-6, 111-13, 121-2, 133, 142, 151-2, 160, 164, 170, 183-4, 202-4, 207-8, 211-12, 216, 223, 227, 231, 243-4, 248, 250, 254-5, 257-8, 256
mysticism 55, 65, 70, 190-1, 193, 223, 261-2
mystical 17-18, 37, 50, 53, 61-2, 64-6, 68-71, 73, 77, 80, 82, 91, 101, 104, 107, 144-5, 161, 187, 192-3, 237-8
myth/s vii, xiii, xiv, 1, 4, 5, 7-8, 16, 31, 37, 39, 58-9, 61, 64, 67-8, 72, 82-3, 86, 89, 103, 105, 113-14, 123, 131, 136, 153, 155, 165, 173, 177-80, 182, 184-6, 188, 190-1, 193, 201-2, 210-12, 214, 217, 219, 225, 228, 237, 239-40, 244-6, 250, 252, 254, 256, 260-2, 264

names/naming 34, 41, 170, 172, 191, 193
Nature xii, xiv, xvi, 4, 8, 15, 19, 26-7, 34-5, 43, 51, 54, 60, 70, 81, 85, 88-9, 92, 101-2, 105, 110, 112, 132-3, 149, 151-4, 162, 165, 171, 179-85, 190-2, 196-7, 203-4, 209, 225, 231, 244-5, 261, 264
Newton, Isaac (1643-1727) xiv, 229
Ngugi wa Thiong'o (1939-2013) 35, 130, 201, 215, 247, 257, 265-6
Nietzsche, Frederick (1844-1900) xvi, 130, 228
Nigeria xv, 70-2, 74, 104, 117-19, 123, 126, 146, 167, 169-70, 223, 229, 236, 255
Nigerian Civil War (1967-70) 33-4, 71, 117-20, 124, 126-7, 168, 172, 226, 232, 236, 255
  Biafra 34, 71, 96, 111, 117, 119-20, 125, 146, 167, 232, 234, 236, 255-6

Norse/Scandanavian sagas 202–5, 210, 212, 239
  Epic of Gilgamesh 34
  Lay of Rig 202, 204
  Poetic Edda 202–3, 264
  Prophecy of the Seer/ess 203, 211
  Prose Edda of Snorri 202–3
Ntuli, Pitika 70–1, 251
numerology 9, 62, 64, 192–3, 262

Obiechina, Emmanuel 6–7, 10, 243
Odysseus 145
Ofeinum, Odia xv
Ogun (Yoruba god), defined 121, 225
Okri, Ben
  An African Elegy (1992) 25–8, 30, 43, 68, 132, 167, 245, 260
  Astonishing the Gods ([1995] 2015) 53, 57–64, 68, 88, 170, 217, 219, 228, 248, 252, 262, 264–5
  A Time for New Dreams (2011) vii, 3, 5–9, 14, 21–2, 25, 28–30, 69–70, 76–7, 82, 85, 87, 105, 116, 129–30, 135, 137, 144, 151, 154, 173, 226, 243, 245, 251–4, 257, 258–61, 265
  A Way of Being Free ([1997] 2015) viii, xiv, 9, 15, 29, 31, 33, 36–7, 48, 54, 58, 62–3, 69, 71, 73–4, 82, 93–4, 97, 101, 103–4, 118, 125. 141, 144, 146, 153, 161, 168, 170, 199, 210, 219, 235, 243, 245, 247–9, 251–3, 255, 257–60, 265–6
  Birds of Heaven (1996) 1, 3–6, 10–11, 48, 52, 87, 90, 144, 203, 206, 211, 214, 223, 226
  Comédie (2010) 41
  Dangerous Love ([1996] 2015) 71, 232, 250–1
  Flowers and Shadows (1979) 170
  In Arcadia ([2002] 2015) xiii, xxi, 15, 47–8, 52–3, 69, 92, 187–8, 193–4, 227, 244, 247–8, 250, 262, 264–5
  Incidents at the Shrine ([1986] 1993) 117–18, 168
  Mental Fight (1999) 28–30, 47, 57–8, 60, 62, 68, 202, 206, 218, 228, 233, 245, 248, 252, 262, 264
  Prayer for the Living (2019) 259
  Rise Like Lions (2018) 159, 167, 170–1, 173, 184, 260
  Songs of Enchantment (1993) xv, 28, 58, 200, 213
  Starbook (2007) 33, 37–8, 40, 47, 72, 111, 157, 199, 201–12, 214, 217, 219–20, 226–7, 239, 245, 259, 263–5
  Stars of the New Curfew (1988) 203, 223, 232
  Tales of Freedom (2009) 9, 33, 85. 87, 89, 94–5, 118, 151, 217, 232, 247, 251–2, 258–9
  'The Comic Destiny' 33, 35–9, 41–3, 87, 118, 226–7, 243, 246, 255
  The Age of Magic (2014) 36, 71, 80–1, 153, 180, 187–9, 192–5, 236, 238–9, 247, 251, 262–3
  The Famished Road (1991) xv, 9–10, 16, 21, 47, 58, 74, 120, 131, 165, 170, 200–1, 205, 214, 223, 226, 228, 243, 245, 247–9, 255, 257, 259, 260, 265–6
  The Freedom Artist (2019) 9, 120, 170, 243, 255, 261
  The Landscapes Within (1981) ix, 35, 69–72, 75–82, 109, 111, 170, 195, 231–2, 247, 250–2, 254, 260–3
  The Magic Lamp: Dreams of Our Age (2017) viii, 4, 146, 157, 159–62, 165, 177, 179–80, 182, 185, 235–8, 259–61
  'The Muse of Archaeology' (2016) 129, 134, 136, 149, 156, 257, 259
  The Mystery Feast (2015) 62, 69, 73–4, 177, 237, 247, 249, 251, 261
  The Outsider (2018) 168, 260
  Wild (2012) xv, 13–14, 18, 70, 102, 104, 109, 111, 116, 129–32, 134, 141, 155, 180, 223–4, 234–5, 237, 244, 253, 256
Olu-Oloabi, K. 126, 255
Omotoso, Kole 121, 255
ontopoiesis/ontopoietic, defined xiv, 4–5, 7–8, 16, 18, 22–33, 25–6, 28, 30, 69, 74, 80, 86–7, 93, 97, 101, 103, 105, 109, 120, 135, 137, 144, 158, 163, 179, 185, 188, 197, 226, 231, 234, 245–6, 252–3
oral/tradition xvii, 26, 145, 147
Ovid, Publius Ovidus Nosa (43 B.C.–17 B.C.) 161, 179–80, 183

Paracelsus, Theothrastus von Hohenheim (1493–1541) xiv, 106
  'Tria Prima' defined xiii–iv, 193
Paradise xvii, 20, 35, 38, 41, 48, 51, 67, 93, 150, 183, 191–2, 194, 211, 243
paradox/ical xvii, 6–8, 10, 14, 16, 18–19, 27, 40, 65–6, 81, 86–7, 89, 91–5, 97, 103, 116, 118, 126, 133, 144, 147, 151–2, 183, 191, 193–5, 208–10, 216
paremiology, defined xii, 3, 10, 141–2, 148, 235, 243, 257
Perennial Tradition 58, 65, 228, 231, 248–9
petro-magic-realism/petro-fiction 71, 79, 119, 223, 261
phenomenology 8, 16, defined 26, 28–9, 69, 97, 101, 106, 114, 120, 231, 244, 246, 252–3, 260, 263
Philosopher's stone 180, 188
Plato (B.C 427–347 B.C.E.) 59, 69, 78, 80, 122, 142–3, 159, 162, 182, 196, 200, 202, 214, 249, 251, 258, 264
Pope, Alexander (1688–1744) 215, 266
postcolonial/ity xi–xii, xv–xvi, xix, 36, 38, 199, 214, 223, 249, 263
postmodernism/postmodernist/ity xiii, 3, 41, 66, 86, 88, 109–11, 114–16, 145, 148, 179, 183, 208, 210, 247, 253
post-structuralist 88
Poussin, Nicolas (1594–1665) 47, 50, 52, 188
  Les Bergers d'Arcadie 15, 47, 52–3, 55, 188, 194
Prometheus 136, 145
Proteus/ean 177, 184–6, 212, 237, 261
protorationalism/ist 33, 35, 158
proto-reality 41, 69, 72
Proust, Marcel (1871–1922) xx, 39
Pushkin, Alexander (1800–1837)
  Eugene Onegin 95
Pythagoras/Pythagorean (c. 570 B.C. –495 B.C.E.) 180, 237

Quayson, Ato 35, 58, 62, 64, 201, 239, 247, 250, 265

Ra (Egyptian Sun god) 103, 105–6, 113
Riccoeur, Paul (1913–2005) 116
river/s 15–17, 21–2, 25, 33–4, 65, 94, 102–3, 106, 110, 112, 121, 124, 131, 133, 148, 164, 180, 185, 192, 194, 204–5, 208, 218, 225
riverbed/s 20, 169–72
Robbe-Grillet, Alain (1922–2008) 48, 148
Roh, Franz (1890–1965) 180, 237, 261
romantic/ism xiii, 8, 26, 43, 54, 88
Rowley, George 54–5, 69–70, 74, 82, 248, 251
Russell, Bertrand (1872–1970) 103, 143, 179, 234, 253, 258, 261

sacred geometry 48, 111, 180, 189
Said, Ali Ahmed, 26–7, a.k.a 'Adonis' 86, 97–8, 245, 252
Saro-Wiwa, Ken (1941–1995) 126, 167–8, 236
Schopenhauer, Arthur (1788–1860) 6
Schreiner, Olive (1855–1920) 47, 52
serendipity/ous/ly 3, 5, 27, 85–7, 89, 91–8, 151, 153, 182, 232
Shakespeare, William (1564–1616) xix, 31, 145, 220, 244
  Ham 40, 42, 244
  1H4 224, 244
  KL 43
  Oth xiv
shaman/ism/inSanusi/griot 21, 71, 91, 93, 97, 152–4, 164–5, 177–8, 209, 250, 258
Shaw, George Bernard (1856–1950) 6
Shelley, Percy Bysshe (1792–1822) 113, 136, 170, 173, 183, 262
Sidney, (Sir) Philip (1554–1586) 52, 165
silence/s xv, 18, 25, 28, 35, 42, 51–2, 65, 67–9. 73, 86, 105, 131, 148, 181, 200, 206–7, 211, 213–4, 218, 263
Sir Gawain and the Green Knight (Gawain Poet, late 14th century) 192
slave/trade/slavery xvi, 33–5, 39–43, 71, 103, 105, 113, 202–3, 206, 208–9, 227
Smith, Adam (1723–90) 111
Smith, Jadwiga 4, 162, 158, 163, 223, 244, 256, 260
Smuts, Jan Christiaan (1870–1950) 229–30, 250
Socrates (B.C. 470–399), Socratic dialogue 13, 65, 80, 143, 197
Soyinka, Wole 4, 6–8, 14, 25, 29–31, 55, 86–7, 89, 123–4, 126, 167, 184, 186,

205, 215–16, 225, 228, 238, 244–5, 248, 252, 255, 256, 261–3, 266
sublime/sublimity xii–iii, 18, 51, 62, 67, 97, 104, 111–2, 115, 141–8, 164, 169, 180, 196, 203, 207–8, 214, 235, 237, 257
'stoku/s', defined xvi, xxi, 85–98, 145, 149, 151–5, 159, 232, 252, 256, 258–9
Sufism 58, 67, 190–192, 195, 197, 239
symbol/ism/ist xi–xiv, xvi, 10, 27, 33, 35–7, 47, 55, 59, 65, 67, 74–6, 79, 82, 88, 90–1, 93, 95–6, 102, 107, 111, 121–3, 131–2, 134, 137, 141, 153–4, 160–1, 169, 180–1, 183, 185, 188, 192, 194, 199, 208, 226, 229, 246, 250, 255

Tao Thê Ching/Taoism 55, 92, 109, 215, 217, 238
Tarot 193
The Book of Common Prayer 27
The Dream of the Rood 27
The Panchatantra 34, 246
Theocritus (c. 300–c. 360 B.C.E) 54
Tiresias 219
Tolkien, J. R. R. (1892–1973) 42, 95, 247, 265
    'eucatastrophe' 95
    The Hobbit 42
Tolle, Eckhart 74, 102, 106, 109, 115, 251, 253–4
transgender studies xix
transhuman/ism/ist xii, 3, 5–6, 8, 147, 158–60, 164–5, 173, 243, 259–60
truth xiv, 4, 15, 20, 22, 31, 34, 39, 59, 61, 66, 77, 81, 83, 85, 90, 92, 97, 103, 126, 130, 134–5, 142, 154, 159, 168, 173, 177, 179, 188, 196, 202–3, 206, 214, 216, 218, 225, 240
Tymieniecka, Anna-Teresa (1923–2014) 4, 28–9, 31, 69, 74, 78, 86–7, 101, 104–7,
109, 114, 120, 163, 179, 188–9, 223–4, 226, 231, 234, 244–6, 251–4, 256, 260, 262

'ubuntu' xvi, 22, 107, 225, 245
Urhobo/Urhobo cosmogony 64, 118, 168, 202, 217
utopia/n xi, 36, 63, 67, 102, 112, 116, 212, 254

Van der Post, (Sir) Laurens (1906–1996) 157, 260
Vermeer, Jan (1632–1675) 50, 248
Virgil, Publius Virgilius Maro (B.C. 70–19 B.C.E.) 20, 54, 110, 182, 192, 262
    Aeneid 182. 238
    Eclogues 110, 225
virtue 7, 36, 39, 90, 180, 226, 237

Wiesel, Elie 117–19, 121–2, 124–5, 256
Wilson, Edward O. 38, 149, 150, 235, 237, 247
    The Diversity of Life 247, 259, 262
Wisdom Corpus xiii–xiv, 3–4, 131, 145, 237
Wordsworth, William (1770–1850) xii–xiii, 142, 258
    'Imitations of Immortality' 202, 240
    'Tintern Abbey' 105, 148, 235
    'To Daffodils' 105

Yeats, W. B. (1865–1939) 150–1, 153–4, 184, 259
    'Chosen' 236
    'The Second Coming' 151, 153
Yoruba 21, 119, 225, 232

ziggurat xiv, 155, defined 175, 190, 199, 201, 207–8

www.ingramcontent.com/pod-product-compliance
Lightning Source LLC
Chambersburg PA
CBHW072126290426
44111CB00012B/1789